Learning in Adulthood

Sharan B. Merriam

Rosemary S. Caffarella

Learning in Adulthood

A Comprehensive Guide

Second Edition

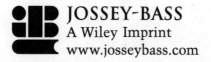
JOSSEY-BASS
A Wiley Imprint
www.josseybass.com

Published by Jossey-Bass
A Wiley Imprint
989 Market Street, San Francisco, CA 94103-1741   www.josseybass.com

Jossey-Bass books and products are available through most bookstores. To contact Jossey-Bass
directly call our Customer Care Department within the U.S. at 800-956-7739, outside the U.S.
at 317-572-3986 or fax 317-572-4002.

Jossey-Bass also publishes its books in a variety of electronic formats. Some content that
appears in print may not be available in electronic books.

Library of Congress Cataloging-in-Publication Data

Merriam, Sharan B.
    Learning in adulthood : a comprehensive guide / Sharan B. Merriam, Rosemary S.
Caffarella. — 2nd ed.
        p.   cm.—(The Jossey-Bass higher and adult education series)
    Includes bibliographical references and indexes.
    ISBN 0-7879-1043-0 (cloth : perm paper)
    1. Adult learning.   I. Caffarella, Rosemary S.   II. Title.   III. Series.
    LC5225.L42   M47   1999
    374—ddc21   98-25498

SECOND EDITION
HB Printing   10 9 8 7

The Jossey-Bass

Higher and Adult Education Series

Contents

—ᨓ— Preface

Learning in adulthood is an intensely personal activity. Yet at the same time, a multibillion-dollar enterprise has arisen in response to adult learning interests—an enterprise that spends more dollars than elementary schools, high schools, and postsecondary schools combined. Indeed, the field of adult and continuing education is characterized by a bewildering array of programs, agencies, and personnel working to assist adults in their learning. It is precisely the focus on adults as learners, however, that unites an otherwise extraordinarily diverse field. It is also the nature of *adults* as learners and the distinguishing characteristics of the adult learning process that differentiate adult education from other kinds of education. To facilitate the process of learning, it is especially important to know who the adult learner is, why adults are involved in learning activities, how adults learn, and how aging affects learning ability. *Learning in Adulthood* addresses these topics among others.

What we said nearly a decade ago about the literature on adult learning in the Preface to the first edition of *Learning in Adulthood* is even more true today. There is a voluminous literature on adult learning, ranging from technical articles on various aspects of adult learning to handbooks, guides, and pamphlets summarizing material for the new instructor of adult students. Should one go to the Educational Resources Information Center (ERIC) database, which catalogues journal articles, monographs, conference proceedings, papers, and so on, or to random exploring on the World Wide Web, one encounters thousands of citations under the topic "adult learning." Further, dozens of books with either a central or secondary focus on adult learning have been published in the past decade.

This second edition of *Learning in Adulthood* builds on material in the 1991 edition, bringing together the important contributions of the past decade or more to our understanding of adult learning. This edition is more than a restatement of earlier work with new material tacked on. It is a comprehensive overview and synthesis of what we know about adult learning: the context in which it takes place, who the participants are, what they learn and why, the nature of the learning process itself, the development of theory in adult learning, and other issues relevant to the practice of adult learning.

The book also takes into account recent work in sociology, philosophy, critical social theory, and psychology. In most writing on adult learning, the sociocultural perspective has been widely neglected in favor of the predominant orientation to the individual learner and how to facilitate her or his learning. In addition to the focus on the learner, we attend to the *context* in which learning takes place and to learners' interactive relationship with that context and with the learning activity itself. We look at how the social structure influences what is offered and who participates, how the sociocultural context creates particular developmental needs and interests, and how social factors such as race, class, and gender shape learning. Along with the attention given to the sociocultural context of learning are chapters that examine social issues with an impact on the provision of learning opportunities for adults and the ethical issues inherent in instruction and program planning for adults. Only recently has the sociocultural context received attention in the literature and at gatherings of adult educators.

This book is intended primarily for educators of adults. We have organized the material so that it will make sense to readers who are new to adult education and at the same time will challenge those who are already familiar with the knowledge base of the field. The organization and presentation of this material reflect our efforts over the years to find the best way to organize courses, workshops, and seminars in adult learning and development for audiences with varying levels of expertise. We have endeavored to put together a book that is at once readable, thorough, and up-to-date in its coverage. In particular, the book is designed for use in courses in adult learning. In addition to those associated with the field of adult education itself, however, those in counseling, health, social work, human resource development, administration, and instructional technology and in such institutions as libraries, churches, business and industry, and higher education often deal on a daily basis with adult learners. We also intend this book to be a resource for practitioners in these fields who would like to know more about adult learners and the learning process.

OVERVIEW OF THE CONTENTS

This second edition of *Learning in Adulthood* is divided into five parts. Part One describes the context of adult learning. Part Two focuses on adult learners from a developmental perspective. The chapters in Part Three explore various components of the learning process. Part Four focuses on the learning transaction with adults, and Part Five addresses ethical issues and presents our synthesis of the adult learning literature.

The chapters in Part One describe the context of adult learning. Chapter One sets the sociocultural context for adult learning in North America. In it, we discuss three forces—demographics, the global economy, and technology—that have shaped adult learning today. It is important to understand how the interaction of those three factors has led to changes in both what adults want to learn and the learning opportunities provided for them. Directly related to the sociocultural context of adult learning are the nature and types of learning opportunities available to adults. These range from those offered by educational and noneducational institutions, such as hospitals and government agencies, to nonformal and community-based agencies, to incidental and informal learning that take place through self-directed learning. This range of settings and the ways in which they influence learners and the learning process are the subject of Chapter Two. Chapter Three summarizes the literature on who participates in primarily formal adult learning activities, why people participate, and what they choose to learn. The chapter examines six models of participation that attempt to explain and even predict who participates in formal adult learning activities. The last chapter in Part One takes a critical look at key questions of access and opportunity, and examines the gaps between the rhetoric and the reality in the provision of formal and nonformal learning activities in our society.

Central to the practice of adult education is the adult learner. Part Two focuses on adults' developmental characteristics. Beginning with biological and psychological perspectives on adult development in Chapter Five, our focus moves to sociocultural and integrated perspectives on development in Chapter Six. The work on adult development in recent years places less emphasis on age and stage models and more on the effect of such factors as race, gender, class, and ethnicity on development. Much has been written lately about cognitive development in adulthood, and so this is treated separately in Chapter

Seven. Here we review six theoretical models of cognitive development as well as present the concept of dialectical thinking. Chapter Eight reviews the work on intelligence, especially as it has been studied from a developmental or aging perspective. Educators who want to understand adults as learners will profit from the chapters on biological aging, psychological development, sociocultural determinants of growth, and cognitive and intellectual development in this part.

Part Three, "The Learning Process," consists of three chapters. Drawing on several disciplines and summarizing recent work on memory and aging, schema theory, expertise, cognitive and learning styles, and brain-based research, Chapter Nine is one of the few compilations of its kind in an adult learning textbook. In Chapter Ten we look closely at the role of experience in learning: how adult learning not only builds on prior experience but also how experience shapes learning. The concepts of experiential learning, reflective practice, and situated cognition are also examined in this chapter. In the final chapter of Part Three, we review five traditional theories about learning—behaviorism, cognitivism, humanism, social learning theory, and constructivism—along with their implications for adult learning.

The amount of research and writing that has been done in the past decade on adult learning is reflected in Part Four, "The Learning Transaction with Adults." Accompanying this growth has been the development of models and theories to help explain and guide practice, as well as to direct future research efforts. We begin Chapter Twelve with a description and critique of the best known of these theories: Knowles's (1980) concept of andragogy. Based on five characteristics of adult learners, andragogy focuses on how adults learn. We also cover less-well-known models of adult learning by Cross (1981), McClusky (1970a), Jarvis (1987a), and Knox (1980). In Chapter Thirteen we explore the rich array of work that has been completed on self-directed learning. Addressed are the goals and processes of self-directed learning, the concept of self-directedness as a personal attribute of the learner, and the major challenges to be considered in building future research and theory. There has been so much research and theory-related activity recently with regard to transformational learning that we felt the material warranted a separate chapter in this edition of *Learning in Adulthood*. Chapter Fourteen summarizes the development of transformational learning and examines unresolved issues inherent in this approach to adult learning. Chapter Fifteen is also new to this edition; in it, we discuss three perspectives that focus on power relations in the learning transaction: critical theory, postmodernism, and feminist theory and pedagogy. These theories are reviewed for their contributions to our understanding of adult learning.

Finally, in Part Five, we step back from the accumulated knowledge base and examine how values and beliefs affect the practice of adult learning. Chapter Sixteen focuses on ethical issues in the teaching-learning transaction and in program planning. We explore the nature of ethical practice and adult education, and describe three frameworks with which educators of adults can address ethical dilemmas they face as instructors and planners. Chapter Seventeen, the final chapter, summarizes and integrates the material on adult learning presented in earlier chapters. It also reflects how we ourselves have come to think about learning in adulthood.

ACKNOWLEDGMENTS

This edition of *Learning in Adulthood* is a direct response to the field's burgeoning literature base on research and theory in adult learning and the need for a single, comprehensive, up-to-date textbook to use in our adult learning classes. In a very real sense, it has been the students in our programs and the participants in our workshops and seminars who have challenged us to revise and update the original edition of *Learning in Adulthood*. Others, of course, have been of invaluable assistance at various stages of the project. Gale Erlandson, our editor at Jossey-Bass, was instrumental in helping us conceptualize the book and in assisting us through the process. Colleagues Bruce Barnett, Ralph Brockett, Carolyn Clark, Jean Fleming, Flo Guido-DiBrito, Catherine Hansman, Ed Taylor, Libby Tisdell, Arthur Wilson, and Lynn Zinn unselfishly took time out from their own work to read and critique draft chapters. Their comments, insights, and suggestions considerably strengthened this book. Special thanks also go to Janet Anderson, Lynda Hanscome, and Patricia Reeves, graduate research assistants, for tracking down references and assisting in editing. To all of you we offer our heartfelt thanks. Finally, we thank our family members and friends for their support and patience over the last year.

Athens, Georgia   SHARAN B. MERRIAM
Greeley, Colorado   ROSEMARY S. CAFFARELLA
August 1998

⁓⁓⁓ The Authors

Sharan B. Merriam is professor of adult education at the University of Georgia. Her research and writing activities have focused on the foundations of the field, adult development and learning, and qualitative research methods. She has served on steering committees for the annual North American Adult Education Research Conference and the Commission of Professors of Adult Education. For five years she was coeditor of *Adult Education Quarterly,* the major journal of research and theory in adult education. Her books include *Lifelines: Patterns of Work, Love, and Learning in Adulthood* (1991, coauthored with M. C. Clark); *A Guide to Research for Educators and Trainers of Adults* (1995, 2nd ed., with E. L. Simpson); *The Profession and Practice of Adult Education: An Introduction* (1997, with R. Brockett), winner of the 1997 Cyril O. Houle World Award for Literature in Adult Education; and *Qualitative Research and Case Study Applications in Education* (2nd ed., 1998).

Rosemary S. Caffarella is a professor in the Division of Educational Leadership and Policy Studies at the University of Northern Colorado. Her research and writing activities have focused on adult development and learning, program planning and evaluation, and leadership development. She has served as chair of the Commission of Professors of Adult Education, on the steering committee for the annual North American Adult Education Research Conference, and on the board of directors of the American Association for Adult and Continuing Education. In addition, she has served or is serving as a consulting editor for *Adult Education Quarterly, Adult Learning,* and *The Canadian Journal for the Study of Adult Education.* Caffarella is the author of numerous books, book chapters, and articles. Her latest book, *Planning Programs for Adult Learners: A Practical Guide for*

Educators, Trainers, and Staff Developers, was published in 1994. Her other books and monographs include *Experiential Learning: A New Approach* (coedited with L. Jackson, 1994) and *Psychosocial Development of Women: Linkages to Teaching and Leadership in Adult Education* (1992).

Learning in Adulthood

The Context and Provision of Adult Learning

I t is very much the perspective of this book that learning is a personal process. It is also the perspective of this book that the context of adult life and the societal context shape what an adult needs and wants to learn and, to a somewhat lesser extent, when and where learning takes place. As Jarvis (1987a, p. 11) observes, learning "is intimately related to [the] world and affected by it." The four chapters in Part One explore the sociocultural context of the United States, the range of learning opportunities available to adults in this context, who takes advantage of these opportunities and why, and why access to these opportunities is limited to certain segments of society.

Chapter One describes three factors characteristic of American society today that affect what adults want to learn. First, dramatic changes are occurring in the demographic base of our society. Adults outnumber those under eighteen years old for the first time ever. Moreover, the percentage of the population over age sixty-five continues to grow, commanding the attention of policymakers, businesspeople, and educators like. Our population as a whole is also better educated than ever before, and there is more cultural and ethnic diversity. Therefore, there are simply more adults seeking learning opportunities, as well as more groups of adults with special learning needs.

The second and third factors shaping the learning enterprise are the global economy and technology. These are very much interrelated, of course; technology has had an enormous impact on the economy. Robotics and automation displace production workers but create other jobs; technology has fostered whole new work structures such as telecommuting; and so on. The effect of the global economy and technological advances on the nature of adult learning is staggering. Adults find that they must continue their learning past formal schooling in order to function at work, at home, and in their communities. The need for new knowledge, for updating old information, for retraining, has resulted in a multibillion-dollar educational enterprise.

Some of this learning takes place in formal settings sponsored by a myriad of institutions and agencies. As might be expected, business and industry and educational institutions offer a large number of adult learning opportunities, but so do the military, cooperative extension, churches, hospitals, and other institutions. Chapter Two, "Learning Opportunities in Adulthood," explores how the context of institutions influences the learner and the learning process. Also reviewed are learning opportunities that are nonformal, such as those offered by community-based agencies, and informal, incidental, and self-directed opportunities, as might happen in the course of the workday or by watching a television program. In addition, the concept of the learning organization, which looks at the organizational unit itself as a learning entity, is discussed.

Chapter Three profiles who participates in adult learning, why adults participate, and what an adult chooses to learn. Most of this information on participation and motivation is in reference to formal learning, such as that provided by educational institutions and employers. Estimates as to the percentage of the adult population who participate in learning have steadily risen over the past thirty years, with the most current study suggesting that approximately 40 percent of all adult Americans participate. Studies of self-directed learning and other nonformal types of education put the percentage even higher. Clearly, adult learning comprises an important activity for today's adults. Finding out what motivates adults to participate and what deters participation is important information, especially for program developers. This chapter also reviews these motivational studies. Finally, the search for an explanatory framework or model of participation has led to the development of numerous models. Six of these models are reviewed and critiqued in the last section of this chapter.

The final chapter in Part One is a synthesis of the information on factors in the context that shape adult learning, the nature of the provision of adult learning opportunities, and who actually does participate and why. The result is a discussion of access and opportunity in adult education. The gap between the better educated who seek out continuing education and those who do not continues to widen. Adult learning seems to have become a vehicle for solidifying a socioeconomic structure that limits access and opportunity, contrary to the stated goal of equal access to education in our society. Chapter Four examines the rhetoric, which espouses one set of values, and the reality, which demonstrates another, in the provision of adult learning opportunities. The chapter is organized around three questions: Who in our society decides what the learning opportunities will be? To what goals are the learning activities directed? And who benefits from these activities?

CHAPTER ONE

Adult Learning and Contemporary Society

Learning, even self-directed learning, rarely occurs "in splendid isolation from the world in which the learner lives; . . . it is intimately related to that world and affected by it" (Jarvis, 1987a, p. 11). What one wants to learn, what is offered, and the ways in which one learns are determined to a large extent by the nature of the society at any particular time. Contrast the young male apprentice of colonial times learning to be a blacksmith with today's middle-aged woman learning data processing, for example, or the preparation needed to become a medical doctor at the turn of the century—less than a high school diploma—with today's long and specialized training.

It can also be argued that the nature of society at any particular point in time determines the relative emphasis placed on *adult* learning. In preindustrial societies, the rate of change was such that what a person needed to know to function as an adult could be learned in childhood (Jarvis, 1983). In societies hurrying to catch up, however, and in our own society with its accelerated rate of change, the urgency of dealing with social realities lies with adults. Society no longer has the luxury of waiting for its youth. As Belanger (1996, p. 21) notes, "The question is no longer whether adult learning is needed, and how important it is. The issue today is how to respond to this increasing and diversified demand, how to manage this explosion." Youth, in fact, "who are sent out into life with a dwindling sackful of values, . . . face a situation in which they have to keep filling up their sack. This leads adult education to take 'lifelong learning' as its motto. The duty to be free (with the pressure to realize oneself) is the duty to go on learning. . . . The hole in the ozone layer provides the stimulus for courses to which people turn for advice, mad cow disease pushes up the numbers attending vegetarian cooking courses, and backache creates a need for posture classes" (Geissler, 1996, pp. 35–36). Ironically, to some observers, adult education finds itself in the position of being "both a victim and a perpetrator of the modernization process" (Geissler, 1996, p. 37).

To some extent, the learning that goes on in adulthood can be understood through an examination of the social context in which it occurs. How is learning in adulthood shaped by the society in which it takes place? How does the sociocultural context determine what is learned and by whom? What is it about the American context in particular that promotes learning in adulthood?

This chapter explores three dimensions of the current sociocultural context that are shaping the nature of adult learning in today's world: demographics, the global economy, and technology. Although we present each of these separately at first, these three factors are very much interrelated, and thus their convergence and subsequent impact on learning in adulthood are discussed in the final section of this chapter.

DEMOGRAPHICS

Changing demographics is a social reality shaping the provision of learning in contemporary American society. Demographics is about people, groups of people, and their respective characteristics. For the first time in our society, adults outnumber youth, there are more older adults, the population is better educated than ever before, and there is more cultural and ethnic diversity. For various reasons, individuals and groups of people seek out learning experiences; for other reasons, society targets learning activities for certain segments of the population. Thus, certain learning activities are learner initiated and others are society initiated in response to the changing demographics. The field is concerned with the growth and development of adult learners, while at the same time, there are emerging groups of learners with special needs.

To begin, there are simply more adults in our society than ever before, and the population will continue to age. In comparison to colonial times when half the population was under age sixteen, in 1990, fewer than one in four Americans were under age 16 and half were age 33 or older (U.S. Bureau of the Census, 1992). The median age of the American population of 34.0 years in 1994 is expected to increase to 35.5 in 2000, and 39.1 in 2035 (U.S. Bureau of the Census, 1995). The so-called baby boomers—the seventy million people born between 1946 and 1964—are a contributing factor to this change in the population. Cross (1981, p. 6) notes that such a large cohort, "because of its political and economic strength, manages to gain the attention of the society throughout the life span of the cohort. Because of its sheer size, it has commanded the attention of education, industry, and government." Although we might hear more about youth, they have less of an impact on the economy than the boomers. "People over fifty represent 26 percent of the population, are owners of 80 percent of all money in banks and S&Ls, holders of 77 percent of the nation's financial assets, and buyers of 48 percent of all luxury cars" (Wagschal, 1997, p. 25).

The shift from a youth-oriented to an adult-oriented society is solidified by the increasing numbers of older adults in the population. In 1987, for the first time ever, Americans over the age of sixty-five outnumbered those under twenty-five (Spear and Mocker, 1989). Furthermore, the oldest old, those over eighty-five years old, are the fastest-growing segment of the older population. As of January 1, 1995, there were over three and one half million adults over eighty-five years old, an increase of 18.5 percent from the 1990 census (U.S. Bureau of the Census, 1995). Older adults are also increasingly better educated, in better health, and economically better off than previous cohorts. Society is already heeding their learning needs with policies like tuition waivers for higher and continuing education programs and specially designed programs, such as the popular Elderhostel program and learning-in-retirement institutes. There has also been a subtle change in the philosophical rationale—at least among those working in the fields of gerontology and educational gerontology— underlying the provision of education for this group. Along with an economic rationale (the better educated need fewer social services) and social stability rationale (millions of healthy retired people need something to do) is an awareness that older adults as well as younger ones have an unending potential for development. Williamson (1997, p. 175) suggests that our culturally endorsed notion about what represents "appropriate" learning over the course of the life span tends to "reinforce prevailing myths about retirement and aging as processes of withdrawal and decline." This mind-set ignores the exciting possibilities for personal growth and societal contributions among older members of the population. A more inclusive educational model would promote lifelong learning as a process to make young and old alike "'connoisseurs of the past, implementers of the present and visionaries of the future'" (Berman cited by Williamson, 1997, p. 174).

Thus, more adults and an increase in the number of older adults are two demographic factors influencing the provision of learning activities in our society. So, too, is the rising level of education characteristic of our population. This is dramatically illustrated by the fact that over 80 percent of today's twenty year olds have completed four years of high school compared with less than half (49 percent) of those in their grandparents' generation (Mercer and Garner, 1989). Since previous education is the single best predictor of participation in adult education, the rising educational level of the adult population is a contextual factor of considerable import. Participation data from the Center for Education Statistics show, for example, that 16 percent of adults with fewer than four years of high school participate in organized adult education, while 31 percent of high school graduates and 58 percent of college graduates participate (Kim, Collins, Stowe, and Chandler, 1995). Nevertheless, even as the educational attainment level of the population as a whole continues to rise, an alarming number of high school students drop out before graduating. And "as a high school education becomes the minimum educational standard, those who drop out are more likely to become members of an educational underclass, from which adult education (especially in the form of adult basic and secondary education) may be the only hope of escape" (Rachal, 1989, pp. 10–11). Unfortunately, 1995 data from the National Center for Education Statistics "show that adults with less than a high school diploma were least likely to participate in adult education activities overall, in credential programs, and in work-related courses, and only 5 percent of these adults participated in adult basic education or GED preparation" (Kim, Collins, Stowe, and Chandler, 1995, p. 3). The recent change in government welfare policies limiting time on welfare combined with better education and training opportunities may have a positive effect on raising the level of participation by this population.

Another demographic characteristic of the social context is the growing cultural and ethnic diversity of America's population. Briscoe and Ross (1989, p. 584) point out that "not only is America graying, the skin color of America is also changing." In contrast to the influx of European immigrants at the end of the nineteenth century, today's immigrants are more likely to come from Asia and Latin America. If current trends in immigration and birthrates persist, it is projected that between the years 2000 and 2005, the Hispanic population will account for 37.7 percent of the total population growth, Asian–Pacific Islanders about 19.5 percent, and African Americans 17 percent (Gardner, 1996a). By the year 2000, Hispanics will be the largest minority group in America, with African Americans the second largest (Briscoe and Ross, 1989). Furthermore, the average age of minority populations is decreasing, while the majority population is growing older. For example, "Hispanics will be the youngest population with one-half under 26 years of age while the white population will remain the oldest" (Gardner, 1996a, p. 59). Briscoe and Ross (1989, p. 584) report that "minorities also tend to be clustered in metropolitan areas, and, in the future, fifty-three major U.S. cities will have minority populations that outnumber the present majority population." Not only is the composition of the minority population changing, but so too are the overall numbers. By the year 2000, minorities are expected to compose 29 percent of the population; by 2050, minorities will account for nearly 47 percent of the overall population (U.S. Bureau of the Census, 1995).

The implications of these population trends for society in general and adult education in particular are staggering. Although changing demographics offer a tremendous opportunity for capitalizing anew on the merits of many peoples from many lands, there are also risks (Henry, 1990, p. 29). Minority adults, for example, are disproportionately represented among the unemployed, the low-income stratum, and the less educated. These characteristics are correlated with low rates of participation in organized adult education. The nation's minorities constitute a sizable resource. Briscoe and Ross (1989, p. 586) stress the urgency of the problem: "The consequences to North American society of leaving this resource undeveloped are great. It is likely that young people who leave school early will never participate fully in society or in the decision-making processes of government, and that they will neither enjoy the benefits of good health, nor experience the upward mobility needed as adults to make them full contributors and partners in shaping and participating in the larger society. One cause of the problem is educational institutions not responding quickly enough to change, even though educators are aware of the impact they can have on societal systems."

The growing ethnic and cultural diversity of our population has been identified by Naisbitt and Aburdene (1990) as one of the mega-trends for the twenty-first century. They have observed that "even as our lifestyles grow more similar, there are unmistakable signs of a powerful countertrend: a backlash against uniformity, a desire to assert the uniqueness of one's culture and language. . . . Outbreaks of cultural nationalism are happening in every corner of the globe" (p. 119). Adult educators are slowly becoming aware of the instructional implications of the fact that "as our outer worlds grow more similar, we will increasingly treasure the traditions that spring from within" (Naisbitt and Aburdene, 1990, p. 120).

In summary, the composition of society is an important factor in the provision of learning opportunities for citizens of all ages. In the United States, there are more adults than youth, there is a growing number of older adults, the population as a whole is better educated than ever before, and there is a large minority population. The field of adult education with its orientation to the learners themselves is especially sensitive to these demographic trends—whether by focusing on individual growth or by diagnosing and addressing the needs of special groups.

THE GLOBAL ECONOMY

A second dimension of the social context that has a direct bearing on learning in adulthood is the economic structure. Clearly the American economy is changing and with it the learning needs of adults. In particular there is a recognition of global interdependence, a shift to a service economy, and a change in composition of the labor force.

Americans have become increasingly conscious of the interrelatedness of their lives with the rest of the world. Naisbitt and Aburdene (1990, p. 19) identify the global economy as one of the megatrends for the twenty-first century: "We are in an unprecedented period of accelerated change, perhaps the most breathtaking of which is the swiftness of our rush to all the world's becoming a single economy.

Already it may be said that there is no such thing as a U.S. economy, as enmeshed is it in all the other economies of the world." The globalization of economies worldwide is creating a competitive atmosphere that has dramatic implications for adult learning. Petrella (1997) paints a vivid picture of this relationship:

> The globalisation of economies is therefore launching every company, every town, every region, every country into an open confrontation with other companies, towns, regions and countries in arenas from which will emerge triumphant, or at least as survivors, only the strongest, the most competitive, those with the oldest battle scars and those who were astute enough to prepare themselves in good time for the new scuffles associated with globalising markets. Competition, everyone competing against everyone else across the globe, is thus now considered as being the major "must" for every economic agent, whether private-sector or public-sector.
>
> To be competitive in a liberalised, deregulated, privatised and glob-alising market, every company is obliged, so the theory goes, to adopt a strategy of reducing production costs and improving the quality and range of its goods and services. . . . One of the most efficient options open to companies for achieving this goal is that of making "aggressive" and intelligent use of human resources, especially those segments thereof which are at the various extremes: the best and the worst qualified, the best and worst paid, the oldest and the youngest. [p. 25]

What does all this mean for adult learning? For one thing, "it does a worker very little good to train specifically for a job with a company that outsources the position, downsizes, or sells to a foreign owner who reorganizes or 'reengineers' the company, selling off pieces, leaving the worker trained and unemployed" (Tomlin, 1997, p. 20). Global economics has led to changing work practices, which require different kinds of preparation and training. This has resulted in the control of education shifting to business. Business is "almost unintentionally evolving new meanings for learning and new methods of delivering education. And it is doing so in ways that are consistent with its fundamental role as business, competitively filling unmet needs in the marketplace. All business visions are anchored in this fundamental belief" (Davis and Botkin, 1994, p. 34). The emphasis now is on improved product and service quality, greater worker responsibility, and teamwork approaches. Adult education and human resource development, in particular, have responded with broad-based workplace literacy programs and training and development packages designed to address a wide range of economy-driven needs. Participation rates also reflect the increasingly job-oriented nature of adult education in America. While in 1969, "adult education courses were nearly evenly split between job-related and non-job-related," in the most current study of participation, "fully 90.6 percent of adults cited career or job-related reasons for educational participation. Clearly, there is a marked increase in the employment orientation of adult education in the United States" (Valentine, 1997, p. 5).

The global economy is having an impact on learning in broader ways too. We have become, in the words of Usher, Bryant, and Johnston (1997, p. 4), "a culture of consumption. . . . The factory, the assembly line, large-scale manufacturing—are being increasingly displaced by centres of consumption—financial services, small-scale specialised enterprises, shopping malls and superstores, entertainment complexes, heritage and theme parks." This shift is evidenced in a changing relationship between educator and learner to one of a "market relationship between producer and consumer. Knowledge is exchanged on the basis of the performative value it has for the consumer" (p. 14). Educational institutions themselves "become part of the market, selling knowledge as a commodity and increasingly reconstructing themselves as enterprises dedicated to marketing their commodities and to competing in the knowledge 'business'" (p. 14). In a recent article on a community college in Arizona, for example, "its booming enrollment and low overhead" were attributed to the college's "treat[ing] students like customers" and a philosophy whereby education is seen as "a commodity that can be adapted to what the market demands" (Healy, 1998, p. A32).

A second economic shift has been from a society employed in producing goods to one employed in providing services. The decline in industrial labor stems from automation and competition from other countries with low labor costs. Dislocated workers from both the industrial and agricultural sectors, with few if any transferable skills, find themselves in low-skill, low-paying service jobs. Ironically, "the ready supply of displaced workers with limited employable skills will lead to low wages in parts of the service sector and thus will promote the general growth of service-related business" (Charner and Rolzinski, 1987, p. 8). Tomlin (1997, p. 20) cites research that estimates "that the U.S. alone will create 10,000 new jobs a day, every day for the next ten years" and that "many of these jobs will be in the service sector, many more will be in careers that have yet to be invented. These new workers do not yet know what or how they will need to learn."

Concurrent with the shift to a service economy is the shift to what has been called the information society. Our economy increasingly is based on information rather than heavy industry: "Already more workers are engaged in generating, processing, analyzing, and distributing information than are engaged in agriculture, mining, and manufacturing combined" (Hart, 1983, p. 10). Fay, McCune, and Begin (1987, p. 20) estimate that by the year 2000, "80 percent of all workers in the United States will be employed in the information industry. . . . This will have a major impact on workers as economic units. In an industrial age, workers are expendable cogs in the machine; in an information age (and to a lesser extent, in a service age), human capital is the most valuable capital an organization has." The implications for learning—and in particular for work-related training—are enormous. Already the amount spent annually by business, industry, and government agencies on job-related training is in the billions of dollars and exceeds that spent on public higher education (Rowden, 1996b). Furthermore, since skills learned in preparation for a job or career cannot keep pace with the demands of the world of work, the ability to learn becomes a valuable skill in and of itself.

Developing simultaneously with the emphasis on learning to learn is the notion of the learning organization (see Chapter Two). To survive in the global economy, an "organization needs to evolve into 'a learning organization' whereby new and expansive patterns are permitted, allowing employees to learn individually and collectively (continually learning how to learn)" (Gardner, 1996b, p. 43). The growing body of literature on the learning organization positions learning, information processing, and problem-solving skills as central to the survival of both the individual worker and the organization. Ulrich (1998) underscores how globalization necessitates the creation of learning organizations. Globalization requires companies "to move people, ideas, products, and information around the world to meet local needs. They [companies] must add new and important ingredients to the mix when making strategy: volatile political situations, contentious global trade issues, fluctuating exchange rates, and unfamiliar

cultures. They must be more literate in the ways of international customers, commerce, and competition than ever before. In short, globalization requires that organizations *increase their ability to learn* and
collaborate and to manage diversity, complexity, and ambiguity"
(p. 126, emphasis added).

Closely related to shifts to a service and information economy are
changes in America's labor force. The largest job-growth categories
are jobs related to service—cashiers, orderlies, fast food workers—
and to information and technology—computer programmers and
operators, engineers, teachers, and so on (Rachal, 1989). Not sur-
prisingly, women, minorities, and the elderly are overrepresented in
the lower-paying service jobs. Since the middle of this century, however, the labor force has changed from one dominated by blue-collar
occupations to one where the majority of jobs are considered white
collar. Significant changes in the composition of the workforce are
also occurring along racial and ethnic lines. Although white non-
Hispanic workers account for the vast majority of workers (73 percent in 1996), "their rate of growth is considerably below that for the
black, Asian, and Hispanic groups. Continued rapid growth of the
Hispanic population makes it likely that this group will become
the second largest ethnic grouping, replacing blacks, by 2006" (Bowman, 1997, p. 4). Perhaps the greatest change of all has been the
steady increase of women in the workforce. In 1960, 37.7 percent of
women in the population were members of the workforce; in 1994,
58.8 percent participated; and the rate is estimated to be 61.6 percent by the year 2000 (U.S. Bureau of the Census, 1995). Economic
necessity and the freeing of occupations traditionally assigned to
men have contributed to this change. Cross (1981) observes that "the
revolution in women's roles is the result of two complementary
forces. On the one hand, social and technological changes push
women out of the home; on the other hand, new opportunities in
education and the labor market pull women into the new worlds of
work and education" (p. 26).

In summary, economic factors are shaping the nature of our society and, by extension, the nature of learning that adults are most likely
to undertake. A global economy, the shift to a service and information
society, and consequent changes in the configuration of the labor force
are determining to a large extent where learning takes place, what is
offered, and who participates.

TECHNOLOGY

There is no more apt metaphor for reflecting the rate of technological change than the computer. Itself a major component of our highly technological age, computer language has invaded the ways in which we talk of adult learning. We process students and information; we plan learning activities with an eye to inputs, flow, and outputs; we provide feedback to individual learners and to programs. Indeed, we program learning experiences and ourselves. Technology has had an enormous impact on society and adult learning. It has been instrumental in bringing about the so-called information society, which has created new jobs and eliminated others. The technology-driven information society has also affected adult education.

The move to an information society has been a function of technological developments associated with an information explosion. Within a short span of time, electronic, communication, and information technologies have changed society as a whole and affected how people go about their daily lives. From ordering pizza by computer, to making telephone calls from one's car, to faxing a request to the local radio station, everyday life has been irrevocably influenced by technology.

Concurrent with these technological advances has been an information explosion. It has been estimated that the amount of information in the world doubles every seven years (Apps, 1988, p. 23), and some have projected that information will "soon double every 20 months" (Whitson and Amstutz, 1997, p. 1). Others have speculated that half of what most professionals know when they finish their formal training will be outdated in less than five years, perhaps even months for those in technology-related careers. Thus, the need for continuing education has dramatically escalated with the increase in knowledge production. Not only is there considerably more information than ever before, but links with technology have made its storage, transmission, and access more feasible than ever before. Laser technology in particular is revolutionizing the dissemination of information, as well as its storage and retrieval. A compact disk using laser technology makes it possible to store huge amounts of information in a very small space, and the Internet and World Wide Web have become repositories for more information than any one person could access in a lifetime. Further, the merging of the three technologies of communications, computer, and video-image handling promises to have a significant impact on teaching and learning. "Communications provides the ability to transfer information; computers offer interactivity, control, and storage of information; and video uses images and sound as well as text to enhance information. General-purpose microcomputer workstations have become available that integrate all three technologies. . . . Workstations integrating the three technologies will be the fundamental, conceptual prototypes for much of the hardware designed and developed for use in all organizations, including schools" (Picciano, 1998, p. 254).

Boucouvalas (1987) and others make the case that a major societal shift, such as moving from an industrial to an information society, results in profound changes in the society's structure. In an industrial society, machine technology extends physical ability; in an information society, computer technology extends mental ability. Material wealth has major value in an industrial society; knowledge and information are key assets in an information society. The social structure changes from hierarchies and bureaucracies to multicentered and horizontal networks; labor movements versus citizen movements are the locus for social change (Boucouvalas, 1987). These changes in society's underlying structure can be seen most dramatically in changes in the workforce. As noted earlier, the shift is eliminating certain classifications of work while creating others not yet dreamed of.

In addition to the creation and elimination of jobs, technological changes are affecting workers in other ways, such as where work is done. As Gardner (1996b, p. 48) observes, "Computer technology frees labor from a particular location. . . . Knowledge workers can work anywhere; they simply have to have access to a computer connection. Even within the team framework, workers can stay engaged in their mutual tasks even if not in close proximity to each other. Delocalizing work has been touted as one of the more appealing aspects of technological advances in the workplace." Telecommuting, or "home work," some predict, has increased because of the new technologies, and it is considered desirable because it fits in with alternative family patterns (such as more single-parent families), worker concerns for control of time and worksite, and organizational efforts to cut costs and remain flexible by contracting out for services rather than hiring more workers. Estimates of the number of people who currently telecommute vary because of different interpretations of this new work structure. However, estimates for the mid-1990s range from 7 million (Piskurich, 1996) to 8.4 million (Hill, Hawkins, and Miller, 1996).

Yet others have cautioned against the unquestioning adoption of technology in the workplace. Attewell (1996, p. A56) points out that information technologies have created a "productivity paradox" in the workplace. Designed to get more work done more efficiently by fewer employees, information technologies have instead offered more ways to communicate, increased the demand for information, and raised the level of expectations with regard to the print and graphic presentation of material. One result has been a displacement of clerical workers with higher-skill-level professional and managerial workers.

Clearly, technology and the information age that it spawned are changing the nature of adult learning. Professionals whose knowledge becomes outdated in a few years, auto mechanics who must now master sophisticated electronic diagnostic systems, adults who must learn new ways to bank or shop from home computers: all must be able to function in a fast-changing society, and this necessitates continued learning. Technology is not only making learning mandatory, it is providing many of the mechanisms for it to occur. Computer-assisted instruction, teleconferencing, interactive videodisk, the Internet, and the World Wide Web are expanding the possibilities of meeting the growing learning needs of adults.

Simultaneous with the development of technologically sophisticated delivery systems is the development of new roles for educators and trainers. Having access to unlimited information is not the same as being able to search efficiently for the most significant information, or to even know what is most significant. Heclo (1994, p. B2) states that "in the long run, excesses of technology mean that the comparative advantage shifts from those with information glut to those with ordered knowledge, from those who can process vast amounts of blab to those who can explain what is worth knowing and why." Ratinoff (1995, p. 163) points out that the information explosion has had both positive and negative effects: "On the positive side, the myths and riddles of power are more exposed to public scrutiny. To fool all people is very difficult under the present circumstances." On the downside, "information has been growing faster than the individual and institutional capacities required to make sense of the new diversity of signals and messages" (p. 164). The result of this information overload has been "a social craving for simplifications, a popular demand for translating simplicity into action and a preference to reduce action to means" (p. 165). The need for order among information chaos has led to "closing the alternatives. Pre-conceived beliefs, analytical parsimony and political correctness" take the place of grappling with too many alternatives and information overload (p. 173). What is needed, Ratinoff (1995, p. 165) suggests, is to consider "the interaction between the quantity and quality of knowledge."

Whitson and Amstutz (1997) suggest a number of strategies for dealing with the information and technology overload. First, adult educators should "build more and better connections with those who directly teach information access skills," especially librarians, but also computer specialists (p. 133). Educators can also focus on developing students' "higher level thinking skills" such that judgments can be made about the credibility and usefulness of information (p. 137). Since much information is available electronically through the Internet and the World Wide Web, the authors underscore the need for educators themselves to become comfortable in this environment, to the point that they can help learners take advantage of technology. Finally, "we have an obligation to consider the ethical implications of our information access processes. . . . The rights of poor people to have access to information and the ways in which information should be made accessible to them are important concerns. We need to resist the growing tendency for business, industry, and government to control access to information" (p. 141).

With regard to the ethical questions of access and equity, Winner (1991, p. 164) alerts us to the myth that "a widespread adoption of computers and communications systems, along with broad access to electronic information, will automatically produce a better world for humanity." The more affluent and better-educated adults with home computers have access to information and instructional packages that make them even more informed. On a global level, the "have" nations can communicate and exchange information in ways that will never be a reality to the majority of the world's people. Even job training necessitated by technological change tends to favor the haves. Levison (1995, p. B5) warns against fostering a technology-based social elite where knowledge workers become insulated "from disturbing news and contrary opinions, isolating them from the concerns and problems of the nation's have-nots."

On the other hand, technology's potential for increasing access to learning for people of all ages and possibly all economic levels is unlimited. In more and more communities, computers can be found in libraries, restaurants, laundromats, and other public places. In addition, what is known as WebTV—where for a few hundred dollars one can access the World Wide Web through the television—holds the potential for bringing most of society onto the information superhighway. Naisbitt and Aburdene (1990) argue that technology is "empowering." In their opinion, "there are fewer dictators on the planet today because they can no longer control information. . . . Computers, cellular phones, and fax machines empower individuals, rather than oppress them, as previously feared" (pp. 303–304).

THE CONVERGENCE OF DEMOGRAPHICS, ECONOMICS, AND TECHNOLOGY

Demographics, economics, and technology forces are closely entwined with each other. Advances in technology, for example, are interrelated with changes in the economic structure. Automation and robotics displace production workers but create other jobs. Technology creates alternative work structures. The need to be competitive in the world market leads to further technological sophistication. Demographics and economics are clearly related. The baby boom cohort that is now in the labor force, for example, is saturating middle and upper management career levels, forcing younger people to consider career alternatives. As another example, the growing number of older adults in our society is having several effects on the economy. Some older adults are being asked to retire early to make room for younger workers; with increased longevity and good health, others are pursuing second or third careers; and some employers, especially those in the service sector, are recognizing the human resource potential of this group and are actively recruiting older workers.

　　Embedded in this convergence of demographics, economics, and technology is a value system based on the political and economic structure of capitalism. More than a decade ago, Beder (1987, p. 107) explained how these three forces are linked within the value system: "The beliefs undergirding the capitalist system emphasize material values. The health of the system is gauged in terms of national wealth as embodied in the gross national product, and social equality is assessed in terms of economic opportunity—the potential of members of the underclasses to amass more income. Hence, the political and social systems become directed toward . . . economic productivity, and economic productivity under the rationale of human capital theory becomes the predominant rationale for all publicly funded social interventions including adult education." This value system directly shapes adult education in the United States in several ways. First, economic productivity becomes "the dominant rationale for all public subsidy of adult education" (p. 109). Second, social justice becomes equated with economic opportunity in that "the just society is a society that provides opportunity for members of the underclasses to amass more income and material goods" and adult education "helps learners acquire the skills and knowledge" to do so (p. 109). The emphasis is on productivity and efficiency, both of which benefit from advances in technology. Thus technology, in the service of economic productivity, converges with changing demographics in shaping the adult learning enterprise.

The global economy in particular seems to be shaping adult learning and the face of adult education worldwide. Youngman (1996, p. 9) points out that the collapse of the Soviet Union and the Eastern bloc has resulted in a "'new world order' and the dominance of a small group of advanced capitalist countries led by the USA. . . . This new stage [of imperialism] is distinguished by changes taking place in the world economy, driven by the technological revolution and the internationalization of production and trade by the multinational corporations." The implications for adult education reside in the cultural dimension of the new global economy: "Ideologies, language, social values, patterns of behavior, modes of consumption, and cultural institutions in the South are powerfully influenced from the North through the media, advertising, tourism, and other means which shape the way people think and act. Education as an agency of the legitimation and reproduction of the capitalist order is a crucial element of cultural imperialism" (Youngman, 1996, p. 11).

A number of writers would like to see the values and purposes of adult education reexamined in the wake of the wide-scale social and economic changes taking place. In a postmodern world characterized by large-scale changes in global activity resulting in economic, social, and political uncertainty, adult education tends to be an entrepreneurial instrument of the so-called new world order. Adult education is particularly sensitive to a restructured workplace, reliance on technology to produce knowledge, and a market demand for multiskilled workers. Petrella (1997) emphasizes the decreased importance placed on individuals in the new market economy in observing that humans as "resources" take precedence over humans as human beings. As well, knowledge has become an important business commodity that is readily marketed, due, in part, to the explosion of the Internet and other information technologies (Gardner, 1996b; Usher, Bryant, and Johnston, 1997). Finger (1995) and Youngman (1996) believe that adult education is in danger of losing its social action orientation as it focuses on helping "individuals face up to the overwhelming economic and other challenges that threaten their identities and survival in the increasingly dense jungle of a postmodern society" (Finger, 1995, p. 115).

While globalization has extended economic and cultural boundaries, it has also served to fragment society in many ways. For example, although minorities and other ethnic groups may be perceived as valuable contributors within society, conflict results when scarce educational and other resources are allocated. Minority groups may become more isolated from mainstream society. In other ways, too, individuals within society may experience fragmentation as they struggle to make sense of their disordered and sometimes disrupted lives. In a time when nations, companies, and families are splintering, there is little sense of security. As Gardner (1996b, p. 53) points out, "not even in the entrepreneurial world will security be held out as a term of employment. College graduates place their highest priority on finding a secure job. Their challenge, however, has become one of redefining their expectations and finding security in their skills and experiences; a process few have taken seriously nor know how to do."

If the postmodern world is characterized by fragmentation and diversity, it is also characterized by new alliances and interactions. Demographics, the global economy, and technology have come together in adult education in the blurring of the field's content and delivery mechanisms. For example, adult education has been variously divided into formal, nonformal, and informal learning activities (Coombs, Prosser, and Ahmed, 1973). Formal learning takes place in educational institutions and often leads to degrees or credit of some sort. Nonformal learning refers to organized activities outside educational institutions, such as those found in learning networks, churches, and voluntary associations. Informal learning refers to the experiences of everyday living from which we learn something. Today, many formal providers offer learning experiences that are noncredit, leisure oriented, and short term. Similarly, nonformal learning and informal life experiences can be turned into formal, credit-earning activities.

Another blurring can be noted in higher education (Apps, 1989). Once composed of learners eighteen to twenty-two years old, the student body has grayed along with the population. In fact, students twenty-five years of age and older now make up close to 50 percent of all college enrollments in the United States (The College Board, in press). Similar subjects may be taught at the local community college for credit and at the public adult school for noncredit. The part-time adult student taking a course during the day at a college is an adult learner as much as the sixteen year old studying for a high school diploma in a local evening class. There is also a blurring between higher education and business and industry. Many postsecondary institutions have business institutes that provide training and development services to business. Conversely, a growing number of private companies, such as McDonald's Hamburger University and the Rand Graduate Institute, are offering accredited degrees (Eurich, 1985, 1990).

Finally, a blurring of content and delivery is found in such popular slogans as "workplace literacy," "learning to learn," "critical thinking," and "media literacy." Educators, employers, and society at large are focusing attention on developing the skills needed to be productive and informed members of a fast-changing and highly technical society. With the erosion of boundaries in the content and provision of adult learning, we may be witnessing the emergence of what has been called the learning society. Taking human beings rather than educational institutions as its beginning point, the learning society is a response to the social context. Jarvis (1983, p. 51) concludes that "it may be possible to detect its emergence as rapidly changing levels of technology provide people with the social conditions necessary for, and make people aware of, the opportunities to extend their learning throughout the whole of their lives."

SUMMARY

Adult learning does not occur in a vacuum. What one needs or wants to learn, what opportunities are available, the manner in which one learns—all are to a large extent determined by the society in which one lives. This chapter has discussed several characteristics of American society today that are shaping the nature of learning in adulthood.

Demographics, the global economy, and technology are three forces affecting all of society's endeavors, including adult learning. With regard to the American population, adults outnumber youth, there are more older adults, adults are better educated, and there is more cultural and ethnic diversity among the population than ever before. We have entered a world economy in which "individuals become 'linked' into an international order . . . by virtue of economic and material interdependence" (Beder, 1987, p. 106). Technology has contributed to, if not caused, the shift to an information society, which is creating dramatic changes in the workforce. Although we have treated them separately, these three forces are interactive and firmly embedded in the American capitalist value system. Adult education both reflects and responds to the forces prevalent in the sociocultural context. Among the implications discussed in the chapter are the field's responsiveness to special groups of people, the economic productivity rationale behind much of adult education, the potential of technology for enhancing or impeding learning, and the blurring of content and delivery in current adult education.

CHAPTER TWO

Learning Opportunities
in Adulthood

W henever we ask adults about their learning, they most often mention education and training programs sponsored by the workplace, colleges and universities, public schools, and other formal organizations. They first picture classrooms with "students" learning and "teachers" teaching in a highly structured format. Yet when we ask these same adults about what they have learned informally over the last year, they typically respond with descriptions of learning activities outside these formal settings. They discuss, for example, remodeling a house, which has involved everything from reading and talking with friends to conversations with carpenters, plumbers, and electricians. Or they may focus on a major change in their life, such as an illness, parenthood, or divorce, which has precipitated numerous learning events, sometimes over an extended period of time. In considering the spectrum of learning opportunities available to adults, it is important to acknowledge all of these arenas of learning, from the highly structured to the more informal ways adults go about learning.

Why is it important that educators of adults recognize that learning happens in so many and varied places in the lives of adults? First, appreciating and taking into consideration the prior knowledge and experience of learners has become a basic assumption of our practice as educators of adults, wherever this knowledge was learned (Knowles, 1980). In working with welfare recipients, for example, instructors might recognize that parents on welfare have had to learn how to take care of their children on constrained budgets, keep their families safe and healthy under difficult living conditions, and in general make do with very little. Rather than asking questions about how they have learned to do this successfully, what is focused on most often is their lack of formal education and skills training. Formal schooling and skills training are important, but so are the ways they have informally learned about life skills that have kept them fed and clothed. Likewise, workshop leaders putting on staff development programs in schools might learn as much as possible about the background and experience of the teachers in that school and what their knowledge base is with respect to the content of the workshop. There is nothing that turns off teachers more in these programs than being treated as if they know very little about the subject matter, especially if they have been dealing with it on a daily basis.

Second, if educators assisted learners in recognizing the many places and ways they have gone about learning in adulthood, more adults might see themselves as active learners. As a result, they may be less cautious about learning new things and even be more willing to enter formal programs of learning. One of our favorite stories is about a duck carver who was interviewed as part of a study on self-directed learning (Berger, 1990). This man, who considered himself both a nonreader and "definitely not a very good student," taught himself how to carve ducks. He started this process by carving some ducks by himself and then taking them to duck carving shows, where he could talk with other artists about his initial attempts. In addition, he read every book he could get his hands on related to duck carving (and remember that he thinks of himself as a nonreader). He now raises ducks so he can have live models, in itself another learning project. As a result of the interview process, this man saw himself as much more of a learner than he had before. Our hope is that as more individuals view themselves as active and competent learners, at least in some areas, they might be better able to address the many life challenges that come in adulthood, through both formal and informal learning modes.

In exploring the spectrum of learning opportunities in adulthood, we first discuss each of the major arenas in which adult learning occurs: learning opportunities sponsored by formal institutions, nonformal community-based learning activities, and learning that is more informal or self-directed in nature. This is followed by a description of how these learning opportunities are designed for adults. The chapter closes with an exploration of a new site for learning: the learning organization.

WHERE LEARNING OCCURS

In this section we present a framework for three types of opportunities within which learning occurs for adults: formal institutional settings, nonformal settings, and informal or self-directed contexts. This framework is an adaptation of one proposed by Coombs, Prosser, and Ahmed (1973), in which they classified lifelong learning according to three broad categories. The major difference between their conceptualization and our framework is that we have added the concepts of self-directed learning (which is synonymous with their definition of informal learning) and indigenous forms of learning. Although we are aware of the problems of trying to divide the landscape of learning opportunities into three separate categories, we are assuming that all three categories are of equal importance in the adult learning enterprise. There will always be overlaps among the three major categories of the framework, something educators of adults can capitalize on when designing educational activities.

Formal Institutional Settings

For most people, learning in adulthood brings to mind classroom settings. We envision adults encased in four walls of various shapes and sizes, learning in a variety of ways, from formal lectures to small-group interactions. When we ask participants what they remember as positive about learning in formal settings, they often cite well-organized, knowledgeable, and caring instructors; participatory instructional methods and well-crafted lectures; relevant and useful materials; and respect for them as adults and learners. And, conversely, when we ask participants to recall some of their worst experiences, they talk about arrogant instructors who have no sense of them as people or learners, poorly delivered content whatever the method used, and poorly organized and irrelevant materials.

In more recent years, as the use of technology has increased in the delivery of learning programs, our picture of learning in formal settings has expanded dramatically. We now see learners doing individualized or group learning in computer labs, participating in interactive teleconferences, and interacting from their homes with fellow participants and instructors via the Internet. So, too, have our participants' reactions to learning in formal settings changed. They now add to the traditional comments from the positive side hardware and software that is user friendly and works, and on a more negative note, the continuing crashing of systems or unintelligible software programs. The stand-alone and interconnected systems of formal settings for adult learning have indeed become very differentiated and complex.

Numerous writers have described systems for classifying the vast array of formal settings that provide learning opportunities for adults (Merriam and Brockett, 1997). One of the most useful categorizations of formal institutional settings has been given by Darkenwald and Merriam (1982). Building on the work of Knowles (1964), they describe a four-part typology:

1. *Independent adult education organizations.* These organizations exist for the primary purpose of providing learning opportunities specifically for adults. They can be community based—for example, learning exchanges and grassroots organizations—or they can be private, such as literacy groups (Literacy Volunteers of America, Laubach Literacy International, and the like) and proprietary schools or residential centers such as the Highlander Center for Research and Education, which fosters social change and encourages thoughtful community citizenship.

2. *Educational institutions.* This category includes educational institutions, including public schools and postsecondary institutions of all sorts, that have had as their primary mission serving youth. In more recent years, the populations of some of these institutions have changed so dramatically that they are now reaching more adult learners than the traditional-age students, such as many community colleges and selected postsecondary institutions. In addition, some educational institutions have been established for the primary purpose of serving adults (for example, Empire State College in New York). The Cooperative Extension Service, whose primary mission is "to disseminate and encourage the application of research generated knowledge and leadership techniques to individuals, families, and communities" (Forest, 1989, p. 336), is also included in this category.

3. *Quasi-educational organizations.* Whether public or private, these organizations consider the education of the public to be an integral part of their mission, and they view education as an allied or corollary function of their primary mission. This category includes cultural organizations (libraries, museums, and the mass media) and community organizations such as service clubs and religious and civic organizations.

4. *Noneducational organizations.* These are similar to quasi-educational organizations in that their primary mission is not educational; the difference is that rather than viewing education clearly as an allied function, noneducational organizations consider it a means to some other end. Furthermore, educational opportunities are mostly geared to the organization's employees instead of to the public, although they may sponsor some educational activities for the general public. For example, business and industry exist to make a profit. To the extent that education (more often called "training" or "performance improvement programs" in this setting) can increase profits, these institutions support it. Government agencies at the local, state, and federal levels are also engaged in extensive training and education, as are the armed forces, unions, and correctional institutions (Merriam and Brockett, 1997, pp. 106–107).

Although these settings are considered to be of a formal nature, some could also be more appropriately categorized as nonformal learning opportunities for adults, even those that are labeled independent adult education organizations. For example, some programs for adults offered by the Young Women's Christian Association (YWCA) or many community-based social action adult education programs could be categorized as nonformal learning settings. We go back to one of our assumptions about the framework we have chosen to use: there will always be overlaps among the three major categories of the framework.

Nonformal Settings

The term *nonformal education* has been used most often to describe learning opportunities outside formal educational settings that complement or supplement the needs of underserved adults or learners in developing nations (Bock and Bock, 1989; Brennan, 1997; Kidd, 1982; Merriam and Brockett, 1997). Typically, according to Merriam and Brockett (1997, pp. 169–170), the nonformal adult learning opportunity is "less structured, more flexible, and more responsive to localized needs. It also is expressly concerned with social inequities and often seeks to raise the consciousness of participants towards social action." Early programs of nonformal education were often associated with literacy initiatives and other community development programs in Third World countries.

Although this description of nonformal education is accurate for nonformal learning opportunities in most developing nations and for some programs in the more developed countries, in these latter countries many of the adult learning opportunities that could be placed in this nonformal category often more closely resemble programs in formal educational institutions. So does using this term *nonformal learning opportunities* have utility today? We believe that it does, both in terms of recognizing the many educational programs in developing nations as well as focusing on the community-based programs of adult learning in all environments that fit the parameters of less structure, more flexibility, and concern with social inequalities. In addition, another type of learning usually associated with nonformal education, that of indigenous learning, is again being recognized as an important form of learning (Brennan, 1997). Therefore, in describing nonformal educational learning opportunities, we focus principally on two types of these opportunities: community-based adult learning programs and indigenous learning.

COMMUNITY-BASED LEARNING OPPORTUNITIES. Varied pictures come to mind when we talk about community-based learning opportunities (*Adult Learning,* 1996; Beder, 1996; Cunningham and Curry, 1997; Galbraith, 1990; Hamilton and Cunningham, 1989; Harris, 1997; Hill, 1998; Peterson, 1996). We see people gathered in churches, the local community center, or the town square organizing to overcome a specific problem or issue they believe to be important in improving life in their community. These problems have ranged from addressing racial hatred and inequality to ensuring adequate housing and sanitary living conditions. Other images of community-based learning programs include men and women learning to read and write while at the same time gaining marketable job skills; farmers being introduced to new methods and crops as a way to build economic control over their lives; and spouses who batter being taught nonviolent ways of handling their anger and frustration. In addition, some traditional organizations, such as the Red Cross and the YMCA, also offer nonformal educational programs.

A common thread to all of these programs is their focus on social action and change for the betterment of some part of the community. Educators who work in these programs believe that education and training can be a powerful tool in assisting learners to take control over their own lives. Sometimes these programs are not welcomed by the mainstream community, especially if one of their major purposes is to challenge the existing way of life, including the current social and economic structures of that community. Vivid examples include the worldwide human rights movement, the continuing struggle to eliminate poverty and hunger, and the end to discriminatory practices based on race, class, and gender.

Working with adults in community-based learning settings has both its blessings and its curses. Being able to exercise flexibility in administration and programming is often recognized as its major benefit. Because these types of organizations "start small and are typically organized as free-standing organizations with fairly simple structures . . . , they can often move relatively quickly to identify problems and develop programmatic solutions" (Hemphill, 1996, p. 21). This can translate into quicker response times, in terms of both developing funding proposals and getting resources to where they are needed. "New people can be brought in (or unfortunately let go more quickly) as needed. Curricula can be rapidly developed or revised. Teaching assignments can be quickly modified" (Hemphill, 1996, p. 22). Being able to move more quickly does mean that checks and balances must be in place to ensure both a focused program direction based on community needs and quality learning opportunities that are useful. In addition, people attracted to work in community-based adult learning programs, whether paid or volunteer staff, often come with a passion for a cause that gives them the drive to stay with this work, even under the most trying conditions. On the downside, the very nature of many community-based organizations often puts them on the path of the unending search for resources. This continuing search for and worry about resources, in combination with long and often difficult working conditions, can lead to staff burnout very quickly, even for the most committed of individuals.

INDIGENOUS LEARNING. Indigenous learning is learning linked with a culture. It refers to processes and structures people within particular societies have used to learn about their culture throughout their history (Brennan, 1997). Often steeped in oral traditions and art forms, conscious use of indigenous forms of learning can enhance nonformal and perhaps even formal educational programs. Storytelling, for example, is often used by African American women to teach about the joys and sorrows of life. When teaching these women, instructors could incorporate storytelling as a major method of learning about the topic at hand, from surviving in modern-day organizations to basic literacy skills.

Descriptions of indigenous forms of learning can be found in both scholarly and more popular literature (Brennan, 1990; Cajete, 1994; Kidd and Coletta, 1980; Morgan, 1994; Ocitti, 1990). Cajete (1994) eloquently describes the tribal foundations of American Indian education, which he sees as "shared by Indigenous cultures of the world" (p. 33). In tracing these foundations, Cajete observes:

> We are tracking the earliest sources of human teaching and learning. These foundations teach us that learning is a subjective experience tied to a place environmentally, socially, and spiritually. Tribal teaching and learning were intertwined with the daily lives of both teacher and learner. Tribal education was a natural outcome of living in close communion with each other and the natural environment. The living place, the learner's extended family, the clan and tribe provided the context and source for teaching. . . . Informality characterized the greater part of American Indian teaching and learning. . . . However, formal learning was usually required in the transfer of sacred knowledge.
>
> *Hahoh* is a Tewa word sometimes used to connote the process of learning. Its closest English translation is to "breathe in." *Hahoh* is a sacred metaphor describing the perception of traditional Tribal teaching—a process of breathing in—that was creatively and ingeniously applied by all tribes. . . . Through these methods [such as storytelling, dreaming, tutoring, and artistic creation], the integration of inner and outer realities of learners and teachers were fully honored, and the complementary educational processes of both realities were fully engaged. [pp. 33–34]

Cajete beautifully expresses what teaching and learning mean to him: "A parable that often flashes through my memory during times of quiet, deep relaxation, or just before I fall asleep: 'It is an essential, life-sharing act of each generation of a People to nurture that which has given them Life and to preserve for future generations the guiding stories of their collective journey to find life'" (p. 187).

Brennan (1997, p. 191) has observed "that the lack of attention to the indigenous learning structure may have been initially the work of missionaries who viewed indigenous culture as inferior and non-Christian and therefore to be ignored or if necessary repressed." He goes on to suggest a four-stage process for recognizing indigenous learning as an essential part of the nonformal system of learning for adults. In Stage One, approaches or techniques that may be relevant to educational or developmental activities are identified—for example, the role of traditional dance and music and the use of legends, myths, tales, and proverbs (Adams, 1987, as cited by Brennan, 1997; Kidd, 1982; Kidd and Coletta, 1980). Stage Two involves classifying these approaches and techniques into a system that educators in more formal settings can understand and integrate into their own ways of thinking. "The third stage," he writes, "is associated with advocacy for the exploration of a broader indigenous learning 'system' . . . [and] the fourth stage is represented by the development of more detailed and comprehensive learning 'systems' for a particular cultural group (Brennan, 1997, pp. 192–193). Indigenous forms of learning could also be seen as informal or self-directed learning as was described by Cajete and is examined in the next section.

Informal or Self-Directed Contexts

Informal learning or self-directed contexts are the last form of learning opportunities we discuss. Although these two terms have not often been used interchangeably, both describe similar phenomena. What characterizes both informal and self-directed learning from learning in formal and nonformal settings is that this form of learning occurs most often in learners' natural settings and is initiated and carried through primarily by the learners themselves (Candy, 1991; Coombs, 1985; Merriam and Brockett, 1997; Watkins and Marsick, 1993). Although well accepted today as the way most adult learning happens, many times adults do not even recognize they are learning even when they are actively engaged in informal or self-directed learning activities at work or at home. What also confounds understanding this form of learning is that incorporating methods of self-directed learning into formal and nonformal settings has become a major focus of practice for some adult educators. We describe first informal or self-directed learning carried forth primarily through learner initiatives and actions, then present an overview of how instructors in formal settings have organized their instructional processes around tenets of self-directedness.

INDEPENDENT PURSUIT OF LEARNING. Charlie has a passion for model railroading. He spends hours in his basement planning his layout, tinkering with his equipment, and laying track. He subscribes to every railroad magazine published and talks shop with acquaintances who also have model trains. Every once in a while, he attends a model railroad show, but for the most part, this is a hobby he enjoys pursuing on his own. Over the years he has learned a great deal about model railroading and is proud of his layout, though as he says, "I'll never be totally satisfied. There are always new things coming out which I like to fiddle with."

Trudy has just learned that she has breast cancer. Once over the initial shock, she decides to take an active role in planning her treatment. So that she can speak intelligently with the myriad of medical personnel she knows she must face, she gathers as much information as she can about the disease from a number of sources, including the American Cancer Society, her local Reach for Recovery Program, the Internet, and an oncology nurse who is a friend of a friend. Moreover, she learns of a local support group for cancer patients and decides to join for both information and emotional solace, thereby choosing a nonformal learning opportunity as part of her own self-directed efforts. Her husband and best friend have joined her in her fight, and both are reaching out to a number of different sources for advice and counsel.

These scenarios, representing the independent pursuit of learning in natural settings, with or without the support of institutional resources, are very common in adult life (Candy, 1991; Percy, Burton, and Withnall, 1994). Yet even with the many verification studies that have been completed (Brockett and Hiemstra, 1991; Caffarella and O'Donnell, 1987), self-directed learning in this form is not recognized by many adults, or even some educators of adults, as "real learning." There are a lot of Charlies out there, learning all kinds of things on their own, from model railroading to making quilts and crafting clay pots. Some find friends or independent mentors to assist them in their learning, and some deliberately choose institutional resources that might be helpful to them as part of their self-directed activities. There are also numerous Trudys whose self-directed learning activities "arise from and seek to resolve a problem or situation" (Candy, 1991, p. 199). These learners often combine resources in their natural environments with those supplied by institutions, from educational materials to people who can assist them with their learning. What becomes evident is that this independent pursuit of learning does not necessarily mean learning alone, a major myth about this form of learning (Brockett, 1994). Rather, adults often use other people and even groups, whether they are institutionally based or not, in their self-directed learning pursuits.

A WAY OF ORGANIZING INSTRUCTION. The majority of descriptions of how instructors of adults have capitalized on adults' independent pursuit of learning, to capture and maximize in their classes and activities what adults already do in informal or self-directed contexts, are of programs in formal settings (Brockett and Hiemstra, 1991; Candy, 1991; Straka, 1997). Only a few authors have addressed implementing informal or self-directed learning approaches in nonformal settings (for example, Rowland and Volet, 1996). The following scenarios represent two different ways that instruction has been organized in formal settings to use what we know about how adults typically go about learning in their natural settings.

Carolyn has asked her students in a graduate class in adult education to work with her in designing the class. As part of this process, she has requested that students choose from learning objectives that she has developed for the class and/or develop their own. In addition, she has challenged them to think about how they would like to learn the material and be evaluated on their learning. Carolyn has provided them with written resources to help guide them through this process, and she has suggested that some students may want to design their own program of study, while others may feel comfortable using the more structured course syllabus materials she has provided. However students choose to put together the class for themselves, she has asked that a formal learning contract be developed by either individuals or teams of students. In addition, Carolyn has agreed to facilitate the class according to what needs are expressed by the students, as well as to present some basic concepts and ideas that she believes are appropriate for all students to understand about the subject they are studying.

Barbara, director of training for a large health care organization, has been asked to develop self-directed learning options for staff as part of the company training program. One of the guidelines for this program is that the training must relate directly to the organization's mission and product orientation; otherwise she has been given free rein to complete this task. She and her team of people from throughout the organization have identified several options that allow staff to work individually or in small work teams. Among these options are individual professional development plans, self-directed work project teams, computer-assisted packages, and collaborative action research projects.

What is common in both of these scenarios is that the instructor and program manager are working to give more control to learners about what and how they learn, and on what criteria and who should evaluate that learning. In addition, these educators are trying to foster within their learners a more independent way of going about the learning process, whether these learners choose to learn on their own or within self-selected dyads or groups. In fact, many types of organizations, from colleges and universities to business and industry, use informal or self-directed ways of learning, in many forms, as a way to organize instruction (Caffarella and Caffarella, 1986; Cranton, 1994a; Piskurich, 1993; Wilcox, 1996).

In summary, we have presented a framework that encompasses three types of settings or contexts within which learning in adulthood occurs. The first two settings, formal and nonformal, involve some form of organizational or community sponsorship. The third opportunity, informal or self-directed learning, is more of a hybrid. Although the majority of learning opportunities within this last category are planned and initiated primarily by learners in natural settings (such as the home, on the job, or through recreational pursuits), the learning processes and methods used in self-directed and informal learning have been incorporated by some formal and nonformal settings into the way they carry through their instructional programs.

THE DESIGN OF LEARNING OPPORTUNITIES

Understanding how learning is designed in formal, nonformal, and informal or self-directed ways is a good way to gain a clear picture of the range of learning sites and opportunities that are available to adults and the overlapping nature of our categories. To that end, we describe how learning opportunities are designed for adults. Houle (1996) has provided the most comprehensive categorization of educational design situations, ranging from a focus on the individual to mass audiences. Note, from Table 2.1, which outlines Houle's eleven major categories of design situations, the emphasis on both self- and other-designed situations, including the formation of new institutions to address the learning needs of adults. These design categories can be used to think through the most effective way to design educational programs for adults, whether they are housed within formal and non-formal settings or are more informal or self-directed in nature.

Within Houle's categories for educational design situations is a recognition of self- and other-designed learning opportunities. In terms of thinking through this central theme of other- versus self-designed learning opportunities, Knowles (1980, 1987), Pratt (1988), Hiemstra and Sisco (1990), and Hiemstra (1994) have provided clear guidelines. In instructor-designed learning activities, the teacher or facilitator of the learning activity is primarily responsible for planning, implementing, and evaluating the learning experience. Instruc-

Individual

1. An individual designs an activity for herself
2. An individual or a group designs an activity for another individual

Group

3. A group (with or without a continuing leader) designs an activity for itself
4. A teacher or group of teachers designs an activity for, and often with, a group of students
5. A committee designs an activity for a larger group
6. Two or more groups design an activity that enhances their combined programs of service

Institution

7. A new institution is designed
8. An institution designs an activity in a new format
9. An institution designs a new activity in an established format
10. Two or more institutions design an activity that enhances their combined programs or service

Mass

11. An individual, group, or institution designs an activity for a mass audience

Table 2.1.   Major Categories of Educational Design Situations.
Source: Adapted from Houle, 1996, p. 57.

tor-designed activities may be done by individual instructors or by a team of instructors. This instructor-designed learning is what adults have come to expect in formal settings.

When more self-directed methods are introduced, some learners at first shy away from being involved. Some even feel cheated and angry; they think that they are being asked to do what they consider to be the "teacher's job." Other adults in formal settings readily embrace the more learner-centered form of planning learning activities, and like the opportunity to have a greater voice in what and how they will learn. This greater control by individual learners can be seen in such practices as self-directed work teams, individually designed professional growth plans, and classes where instructors and participants mutually plan their learning activities (Caffarella, 1993a; Maher, 1994; Piskurich, 1993).

The andragogical model of instruction, described by Knowles (1975, 1980, 1987), is the best-known learner-centered or learner-directed model of instruction. In addition, this model has been applied to more informal and self-directed learning arenas (for example, Caffarella, 1993b; Rowland and Volet, 1996). Although on the surface this model is similar to other instructional models (diagnosing learning needs, formulating objectives, designing a pattern of learning experiences, evaluating results), there is one key difference: the learner is viewed as a mutual partner or, when learning in natural settings, as the primary designer of the learning activities. Although Knowles himself (1984, 1987; Knowles and Associates, 1984), as well as others (Brookfield, 1986; Hiemstra and Brockett, 1994; Hiemstra and Sisco, 1990), have provided rich descriptions of how his model and its variations have been used in formal settings, we believe that the andragogical model of instruction has not been used a great deal in actual practice, except in nonformal or self-directed situations. Adult learning in formal settings, whether that learning is face to face or through the use of various instructional technologies, remains primarily instructor designed and directed.

There has been a call for the merging of these two extremes of instructor-directed and learner-directed designs to account for the learners' characteristics and skills and the content being taught (Candy, 1987, 1991; Grow, 1991; Pratt, 1988). Pratt (1988) has provided the most comprehensive framework for combining these two ways of designing learning activities. As illustrated in Figure 2.1, he proposes four ways of looking at learning situations based on the

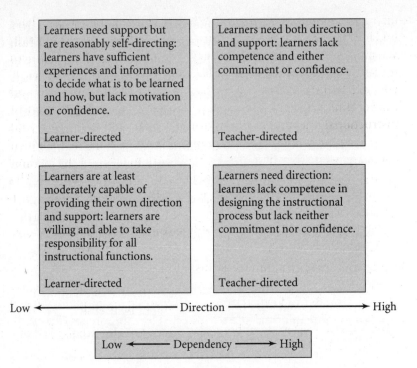

Low ⟵——————— Direction ————————⟶ High

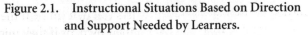

**Figure 2.1.   Instructional Situations Based on Direction
and Support Needed by Learners.**
Source: Pratt, 1988, p. 167. Adapted with permission.

direction and support needed by the learner: (1) learners need both
direction and support, (2) learners need direction, (3) learners need
support but are reasonably self-directed, and (4) learners are at least
moderately capable of providing their own direction and support. The
key variable that separates each quadrant is the learner's competence
in deciding what to learn and how to carry out the learning process
and his or her commitment and confidence to do so.

Pratt's framework can be helpful for both instructors and planners
in formal and nonformal settings and for individuals and groups of
learners who want to plan their own learning activities. In choosing
whether to use more instructor-directed or learner-directed instruction in formal settings, educators and trainers must assess learners'
abilities and commitment to planning and carrying out specific learning activities. In designing a class on woodworking, for example, an

instructor may give free run of the shop to expert hobbyists who have told her they want to become more creative in their work. In contrast, she may require those who have never done woodworking before to follow her specified regimen for learning the basic skills. Instructors who are willing to use a combination of instructor-directed and learner-directed approaches must be capable of assuming a variety of instructional roles and using a range of formats and techniques. And learners in more nonformal programs or those learning on their own could see where they fit in Pratt's framework in terms of the amount and types of assistance they may need for their learning projects. The following questions would be helpful for them to think about:

- How much do they know about the content or skill to be learned?
- Do they really want to learn this?
- Are they confident they can learn the material or skill on their own? If not, what kind of assistance might be useful?
- Do they have a sense of how to go about learning what it is they want to know or do?

In responding to these questions, learners can determine if they really can go about learning this material on their own, or if they might better combine some formal educational program with their own learning strategies.

Although the major focus of designing learning activities has been for individual learners or groups of learners, a recent trend has been to look at the organizational unit itself as a learning entity. This has led authors to speculate on what these learning organizations are all about and what educators of adults can do to foster learning organizations.

NEW FRONTIERS IN LEARNING OPPORTUNITIES: THE LEARNING ORGANIZATION

Attention in the literature and in practice to the concept of the learning organization has grown over the past decade. Watkins and Marsick (1993, p. 8) define the learning organization as "one that learns continuously and transforms itself. Learning takes place in individuals, teams, the organization, and even in the communities with which the organizations interact. Learning is a continuous, strategically used process—integrated with, and running parallel to [the] work [of the organization]." This learning capability improves an organization's capacity to respond quickly and in novel ways, thus increasing its ability to foster innovation and change. Organizations with this ability to make rapid changes may have a competitive advantage in the marketplace (Moingeon and Edmondson, 1996).

There is skepticism and even controversy as to whether organizations can really learn or whether "it is actually individuals in organizations that do the learning" (Rowden, 1996a, p. 107). Yet evidence is growing that understanding the learning organization is critical to fostering the growth and development of organizations and people who are associated with these organizations (Di Bella and Nevis, 1998; Leithwood, Leonard, and Sharratt, 1998; Senge, 1990; Watkins, 1996).

Grounded in the early work of Argyris and Schön (1974, 1978), among others, numerous writers have described what is needed to create a learning organization (Di Bella and Nevis, 1998; Moingeon and Edmondson, 1996; Pedler, Burgoyne, and Boydell, 1991; Senge, 1990; Starkey, 1996; Watkins and Marsick, 1993). One of the most often quoted sources is Senge's book, *The Fifth Discipline* (1990). It is Senge's contention that "organizations learn only through individuals who learn" (p. 140). With that assumption at the center of his theory, he describes five core disciplines, or "component technologies," that individuals must adopt for the learning organization to become a reality. Senge views systems thinking as the cornerstone of the learning organization. He believes that it is critical for people to shift their thinking from "seeing parts to seeing wholes, from seeing people as helpless reactors to seeing them as active participants in their reality, from reacting to the present to creating the future" (p. 69). Without this shift in thinking, he views the other four disciplines (developing personal mastery, changing mental models, building shared vision, and participating in team learning) as useless.

In a similar vein, Watkins and Marsick (1993) have outlined six "action imperatives" needed to create and sustain learning organizations. The first imperative is to create continuous learning opportunities at all levels of the organization. These opportunities range from on-the-job learning experiences to hosting global dialogue teams, with the goal that learning becomes an integral part of the everyday work life. To promote this continuous learning, two other action imperatives are brought into play: inquiry and dialogue, and collaboration and team learning. These learning strategies seem to form the heart of most organizational learning efforts, with the emphasis on the collective and interdependent nature of these processes. The fourth imperative, establishing systems to capture and share learning, involves "building organizational capacity for new thinking that is then embedded and shared with others" (Watkins and Marsick, 1993, p. 15). This fourth imperative, along with the fifth, of empowering people toward a collective vision, mirrors Senge's disciplines of changing one's mental models and building shared vision. The final imperative, connecting the organization to its environment, acknowledges the connections between the organization and its external constituents, including its customers and the various local, national, and international communities that affect the work of the organization. These connections are symbiotic; not only do the external constituents affect the organization, but the organization also affects these external groups.

In emphasizing the collective nature of organizational learning, Dixon (1997) has offered the metaphor of the hallway as a useful analogy for thinking about the process of building and sustaining learning organizations. She defines hallways as "places where collective meaning is made—in other words, meaning is not just exchanged, it is constructed in the dialogue between organizational members" (p. 25). Although the dissemination of complete and accurate information is needed to enable this process to work, it is not sufficient to promote shared meanings among people. Dixon contrasts this accessible meaning of the hallways to that of private meaning, which is knowledge known only to individuals and not accessible to others. Collective meanings of organizational members are held in what she terms the organization's storeroom. This collective meaning, which includes norms, strategies, and assumptions about how the organization functions, is the glue that holds the organization together. She acknowledges that this collective meaning, if not allowed to be questioned, can have a negative impact on organizations' being able to learn and change. Dixon goes on to assert that "hallways are the only spaces in which it is possible for an organization to learn" (p. 27) and outlines various examples of hallway learning, from "whole systems in the room" to the use of action learning, learning maps, and the appreciative inquiry approach. Finally, Dixon outlines seven critical elements that characterize hallway learning: (1) reliance on discussion, not speeches; (2) egalitarian participation; (3) encouragement of multiple perspectives; (4) nonexpert-based dialogue; (5) use of a participant-generated database; (6) the creating of shared experiences; and (7) the creation of unpredictable outcomes. We find the last element especially intriguing; it asks those of us who choose to create learning organizations to move away from the predictable aspects of learning and into the realm of reframing problems in unexpected ways and finding possibilities never thought of before.

In addition to providing opportunities for hallways of learning in organizations, authors have cited other factors that facilitate the creation of learning organizations. Di Bella, Nevis, and Gould (1996) have provided the most comprehensive list of these facilitating factors. Their first three items are similar to those indicated by Senge (1990) and Watkins and Marsick (1993): scanning imperative (of external happenings in one's environment), continuous learning, and a systems perspective. They also include seven other factors (Di Bella, Nevis, and Gould, 1996, p. 43):

1. *Performance gap.* Shared perceptions of a gap between actual and desired performances are viewed as opportunities for learning.

2. *Concern for measurement.* Discourse over defining specific, quantifiable measures when venturing into new areas is seen as a learning activity.

3. *Experimental mind-set.* Changes in work processes, policies, and structures are viewed as a continuous series of tryouts, and small failures are encouraged.

4. *Climate of openness.* Information is accessible, problems and errors are shared and not hidden, and conflict is acceptable.

5. *Operational variety.* Pluralistic, rather than monolithic, definition of valued internal capabilities (for example, response modes, procedures) is fostered.

6. *Multiple advocates.* Top-down and bottom-up initiatives are possible.

7. *Involved leadership.* Leaders at significant levels articulate vision and are actively engaged in implementing that vision.

In contrast, there are a number of barriers or inhibitors to creating learning organizations (Marsick and Neaman, 1996; Marsick and Watkins, 1994; Watkins and Marsick, 1993). Among the most critical are the inability of organizational members to recognize and change their existing mental models, the lingering power of individualism in organizations versus the spirit of collaboration and team learning, the lack of skills and developmental readiness by people to undertake "system-wide learning," and "truncated learning or the ghosts of learning efforts that took root because they were interrupted or only partially implemented" (Watkins and Marsick, 1993, p. 240).

We believe that the concept of the learning organization offers a whole new way of working and thinking for educators in both formal and nonformal settings. It allows us to move beyond planning just for individuals and groups of learners in terms of affecting both learning processes and outcomes. Creating learning organizations, whether we are associated with educational, quasi-educational, or noneducational institutions, provides a way to foster learning communities that are open to change and innovative practices.

SUMMARY

Learning opportunities for adults are found in a variety of settings, from formal institutions to one's home or place of employment. The importance of understanding this vast array of learning opportunities for adults is twofold: acknowledging prior knowledge and experiences of learners wherever gained is important to the practice of adult educators, and individual learners, even those without formal schooling, may be better able to recognize their abilities and skills as lifelong learners.

There are three major types of opportunities in which learning occurs for adults: formal settings, nonformal settings, and informal or self-directed contexts. Although the categorization of these learning opportunities and the language used within these categories helps us to think about learning, what is more crucial is the recognition that learning opportunities come in many sizes, shapes, and forms. The most critical actions that educators of adults can take is to recognize the equal importance of the various types of adult learning and advocate that people use them in whatever situation or setting they find themselves.

Designing and facilitating educational activities, no matter what the setting or context, can be done in a number of ways, whether the primary planners are individuals, informal groups, or people in institutional settings. Instructor-designed learning, where the teacher or program planner is primarily responsible for planning, implementing, and evaluating the learning, is predominant in formal settings. In contrast, learner-centered design crosses all three arenas of learning, although it is primarily used in the informal or self-directed context. More recently there has been a call for the merging of these two design frameworks, with both educators and learners making informed choices about what planning process to use depending on the specific situation and the learner's prior knowledge, abilities, and motivation.

The chapter concluded with an exploration of the learning organization as the newest frontier in educational opportunities for adults. In learning organizations, learning—whether done by individuals, groups, or the organization as a whole—is a central, valued, and integral part of organizational life. The heart of the learning organization is the willingness of organizations to allow their employees and other stakeholders related to the organization to suspend and question the assumptions within which they operate, then create and examine new ways of solving organizational problems and means of operating. This process requires that people at all levels of the organization be willing to think within a systems framework, with the emphasis on collective inquiry, dialogue, and action. Creating learning organizations could allow educators of adults, whether they are associated with formal or nonformal settings, to develop learning communities in which change is accepted as the norm and innovative practices are embraced.

CHAPTER THREE

Participation in Adult Education

—〜〜—

Adult education is a large and amorphous field of practice, with no neat boundaries such as age, as in the case of elementary and secondary education, or mission, as in the case of higher education. Adult education with its myriad content areas, delivery systems, goals, and clienteles defies simple categorization. In the previous chapter, we looked at the spectrum of settings where adult learning takes place, ranging from formal institutional settings, to nonformal community-based sites, to one's home, as in the case of many self-directed learning activities. One way to grasp something of the field is to find out who is involved in the activity itself—hence, studies of participation.

Historically, participation in adult education is largely a voluntary activity. Not only is there curiosity about who volunteers to participate, but without volunteer learners, there would be a much smaller enterprise of adult education. Providers of adult education therefore need to know who is participating, why they are participating, and what conditions are likely to promote greater participation. Conversely, knowing who is *not* involved can be important information for providers who wish to attract new learners. Interestingly, the report of the first national study of participation is titled *Volunteers for Learning* (Johnstone and Rivera, 1965).

Knowledge about participation is useful to policymakers in terms of funding and to those who plan and implement programs. At the federal level, for example, funding for literacy and other programs is a function of who is now participating, in conjunction with the perceived needs of nonparticipants. Along with current numbers and rates of participation of various segments of the adult population, other sociopolitical and economic factors play important parts in federal policy formation, not the least of which is the desire to maintain a stable democratic and globally competitive society. For those who plan learning activities and instruct adults, it is certainly helpful to know as much as possible about the clientele being served.

This chapter offers a descriptive profile of who participates in adult learning activities. The emphasis is on formal, institutionally based programs, because that is where the bulk of information lies. There are no national studies of participation in nonformal adult education activities that we could find; as for participation in self-directed learning, only one national study has been conducted. There are, however, many studies on what motivates adults to participate *or not* in adult education. Why an adult might choose to participate is also discussed in this chapter. Finally, we review attempts to build models that explain and predict participation.

WHO PARTICIPATES?

In 1962 an "inquiry into the nature of adult education in America" was funded by the Carnegie Corporation and carried out by researchers Johnstone and Rivera (1965) at the National Opinion Research Center (NORC) in Chicago. The study sought to describe participation in formal and informal educational activities, assess attitudes and opinions held by adults concerning education, describe the organizations delivering adult education in a typical urban community, and focus on the educational and work experiences of young adults aged seventeen to twenty-four. The findings of this first national study have provided a baseline against which the findings of subsequent studies have been compared.

Since comparisons are made, it is important to know how *adult education* and *adult* are defined in this study. Realizing the import of this function, Johnstone and Rivera (1965, p. 26) struggled to come up with a definition of an adult educational activity that was broad enough to capture systematic efforts at learning but not so broad as to include "a host of activities . . . which would fall beyond the range of any reasonable or workable definition of adult education." They decided that an adult education activity would have as its main purpose the desire to acquire some type of knowledge, information, or skill and that it would include some form of instruction (including self-instruction). They thus measured involvement as a full-time adult student, as a part-time participant in adult education activities, and as a participant in independent self-education. An adult was defined as anyone either age twenty-one or over, married, or the head of a household. Interviews with a random national sample of nearly twelve thousand households formed the data set.

Using the above definitions, Johnstone and Rivera estimated that 22 percent of American adults participated in "one or more forms of learning" between June 1961 and June 1962 (p. 1). They also discovered that what adults were learning was largely practical and skill oriented rather than academic: "Subject matter directly useful in the performance of everyday tasks and obligations accounted for the most significant block of the total activities recorded. Together, the vocational and home and family life categories alone represented 44 percent of all formal courses studied and 47 percent of the subjects people studied on their own" (p. 3).

This landmark study also identified the major demographic and socioeconomic variables characteristic of participants. Age and formal schooling were delineated as the major correlates of participation in adult education. Johnstone and Rivera's often-quoted profile of the typical adult learner has held up, with minor deviations, in all subsequent national studies of participation. Their profile is as follows: "The adult education participant is just as often a woman as a man, is typically under forty, has completed high school or more, enjoys an above-average income, works full-time and most often in a white-collar occupation, is married and has children, lives in an urbanized area but more likely in a suburb than large city, and is found in all parts of the country, but more frequently in the West than in other regions" (p. 8).

Beginning in 1969, the National Center for Education Statistics (NCES) in the U.S. Department of Education undertook a set of triennial surveys of participation of adults in education. The results of the first six surveys (1969, 1972, 1975, 1978, 1981, 1984) and two studies in 1991 and 1995 can be loosely compared with each other to reveal participation trends. In these surveys, adult education is equated with organized instruction: "Adult education is defined as any course or educational activity taken part-time and reported as adult education by respondents seventeen years old and over" (U.S. Department of Education, 1986). Changes in methodology and sample design over the years warrant caution in making comparisons (Collins, Brick, and Kim, 1997). Nevertheless, certain trends emerge.

The first trend is that the numbers of adults participating part time in organized instruction has increased from a low of 10 percent in the 1969 survey, to 14 percent in 1984, to 38 percent in 1991, and to 40 percent in 1995. The 40 percent figure obtained in 1995 is congruent with a subsequent study of participation by the United Nations Educational, Scientific, and Cultural Organization (UNESCO) that found that 41 percent of the American adults in the study sample participated in some form of education (Valentine, 1997). In a recent report comparing the NCES study findings with the UNESCO study, Valentine summarizes the following trends:

- In 1969 and the years immediately following, men were disproportionately represented among participants. By 1984, participation rates had equalized, with women participants outnumbering men in both job-related and non-job-related activities. In the 1991 and 1995 NCES reports—and in the present [UNESCO] study—there is no significant difference in men and women's participation rates.

- In 1969, adult education courses were nearly evenly split between job-related and non-job-related. In the late seventies, job-related courses began to gain ascendancy, and by 1984, job-related courses dominated 2 to 1. This trend continued through June 1993 (Kopka and Peng), though the 1995 study places this ratio closer to 1 to 1. In the current UNESCO study, fully 90.6 percent of adults cited career or job-related reasons for educational participation. Clearly, there is a marked increase in the employment-orientation of adult education in the United States. Also clear, however, is the fact that methodological differences must be blamed for a large proportion of the observed differences in percentage.

- Since 1969, whites were overrepresented among participants. This trend continues through the 1990–91 report. (Comparable figures have not yet been released for the 1994–95 data.) The current

UNESCO survey, unfortunately, does not include analyses based on race and ethnicity. Even without current data, it is safe to assume that "minority" groups in the United States are underrepresented in most types of adult education endeavors. [1997, pp. 6–7]

Johnstone and Rivera's profile of the typical adult learner has changed little over the past thirty years. Compared to those who do not participate, participants in adult education are better educated, younger, have higher incomes, and are most likely to be white and employed full time. Except for race, which was not a variable, the most recent UNESCO study findings are congruent with this profile. As can be seen in Table 3.1, better-educated, younger, married or single (never married), American-born versus immigrants, and adults employed full-time in professional and technical occupations are most likely to participate in adult education.

Among the other national studies, two are worth mentioning for their somewhat different emphases. Aslanian and Brickell (1980) sampled 1,519 adults over age twenty-five, of whom 744, or 49 percent, reported having learned something formally or informally in the year prior to the study. Although the focus of this study was on reasons that adults gave for their participation, the authors present a profile of learners compared to nonlearners. In contrasting the 744 learners with the 775 nonlearners, learners were found to be younger and better educated; they also had higher incomes, were employed, lived in urbanized areas, were white, were engaged in professional and technical work, and were single or divorced.

The second study, by Penland (1979), had a considerably different focus from the other work reviewed here. Penland was interested in corroborating Tough's (1979) findings that more than 90 percent of adults are engaged in independent learning projects (see Chapter Twenty). Briefly, Tough felt that adults were engaged in learning as part of their everyday lives—learning that was not necessarily institutionally based and not easily recognized by the learners themselves due to the association of learning with formal instruction. Consequently, Tough and Penland asked adults to think about major learning activities that were clearly focused efforts to gain and retain knowledge or skill. A learning project had to have occurred over at least a two-day period, totaling at least seven hours of learning. Respondents in both studies were given a list of things people learn about—a foreign language, gardening, raising children, and so on.

Attribute	Participation Rate (percent)
Level of Education	
Did not complete secondary school	15.3 percent
Secondary school diploma	31.7
Postsecondary degree	62.3
Age	
17–24 years	47.6 percent
25–34 years	44.1
35–44 years	44.3
45–54 years	42.1
55–64 years	26.3
Marital Status	
Single	43.6 percent
Married	41.7
Widowed, divorced, or separated	33.9
Country of Origin	
United States	42.8 percent
Other	29.1
Type of Community	
Nonurban	43.9 percent
Urban	33.8
Employment Status	
Employed	47.8 percent
Unemployed, looking for work	27.5
Homemaker	13.5
Retired	12.5
Student	91.8
Other	16.3
Size of Company	
Fewer than 200 employees	36.0 percent
200 or more employees	58.0
Occupation	
Government	57.7 percent
Professional and technical	70.0
Clerical	52.6
Service	39.4
Crafts, manufacturing, and skilled agriculture	25.2
Nature of Job	
Employee with no supervisory responsibilities	40.0 percent
Employee with supervisory responsibilities	61.5
Self-employed	33.0

Table 3.1.   Personal Attributes of Participants.

Source: Valentine, 1997. Reprinted from Paul Belanger and Sofia Valdivielso (eds.), *The Emergence of Learning Societies: Who Participates in Adult Learning?* Copyright 1997, Chapter 6, with permission from Elsevier Science.

Penland's 1,501 respondents were selected from the U.S. population by means of a modified probability sample. He found that "almost 80 percent (78.9) of the population of eighteen years and over perceive themselves as continuing learners whether in self-planned or formal courses" and "over three-quarters (76.1 percent) of the U.S. population had planned one or more learning projects on their own" (p. 173). Furthermore, of the nine areas of study, personal development and home and family ranked highest in popularity, followed by hobbies and recreation, general education, job, religion, voluntary activity, public affairs, and agriculture/technology.

In summary, although participation rates vary depending on how adult and adult education are defined, the profile of the typical adult learner has remained remarkably consistent across studies. Next we discuss why adults do or do not choose to participate in learning activities.

WHY ADULTS DO OR DO NOT PARTICIPATE

Adults are busy people. Most spend at least eight hours a day working and often as many hours attending to family, household, and community concerns. Why do as many as 79 million of these adults (Valentine, 1997) enroll in adult education classes, seek private instruction, or engage in independent learning projects? Teachers, counselors, administrators, and policymakers all have a keen interest in understanding why people do or do not participate in learning activities. One approach to answering this question is to ask people their reasons for participating, and this has been done as part of the national survey studies already cited. Another approach is to try to determine the underlying motivational orientations or barriers to participation of certain groups of learners. These approaches are discussed below.

Survey Studies

Hundreds of local, state, and national studies have asked adults their reasons for engaging in educational pursuits. In most of these studies, respondents are presented with a list of reasons that people might participate and asked to indicate which ones apply to them. Most respondents report multiple reasons. If asked to indicate the main reason (as they were in the NCES surveys), however, they most commonly cite job-related motives.

The strength of employment-related motives was first uncovered by Johnstone and Rivera (1965). Thirty-six percent of respondents indicated that they were "preparing for a new job or occupation" (p. 144), and 32 percent said they participated in education "for the job I held at that time." The authors concluded that "vocational goals most frequently direct adults into continuing education" (p. 144). The eight surveys of participation conducted by the NCES have consistently revealed job-related reasons as the most frequently cited, with personal development courses a close second in the most recent study, from 1995 (Kim, Collins, Stowe, and Chandler, 1995). Figure 3.1, which is drawn from the 1991 NCES study (cited by Kopka and Peng, 1993), shows the relative importance of work-related reasons by age group. In the most recent UNESCO survey, fully 90.6 percent cited career- or job-related reasons for participation, and 9.4 percent cited "personal interest" (Valentine, 1997). When asked about the goal of the learning activity, the largest percentage (58 percent) said it was professional or career upgrading, 18.3 percent "other," 17.6 percent to earn a college or university degree, 3.8 percent to earn a vocational or apprenticeship certificate, and 2.3 percent to complete secondary school (Valentine, 1997). Clearly, there is a strong linkage between one's work life and participation in adult education. Cross (1981) explains this relationship as quite logical given most adults' life situations:

> People who do not have good jobs are interested in further education to get better jobs, and those who have good jobs would like to advance them. Women, factory workers, and the poorly educated, for example, are more likely to be pursuing education in order to prepare for new jobs, whereas men, professionals, and college graduates are more likely to be seeking advancement in present jobs. Men are more interested in job-related learning than women are, and young people are far more interested in it than older people are. Interest in job-related goals begins to decline at age 50 and drops off sharply after age 60. Those who are not currently participating in learning activities (most often the economically disadvantaged and poorly educated) are even more likely to express an interest in job-related education than are their more advantaged peers, who can afford the luxury of education for recreation and personal satisfaction. [1981, pp. 91–92]

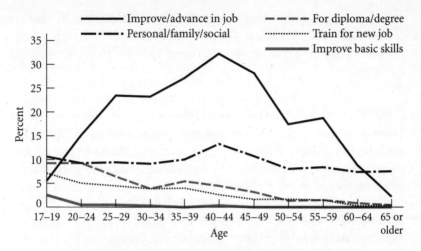

Figure 3.1. Participation Rates in Adult Education and Main Reasons for Participating, by Age, 1991.

Source: U. S. Department of Education, National Center for Education Statistics. *National Household Education Survey, Adult Education Component,* cited in Kopka and Peng, 1993, p. 4.

Approaching people's reasons for participating in adult education from a somewhat different angle, Aslanian and Brickell (1980) sought to test the hypothesis that life transitions motivate adults to seek out learning experiences. They found that 83 percent of the learners in their sample could describe some past, present, or future change in their lives as reasons for learning. The other 17 percent were engaged in learning for its own sake—that is, to stay mentally alert—or for the social aspects or because learning is a satisfying activity. Those going through transitions, such as marriage, retirement, job changes, birth of children, and so on, were able to identify specific events, such as getting fired or promoted, that triggered their transition. The authors noted seven kinds of transitions. Those relating to career and family accounted for 56 percent and 16 percent of the transitions, respectively. The other transitions, in descending importance, concerned leisure (13 percent), art (5 percent), health (5 percent), religion (4 percent), and citizenship (1 percent). "To know an adult's life schedule," the authors conclude, "is to know an adult's learning schedule" (pp. 60–61).

The survey studies have been helpful in identifying reasons adults give for participating in learning activities. Since most adult learners are employed and derive much of their identity from their work, it is not surprising to find that at least half of them are involved in education for job-related reasons. Other investigations have sought to go beyond these self-reported data in trying to understand the why of participation.

Motivational Orientations of Learners

Interest in categorizing the various reasons given for participating in adult learning has spurred a line of inquiry in addition to the survey studies. This area of investigation was initiated with the publication by Houle in *The Inquiring Mind* in 1961. Choosing a small, select sample of twenty-two adults "conspicuously engaged in various forms of continuing learning" (p. 13), Houle conducted in-depth interviews that explored his subjects' history of learning, factors that led them to be continuing learners, and their views of themselves as learners. An analysis of the interview data revealed three separate learning orientations held by the adults. The now-famous typology consists of *goal-oriented* learners, who use education as a means of achieving some other goal; *activity-oriented* learners, who participate for the sake of the activity itself and the social interaction; and *learning-oriented* participants, who seek knowledge for its own sake.

Houle's research stimulated a number of studies attempting to affirm or refine the original typology. Sheffield (1964), for example, used Houle's interview transcriptions to develop an instrument to measure adults' learning orientations. Through factor analysis, he came up with five orientations, two of which could be subsumed under two of Houle's categories. Burgess (1971) and Boshier (1971) also developed scales in which the items have been shown to cluster into between five and eight factors.

By far the most extensive work has been done with Boshier's forty-eight item Education Participation Scale (EPS), later refined to forty items. Used first by Boshier in New Zealand, it was subsequently used by Morstain and Smart (1974) with 611 adults in evening credit courses at a college in New Jersey. Their six-factor solution extended Houle's typology somewhat:

1. *Social Relationships.* This factor reflects participation in order to make new friends or meet members of the opposite sex.

2. *External Expectations.* These participants are complying with the wishes or directives of someone else with authority.

3. *Social Welfare.* This factor reflects an altruistic orientation; learners are involved because they want to serve others or their community.

4. *Professional Advancement.* This factor is strongly associated with participation for job enhancement or professional advancement.

5. *Escape/Stimulation.* This factor is indicative of learners who are involved as a way of alleviating boredom or escaping home or work routine.

6. *Cognitive Interest.* These participants, identical to Houle's learning-oriented adults, are engaged for the sake of learning itself.

Boshier himself conducted an extensive test of Houle's typology using his EPS scale (Boshier and Collins, 1985). Using cluster analysis instead of factor analysis, because the technique is more congruent with Houle's original conceptualization of three separate but overlapping orientations, he analyzed the responses of 13,442 learners from Africa, Asia, New Zealand, Canada, and the United States. Boshier and Collins were able to effect a three-cluster solution "loosely isomorphic with Houle's topology" (p. 125). They found that "Cluster I consisted of the Cognitive Interest items and was congruent with his learning orientation." Cluster II, the activity orientation, "was multifaceted and composed of items normally labeled Social Stimulation, Social Contact, External Expectations, and Community Service" (p. 125). Cluster III consisted of the Professional Advancement items and thus resembled Houle's goal orientation. The authors note that although their three-cluster solution is "loosely isomorphic," the grouping of items to make up the activity cluster that matches Houle's typology is "overly generous." They conclude that "Houle's intuition has been partly collaborated; two of the six clusters were as he described them" (p. 127).

A more recent study using Boshier's EPS analyzed responses from 1,142 students in programs at a large state university (Fujita-Starck, 1996). Results confirmed the seven-factor typology proposed by Boshier in 1991 (communication improvement, social contact, educational preparation, professional advancement, family togetherness, social stimulation, and cognitive interest). The author also found the scale to be reliable "in differentiating among a diverse group of students with varying reasons for participating in continuing education" (p. 38).

Despite the limitations of this line of research (Courtney, 1992; Long, 1983), it has become evident that learners' motivations for participating in adult education are many, complex, and subject to change. The search for an underlying motivational structure related to participation is likely to continue, however, for such knowledge "can assist educators and administrators in identifying and meeting the needs of a wide spectrum of learners relative to program content, as well as the time, duration, and location of related activities" (Fujita-Starck, 1996, p. 39).

Barriers to Participation

Knowing why adults participate in adult education does not tell us why many do not. That is, we cannot assume that those who are not participating are happily employed and satisfied with their family, community, and leisure activities. In fact, one of the field's biggest mysteries is why more adults, especially those who might benefit the most, are not involved in adult education. This question has prompted research into why adults do not participate in adult education.

The two most often cited reasons for nonparticipation are lack of time and lack of money. These are socially acceptable reasons for not doing something, of course, and probably very legitimate reasons for adults who are busy people trying to become or stay economically solvent and take care of their families and themselves. Johnstone and Rivera (1965) in their national study of participation found that 43 percent cited cost as a reason for not attending adult education courses and 39 percent said they were too busy. These were also the two major reasons for nonparticipation cited in the UNESCO study (Valentine, 1997). Forty-five percent of respondents said lack of time was a barrier for job-related education; this figure climbs to 60.1 percent for non-job-related education. Interestingly, 33.4 percent gave cost as a barrier for job-related education, but 25.4 percent reported cost as a barrier for non-job-related education (Valentine, 1997). For both types of education, "family responsibilities" was cited as the next most salient barrier.

Reasons that adults do not participate have been clustered by several researchers into types of barriers. Johnstone and Rivera (1965) clustered ten potential barriers into two categories: external, or situational, and internal, or dispositional, barriers. External barriers are "influences more or less external to the individual or at least beyond the individual's control" (p. 214), such as cost of the program. Internal barriers reflect personal attitudes, such as thinking one is too old to learn. Older adults, for example, cited more dispositional barriers, and younger people and women were more constrained by situational barriers. On the other hand, Valentine's (1997) analysis of the UNESCO data revealed that situational barriers affected both men and women: "Women were more likely than men to report that family responsibilities interfered with both job-related and non-job-related education. Men were more likely than women to report that work demands interfered with non-job-related education."

To situational and dispositional barriers, Cross (1981, p. 98) added a third cluster: institutional barriers, consisting of "all those practices and procedures that exclude or discourage working adults from participating in educational activities." Darkenwald and Merriam (1982) also cite institutional and situational barriers but divide the dispositional barrier into psychosocial obstacles (beliefs, values, attitudes, and perceptions about education or about oneself as a learner) and informational, which reflects the lack of awareness as to what educational opportunities are available.

Darkenwald and colleagues have gone beyond the three-part or four-part barrier typologies in developing a scale of deterrents to participation that can be factor analyzed to reveal the structure of reasons underlying nonparticipation (in much the same way the EPS does for participation). A form of the Deterrents to Participation Scale (DPS) used with the general adult public revealed six factors of nonparticipation: lack of confidence, lack of course relevance, time constraints, low personal priority, cost, and personal problems (such as child care, family problems, and personal health) (Darkenwald and Valentine, 1985). In a later analysis of the same data, Valentine and Darkenwald (1990) derived a typology of adult nonparticipants. According to their analysis, the adult nonparticipants in the general public cluster into five distinct groups. People are deterred from participating by personal problems, lack of confidence, educational costs, lack of interest in organized education generally, or lack of interest in available courses.

Viewing participation from the perspective of barriers lends another dimension to the field's attempt to understand why some adults participate in adult education and others do not. But this perspective tells only part of the story. The bulk of research in North America on nonparticipation has been from the perspective of the *individual's* motivation, attitudes, beliefs, behaviors, position in the life cycle, and so on. This has not always been the case, however, as Courtney (1992) points out in his historical analysis of participation research. Prior to the 1960s, a popular topic among researchers was social participation. General social participation refers to the extent to which a person is an active participant in family and community life; participating in adult education activities was considered just one component of social participation. Benn (1997) has recently revisited this notion of social participation in a survey study of 259 adults in a range of educational programs. She concludes that the extent of one's general social activity affects learning activity, a finding that has implications for marketing and recruitment: "Rather than blanket publicity, a more effective approach might be to advertise through social groups and organizations. . . . Adult education does not choose its students, they choose (or do not choose) adult education" (p. 34).

For some, a combination of psychological and social factors acts as a barrier to participation. Rubenson (1998, p. 259) points out that "only when we include structural factors and analyze the interaction between them and the individual conceptual apparatus does an interpretation become possible. Adults' readiness to learn and barriers preventing it . . . can be understood in terms of societal processes and structure, institutional processes and structure and individual consciousness and activity." Hall and Donaldson's (1997) study of why women without a high school diploma chose *not* to participate provides examples of how the social and the psychological interact. Preadult factors such as parents' education, early pregnancies, and economic status formed part of the picture. Lack of a support system was a second factor. Conventional barriers such as lack of time, information, and child care were also operative. The fourth dynamic Hall and Donaldson termed "lack of voice": "At the heart of nonparticipation lies a 'deterrent' so deeply embedded in some women that no theory can fully capture its meaning. The way a woman feels about herself, her self-esteem and self confidence, and the way she can express herself are significant elements in her decision about whether to participate in adult education" (p. 98).

The question of why some adults participate and others do not can also be addressed from a strictly sociological perspective (Bagnall, 1989; Courtney, 1992; Jarvis, 1985; Nordhaug, 1990; Quigley, 1990; Rubenson, 1998; Sissel, 1997). Rubenson (1998, p. 261) characterizes this approach to participation as consisting of two dimensions—"the long arm of the family as reflected in the relationship between social background, educational attainment and participation . . . and the long arm of the job: the increased importance of adult education and training as investment." Nordhaug (1990) examined participation in Norwegian adult education not from the individual participant's perspective, but from variables such as material resources and population density related to the structure of municipalities. Sissel's (1997) study of parent involvement in Head Start programs found that "power relations were expressed in the withholding or allocation of programmatic resources, and functioned to either impede or promote participation" (p. 123). She recommends that more research be conducted on "specific structural factors" (such as race and gender) that "enhance or impede participation" (p. 135). Davis-Harrison (1996) also found race and class to be important variables in investigating the nonparticipation of blue-collar male workers. Finally, in raising the interesting question of just how "voluntary" voluntary participation in continuing education was for government workers in British Columbia, Stalker (1993b) found the concept to be something of a myth. The notion of voluntary participation did not adequately account for issues of power, authority, and control.

Working from this same critical perspective, Jarvis (1985) makes the case for a class analysis in that the middle-class bias found in all studies of participation can be explained by the idea that adult education is organized by the middle class, and the presentation of knowledge is middle class in both language and content. Furthermore, previous school experiences select out "those who were labeled as successful in education" (p. 204), and those who will be labeled successful is pretty much predetermined by one's class, age, sex, and educational background. In a similar vein, Keddie (1980, p. 63) makes the point that what we consider to be "problems" in adult education—attracting more participants from the lower socioeconomic classes, for example—are really society's problems: "That is, change will depend on seeing that the 'problems' lie within the nature of the provision adult education makes and not in those who do not avail themselves of the resources it offers."

In summary, looking at social structure rather than individual needs and interests reveals some very different explanations as to why adults do or do not participate in adult learning activities. These competing perspectives imply different strategies for increasing participation. If individual interests and motivation account for participation, then recruitment efforts would center on responding to an adult's perceived learning needs and stimulating motivation. If, on the other hand, participation or nonparticipation is seen as a function of the social structure, then one would work toward changing society in ways that would facilitate participation (see Chapter Four for a more thorough discussion of social issues in the provision of adult learning opportunities). The most robust explanation of participation is likely to be found in considering *both* the psychological and sociological perspectives.

EXPLAINING AND PREDICTING PARTICIPATION

When one considers the myriad of psychological and sociological variables and the relationships between them that affect participation, it is not surprising that there is as yet no single theory or model to explain or predict participation in adult education. What we have are a number of models, some emphasizing the psychological and some linking the individual with social and environmental forces. Some focus on the decision to participate (Henry and Basile, 1994), others on persistence in the adult education activity (Boshier, 1973). A recent model connects participation, learning, and noninvolvement (Sissel, 1997). Most of the models apply to participation in formal learning activities rather than informal or self-directed learning, and only a few have been tested. Some models are borrowed from other fields and applied to adult students. Tinto's (1993) model of student departure from higher education, for example, has been applied to nontraditional students in higher education (Ashar and Skenes, 1993) and to doctoral graduate students (Lees, 1996). In this section of the chapter we offer a brief overview of a number of models from adult education and then step back and assess model-building efforts generally.

Models of Participation

Models are visual representations of how concepts related to participation interact to explain who participates and perhaps even predict who will participate in the future. Following are summaries of seven such models.

MILLER'S FORCE-FIELD ANALYSIS. One of the earliest efforts to explain participation was presented by Harry Miller in 1967. Miller attempted to link the motivational needs hierarchy of Maslow (1954) with Lewin's (1947) force-field theory. From Maslow, Miller hypothesized that adults from lower socioeconomic classes would participate for job-related and basic skills reasons, whereas participants from higher social classes would seek education to satisfy achievement and self-realization needs. This tendency was also related to one's place in the life cycle: younger people would be more interested than older people in achieving economic security, for example. From Lewin, Miller drew the idea that both negative and positive forces act on the individual, and the direction and sum total of these forces determine an adult's motivation to participate. Miller's model consists of figures depicting forces by arrows, with wider arrows signifying a stronger force at work. There are figures for four social classes (lower lower, working, lower middle, and upper middle) and four content areas (vocational, family, citizenship, and self-development). Figure 3.2 displays the strength of positive and negative forces for education for vocational competence for the lower-lower-class level. Five arrows represent negative forces (such as "hostility to education") and four arrows represent positive forces (such as "survival needs"). The summative level of motivation for this group is relatively low, as indicated by the bar's being below the midpoint of the figure.

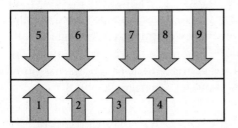

Negative Forces

5. Action-excitement orientation of male culture

6. Hostility to education and to middle-class object orientation

7. Relative absence of specific, immediate job opportunities at end of training

8. Limited access through organizational ties

9. Weak family structure

Positive Forces

1. Survival needs

2. Changing technology

3. Safety needs of female culture

4. Governmental attempts to change opportunity structure

Figure 3.2. Education for Vocational Competence: Lower-Lower-Class Level.

Source: Miller, 1967, p. 21.

BOSHIER'S CONGRUENCY MODEL. Like Miller, Boshier (1973) explains participation in terms of the interaction between personal factors and social factors. According to Boshier, "the model asserts that 'congruence' both within the participant and between the participant and his educational environment determine participation/nonparticipation and dropout/persistence" (p. 256). Drawing from Maslow, Boshier posits that people are either primarily growth motivated or deficiency motivated, with deficiency-oriented people "more at the mercy of social and environmental forces" (p. 256). The model is based on the assumptions that participation and persistence in adult education are determined by how people feel about themselves and the match between the self and the educational environment. As can be seen in Figure 3.3, the cumulative effect of these discrepancies is mediated by social and psychological variables such as age, sex, and social class and subenvironmental variables such as transportation and class size. The arrows in the model suggest that these two groups of mediating variables have had an effect on the person's orientation to learning in the first place.

Moderate testing of the model by the author (Boshier, 1973, 1977) and by Garrison (1987) suggests that it is at least a promising beginning. With a sample of 1,372 university continuing education students, Boshier (1973) confirmed his hypothesis that those with high incongruence scores are more likely to drop out. Garrison (1987), on the other hand, was better able to predict persisters (93 percent) than dropouts (20.8 percent). Boshier (1986) himself has proposed another model drawing on some of the same assumptions underlying the congruency model, as well as taking into account learners' motivation, need, and orientation to future-centeredness. (For a discussion of Boshier's as yet untested revised model, see Bagnall, 1990.)

RUBENSON'S EXPECTANCY-VALENCE MODEL. Rubenson's Expectancy-Valence model (1977) addresses both socialization and structural dimensions, as well as individual orientation. The decision to participate is a combination of the negative and positive forces within the individual and the environment. Expectancy consists of the anticipation of being successful in an educational situation. Valence relates to the value a person puts on being successful; one could be positive, negative, or indifferent. The individual is the center of Rubenson's model because everything depends on a person's perception of the environment and the value of participating in adult education. People develop these perceptions through being socialized by family, school, and

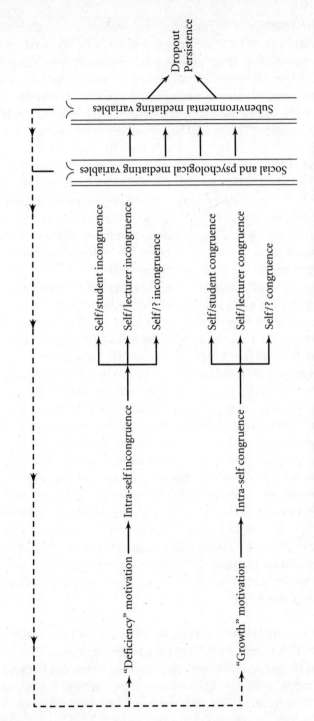

Figure 3.3. **Boshier's Model to Explain Dropout from Adult Education Institutions.**

Source: Boshier, 1977, p. 91.

work. Structural factors in the environment—such as the values of people important to one's self-definition and accessibility of educational programs—directly affect how one sees the environment. Running parallel with socialization and structural factors are the person's current needs. Again, it is how one experiences these needs that determines whether one has a positive, negative, or neutral valence toward the proposed education. This model has yet to be systematically tested.

COOKSON'S ISSTAL MODEL. Based on Smith's (1980) social participation model, Cookson's (1986) model stresses the social dimension of participation. ISSTAL stands for "interdisciplinary, sequential specificity, time allocation, and life span." It is interdisciplinary in that it includes concepts from several disciplines; sequential specificity relates to the causal interconnectedness of variables leading to participation; and time allocation and life span assumptions have to do with viewing participation in adult education as but one form of an adult's overall social participation. Cookson asserts that social participation is a lifelong pattern: "People who exhibit higher levels of [participation in adult education] in their thirties may be expected to display similarly higher levels in their forties, fifties, and sixties" (p. 132).

The model begins with the external context, which includes climate, topography, culture, and social structures. Sociodemographic factors such as age, education, and occupation follow. Midway in the model are four interactive components: personality traits, intellectual capacities, retained information, and attitudinal dispositions. The final component of the model are situational variables that reflect the person's immediate situation and have the most specific influence on the decision to participate. Cookson (1987) tested his model in two studies conducted in British Columbia. Fifty-eight independent variables were used to operationalize the model with fifty male low-income heads of household and four hundred men and women in public evening school classes. None of the variables proved significant with the male-only group, and only three were significantly related to participation in the other study.

DARKENWALD AND MERRIAM'S PSYCHOSOCIAL INTERACTION MODEL. Darkenwald and Merriam's (1982, p. 142) model emphasizes "social-environmental forces, particularly socioeconomic status, not because individual traits or attitudes are unimportant but because less is known about their influence on participation." This model, shown in

Figure 3.4, has two major divisions: preadulthood and adulthood. In the preadulthood phase, individual and family characteristics, particularly intelligence and socioeconomic status, determine the type of preparatory education and socialization a person undergoes in becoming an adult. The adult's socioeconomic status is the direct result of these preadulthood experiences. The adulthood phase consists of six components, each of which can have a high, moderate, or low value. Socioeconomic status (SES) is followed by learning press, defined as "the extent to which one's total current environment requires or encourages further learning" (p. 142) and directly related to SES. The other components of the model are perceived value and utility of adult education, readiness to participate, participation stimuli, and barriers. Participation stimuli are specific events that prod adults into considering an educational activity.

Cervero and Kirkpatrick's (1990) test of the model found that the preadulthood variables, especially father's level of education, explained a significant amount of participation for both credit and noncredit activities.

HENRY AND BASILE'S DECISION MODEL. Henry and Basile's (1994) model is unique in its incorporation of *both* motivational factors and deterrents to participation to help explain adults' decision to participate in formal adult education. The starting point for the model is the target population and its characteristics, such as age, sex, race, education, and occupation. Reasons for enrolling, such as improving one's work situation, meeting new people, or dealing with major life changes, are related to sources of information about learning opportunities. This leads to three more factors—course attributes, deterrents, and institutional reputation—all of which are taken into account in the decision to take the course or not. The authors explain that "in some cases, a strong motivation may be overcome by the lack of a specific course offering, or by some negative impressions of the program or institution. In other cases, a strong institutional reputation and availability of a convenient course may induce participation despite a weak motivational interest. The conceptual framework allows the empirical investigation of these complex relationships" (p. 70). They tested their model with a group of 138 learners who enrolled in a continuing education course and 180 nonparticipants who had sought information about a course but had failed to enroll. The findings of their study confirmed the complexity involved in "a simple decision to participate in a course

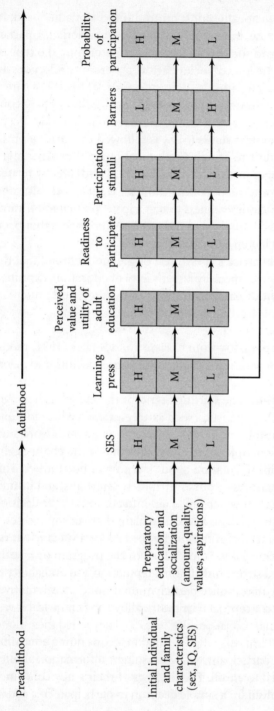

Figure 3.4. Psychosocial Interaction Model of Participation in Organized Adult Education.

Note: H = high, M = moderate, L = low.

Source: From *Adult Education: Foundations of Practice,* by Gordon Darkenwald and Sharan B. Merriam. Copyright © 1982 by Harper & Row, Publishers, Inc. Reprinted by permission of Addison-Wesley Educational Publishers Inc.

. . . that both motivations and deterrents influence the decision to participate" (p. 80). The authors note that vocational reasons were a particularly strong motivator with these adults: "According to our data, work-related factors pile up in favor of participation: typical is a person who has a job-related interest, received a course brochure at work, and has an employer who is willing to pay the course fees" (p. 80).

CROSS'S CHAIN-OF-RESPONSE MODEL. Drawing on a synthesis of the common elements in Miller's (1967), Boshier's (1973), and Rubenson's (1977) models, Cross (1981, p. 124) proposed "a conceptual framework designed to identify the relevant variables and hypothesize their interrelationships." She assumes that participation in a learning activity is the result of a chain of responses to both psychological and environmental factors.

The chain of responses (COR) begins with the individual, as depicted in Figure 3.5. Self-evaluation (A) is one's assessment as to whether achievement in an educational situation is possible. This evaluation combines with attitudes about education (B). Echoing Boshier's notion of growth-motivated or deficiency-motivated learners, Cross comments on the linking of points A and B: "There is a relatively stable and characteristic stance toward learning that makes some people eager to seek out new experiences with a potential for growth while others avoid challenges to their accustomed ways of thinking or behaving" (p. 126). Point C—the importance of goals and the expectation that participation will meet them—is equivalent to Rubenson's notions of expectancy and valence. Expectancy is closely related to points A and B "in that individuals with high self-esteem 'expect' to be successful" (p. 126). Positive attitudes and self-evaluation usually result in an expectation to succeed, thus making motivation to participate relatively high at this juncture in the model.

Cross's COR model is the first to incorporate life events and transitions. Life transitions (D) are those events and changes that all adults encounter as they move through the life cycle. Graduation, marriage, retirement, and so on precipitate transitions that, according to one study, account for 83 percent of the motivation to participate in adult education (Aslanian and Brickell, 1980).

Points E and F are environmental factors that may decide whether one participates in education. Barriers can be overcome and opportunities taken advantage of if one has the information needed to proceed (point F). "Without accurate information, point E in the model

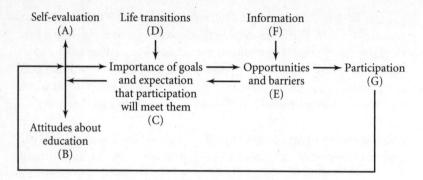

**Figure 3.5. Cross's Chain-of-Response Model for
Participation in Adult Education.**
Source: Cross, 1981, p. 124.

is weak because opportunities are not discovered and barriers loom large" (p. 127). If responses all along the chain are positive, the result will be participation (point G).

Cross says that the model is not really as linear as these steps might suggest. It is also a reciprocal model, in that participation in adult education (G) can affect how one feels about education (B) and oneself as a learner (A).

Although this model does have environmental components, it is primarily a psychological model with its focus on the individual progressing through the chain of response. For Cross, the psychological factors are most important: "If adult educators wish to understand why some adults fail to participate in learning opportunities, they need to begin at the beginning of the COR model—with an understanding of attitudes toward self and education" (p. 130). Gooderham (1993), however, feels that antecedent sociological factors are what shape the factors in Cross's model. In his framework for understanding adults' pursuit of higher education, for example, he proposes that one's attitude to formal learning (point B in Cross's model) is actually determined by the antecedent factors of "social origin" and "degree of success at school" (p. 37).

Assessment of Model-Building Efforts

All these models of participation point to the complexity of the topic of explaining and predicting participation in adult education. Each model is an attempt to account for who participates and why, as well as stimulate new research directions. All the models posit an "interaction between the individual and his or her environment" (Cross, 1981, p. 123). The relative weight of these two factors varies from model to model—from the emphasis on the individual's orientation in Boshier's model to the external context and social background stressed in the ISSTAL model. Moreover, most of these models attempt to explain participation in institutionally sponsored learning activities—that is, after all, what most educators are interested in. Of the seven models reviewed here, only Cross's seems capable of explaining participation in self-directed learning activities. Bagnall (1989, p. 256) points out that these models assume the learner's physical presence, which is only one way to think of participation. Participation can also be thought of as involvement (the extent to which the learner is actively engaged in the learning event) and control (the extent to which the learner controls the content, goals, or outcomes of the event).

There are some unique features in the different models. Rubenson, for example, makes use of member and reference groups whose norms determine one's perceptions of the usefulness of education. Fingeret's (1983) research on illiterate adults, in which she explores the effects of their membership in a social network, lends support to the validity of this concept for explaining participation. That is, many illiterates may fail to join literacy classes because their literacy needs are met through an exchange of goods and services and the groups with whom they identify do not promote education as a means of dealing with their literacy needs. Cross includes life transitions as an important determinant of participation. This component takes into account the research on adult development, in particular the potential of periods of change in the adult life cycle for precipitating learning needs. Aslanian and Brickell (1980), discovering that 83 percent of the learners were participating in adult education because of some past, present, or anticipated change in their lives, provide strong support for the life transition component of Cross's model. Unique to Darkenwald and Merriam's model is learning press, which includes general social participation, occupational complexity, and lifestyle—all of which, in combination, press one in varying intensity toward further learning. Henry and Basile are the first to combine motivational factors along with deterrents to help predict the decision to participate. Finally, Cookson's ISSTAL model includes an intellectual capacity factor. He notes that when the intellectual capacity factor is operationalized in terms of intelligence test scores, there is a relationship to persistence in adult basic education programs. The practical and ethical considerations involved in obtaining such a score, however, may mitigate against its use in predicting persistence.

It might be asked to what extent these isolated attempts to explain and predict participation have moved the field toward a comprehensive explanation of this phenomenon. On the other hand, a comprehensive theory may not be possible given the number of variables that might be needed to cover the topic adequately. As of this writing, there has been relatively little testing of the models reviewed here, partly because of the difficulty in operationalizing complex variables such as personality traits, structural factors in the environment, and learning press and their interrelationships with each other. Several recent efforts to map these interactions in combination with sophisticated measurement techniques seem promising (Dirkx and Jha, 1994; Yang, 1995; Yang, Blunt, and Butler, 1994). Yang's (1995) work in particular is the first longitudinal study to address how participation affects, and is affected by, personal and social factors across the life span. Continued work in this direction might yet result in a good explanatory model of participation that will be of use to researchers and educators alike.

SUMMARY

Participation is one of the more thoroughly studied areas in adult education. We have a sense of who participates, what is studied, and what motivates some adults and not others to enroll in a course or undertake an independent learning project. This accumulation of descriptive information about participation has led to efforts to fit the pieces together in the form of models that try to convey the complexity of the phenomenon.

Although there were numerous studies of participation in the forty years between the inauguration of the field of adult education and the 1960s, it was not until 1965 that the first national study of participation was published. Johnstone and Rivera's study, with its care in defining participation and selecting methods of data collection and analysis, remains a benchmark contribution to this literature. Subsequent surveys by the National Center for Education Statistics (NCES), Aslanian and Brickell (1980), Penland (1979), and UNESCO (Valentine, 1997) have contributed to this database. Regardless of the study, the profile of the typical adult learner remains remarkably consistent:

white, middle class, employed, younger, and better educated than the nonparticipant. Further, employment-related reasons account for the majority of participant interest in continuing education.

Why adults do or do not participate in adult education is an important question, having implications for both theory and practice. Surveys have uncovered both reasons for and barriers to participation. The work on determining an underlying structure of motivational orientations begun by Houle (1961) has been carried on most notably by Boshier's research using the Education Participation Scale (EPS). Between three and seven factors have been delineated to explain why adults participate. In a similar approach, barriers to participation have been investigated using various forms of the Deterrents to Participation Scale (DPS), developed by Darkenwald and colleagues. Further, explanations of participation have been advanced from a sociological rather than a psychological perspective. In these analyses, people's decisions to participate have less to do with their needs and motives than with their position in society and the social experiences that have shaped their lives.

Finally, seven models of participation were reviewed in this chapter. The value of these models in explaining and predicting participation has yet to be determined through research and testing. Nevertheless, they constitute a contribution to the literature on participation in that they attempt to map the interaction of variables that have been shown to influence a person's decision to participate and subsequent perseverance in the activity.

CHAPTER FOUR

Providing Learning Opportunities

T hat thousands of adults are learning computer skills in company-sponsored training sessions or that others are enrolled in community-based literacy programs and still other adults are undertaking personal learning projects is no accident. The particular learning opportunities available to adults *and* the particular adults who take advantage of them reflect a combination of individual values and interests and larger social and economic factors in place at any point in time. Compare, for example, the use of radio in adult learning in the 1930s with television in the 1970s, with the Internet and the World Wide Web in the 1990s; or compare who attended college in the 1920s with the 1950s and the impact of the GI Bill, with the present, where returning adults make up nearly half of all college enrollments (The College Board, in press). Clearly, there is an interactive relationship between the conditions of learning and the society in which it takes place.

Only recently has attention been given to the social context involved in the provision of learning opportunities for adults. The focus of discussion, research, and writing has been on the individual learner and the individual educator. As Rubenson (1980, p. 13) states, "One gets a picture of the adult educator with a firm grip on the rudder keeping the vessel on the right course. However, no one seems to ask where the wind and the waves are coming from." This chapter explores where the wind and waves are coming from—that is, how the societal trends presented in Chapter One interact with other factors to result in the particular learning opportunities available, as well as the skewed participation patterns characteristic of adult education (see Chapter Three). To structure this discussion, three questions are addressed: To what purposes are the learning activities directed? Who decides what the learning opportunities will be? And who benefits from these learning activities?

FOR WHAT PURPOSE?

Individual educators and individual learners are likely to be fairly explicit about why they are engaged in a particular learning activity. Such easily identified objectives are usually aligned with the content of the activity. Someone may be learning to read to get a driver's license, another's goal is to work on a new computer system, and yet another learner may be studying nutrition to manage a health problem. By asking the same question from a sociohistorical perspective, we get some rather different answers. The primary purpose of adult learning in colonial America, for example, was salvation through being able to read the Bible. After independence there was a shift to civic education; the new democratic republic needed informed citizens and leaders. With industrialization came the need for vocational training and Americanization programs for the thousands of immigrants pouring into industrial centers.

Since the 1920s when adult education first became a field of practice, a number of writers have identified various goals and purposes of adult education. One of the most enduring frameworks is that of Lindeman ([1926] 1989, p. 104), who saw the goals of adult education as twofold: "Adult education will become an agency of progress if its short-time goal of self-improvement can be made compatible with a long-time, experimental but resolute policy of changing the social order. Changing individuals in continuing adjustment to changing social functions—this is the bilateral though unified purpose of adult learning." Inherent in Lindeman's framework is the ongoing tension between individual development versus social change as the primary purpose of adult education.

Since Lindeman, at least seven typologies of goals and purposes of adult education have been added to the literature. There is much similarity among these typologies. As Merriam and Brockett (1997) observe:

> First, there is the absence of any explicit moral or religious purpose, although Apps (1985) does note that this was an aim of adult education in early America. Second, personal growth and development (including liberal education) and occupational and career-related education have been constant goals of modern adult education. Third, . . . while preserving the democratic society is still a powerful rationale for much of adult education, a more recent perspective (as in the goal of "social transformation") sees adult education as a force for challenging and changing the social structure. A fourth observation is the recognition in the more recent typologies of . . . training and human resource development. [p. 22]

Underlying many of the stated purposes of adult education in America is the assumption that the ideal of a democratic society must be maintained, and that education is one way to do this. Individualism, independence, and a Protestant-capitalist work ethic frame the actual provision of adult education in America. Further, *because* this is a democratic society, all individuals have access and the opportunity to benefit through education. We are thus back to Lindeman's dual purpose of adult education of improving both society and the individual. In practice, however, a case can be made that education is "an apparatus for social control" (Cunningham, 1988, p. 133) rather than empowerment, and that adult education in the United States is elitist and exclusionary. Cunningham points to middle-class participation patterns, to the homogeneous, technically oriented training of adult educators, to a "psychology of individual deficit" as a basis for explaining social inequities, and to the erosion of the voluntary nature of adult education as evidence of adult education's elite bias.

Most societies in fact use education to preserve the status quo rather than to bring about change or address inequities. In reviewing the common functions of adult education, Jarvis (1985) points out how they can be used in the service of maintaining the status quo. Adult education maintains the social system and existing social relations in that "the education of adults transmits the dominant culture and in the process it reproduces the cultural system which, in itself, is a force for the retention of the status quo rather than social change" (p. 139). Individual advancement and selection, while appearing to develop individuals, is actually a selective process carefully monitored by the system itself. Another function—offering a second chance and legitimization—also promotes the dominant culture since "second chance education actually produces an appearance of greater equality of opportunity and, hence, reinforces the existing social structures" (p. 143). Even leisure-time pursuits have as a latent function "the retention of stability in the social system at a time when many people do not have work to occupy their time and their minds" (p. 147). Finally, development and liberation can be goals of adult education, although one should be aware that such development and liberation may actually be designed to enable people to fit more easily into the existing social system.

Whatever the stated or actual purposes of a learning activity, adult education is usually a form of social intervention that often begins with a problem that needs to be solved. Of course, what is seen as problematic depends on one's values, social position, and perspective: "Identification of the problem has important ethical implications because it determines selection of the target to which change efforts are directed. Where we intervene depends on where we, with our personal value preferences and perspectives, perceive the problem to lie" (Kelman and Warwick, 1978, p. 13). In the case of social unrest, for example, "those who identify with the status quo are likely to see the problem as a breakdown of social order, while those who identify with the protesters are more likely to see the problem as a breakdown of social justice" (pp. 12–13). The mid–1990s debates and discussions about gays in the military offer another example. For some, the problem was one of their presence being a threat to order and discipline; for others, their exclusion represented homophobia and ignorance.

The problems to which adult educators respond tend to be identified by those who have a value perspective not necessarily shared by the target population. As Cunningham (1988, p. 141) has noted, much program planning is based on an individual deficit model rather than an examination of "the oppressive structures in which people live." Programs are thus designed around learner deficiencies that may or may not be of concern to the learner. A good example of the individual deficit model can be seen in the rhetoric of proposed legislation. The never-funded Lifelong Learning Act had as its purpose to offer "hope to those who are mired in stagnant or disadvantaged circumstances—the unemployed, the isolated, elderly, women, minorities, youth, workers whose jobs are becoming obsolete. All of them can and should be brought into the mainstream of American life. Lifelong learning is a necessary step toward making the lives of all Americans more rewarding and productive" (quoted in Richardson, 1987, p. 2). Richardson offers one explanation why the act was never funded: "Lifelong learning is a fuzzy, shorthand, politically expedient term, offered as a solution to a clump of ill-defined problems which would be thought about more usefully if they were kept separate: age discrimination, worker alienation, rapid social change, the knowledge explosion, poverty, illiteracy, and a host of related educational and social inequities" (p. 3).

Nevertheless, "adult education is given public support when the public can see the connection between education and the solution to a threatening situation" (Griffith and Fujita-Starck, 1989, p. 172). Most "threatening" are challenges to economic stability and social order. The emphasis may shift with changes in society's social, cultural, and economic structures. Literacy education in colonial America was invested in for a greater religious purpose; this gave way to a citizenship orientation in the wake of independence during the mid-eighteenth century, which was eclipsed by vocational training and immigrant education at the turn of the twentieth century. The past thirty years or so have seen a number of schemes to train and retrain workers in response to rapidly changing economical and technological conditions.

In the light of the social forces documented in Chapter One—demographics, economics, and technology—the purposes of adult education today for which there is public support cluster around the United States' sustaining a competitive edge in a global economy. This translates into preparing and then maintaining an informed and efficient workforce. Along with this economic imperative is the assumption that social stability is both a product and a goal of adult education and training. Thousands of restless, illiterate, unemployed, or underemployed adults pose a threat to the stability of the social order, not to mention a drain on social resources. So although the rhetoric of adult education suggests some rather lofty ideals for the purpose of the endeavor, the reality suggests a more conservative purpose: maintenance of the status quo, which today means a capitalist economic system that values individuality, independence, and entrepreneurialism. Thus we see a growing emphasis on human resource development and training, continued provision for basic skill acquisition, and ever-expanding postsecondary opportunities for adults. Rubenson (1998, p. 258) concurs, noting that the recent national policy documents on lifelong learning "reflect an erosion of commitment to equality. Instead the concerns are with accountability standards, relevance to the needs of the economy and cost effectiveness."

WHO DECIDES?

Asking who decides what the learning opportunities should be is the same as asking who has the power to decide. In theory, at least, it is learners themselves who decide what is to be offered. The voluntary nature of much of adult learning reinforces this in that a great number of these activities are characterized by voluntary participation, in contrast to the compulsory nature of preadult schooling. Adults will not volunteer, and will not stay if they do volunteer, in formal or nonformal learning activities that are not responsive to their needs. And since a large proportion of organized adult learning is self-supporting, learners to some extent do decide what is offered. But if learners were the only ones to determine offerings, the entire field of adult education could become a reactive endeavor in which trained personnel become technicians in the service of demanding learners. Furthermore, the provision of learning opportunities would be based solely on who is willing to pay, resulting in a market-driven rather than an educationally inspired enterprise.

The reality, of course, is much more ambiguous. The service orientation of adult education is alive and well, and to some extent learners do influence what is offered. But so do trained adult educators, legislators, employers, and others who may or may not themselves be participants. Nevertheless, the answer to who decides what is to be offered cannot be uncoupled from the question of who finances the various adult learning opportunities. And in North American society, tying these two questions together makes for a very murky answer at best.

The answer is somewhat easier to track in reference to formal adult education—learning that is institutionalized versus nonformal learning that is organized outside the formal system (such as self-help groups and alternative schools). In North America, there are many providers of formal learning opportunities, including government at all levels, employers, educational institutions, and community institutions such as libraries. Because much of the expenditure for this form of learning is hidden under a variety of budgetary labels—at one time more than 270 federal programs alone had some component of adult learning (Griffith and Fujita-Starck, 1989)—it is difficult to measure the relative financial power of various providers.

To complicate the matter, what is offered at any particular time "will almost inevitably relate to the pressures generated in the social system. . . . Social pressures act in such a manner as to create an imbalance in the system to which institutions, other than that generating pressure, respond by seeking to restore the system to some form of equilibrium" (Jarvis, 1986, p. 57). Institutions are currently being pressured to respond to the issues of a low-literate workforce—for example, technological obsolescence and health threats such as AIDS. This notion of mobilizing institutions in the service of maintaining social equilibrium is but one explanation for the shifts in curriculum emphasis.

The problem of who decides what learning opportunities should be available brings into question the extent to which the public good takes precedence over individual freedom. In the case of AIDS, for example, does the government have the right to send an educational brochure to people's homes? Can employers require employees to attend an educational workshop on AIDS? Actually, federal initiatives in response to social concerns through education have been rather limited. This is partially due to the U.S. system in which education falls under state, rather than federal, responsibility.

With the responsibility at the state level, and especially in recent periods of decentralization and deregulation, states are making many of the decisions as to how educational dollars are to be spent. States do have some choice in how they respond to these social pressures, of course. In a study of state policies and practices regarding the provision of adult learning activities, Cross and McCartan (1984) have identified four levels of intervention. The first of these they label the *laissez-faire* approach. Here the state either believes that a free market will best serve the interests of adults, or it simply does not wish to get involved. The second stance, and the most prevalent, is *encouragement.* The state takes no direct action but facilitates the involvement of others through "planning and goal setting, collecting data, promoting local cooperation, or establishing task forces" (p. 4). The third option, *intervention,* is rationalized on the basis of the "state's interest in the efficient use of public resources and in protecting citizens against fraudulent or shoddy educational practices" (p. 125). Finally, states may intervene with *direct support and services,* especially if it is more cost-effective or more equitable to offer a service statewide.

The flip side of the question of public rights in deciding what provisions to offer is the question of individual learning rights. Is there such a thing? Is it related to certain roles, such as citizen, consumer, employee? To what extent does our system of adult and continuing education support, neglect, or reject these different learning rights? In contrast to totalitarian forms of government, a democratic form of government such as found in North America would seem to foster individual learning rights. Do adult learners, for example, have the right to request support for learning about environmental and consumer issues that in turn makes for a more informed citizenry? If adult learners have a right to ask for certain education activities, who is obligated to respond?

In a pluralistic society such as ours, the question of who decides what learning opportunities to offer has no single answer. In reality, for formal learning programs at least, decisions are made by those who pay—whether that means the learners themselves, government, employers, or educational institutions. And those who pay are in positions of power to determine which social pressures will be addressed and how those responses will be structured. Those not in positions of power rarely decide what learning opportunities are offered. Their role is limited to deciding whether to participate.

WHO BENEFITS?

Popular rhetoric suggests that everyone—young or old, well educated or not, rich or poor—can improve his or her life situation through learning. And certainly there are programs that attract or even target every description of adult and every subject imaginable. Theoretically, every adult can choose to participate in any adult learning activity. The reality of the situation, however, is that the vast majority of adults attracted to continued learning are already well educated, middle class, and white (see Chapter Three). "A close look at different forms of adult education reveals," Rubenson (1989, p. 64) points out, "that the better an education pays off in terms of income, status, occupation, political efficacy, cultural competence, and similar matters, the greater the differences in socioeconomic status between participants and nonparticipants." According to Rubenson, the least

payoff and thus the least socioeconomic difference between participants and nonparticipants can be found in self-directed learning
activities. The greatest payoff can be found in higher and continuing
education; there, large socioeconomic differences distinguish participants from nonparticipants. Between these two points on a continuum are community-based organizations and employer-sponsored
education (Rubenson, 1980).

The democratic ideals of equal opportunity and open access make
the current reality of uneven and unequal participation in formal
adult learning particularly worrisome to policymakers, educators, and
researchers. Numerous studies have been undertaken to find out why
a certain segment of our society participates and others do not (see
Chapter Three). Most explanations focus on a person's stated reasons
for nonparticipation, such as cost, time, transportation, and lack of
confidence. When viewed from a social perspective, other explanations emerge. Rubenson (1989, p. 64) argues, for example, that
"through socialization within the family, the school, and, later on, in
working life, a positive disposition towards adult education becomes
a part of some group's habitus but not of others." Jarvis (1985, p. 138)
refers to Bourdieu's concept of "cultural capital" to explain adult education's middle-class bias: "Those most likely to be the recipients of
the dominant culture are those who, as a result of birth and upbring-
ing, have already acquired the cultural capital to receive it." Cropley
(1989, p. 146) further explains how social class in particular structures
participation: "Participation in adult education is thus affected by the
role people play in the groups to which they belong, by the tactics they
prefer for dealing with the external world, by their degree of willingness to accept certain kinds of external authority, their preference for
particular learning strategies, and so on. Furthermore, these characteristics are shared with other people, are acquired in group settings,
and are reinforced by the groups to which people belong, social classes
being among the most important groups." In other words, "Those who
have already been socialized into a culture that is sympathetic to the
dominant culture, or into the dominant culture itself, are more likely
to acquire the fruits of education than those who have not" (Jarvis,
1985, pp. 138–139).

Those adults who have been socialized into valuing and acquiring
these attitudes and skills will be the ones to take advantage of learning opportunities. Since most providers of such opportunities have
themselves acquired the ability to function freely, little effort is

expended on trying to understand and provide for other populations. The modus operandi of most providers is to offer a set of activities that they assume learners will want. A response, however, is predicated on the assumptions that learners know about the program, can attend at the time it is offered, and can afford it; that the subculture of the institution is conducive to their own; and that what is offered corresponds with what is needed (Jarvis, 1985). Rubenson (1989, p. 65) argues that "a system of adult education that implicitly takes for granted that the adult is a conscious, self-directed individual in possession of the instruments vital to making use of the available possibilities for adult education—a system that relies on self-selection to recruit the participants—will by necessity widen, not narrow, the educational and cultural gaps in society."

There are other reasons that certain adults have more access to learning opportunities than other adults. Where one happens to live, what color, age, or sex one happens to be, what one does for a living: all contribute to the participation pattern in adult education. Cropley (1989, p. 146) calls these factors "framework conditions," which "are largely a function of the circumstances in which people live, especially of factors such as the values, attitudes, habits, priorities and the like of the social groups to which they belong, the economic structure of their society, even features of the education system itself." The result is that "some individuals are more equal than others in the choices available to them" (p. 106).

By way of illustrating how these framework conditions can determine who is more likely to benefit from adult learning opportunities, where and how one lives make a difference. It is common knowledge that there is less accessibility in rural areas than in urban or suburban centers. The picture is a bit more complicated than just a rural-urban split, however. Those in small-town rural areas are better off than those living in isolated areas, and some urban centers are as impoverished as the most rural areas. Worldwide, access to learning opportunities in rural areas is a problem at all levels of education. Further, there are those who lack a geographical place altogether—migrant, transient, homeless, and refugee populations. Migrants, for example, "are the most undereducated major subgroup in the United States, with a high school dropout rate larger than that of any other group. . . . Their mobility, their language differences, and the cultural differences experienced as they move from one community to another combine with health and nutritional problems to negatively affect school achievement. . . . Migrant lifestyles revolve around working, moving on to find other work, and working again" (Velazquez, 1996, p. 28). For any of these geographically mobile groups, there is little more than sporadic access to education or social services.

Age is another condition that often determines who benefits from learning opportunities. Not only do older adults have the lowest levels of participation in adult education generally (Kopka and Peng, 1993), older adult workers receive far less training in the workplace than younger workers. In some settings and in other parts of the world, age in combination with sex makes for another condition affecting access. For example, in the United States, since managerial and professional workers and all nonmanual workers receive more training than manual workers—and women are underrepresented in these positions—women, and older women in particular, are much less likely to receive employer-sponsored training than men are (Stacy and Duc-Le To, 1990, 1994).

The answer to the question of who benefits is clear: it is those who have benefited in the past, those who have the "cultural capital" to take advantage of opportunities that are available. More complex are the underlying conditions that structure the interaction among the context, the individual learners, and the provision of learning.

BROADENING THE PROVISION OF LEARNING OPPORTUNITIES

From the foregoing discussion of who decides, for what purpose, and who benefits, one might conclude that adult education is primarily in the hands of a ruling elite whose interest in self-preservation and self-perpetuation determines the answers. Yet adult educators, policymakers, and others close to the enterprise are themselves functioning with worldviews into which they have been socialized. Out of these worldviews come support for social institutions like church and government, and for concepts like equality and freedom that are consonant with one's worldview. Social interventions such as adult education are designed to preserve and sustain what is valued. The problem, Cunningham (1988, p. 135) notes, "is that we have difficulty seeing how we ourselves have constructed our world." But since we have constructed our social reality, we can also change it. The responses we suggest in this section reflect our assumptions that although we may be shaped by our social context, we can also act on it. We believe that adult educators should take a critical stance in examining the extent to which their own values and assumptions perpetuate the inequities of our practice.

Educators and others are in fact becoming aware that the status quo can be changed and that transformations at both the individual and societal levels can happen. Some are rekindling the spirit of social reform that was characteristic of adult education in the early decades of this century, with questions being raised about the role of adult education in promoting social change (Heaney, 1996). Alongside issues of programming, technical competence, budgeting, and needs analysis, issues of quality, access, and equity are again receiving attention in the literature (Hayes and Colin, 1994a; Heaney, 1996; Merriam and Brockett, 1997; Newman, 1994a).

Several writers have suggested what might be done to promote a more equitable system of adult learning. These suggestions fall into two major categories: the development of a critical pedagogy and the support and promotion of community-based learning activities.

Becoming aware of the power of education, and its politically charged nature, is the first step in addressing some of its inequities. Critical pedagogy directly confronts issues of power and control, conflict and oppression, and mandates action to deal with social inequities as they are revealed in learning encounters (see, for example, Bailey, Tisdell, and Cervero, 1994; Collins, 1991; Hart, 1992; Stalker, 1996; Tisdell, 1995; Welton, 1995a).

The first step in the development of a critical pedagogy is to engage in critically reflecting, both individually and collectively, on the field's mission and the provision of learning opportunities. We have tried to model this process by raising the questions of who provides learning for what reasons, and who benefits. Brookfield (1987) has devoted a book to why it is important to develop a critical stance and how adults can become critical thinkers in their family, work, and personal lives and in relation to mass media. Deshler (1990) suggests that through analyzing common metaphors (such as speaking of learning in terms of return on investment), we can "exorcize the 'ghosts' of our socialization so that we can freely choose meanings out of which we want to live our lives" (p. 296). Mezirow (1990a) too suggests a critical thinking agenda for adult learning. In his theory, social transformations can follow individual perspective transformations. "It is also clear," Mezirow says, "that the individual perspective transformation process includes taking action, which often means some form of social action—which in turn can sometimes mean collective political action" (p. 363).

Another arena where the promotion of critical stance can lead to change is the training of adult educators (Bailey, Tisdell, and Cervero, 1994). Baptiste and Brookfield (1997) model just such a stance in their discussion of the meaning of democracy and how it functions in graduate adult education programs. Apps (1987, p. 17) makes the point that adult educators should not isolate themselves from the rest of the education world. It is important to know what happens educationally in school, in the family, in "everyday living, from going to the movies and from the mass media. . . . Unless we begin to be more concerned about the rest of education . . . the field of adult/continuing education will increasingly be concerned with remedial education" (p. 17). From a critical practice position, Cunningham (1988, p. 143) suggests making sure that the content of all programs "is open to competing ideas" and that professional development programming includes "content that goes beyond nationalist concerns, including such subjects as peace education and global resource sharing." Furthermore, she says, the training of adult educators is too "confined to our technology" without coming to "grips with the purposes of that technology. Two basic ethical questions that should be discussed [in the training of adult educators] are (1) who has the power to make decisions on the nature of adult education programs, and (2) who do these programs benefit? To make this point at the basic ethical level in practice is to decide whether our resources should, for example, be addressed to questions regarding andragogy or racism; self-directed learning or sexism; models of evaluation or the emergence of a permanent underclass in our democracy" (p. 140).

The promotion of nonformal, community-based learning activities is a second major strategy in changing the existing situation. Because of their nonformal nature, these programs and those who work in them have had little visibility and even less public support compared to formal, institutionally based programs. As Smith (1994) observes:

> Their main workplace is not the classroom. Shops, launderettes, streets, pubs, cafes, and people's front rooms are the settings for much of their work. Where they do appear in schools and colleges, it is in corridors,

eating areas and student common rooms that they are most likely to be found. Their work is not organized by subject, syllabus or lessons. . . . They are not interested in possessing knowledge as one might own objects. Rather, they look to the way people are with themselves and the world. Such education is, as a result, unpredictable, risky and, hopefully, emancipatory. [p. 1]

In many ways, community-based, nonformal programs are more egalitarian in practice and are closer to the ideals of adult education in a democratic society than many formal programs. Examples of such programs are public issue discussion forums (Oliver, 1987), the National Issues Forum, self-help groups, and community-oriented adult literacy programs (Sissel, 1996, 1997). Typically these groups are citizen entities rather than professionally organized, are voluntary, have as a goal the development of an awareness of their situation, choose to create their own knowledge base rather than accommodate "official" knowledge, and have a strong action component. Hayes and Snow (1989) further differentiate community-oriented programs, in this case literacy programs, from mainstream programs with respect to mission (social change versus individual literacy), instruction (group-devised methods versus standardized curricula), source of problem (flawed society versus flawed individuals), and outcome (group action versus individual achievement) (see also Sissel, 1997).

The two strategies of developing a reflective and critical perspective as well as fostering community-based programs have been merged by a number of writers. In a book on a community-based approach to literacy, Sissel (1997, p. 100) observes that "the creation of community and the promotion of participation with learners require concrete steps. . . . Questioning and reflection are but the first steps toward the transformation of literacy programs into 'learning organizations' (Watkins and Marsick, 1993) that can be increasingly responsive to the needs of learners." Critical literacy is more than just acquiring basic skills of reading and computing. According to Cunningham (1988), it "means encouraging expression by the individual through dialogue, writing, and public expression"; it is promoting the skills necessary in "creating knowledge and action" (p. 143). Critical pedagogy, or critical practice, is most powerful when it originates with and from community-based, social action groups with a vested interest in changing oppressive social structures (Freire, 1970b; Giroux, 1988; Newman, 1994a; Shor and Freire, 1987).

Every society has "valuables" that are deemed scarce and necessary, such as material wealth, knowledge, skill, and power. Whereas politics is the shaping and sharing of power, education is the shaping and sharing of knowledge and skills. Promoting critical thinking and critical pedagogy and supporting community-oriented programs can lead to the creation of knowledge that empowers, which in turn can lead to social change. Cunningham (1988, p. 137) explains how this can come about: "First, the participant-produced knowledge competes with, confronts, and forces change onto the official knowledge; second, the participants, in recognizing that they have produced and celebrated their own view of the world, empower themselves. . . . This can produce interdependence and informed critical thinkers, as opposed to a dependent and 'coping' underclass."

SUMMARY

The provision of adult learning opportunities can be understood by looking at the interaction between the social context in which it takes place and the learners who benefit. Learning encounters are shaped by more than the knowledge base derived from research. The actual and espoused values of the social system in which the learning takes place also shape the learning enterprise. In our society, questions of access and opportunity that trouble the adult learning enterprise reflect the disjuncture between the values we promote in our rhetoric and what actually happens. The gap between the better educated who seek out and can afford continuing learning opportunities, versus those who do not, continues to widen. Government policy and funding tend to support only efforts that directly address employment-related skills and economic return so that the United States can be competitive in a global marketplace. Large segments of the adult population do not respond to these initiatives, however. Those who do participate are already the better educated, the more socially mobile, the ones with higher income. Formal adult learning opportunities, for the most part, thus become a vehicle for solidifying a socioeconomic structure contrary to our stated goals of access and equality.

This chapter has explored the gap between the rhetoric and the reality of three factors in the provision of most formal learning opportunities: for what purposes is the learning activity provided; who decides what is to be offered; and who benefits? The chapter concludes by suggesting that adult educators and others encourage the development of a critical perspective to permeate all aspects of practice, including the training of future adult educators, and that nonformal, community-based activities manifest many of the ideals that the field espouses.

PART TWO

Adult Development and Learning

L earning to read at a local education center, learning about a new computer system at your place of employment, learning to tune up a car engine at a vocational-technical school, learning how to handle teenagers at a local health clinic: all are examples of adult education. Despite the diversity of content and sponsoring agents, these instances have one thing in common: the adult learner, who is at the center of all such learning activities. Understanding how we as adults develop and change as we age, and how developmental issues and the changes we encounter interface with learning in adulthood, are important considerations in facilitating meaningful learning encounters. Part Two of *Learning in Adulthood* focuses on adult learners and their development.

Research has shown that adults are often motivated to participate in learning activities by developmental issues and changes in their lives (Aslanian and Brickell, 1980; Merriam and Clark, 1991). The study of adult development has become a major topic of interest over the past few decades with a resulting burgeoning of information and data-based research. Chapters Five and Six explore the developmental character- istics of adults that are most clearly related to learning. In selecting the information from this large body of research that is most relevant to learning in adulthood, we chose four areas for coverage. Biological and psychological changes in adulthood, the first two areas, are discussed in Chapter Five. The biological perspective acknowledges the physical aging process brought on by the natural mechanisms of aging as well as environmental influences, health habits, and disease. For the most part, there are few effects on adult learning from these biological changes, except for those associated with severe deterioration of sight and hearing, a slowing of reaction time, and disease, especially diseases connected with the central nervous system. In addition, how even these factors affect learning vary widely from person to person.

Also in Chapter Five is an examination of development from a psychological perspective. Psychological models of development can loosely be grouped into three categories: sequential, life events and transitions, and relational. Although the sequential models (for example, Erikson, 1982, and Levinson and Levinson, 1996) have predominated our thinking as adult educators about the linkages between development and learning, the life events and transitions and the relational models have received greater attention in the literature on adult learning within the past ten to fifteen years. Examined in Chapter Six are the two other approaches to development in adulthood: sociocultural factors and what we are terming the integrative perspective on development. From the sociocultural perspective, change in adulthood is determined more by contextual influences, such as social, economic, and historical factors, than by internal mechanisms. Three strands of work from this perspective are highlighted: the importance of social roles; the socially constructed nature of the concepts of race, gender, ethnicity, and sexual orientation; and cross-cultural studies of adult development. The integrative perspective acknowledges the intersections among the biological, psychological, and sociocultural perspectives in framing developmental theory. To move to a richer understanding of learning in adulthood, we suggest that adult educators use multiple lenses or perspectives on development instead of relying on just a single paradigm of development.

Chapter Seven explores cognitive development in adulthood—that is, how adults' thinking patterns change over time. Beginning with a discussion of the pioneering work of Piaget (1972), we present alternative theories and models of adult cognitive development, including a contextual perspective, which has gained more prominence recently.

Dialectical thinking, characterized by the tolerance for contradictions and ambiguity in ways of thinking about similar phenomena in adult life, is explored next as one of the major schemas of mature adult thought. Among the works discussed are those of Riegel (1973), Benack and Basseches (1989), and Kegan (1994). Finally, we consider one of the hallmarks of mature adult thought: wisdom.

The last chapter in Part Two focuses on the concept of intelligence. Beginning with the early work of Thorndike (1928), researchers and educators alike have sought to understand the nature of adult intelligence and how it might be affected by the aging process. This chapter traces the development of the concept of intelligence, highlighting the theories that have helped to clarify the nature of adult intelligence, such as the theories of Gardner (1983), Sternberg (1985, 1996b), and Goleman (1995). In general, the movement has been from viewing intelligence as a single general trait to a more multifaceted construct, with most authors observing that the single general traits theories may be helpful in explaining intelligence in children, but not in adulthood. Also explored are the means of assessing intelligence in adulthood and the shortcomings of the common measurement tools, including the test items themselves and how test scores have been used to influence social policy. Many questions remain about how intelligence is affected by the aging process and whether educators can design interventions to halt the loss of intellectual capacities or strengthen those we have throughout our life spans.

CHAPTER FIVE

Biological and Psychological Development

hat children change as they age is well understood and anticipated; but it is only within the last few decades that it became equally clear that adults also change as they age. It is not unusual to hear someone talk about her "age-thirty transition," "midlife crisis," or "biological clock" running out. Indeed, separating facts, ideas, and theories about adult development from the popularized and fictionalized versions of research findings and then linking those findings to learning in adulthood is the challenge. Efforts to integrate development and learning have focused on why and how we physically age, our psychological makeup, and more recently on how social and cultural forces shape our development (Tennant and Pogson, 1995). In addition, there have been major discussions about how our thinking processes themselves change in adulthood. (See Chapters Seven and Eight.)

The concept of development, as with learning, is most often equated with change. Some view change resulting from development as an orderly progression, while others find little that is preprogrammed. The goal of development is similarly controversial. Some think that adults move toward closely specified goals such as self-actualization (Maslow, 1970) or a fully integrated sense of ego (Loevinger, 1976). Others, like Riegel (1973) and Tennant and Pogson (1995), view development as more dialectical in nature, with development a function of the "constant interaction of the person and the environment" (Tennant and Pogson, 1995, p. 199). Still others view development as a political construct "because different versions of development serve the interests of different groups" (Tennant and Pogson, 1995, p. 199).

Most of the work in adult development has been driven by the psychological tradition and focuses on the individual's internal process of development. Out of this tradition have grown the most prevalent theories of development, which often have been conceptualized as a patterned or ordered progression tied to chronological time. Some theorists, such as Havighurst (1972) and Levinson and Levinson (1996), have been highly specific, tying each developmental period to a particular age, while others (Erikson, 1963, 1982; Vaillant, 1977) have left the age frame open-ended and speak rather of life periods such as young adulthood and middle age. Still others within the psychological paradigm have concentrated on life's transitions, such as marriage, birth of a child, or death. Although the psychological framework for development is most often cited, other perspectives on adulthood, such as biological aging, are equally important, especially when thinking about learning. Moreover, there has been a growing awareness (though some might term it a resurfacing of interest) of how social and cultural forces such as gender, race, and social class affect adult development (Dannefer, 1984; Elder, 1995; Tennant and Pogson, 1995). A number of authors have even called for the creation of "a new perspective that . . . draws equally on biology, psychology, and social science, as well as on the humanities" (Levinson, 1986, p. 13), to understand fully the complex and intricate patterns of development in adulthood.

In this chapter we discuss the developmental characteristics of adults from two major orientations, biological aging and psychological changes, each explained through illustrative theories and ideas. We interweave in the discussion of these theories and ideas how educators and others have linked these perspectives to learning in adulthood. Chapter Six focuses on two additional approaches of adult development: the sociocultural and integrative perspectives.

BIOLOGICAL AGING

Biological aging is a fact of life, although rarely a welcome one. When we ask groups of adults to describe physical changes that have happened to them over the previous five to ten years, there are usually a collective sigh and mumblings about weight gain, graying hair, and the like. It is not a subject most people care to discuss. Yet with advances in nutrition and health care, our overall outlook for continued health and well-being has never been better. As Erikson (1982) so keenly observed, we have moved from an elite of elderlies to a mass of elderlies.

Although life expectancy has almost doubled since the beginning of this century, from approximately forty to seventy-six years, our capacity to live longer does not mean we have been able to halt the primary process of aging—those time-related physical changes governed by some kind of maturational process, as in vision and hearing, for example, that happen to all of us (Bee, 1996; Lefrancois, 1996). Although life expectancy has increased, the human life span, usually given as 110 to 120 years, has not changed. Rather, our increased longevity stems from overcoming some of the problems related to secondary aging—aging that is "the product of environmental influences, health habits, or disease and is . . . not shared by all people" (Bee, 1996, p. 83). Improved nutrition, hygiene, medical discoveries, and lifestyle changes have accounted for most of this increased longevity.

Since most bodily functions reach their maximum capacity and efficiency in young adulthood, this period is a time of optimal health, physical strength, and endurance for many adults (Berger, 1998). Decline in the actual functioning of the major biological systems is slow. The fourth and fifth decades tend to be the physiological turning point for most adults, although the effects of these changes may not be felt until the sixth or seventh decade of life (Bee, 1996; Berger, 1998). The most obvious changes are the ones we see when we return to our twenty-fifth college reunion. Suddenly our classmates look middle-aged. We see gray and thinning hair, more wrinkles, and different contours of the body. Yet these changes, although noticeable, really have little effect on our physical functioning, unless we take to heart the negative stereotypes society has placed on "looking old." Less obvious to the eye are the more pervasive internal changes. For example, most adults begin to experience changes in their vision, their cardiovascular systems, their bones and connective material, and their reproductive function (for women) sometime in their forties and early fifties.

Yet it is not until the sixties and the seventies, when the degenerative biological process overtakes the regenerative process for most adults, that major effects on all structures and functions of the body are seen. Even these major changes are being questioned in the popular and scientific literature alike, implying "that virtually all previously presumed changes with age are either illusory or insignificant" (Bee, 1996, p. 84). Still, for most adults "there are real changes occurring with age. It is important not to exaggerate those changes, but neither should we gloss over or ignore them" (Bee, 1996, p. 84). Although it appears that we will all experience many major changes in our physical beings at some point in our lives, the effect of these changes on our capacity to learn is largely unknown. In fact, many of these changes may prove to be very minor, except in cases of underlying disease processes. Three specific physical changes have been shown to affect learning in adulthood: changes in two of the senses, changes in the central nervous system, and changes as a result of major disease processes.

Senses

Deterioration in the ability to see and to hear can create problems with the learning process. Specific changes in vision are well documented (Kline and Scialfa, 1996; Marsh, 1996). One of the most notable changes is in the ability to perceive small detail on the printed page and computer screen. A loss of close vision starts to decline for most people between the ages of forty and fifty and results primarily from the lens's becoming larger and denser and losing elasticity. By the age of seventy-five, poor visual acuity is common, although many problems can be corrected with eyeglasses or surgery.

A second major sight-related change concerns light. As people age, they need more illumination to see both near and far (Bee, 1996; Marsh, 1996). This results from a combination of lens and iris changes that allow less light and a different quality of light to reach the retina. These latter changes make those especially past the age of seventy less responsive to sudden changes in illumination, such as oncoming headlights. In addition, "peripheral vision, depth perception, color vision, and adaption to the dark also become poorer and sensitivity to glare increases" with age (Lefrancois, 1996, p. 505).

While changes in vision happen primarily at set periods in life, hearing loss is a progressive but gradual process throughout adulthood. Most adults do not notice any discernible change until their fifties and sixties, when sounds, especially in the high-frequency range, become more difficult to hear (Kline and Scialfa, 1996; Marsh, 1996). This loss is most often noted by males, who are more affected than females by hearing loss. Even greater hearing losses are noticed in the seventh and eighth decades. An estimated 35 percent of the population has some detectable amount of hearing difficulty between the ages of seventy-five and eight-five, and 51 percent of the population over age eight-five experiences hearing impairment (Bee, 1996). According to Bee (1996, p. 92), the basic cause of this loss appears to be "from wear and tear on the auditory nerves and structures of the inner ear." One of the obvious results of this loss of hearing is the difficulty of older adults to understand the spoken word. Some people become completely deaf, but most often people who are hard of hearing miss pieces of words and phrases, so they may not understand what was said. As some grandchildren have observed, asking their grandparents one question often elicits an answer to a totally different question. Some hearing losses can be compensated for with the use of hearing aids or by adding such devices as amplifiers in large meeting rooms, but such adjustments do not often help those with major hearing losses. Those with acute hearing loss and the people who interact with them often become frustrated with the whole communication process, and adults with serious hearing losses may become increasingly isolated.

The aging of the eyes and ears "serves as a good example of how the effects of aging need not interfere with the capacity for learning" (Cross, 1981, p. 156). Except for major degenerative and other disease processes, corrective measures, such as the wearing of eyeglasses and teaching people to find alternative ways of communicating, can help ensure the best use of the vision and hearing that remain. Adults learning on their own have fewer problems than those who choose to learn in formal settings. For the most part, our institutions do not take into consideration the physical differences of adult learners. Both teachers and learners must see to it that the educational environment is conducive to all adult learners, ensuring, for example, that rooms are adequately illuminated and acoustics are good.

The Nervous System

Consisting of the brain and the spinal cord, the central nervous system forms the primary biological basis for learning. We have only limited knowledge about how changes in this system affect learning in healthy adults as they age (Bruer, 1997; Scheibel, 1996). For example, although we know that both the weight and the number of cells in the brain decline and the connections between these cells become less numerous with age, we do not know what impact, if any, these changes have on the learning process. During the perinatal period, for example, unborn babies lose many more cells as a consequence of normal brain maturation than the cell loss adults experience later in life (Scheibel, 1996).

The most consistent finding related to changes in the central nervous system has to do with declining reaction time as people age (Bee, 1996; Lefrancois, 1996; Schaie and Willis, 1986). Reaction time is usually measured as the time it takes a person to complete a psychomotor task, such as putting together a puzzle or responding to a specific stimulus by hitting a lighted button. Although "it is not true that all elderly people are markedly slower than young people . . . , on the average people over the age of 65" react less rapidly (Lefrancois, 1996, p. 506). Numerous explanations have been posited for this change, such as possible sensory deprivation or changes in actual brain activity (Baltes and Lindenberger, 1997). Not only are the physiological causes unclear, but it has also been found that such factors as the nature of the task and a person's familiarity with the task also affect reaction time. (Additional implications of the slowing of reaction time with regard to memory and other intellectual processes are discussed in Chapters Eight and Nine.)

Disease Processes

As one grows older, it becomes difficult to distinguish between the normal or primary aging processes and those physical changes that are disease related. Although changes in health can affect the ability to learn at any age, the greatest effect is felt in older adulthood, when "the concept of disease as distinguishable from normal aging (i.e., physical changes unrelated to disease) has many implications for studying cognitive processes" (Elias, Elias, and Elias, 1991, p. 27).

Although a number of health impairments may affect the learning process, two specific disease processes affect learning profoundly, depending on the severity and stage of the disease (Bee, 1996; Lefrancois, 1996). The first is cardiovascular disease, especially when it results in a stroke or cerebrovascular incident in which the blood supply is cut off to a part of the brain. This can lead to a loss of memory and aphasia, restricting the ability to reproduce verbal speech. Moreover, other physical changes, such as loss of mobility, can occur, depending on which part of the brain is affected. If the stroke is mild or intervention comes quickly, full or at least partial functioning may be restored so that people can once again communicate normally and be cognizant of the world around them. In the case of massive brain damage, chronic organic brain disorder might result—the second class of health problems that, even in their milder forms, affect learning. One of the major causes of chronic brain dysfunction is Alzheimer's disease. Alzheimer's disease often develops so slowly that it may take years to recognize, although certain forms of the disease appear to develop more rapidly. The cause of this disease process is not known, but its effects become very apparent over time. Symptoms range from impaired memory and disorganization of thought, to changes in judgment and emotion, and finally to the inability to care for oneself.

In addition to these direct effects, disease processes indirectly influence adults' ability to learn. Pain and fatigue often accompany both acute and chronic illnesses, leaving one with little energy or motivation to engage in learning activities. Different medications and treatments may affect the way one thinks and behaves, side effects that may go unrecognized. Moreover, the financial drain on resources may be enormous, particularly in coping with chronic illness, leaving little support for learning activities of any kind.

PSYCHOLOGICAL CHANGES

The psychological perspective encompasses a broad array of ideas on how adults develop over the life span. The focus of this framework is how development occurs within the individual, whether development is primarily an internal process or results from interactions with the environment. The material can be divided into three major categories: cognitive development, intelligence and aging, and psychological development. Because the categories of cognitive development and intelligence and aging are fundamental to understanding learning in adulthood, they are discussed in depth in Chapters Seven and Eight, respectively. Here we focus on the third category: psychological development.

A number of diverse concepts have been placed in the category of psychological development, including the theories of ego development (Erikson, 1963; Loevinger, 1976), self development (Gould, 1978; Jordan, 1997c; Josselson, 1996; Kegan, 1982, 1994; Levinson and others, 1978; Levinson and Levinson, 1996; Vaillant, 1977), moral development (Gilligan, 1982; Kohlberg, 1973; Kohlberg and Ryncarz, 1990), and faith and spiritual development (Fowler, 1981; Jones, 1995). The common theme in this vast array of work is the changing nature of the internal self as we develop.

The literature on psychological development is grounded primarily in clinical studies and qualitative biographies obtained through in-depth interviews. In addition to the limited nature of the research designs, the samples, except in a few notable studies (Clausen, 1993; Costa and McCrae, 1980, 1994; Eichorn and others, 1981; Neugarten and others, 1964), have been relatively small and highly selective. Subjects of the most often quoted studies have been primarily white and middle class. There also was a male bias in many of the earlier studies (for example, Kohlberg, 1973; Levinson and others, 1978). More recently there has been a substantial increase in the study of women's development (see, for example, Caffarella and Olson, 1993; Estes, 1992; Gilligan, 1982; Jordan, 1997c; Jordan and others, 1991; Josselson, 1996; Levinson and Levinson, 1996). Although the majority of subjects of many of these studies have also been white and middle class, there is a growing trend to acknowledge class, race, ethnicity, and sexual orientation as critical factors in affecting development (D'Augelli and Patterson, 1995; Etter-Lewis and Foster, 1996; Jordan, 1997c; Ponterotto, Casas, Suzuki, and Alexander, 1995). Still the theory building in psychological development is at best tentative in terms of people of color, gay men and women, and people from different social backgrounds and cultures.

Although this material on psychological development is somewhat tenuous and at times unclear, adult educators over the years, such as Knox (1977), Cross (1981), Merriam (1984), Daloz (1986), and Tennant and Pogson (1995), have proposed a number of useful ideas on how this material can help us understand learning in adulthood. We especially like Daloz's notion of using these developmental theories as alternative maps of how adults can develop—without saying which specific roads should be taken or whether in some cases this developmental journey should be taken at all (Daloz, 1986, 1988b). This best fits our stance: that there is no right or best way of developing as we age. With this caveat in mind, we have organized the literature into three categories: sequential models of development, life events and transitions, and relational models. Interwoven within each major theme are implications for learning in adulthood.

Sequential Models

Although all of the sequential models provide for an unfolding of adult life in a series of phases or stages, they have different end points, from becoming autonomous and independent to finding wisdom and a universal sense of faith and moral behavior. Levinson and his colleagues (Levinson, 1986; Levinson and Levinson, 1996; Levinson and others, 1978), Gould (1978), and Sheehy (1976, 1995) assert that development is bound to very specific ages. Levinson and Levinson (1996), for example, from their studies of both men and women, suggest that people evolve through an orderly sequence of stable and transitional periods that correlate with chronological age. One's life structure, that is, "the underlying pattern or design of a person's life at any given time" (Levinson and Levinson, 1996, p. 22), tends to be established and maintained during stable periods and then questioned and changed during transitional periods. The specific time periods they outline for both men and women are as follows (p. 18):

Early Adult Transition	*Ages 17–22*
Entry Life Structure for Early Adulthood	Ages 22–28
Age 30 Transition	Ages 28–33
Culminating Life Structure for Early Adulthood	Ages 33–40
Mid-Life Transition	*Ages 40–45*
Early Life Structure for Middle Adulthood	Ages 45–50
Age 50 Transition	Ages 50–55

Culminating Life Structure   Ages 55–60
for Middle Adulthood

    Late Adult Transition   *Ages 60–65*

    Era of Late Adulthood   Ages 60–?

Components of this changing life structure include marriage and family, occupation, friendships, relationships to politics, religion, ethnicity, and community, and leisure, recreation, and memberships and roles in many social settings. The "*central components* are those that have the greatest significance for the self and the life. They receive the greatest share of one's time and energy, and they strongly influence the character of the other components" (Levinson and Levinson, 1996, p. 23).

Although Levinson and his colleagues hold that both men and women follow these alternating sequences of structure building and transitional periods, these periods "operate somewhat differently in females and males. . . . Women . . . work on the developmental tasks of every period with different resources and constraints, external as well as internal" (pp. 36–37). Levinson and Levinson's central concept for these differences in gender is gender splitting, which "refers not simply to gender differences but of a splitting asunder—the creation of a rigid division between male and female, masculine and feminine, in human life" (p. 38). More specifically they describe four forms of gender splitting that have an impact on how the life structure evolves in men and women (pp. 38–39):

1. The splitting of the domestic sphere and the public sphere as social domains for women and for men;

2. The Traditional Marriage Enterprise and the split it creates between the female homemaker and the male provisioner;

3. The splitting of "women's work" and "men's work";

4. The splitting of feminine and masculine in the individual psyche.

This framework of relating development to specific age periods has led a number of educators to propose a link between age-appropriate tasks and behavior and the fostering of learning activities for adults. Havighurst (1972) was one of the earliest writers to link these ideas into what he termed the *teachable moment*. The idea of the teachable moment is grounded in the concept of developmental tasks—tasks that arise at a certain period in a person's life, such as selecting a mate, starting a family, and getting started in an occupation. Although the time frame and some of the tasks Havighurst suggested are somewhat dated, the idea of specific life tasks' giving rise to a teachable moment is not. Knowles (1980, p. 51) has also viewed developmental tasks as producing "a 'readiness to learn' which at its peak presents a 'teachable moment' " and outlines his own list of "life tasks" for young, old, and middle-aged adults.

For other theorists writing from a sequential perspective, there is a step-wise upward movement, but it is not necessarily tied to chronological age (Erikson, 1963, 1982; Erikson, Erikson, and Kivnick, 1986; Fowler, 1981; Kegan, 1982; Kohlberg, 1973; Loevinger, 1976; Vaillant, 1977). These scholars assert that whether the stages or steps they describe are related to age or not, they are hierarchical in nature and therefore build on one another. There is disagreement among these writers about what causes the movement between stages and whether this movement is upward only to higher stages or whether it is back and forth across stages. Kohlberg (1973) and Loevinger (1976), for example, view the movement as primarily upward only and internally driven, while Erikson (1982) perceives it to be a function of internal and environmental forces and allows for movement back and forth between the stages throughout the life cycle.

Erikson is by far the most often quoted theorist representing sequential development from this perspective. Erikson has posited eight stages of development, each representing a series of crises or issues to be dealt with over the life span. For each stage there is a choice between opposites—one negative and the other positive—and it is imperative that persons achieve a favorable ratio of positive over negative prior to moving to the next stage. In young adulthood, the successful resolution between intimacy versus isolation results in love. In middle adulthood, resolving the tensions between generativity and self-absorption allows people to care for others; in older adulthood, resolutions between integrity versus despair provide the capacity for wisdom. Although Erikson characterized his fourth stage, that of identity versus identity confusion, as being tied primarily to the period of adolescence, researchers in adult development have also included the examination of this stage as part of their research on adults (for example, Josselson, 1987). Erikson maintains that as adults we may revisit earlier stages to resolve or re-resolve conflicts from earlier periods in different ways. For example, because of a loss of a spouse, we may need to work again through issues of both intimacy and identity. In addition, Erikson, Erikson, and Kivnick (1986) go on to suggest that it is vital involvement in old age and the interdependence among people that allow adults to complete the life cycle successfully and leave a positive legacy for the next generation.

Cross (1981, p. 240) proposes that "if one accepts a hierarchy of developmental stages, and if one believes that the role of educators is to help each individual develop to the highest possible level, then the role of educators is to challenge the learner to move to increasingly advanced stages of personal development." One way of accomplishing this is to assist adult learners in examining the basic assumptions on which they operate in order to help them move to these higher levels of development and thinking. The process of facilitating adult learning in this manner has been best described by Daloz (1986, 1988b), Krupp (1987, 1992), Levine (1989), Mezirow and Associates (1990), and Kegan (1994). For example, Daloz, who has directly linked his work with developmental theory, clearly uses the work of Kegan (1982) and others as the foundation for his notions of helping learners through their "transformational journeys" through formal mentoring and teaching activities.

Life Events and Transitions

One of the alternatives to the paradigm of development as a set of sequential stages is the concept of life events and transitions (Brim and Ryff, 1980; Creel, 1996; Evans, Forney, and Guido-DiBrito, 1998; Hultsch and Plemons, 1979; Schlossberg, Waters, and Goodman, 1995). In this framework, "life events are benchmarks in the human life cycle," markers that give "shape and direction to the various aspects of a person's life" (Danish and others, 1980, as quoted in Sugarman, 1986, p. 131). Unlike the stage and phase theorists, those who describe life events as providing key growth periods do not usually connect these life events to specific age periods, although some events seem to be more tied to age than others (Hughes, Blazer, and George, 1988).

There are two basic types of life events: individual and cultural (Hultsch and Plemons, 1979). Individual life events, such as birth, death, marriage, and divorce, define one person's specific life. Schlossberg (1989) has categorized individual life events into those that are anticipated or unanticipated, nonevents or sleeper events. Nonevents are events that were expected but do not occur, like infertility and the child who never leaves home; sleeper events are ones that you are not sure when they started, such as becoming bored with work or falling in love (Schlossberg, 1989; Schlossberg, Waters, and Goodman, 1995). Societal and historical happenings that shape the context in which a person develops, such as wars, the women's movement, and natural catastrophes, make up cultural life events. A number of factors affect how a person might experience any particular event (Brim and Ryff, 1980; Reese and Smyer, 1983; Schlossberg, Waters, and Goodman, 1995; Sugarman, 1986). Among the most salient are *timing* (the event is congruent with either personal or societal expectations of when it should happen), *cohort specificity* (the event may affect only certain generations, or it may affect different cohorts of people in different ways), and *probability* (normative being high, nonnormative being low) (Brim and Ryff, 1980; Neugarten, 1976; Peterson, 1996; Tennant and Pogson, 1995).

In addition to being viewed as milestones, life events are also seen as a process that may begin well before the event itself happens and continue well beyond it (Reese and Smyer, 1983; Schlossberg, Waters, and Goodman, 1995; Sugarman, 1986). The sequence of this process is not necessarily smooth or continuous. In the case of certain disease processes such as cancer, for example, the prognosis may be terminal, with the resulting event being death. But the process of dying is much more than just the day of death and often takes unplanned twists and turns prior to death itself. There is also a time needed after the event of death for survivors to assimilate the loss and make sense out of a seemingly different world. The notion of life events as a process is often equated with the idea of transitions (Schlossberg, Waters, and Goodman, 1995).

Transitions are viewed as "the natural process of disorientation and reorientation that marks the turning points of the path of growth . . . involving periodic accelerations and transformations" (Bridges, 1980, p. 5). Adults continually experience transitions, whether anticipated or unanticipated, and react to them depending on the type of transition, the context in which it occurs, and its impact on their lives. "Transitions may lead to growth, but decline is also a possible outcome, and many transitions may be viewed with ambivalence by the individuals experiencing them" (Evans, Forney, and Guido-DiBrito, 1998, p. 112).

"Whereas a transition may be precipitated by a single event or non-event, dealing with a transition is a process that extends over time" (Evans, Forney, and Guido-DiBrito, 1998, p. 112). Three authors have provided transition models that are especially helpful in understanding the notion of transition as a process (Bridges, 1980, 1991; Schlossberg, 1989; Schlossberg, Waters, and Goodman, 1995; Sugarman, 1986). Bridges's (1980, 1991) model begins with endings, that is, "letting go of something" (Bridges, 1991, p. 5). People then move into what he calls the neutral zone, "the no-man's land between the old reality and the new. . . . It is a time when the old way is gone and the new doesn't feel comfortable yet" (p. 5). His final phase is that of new beginnings, whereby people consciously choose to launch into their new ways of being and doing. Bridges emphasizes that these phases are not necessarily separate; people often find themselves in more than one phase at a time.

Sugarman (1986), who agrees with Bridges that transition cycles are not an orderly or sequential process, has identified seven stages that accompany a wide range of transitions: (1) immobilization—a sense of being overwhelmed or frozen; (2) reaction—a sharp swing of mood from elation to despair depending on the nature of the transition; (3) minimization—minimizing one's feelings and the anticipated impact of the event; (4) letting go—breaking with the past; (5) testing—exploration of the new terrain; (6) searching for meaning—conscious striving to learn from the experience; and (7) integration—feeling at home with the change. And Schlossberg, Waters, and Goodman (1995) endorse a three-phase model: "moving in," "moving through," and "moving out." Bridges (1980, 1991) stresses that letting go of the past, which is included in all three models, is often overlooked. We want to get on with the change rather than deal with the loss of the way we were before. When first having a child, for example, we must let go of what being childless was all about.

Schlossberg and her colleagues (Schlossberg, 1987, 1989; Schlossberg, Lynch, and Chickering, 1989; Schlossberg, Waters, and Goodman, 1995) specifically describe how people in transition have both strengths and weaknesses—resources and deficits—to cope with the transition. She divides them into "four major categories, the four S's: situation, self, supports, and strategies" (1987, p. 75). How does a person assess the transition—as positive, negative, or indifferent—and what is her sense of control as she encounters and acts on the transition? What are the person's inner strengths for dealing with the transition? What kinds of social supports does the person have? And, finally, does the person have a wide repertoire of strategies for coping with the transition? The ratio of strengths to weaknesses helps to explain "why different individuals react differently to the same type of transition and why the same person reacts differently at different times" (Schlossberg, Waters, and Goodman, 1995, p. 49).

A number of educators have proposed that engaging in learning activities is one way in which adults cope with life events and transitions (Aslanian and Brickell, 1980; Knox, 1977; Merriam and Clark, 1991; Merriam and Yang, 1996; Schlossberg, Waters, and Goodman, 1995; Tennant and Pogson, 1995; Wolf and Leahy, 1998). Indeed, Aslanian and Brickell (1980) found that most adults "learn in order to cope with some change in their lives" (p. 111) and concluded that this learning is tied to a triggering event. The learning resulting from these triggering events is not always related to the event itself. For example, a divorce (the triggering event) may motivate a woman to return to school (the learning activity) so she may become more employable and therefore self-sufficient. These triggering events were most often related to career and family changes, such as moving to a new job or becoming pregnant. Blaxter and Tight (1995) have challenged Aslanian and Brickell's findings that most adults learn as a result of life events. Their study of adult students revealed that their respondents "split into two, almost equal groups: those for whom a clear linkage between their current educational participation and one or more transitional events can be identified, and those for whom no such linkage is readily apparent. Indeed, the latter may be continuously resisting such linkages" (p. 231).

Merriam and Clark (1991, 1992), based on a qualitative study of work, love, and learning in adult life, also found that issues related to one's work life and personal life, including family changes, are sources of learning. Furthermore, respondents identified the learning related to these events as highly significant, to the point, in some cases, of bringing about a change in their worldviews. Merriam and Yang (1996), using a totally different methodology, confirmed these findings, with "work-related variables . . . being particularly powerful in predicting" developmental changes.

Merriam and Clark (1991, 1992) also found links between the transition times created by these life events and learning. They observed that more learning happens in periods that people perceive as good versus bad times. Yet although nearly ten times more significant learning occurred in the good times than in the bad, learning that is more likely to be transformative occurred in the bad times. In other words, the more difficult the transition is perceived to be by learners, the more potential this transition may have for learning, and especially for changing how learners see themselves and their worlds.

Merriam, Mott, and Lee (1996) also explored transition times that resulted in what they termed negative learning versus growth and development. They speculated that learning from life experience can also result "in debilitating, growth-inhibiting outcomes" (p. 1). Intensive interviews were held with eighteen adults who self-identified a negative outcome from a life experience. The researchers found that these respondents interpreted their experiences negatively if some defining aspect of themselves had been challenged. For example, becoming divorced challenged one man's definition of self as a caretaker; being attached challenged another women's sense of self as in control. When this challenge was too daunting or made them feel too vulnerable, these respondents made sense of the experience by adopting self-protective behaviors or attitudes, "including blaming others, becoming angry, withdrawing or becoming distrustful" (p. 18). Therefore, rather than opening themselves up to what we might term positive learning or growth, they closed themselves off. Another major finding from the study was that "when and if the threat to the self was reduced by time, having support, and gaining a larger perspective and personal agency, the process began to reverse itself toward more growth-oriented outcomes" (p. 21). Thus, to extract deeper and more expanded leaning from some of our most difficult times, adults often need an extended period of time and the active support and caring from others.

Building on this work, as well as the work of others, such as Mezirow (1981) and Daloz (1986), Merriam and Heuer (1996) have proposed a useful model for extracting meaning from our more complex life-altering transitions (see Figure 5.1). More specifically, this model addresses life experiences that are difficult to accommodate or explain. For example, there is a poor fit between the event and the person's current meaning system. Or there is a challenge to the fundamental assumptions, beliefs, or values a person holds about life. In taking on this challenge, adults must be willing to engage themselves cognitively, affectively, and even physically with the experience and be given the time and support to do so. For example, many parents have their fundamental belief systems about sexuality and the meaning of family heavily challenged when they learn their son or daughter is gay. They may refuse to think about it, react in anger, or become highly stressed. As these parents continue to work through this challenge to their way

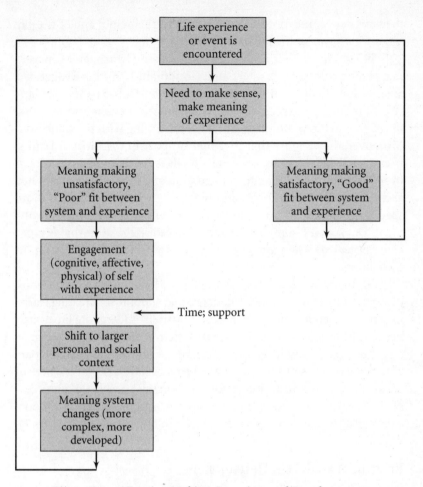

Figure 5.1.   Meaning Making, Learning, and Development.
Source: Merriam and Heuer, 1996, p. 252.

of thinking and being, Merriam and Heuer posit that they need to move in their thinking beyond just their personal experience of learning their child is gay to "the larger context, both personal and socio-cultural, in which [they] live. In doing so, space is created whereby the self can be defined or restructured" (p. 251). One way they might do this is to go into counseling or join a parent support group, where they can share stories and ways of coping with this new reality in their lives. Another strategy might be to support a local group of community activists for gay rights, whereby they could see the broader lives of people who are gay. Hopefully through all of these learning activities, they might become more accepting both of their child and of the gay lifestyle as a way of life for many people.

Schlossberg and her colleagues (Schlossberg, Lynch, and Chickering, 1989; Schlossberg, Waters and, Goodman, 1995) have suggested areas of knowledge and skill that would be helpful to people in transition, including exploration of the transition event and process, problem-solving techniques, and skills for coping with the transition. Moreover, they believe that personal support in the form of family, friends, self-help groups, or professionals is needed to help adults in transition examine their current situation and future scenarios. They and others, like Daloz (1986) and Bloom (1995), have provided more specific guidance for how this could be done in a learning environment. Daloz and Bloom believe that a mentoring relationship is especially powerful when adult learners are in periods of transition in their lives.

And finally, Wolf and Leahy (1998, p. 4) have edited a useful book that gives educators of adults "guidance and support for creating learning environments to meet the needs of learners undergoing life transitions." These authors explore five specific transitional areas (such as career changes, homelessness, and caring for and loss of an aging parent) and examples of specific ways educators have assisted learners in responding to these transitions. Although many learners do not necessarily "speak of their own [transitional] circumstances, the educational community would do well to prepare for and honor such growth" (p. 7).

Relational Models of Development

Yet another model of development has come from scholars who view the centrality of relationships as key to development. The majority of studies from this framework are grounded in research on women's development, including studies of women's moral development, identity development, and sources of well-being (Baruch, Barnett, and Rivers, 1983; Bateson, 1989, 1994; Brown and Gilligan, 1992; Caffarella and Olson, 1993; Crose, 1997; Estes, 1992; Gilligan, 1979, 1982; Hancock, 1985; Jordan, 1997c; Jordan and others, 1991; Josselson, 1996; Miller, 1986; Peck, 1986). The metaphor of an ever-changing web of interconnectedness is often used to describe how women grow and develop throughout their lives. These webs often have very different patterns, sometimes intricate and other times simple, and yet always changing.

The Stone Center relational model provides an excellent example of a model of development that views relationships as central to development (Jordan, 1991a, 1991b, 1997a, 1997b; Surrey, 1991). This model "goes beyond saying that women value relationships; we are suggesting that the deepest sense of one's being is continuously formed in connection to others and is inextricably tied to relational formation. The primary feature, rather than structure marked by separateness and autonomy, is increasing empathic responsiveness in the context of interpersonal mutuality" (Jordan, 1997a, p. 15). Empathy—being able to understand authentically and be a part of the experiences of others—is central to the relational model. Mutual empathy, "characterized by the flow of empathic attunement between people" (Jordan, 1997a, p. 15), then becomes the key to development. Jordan observes that in Western cultures, "there has been a split along gender lines between the ideal of a separate, autonomous, objective male self and a relational, connected, and empathic female self" (Jordan, 1997a, p. 21). Although most authors agree with Jordan's beliefs that the relational model best fits with women, at least white women within Western cultures, there are others who would argue that the importance of connectedness to development also applies to women of color and perhaps even to men in general (Erikson, Erikson, and Kivnick, 1986; Jones, 1995; Levinson and Levinson, 1996; Tatum, 1997; Turner, 1997).

Numerous scholars, writing primarily from their knowledge of women's development and feminist pedagogy (see Chapter Fifteen), have spoken to the importance of relationships and connectedness to the learning process in adulthood (Belenky, Clinchy, Goldberger, and Tarule, 1986; Caffarella, 1992, 1996; Fiddler and Marienau, 1995; Goldberger, Tarule, Clinchy, and Belenky, 1996; Hayes, 1989; Maher and Tetreault, 1994; Taylor and Marienau, 1995). For example, Belenky, Clinchy, Goldberger, and Tarule (1986) coined the term *connected teaching,* which describes a process of collaborative knowing among learners and instructors, and Fiddler and Marienau (1995, p. 76) offer a model of learner-centered teaching that includes the notion that learning is "promoted by interactions among one's experiences and ideas, and those of others." More specifically, Caffarella (1996, pp. 40–42) advocates that adult educators incorporate four key ideas into their practice relating to the theme of centrality of relationships: "(1) use collaborative interaction as one of the fundamental ways to plan and organize learning experiences; (2) foster a climate for learning where learners and instructors support each other in the learning process, both in and out of formal learning situations; (3) use a cooperative communication style; and (4) recognize that feelings are a critical part of fostering relationships in learning experiences." Although Caffarella speaks to the role of educators in primarily formal settings, these same ideas are also relevant for both nonformal and informal learning activities. This can be seen, for example, in studies of learning through social action programs and through informal or self-directed methods (see Chapters Two and Thirteen).

Recurring Developmental Issues

Recurring developmental issues is yet another way of organizing the literature on psychological development. We have chosen the issues of identity and intimacy as two examples, although other themes could be explored. These themes of identity and intimacy, which some authors equate with the time-honored notions of work and love (for example, Freud, as cited in Rohrlich, 1980; Baruch, Barnett, and Rivers, 1983; Vaillant, 1977), are fundamental to the lives of adults. The theme of intimacy centers on building meaningful relationships, while identity issues focus on questions of who we are and what we believe in. Some developmental theorists, like Erikson (1982) and Levinson (Levinson, 1986; Levinson and Levinson, 1996), place these developmental markers on a time continuum, most often during the adolescent and young adulthood phases. In Erikson's theory, for example, "adolescents face *identity* versus *identity diffusion* and learn the virtue of fidelity. Young adults face *intimacy* versus *isolation* and learn the virtue of love" (Chickering and Reisser, 1993, p. 22). Other scholars, including many who study women's development, argue that these themes are salient throughout adult lives (Apter, 1995; Caffarella and Olson, 1993; Chickering and Reisser, 1993; Josselson, 1996; Merriam and Clark, 1991, 1992).

Josselson (1987, 1996), through her longitudinal study of women, found four pathways to identity formation: guardians, pathmakers, searchers, and drifters. Guardians seem to have always known who they were and where they were going without considering alternative paths. The pathmakers, in contrast, consider and try out alternative ways of being and believing before making any commitments to who they are and what they want to be. Searchers continually struggle with making choices about their identities. They are uncertain about who they are or want to be, but they are trying to figure it out. And drifters "are without commitments and not struggling to make them, either feeling lost or following the impulse of the moment" (Josselson, 1996, p. 36). Josselson (1996, p. 40) stresses that adults can move in and out of these different pathways and that one's "identity continues to be modified through adult life. . . . Identity is always both product and process; it embodies continuity and change."

Our stance is in agreement with Josselson and others: these two major themes of identity and intimacy are salient throughout adult lives, and therefore educators of adults need to be aware of these continuing developmental issues in working with adult learners. Issues of who we are and how we fit in the world are never totally resolved. Rather, finding our identity is "an evolving narrative quest. . . . The story is created and revised across the adult years as the changing person and the person's changing world negotiate niches, places, opportunities, and positions within which the person can live, and live meaningfully" (McAdams, 1994, pp. 306–307). Men and women also revisit issues of intimacy over and over again in their lives through multiple contexts: in families with the birth and growth of children; in the loss of a spouse or partner through divorce or death; and in wider social networks of building friendships, as well as structuring relationships with colleagues at work.

Merriam and Clark's study (1991, 1992) gives a clear picture of the patterns of the intersection of work and love and how these patterns relate to learning. More specifically, these authors discovered three broad patterns: the parallel pattern, the steady/fluctuating pattern, and the divergent pattern. In the *parallel pattern*, work and love are intertwined; "change in one area is reflected by change in the other. The *steady/fluctuating pattern* . . . shows one area remaining steady . . . , while the other fluctuates. In this pattern the steady domain—whether it be work or love—appears to function as a stabilizer or source of security, and people tend to locate their identity in this area" (Merriam and Clark, 1991, p. xv). In the *divergent pattern,* work and love exist independently and often in opposition to one another. Although Merriam and Clark caution against generalizability of these patterns because their sample was limited (well educated, white, and heavily female), they assume these patterns might also be present in more diverse populations. In summary, they view work and love events of people's lives as functioning in two ways: "as a stimulus for other learning, and as a source of learning in and of themselves" (Merriam and Clark, 1991, p. 213). Learning, as noted earlier, was often a result of coping with a specific life event and the transition period triggered by that life event. And finally, learning was most likely to occur when "things were going well in both the work and love arenas. Apparently people need the energy and resources available in good times to engage in significant learning" (p. 213).

A number of authors have suggested specific ways that educators of adults can relate one or both of these two fundamental themes of development to their practice (Beatty and Wolf, 1996; Caffarella, 1992, 1996; Chickering and Reisser, 1993; Maher and Tetreault, 1994; Pratt and others, 1998; Wolf and Leahy, 1998). Pratt and others (1998), for example, in offering five perspectives on teaching, speak to the importance of the nurturing perspective. In this perspective, an instructor is "fundamentally concerned with the development of each learner's concept of self as learner per se" (Pratt and others, 1998, p. 49). "Learners' efficacy and self-esteem issues become the ultimate criteria against which learning success is measured" (p. 164). Pratt stresses that nurturing educators are caring and sincerely interested in their learners and can enter their learners' worlds in an empathic manner. And Caffarella (1996, p. 44) has offered three specific suggestions for responding to these developmental themes of identity and intimacy:

1. Recognize that some [learners] may be wrestling with the issues of who they are and what they want to be as educators, especially in times of major changes in their work situations or [personal lives].

2. Encourage [learners] to find, fashion, and use what has been termed the "authentic self" or one's voice in the instructional process. The heart of sharing one's authentic self is the use of "I" and "we" versus "her" or "them."

3. Have instructors serve as role models in helping [learners] share their changing sense of selves.

Beatty and Wolf (1996) have added to these suggestions by outlining an assistance pattern for older adult learners that includes activities such as establishing relationships of trust and credibility with learners and guiding learners in the pursuit of alternative avenues of change.

SUMMARY

Adult developmental theory and research offer a rich array of material from which numerous implications can be drawn about learning in adulthood. This chapter has reviewed the developmental characteristics of adults from two perspectives: biological aging and psychological change. With regard to biological aging, all adults experience some changes as they age. Many of these changes, such as weight gain, graying hair, and wrinkles, while unwelcome and unsettling perhaps, have no effect on learning. The changes that can affect learning, such as deterioration of sight and hearing, changes in reaction time, and disease, vary widely from person to person. Not all adults will lose their hearing, be unable to complete a task in a specified time, or be impaired by acute or chronic illness. Furthermore, we know that adults compensate for physical changes such that learning may not seem affected at all.

Psychological changes in adulthood have been charted by a number of researchers. This work can be loosely grouped into three categories: sequential, life events and transitions, and relational models of development. The sequential models of development of Levinson, Gould, Erikson, Kohlberg, and others attempt to delineate the common themes of adult life according to what phase or stage of life one is in. The characteristics and concerns of a particular time of life have been linked to learning through what Havighurst (1972) called the "teachable moment." Educators who frame programs according to these models believe their role is to help each individual move vertically to the highest possible stage of development or horizontally through the various life phases.

One alternative to the sequential models of development is the life events and transitions framework. Life events are happenings that shape people's lives. Although life events are usually not thought of as connecting to specific age periods, some seem to be tied more to age than others. Transitions, which are precipitated by life events or even nonevents, are processes that over time can, but not necessarily do, lead to learning and change. Adults often engage in learning as one way to cope with the life events they encounter, whether that learning is related to or just precipitated by a life event. Learning within these times of transition is most often linked to work and family, with the most significant amounts of learning happening during what we would term the good times of our lives. Yet although a great deal more learning happens during the good times than the bad, extracting deeper meanings from these events more often occurs during what we perceive as the difficult times, such as a death in the family, divorce, or serious illness.

A third approach to development, based primarily in studies of women, is grounded in the notion that relationships are central to development. The relational model emphasizes that our sense of self is continuously formed in connection to others, with empathic attunement to others as central. From this model and other writings on women's development and feminist pedagogy has come the emphasis on the importance of relationships and collaboration in learning, including the significance of recognizing feelings as a critical part of fostering relational learning.

The chapter concluded with a discussion of recurring developmental themes. The two themes of identity and intimacy, often equated as the time-honored notions of work and love, are seen as fundamental to the lives of adults. Although some theorists place these themes on a time continuum, others view them as the ones that most adults revisit throughout their lives as relationships and roles in life change. Educators in formal and nonformal settings will likely have at least a few learners in their activities who are wrestling with issues of who they are and what they want to be, especially in times of major changes in their work situations or personal lives. In addition, identity and intimacy issues may lead to seeking out adult learning activities.

CHAPTER SIX

Sociocultural and Integrative Perspectives on Development

Scholars have taken many different perspectives about what development in adulthood is all about. For years, the major assumption was that the nexus of development lay with the individual person, whether those forces were genetically preprogrammed or chosen by that person. This belief led to a plethora of books and manuals on how to get adulthood "right," from the many books on the power of loving ourselves to those that advocate ways to use and enhance own our inborn personalities. More recently, there has been an increasing recognition that explaining development in adulthood is more than just focusing on the individualized self. Rather, emphasis has been placed on our collective selves as defined by society. Equally important to development is how society characterizes defining aspects of adulthood, such as age, race, gender, class, ethnicity, and sexual orientation. For example, older people in many Westernized countries are accorded lesser status than young and middle-aged adults. People of color are shunned by many whites, either openly or through less overt ways, like where they choose to live and whom they associate with. Poor people become invisible in the social structure, other than being told regularly to pull themselves up by their bootstraps and get their lives in order. And gays and lesbians fear losing their jobs or being ridiculed for their lifestyle. In addition, there is an increasing interest in viewing adult development from many perspectives. Although this kind of theorizing is difficult to operationalize, it holds much promise; many adults are aware of the complex and interrelated nature of their biological, psychological, and sociocultural selves.

Highlighted in this chapter are two additional perspectives of adult development: sociocultural factors that influence development and what we are calling the integrative paradigm of development. Addressed first are three strands of work from the sociocultural perspective that have figured prominently in our discussion of the connections of adult development and learning: work on social roles and timing of life events; on the socially constructed notions of race, gender, ethnicity, and sexual orientation; and on cross-cultural studies of adulthood. Interwoven within the discussion of each of these ideas is their connection to adult learning. In the second portion of this chapter we discuss theories exemplifying an integrative perspective of development. The chapter concludes with a short overview of why educators of adults need to consider multiple perspectives of adulthood in their research and practice.

SOCIOCULTURAL FACTORS

The sociocultural perspective of adult development moves us from focusing on how development is primarily an internal process to one which acknowledges the importance of the social world in which we live (Dannefer, 1984, 1989, 1996; Levenson and Crumpler, 1996). Within this perspective the emphasis is placed on how the world about us defines who and what we ought to be as adults based on our age, the color of our skin, whether we are male or female, how rich or poor we are, what our ethnic backgrounds are, and our sexual orientation. Scholars writing from this perspective view "the sociocultural environment as a point of departure" for studying the life course of adults (Elder, 1995, p. 103) and stress the socially constructed nature of how adulthood is defined. Bee (1996, p. 41), for example, has listed how adult lives differ in our society based on social status or social class, which "are typically defined or measured in terms of three dimensions: education, income, and occupation." She goes on to observe that "distinctions between 'blue collar' and 'white collar', or 'middle class' and 'working class', are fundamental status distinctions" (p. 41), at least in North American culture. More specifically Bee asserts that people with higher status, compared to those of lower status, have the following characteristics (pp. 41–42):

- In the United States, over the past several generations at least, the majority of both men and women end up in occupations at the same broad level of social status as their parents.

- Middle class adults, as a group, marry later and have fewer children than do working-class adults. Both of these differences affect the timing of various subsequent adult life experiences, such as the departure of the last child.

- The life course of middle-class adults is more likely to be advantaged in a variety of ways: They are less likely to experience periods of unemployment; they are healthier and live longer; . . . retain a higher level of intellectual functioning longer into old age . . . ; and are, in general, more satisfied with their lives.

Bee has developed similar lists for people of different racial and ethnic, and gender groups.

We offer three salient strands of work from the literature on the sociocultural perspective of adulthood that provide us with different ways of looking at adult development: adult social roles and the timing of life events; the socially constructed notions of race, ethnicity, gender, and sexual orientation and how these affect development; and cross-cultural studies of adulthood. Interwoven within the discussion of each of these strands of work are implications for learning in adulthood.

Social Roles and the Timing of Life Events

The earlier work on the sociocultural dimensions of adulthood focused on social role taking and the notion of the timing of life events. Social roles are defined as both positions and associated expectations determined primarily by normative beliefs held by society (Hughes and Graham, 1990). Examples of these various roles include parent, spouse, worker, child, and friend. Changes in one's social position result from modifications of these roles (such as redefining the role of parent when both parents assume employment) and the taking on of new roles (such as wife to widow or paid worker to retired person). These changes may be initiated by the individual or by others; a parent might ask an older child to take on the role of worker to help pay for her college expenses, for example, or changes in legislative policy might give a specific group in society, such as minorities or women, more or perhaps less control over their own lives. This focus on social roles has fostered a number of research traditions in such areas as career development and marriage and family roles (see Bee, 1996; Berger, 1998; Lefrancois, 1996).

The research on the timing of life events, which is exemplified by the work of Neugarten and others (Neugarten, 1976, 1979; Neugarten and others, 1964; Neugarten and Danton, 1973), suggests that "every society is age-graded, and every society has a system of social expectations regarding age-appropriate behavior. The individual passes through a socially regulated cycle from birth to death as inexorably as he [sic] passes through the biological cycle: a succession of socially delineated age-statuses, each with its recognized rights, duties and obligations" (Neugarten, 1976, p. 16). Although the timing of events has changed somewhat and the deadlines for completing such events have become more variable since Neugarten completed her original work, adults are still very much aware of when they should be doing what (Settersten and Hägestad, 1996). Neugarten goes on to point out that it is not the events themselves that necessarily precipitate crisis or change. "What is more important is the timing of those events. If they occur off-time, that is, outside the 'normal, expectable life cycle' (being widowed in young adulthood or fired close to retirement, for example), they are much more likely to cause trauma or conflict" (Merriam, 1984, p. 22). From this vantage point, the study of adult development then becomes a study of life events construed from socially constructed beliefs, whereas in the psychological tradition, the focus is on the life events themselves as markers and processes. More recent work on this concept of the timing of life events has been completed by such scholars as Clausen (1995), Bengtson (1996), and Settersten and Hägestad (1996).

The idea that learning in adulthood is related to appropriate role taking, as defined by society's expectations, has a long history in adult education, from the early citizenship education program for immigrants to today's workplace learning programs. Several writers have suggested that programs be developed related to the social roles of adults. Kidd (1973) and Knox (1977), for example, explored how changes in social roles can be related to learning activities. Specially, Kidd (1973) outlined a taxonomy suggested by Malcolm Knowles at a UNESCO seminar in Hamburg in 1972 that takes into account not only roles but also the competencies related to those roles. The implied assumption underlying this taxonomy is that learning programs could be built to address these competencies for adults going through role changes or wishing to become more competent in their current roles (for example, family member, worker, and citizen). Even learning on our own may be driven by what society expects of us, such as learning parenting skills or taking care of aging parents. For the most part, adult educators have developed programs around role taking to the age-normative times of life events and have not taken into account those people who are "off-time." More recently there has been some change in this thinking. For example, hospice programs, which both offer support and teach caretakers how to care for dying people, do not discriminate whom they will serve based either on the age of the patient or the caretaker.

Socially Constructed Notions of Race, Ethnicity, Gender, and Sexual Orientation

Researchers have been especially interested over the past decade in the socially constructed notions of race, ethnicity, gender, and sexual orientation as they relate to adult development (Bakari, 1997; Bem, 1993; Cross, 1991; D'Augelli and Patterson, 1995; Etter-Lewis and Foster, 1996; Evans, Forney, and Guido-DiBrito, 1998; Helms, 1993; Mashengele, 1997; Ponterotto, Casas, Suzuki, and Alexander, 1995; Tennant and Pogson, 1995; Wilson, 1996). Discussing these different constructs in relationship to development is difficult because they often overlap and have been given different meanings by researchers. For example, some use the terms *race* and *ethnicity* interchangeably, while others clearly distinguish between these two concepts. What makes it even more difficult to establish the connection between these ideas and development is that adults are rarely just black or white, male or female, homosexual or heterosexual, or of one cultural origin. Rather most adults come in many shades and variations. For example, they may be female, but also white, of Hispanic origin, and a lesbian; or they may be male, but also black of African origin and heterosexual.

Although this complexity makes it difficult to form any generalizations, researchers nevertheless are working to untangle the intersections of race, class, gender, sexual orientation, and ethnicity.

Prominent theories of racial and ethnic identity development grounded at least in part on the assumption that views of adulthood are socially constructed include those of Cross (1991, 1995), Helms (1993, 1995), Phinney (1990), and Sodowsky, Kwan, and Pannu (1995). Cross (1995, p. 98), for example, defines his model of Nigrescence as one "that explains how assimilated as well as deracinated, deculturalized, or miseducated adolescents or Black adults are transformed, by a series of circumstances and events, into persons who are more Black or Afrocentrically aligned." Moving through the five stages of pre-encounter, encounter, immersion-emersion, internalization, and internalization-commitment, though not necessarily in a linear journey, blacks are able to change "the salience of race and culture in [their lives] . . . , define what is important [to them] in adult life, and . . . feel totally new" (pp. 114–115). One of the consequences of this movement is that "a person's conception of Blackness tends to become more open, expansive, and sophisticated" (p. 114). They become more at peace and comfortable with themselves as black and replace "an 'I' or egocentric perspective with a 'we' or 'group' perspective" (Evans, Forney, and Guido-DiBrito, 1998, p. 76). Helms (1993, 1995), on the other hand, proposes a process model of white racial identity that consists of two phases: abandonment of racism and defining a nonracist white identity. In this process individuals give up their white privilege and "abandon cultural and institutional racism as well as personal racism. [Rather, they] actively seek opportunities to learn from other cultural groups. . . . It is a process wherein [persons are] continually open to new information and new ways of thinking about racial and cultural variables" (Helms, 1993, p. 66).

Defining gender influences on development from the sociocultural perspective is somewhat different from the psychological tradition. Although scholars writing from a psychological perspective on women and development also often acknowledge the importance of context and environment in development, they do not necessarily see this as the major determinant in women's development. Rather, they more often speak to the lack of women's voices in developmental theory and how that theory might differ if those voices were included. Researchers drawing primarily on the sociocultural perspective view gender as embedded in our cultural discourses and systems of social organization. The perceived differences between males and females become a way to organize our lives. "It is thus not simply that women and men are seen to be different but that this male-female difference is super-imposed on so many aspects of the social world that a cultural connection is thereby forged between sex and virtually every other aspect of human experience, including modes of dress and social roles and even ways of expressing emotion and experiencing sexual desire" (Bem, 1993, p. 2). Thus, a change in perspective about how women and men grow and develop can happen only if we assist adults in examining what they believe about how men and women "act and be" in terms of the dominant culture in which they live. Bem (1993, p. 2) observes, for example, that at least in the United States, males and male experiences are viewed as "a neutral standard or norm, and females' experience as a sex-specific deviation from that norm."

Theories of sexual identity formation of heterosexuals are discussed quite often in the literature. In fact, most developmental theories, whether psychologically or socioculturally based, are primarily drawn from samples of heterosexual individuals or sexual orientation is either not known or not even considered. What is less common are theories that conceptualize gay, lesbian, and bisexual development and especially those that view development as a social construction. D'Augelli's (1994, p. 317) work represents one such model in that he takes into account "the complex factors that influence the development of people in context over historical time." More specifically he identifies six interactive processes that involve individuals' choosing to give up their prescribed heterosexual identity and the privileges associated with that identity to take on one that is still not well accepted by mainstream society. D'Augelli views this as a relatively slow process due to the prevalent social and cultural norms against homosexual or bisexual orientations. Brooks and Edwards (1997) believe that the sharing of narrative stories of people of different sexual orientations is one way to understand better sexual identity development as well as other developmental issues where culture is acknowledged as a key component of the developmental process. Brooks and Edwards go on to observe that "to experience our lives as different from the dominant narrative is frightening. If this experience is supported by a strong counter narrative such as that of lesbians or certain minority and racial and ethnic groups, we can find a space to live out our knowledge knowing there are others like ourselves. However, when our experience remains unarticulated and inchoate, we come to know ourselves as misfits" (p. 69).

This sentiment to share the narratives of one another's lives has been the impetus for many of the studies that address a mixture of two or more of these categories of race, ethnicity, gender, and sexual orientation (Neuman and Peterson, 1997). One such seminal work are the vivid descriptive studies of Coles and Coles (1978, 1980) of women from all walks of life. Through a biographical approach, the story is told of "the daily battles, the losses, the small victories, the long, burdened marches across time and space" (1978, p. 273) of black, Chicano, Eskimo, and Pueblo Indian women, among others. Coles and Coles conclude that the interwoven factors of gender, race, and social class have had a major impact on these women's lives: "The enemy is a given social order, yes; an economic system, yes; but also and quite distinctly—or as George Eliot might want to say quite definitely—a certain number of men" (p. 232).

More current examples of the use of narratives to tell the stories of development across categories include the work of Etter-Lewis and Foster (1996) and A. Wilson (1996). *Unrelated Kin* (Etter-Lewis and Foster, 1996) tells the stories of women of color: African American, Native American, Asian American, Latina, and non-Western women. Etter-Lewis and Foster observe that "documentation of women's lives has tended to be difficult due to a variety of factors, including women's relatively low social status and marginalization within society" (p. 8). In their work, these authors "place women of color at the center of their communities rather than at the periphery. They are the authorities and standard-bearers of their own lives" (p. 10). Patricia Bell-Scott and Juanita Johnson-Bailey also tell the stories, or what they term the "flat-footed truths," of women of African American origin. "To tell the flat-footed truth means to offer a story or statement that is straightforward, unshakable, and unembellished" (Bell-Scott, 1998, p. xix). Bell-Scott, like Etter-Lewis and Foster (1996), views this as risky business for the twenty-seven creative spirits who tell of their lives as women artists: "This kind of truth telling, especially by and about Black women, can be risky business because our lives are often devalued and our voices periodically silenced" (p. xix). Yet Bell-Scott also observes that there have always been women, both within and outside the African American communities, like Audre Lorde and Anita Hill, "who insist on speaking truths in the face of disbelief and public criticism" (p. xix). Through essays, interviews, poetry, and photographic images, the contributors to *Flat-Footed Truths* (Bell-Scott with John-son-Bailey, 1998) have created extended conversations about "the chal-lenge of telling one's own life . . . , the adventure of claiming lives neglected or lost, . . . the affirmation of lives of resistance, and the optimism and healing of lives transformed" (p. xix).

Wilson (1996, p. 303) speaks directly to the problems of trying to treat "sexual and racial identity as independent developmental path-ways. While this simplifying division may make it easier to generate theory, it may also make it less likely that the resulting theory will describe people's real-life developmental experiences." Wilson describes her experiences of trying to find herself as a lesbian indige-nous American—"a two-spirited person." She notes that it was "in the context of Native spirituality [that] I learned about the traditions of two-spirit people. I acquired strength from elders and leaders who were able to explain that as an indigenous woman who is also a les-bian, I needed to use the gifts of difference wisely" (p. 313). Wilson's strength and identity are, in her words, "inseparable from [my] cul-ture" (p. 315). She also makes the point that the mainstream lesbian and gay communities rarely recognize the two-spirit identity and often discriminate against gay and lesbian indigenous Americans.

Chávez, Guido-DiBrito, and Mallory (1996) have presented an intriguing and complex model of how we learn to value what they have termed "the other": anyone who is different from ourselves in race, ethnicity, social class, gender, or sexual orientation. This diver-sity development model, built on the work of Kegan (1994), Cass (1979), Devine (1989), and others, provides "a framework in which individuals develop in a non-linear way toward valuing and possibly choosing to validate those who are 'other'" (p. 8). As shown in Figure 6.1, the framework consists of five periods: unawareness, awareness, questioning/self-exploration, risk-taking/other exploration, and inte-gration. This process "can be experienced at various ages, simultane-ously [if dealing with more than one form of "the other"], repeatedly, or not at all" (p. 9). The outcome for individuals who go through this process is that they are "able to interact confidently in and out of their own 'culture' and have the ability to affirm choices different than their own" (p. 14). Although this model has not been tested empirically, it holds much promise for understanding how to embrace diversity within our lives.

Numerous scholars, primarily within the past decade, have ac-knowledged the importance of the socially constructed notions of race,

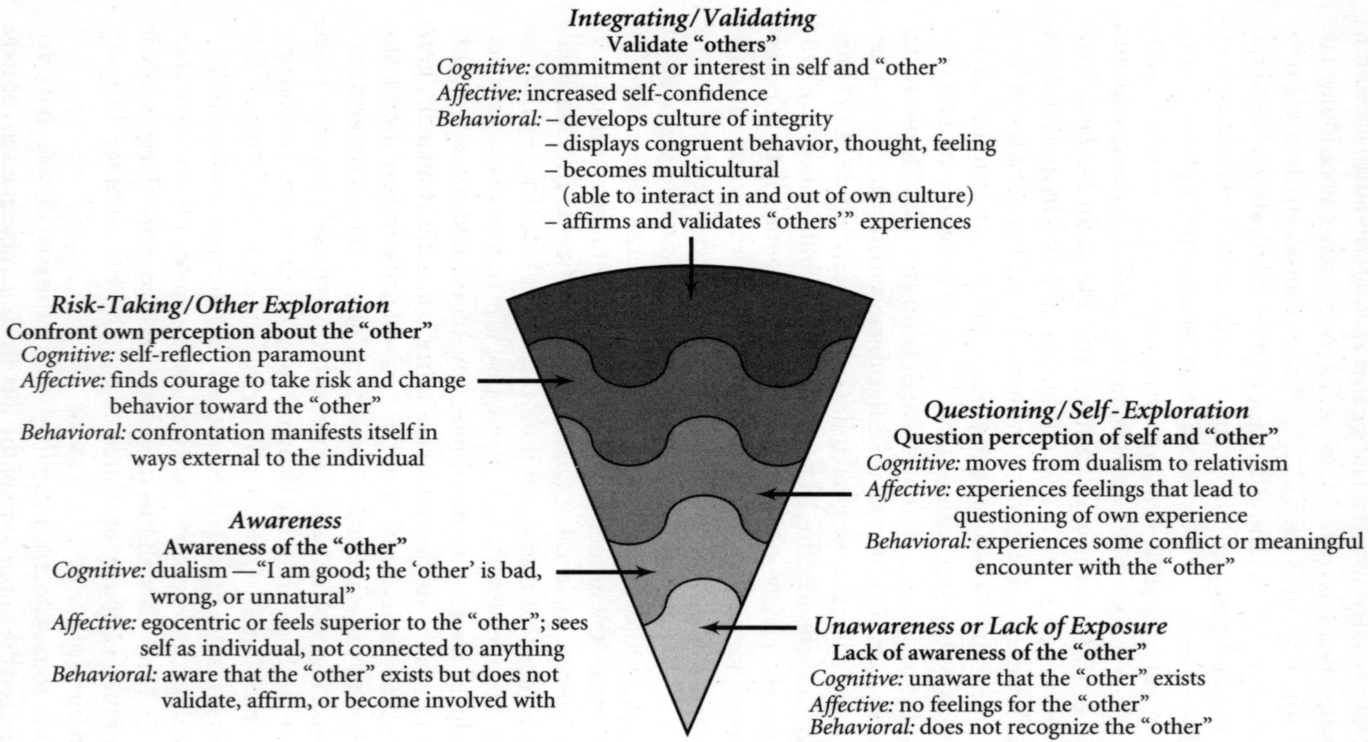

Figure 6.1. Frameworks in Learning to Value the "Other."

Source: Chávez, Guido-DiBrito, and Mallory, 1996.

Integrating/Validating
Validate "others"
Cognitive: commitment or interest in self and "other"
Affective: increased self-confidence
Behavioral: – develops culture of integrity
– displays congruent behavior, thought, feeling
– becomes multicultural
(able to interact in and out of own culture)
– affirms and validates "others'" experiences

Questioning/Self-Exploration
Question perception of self and "other"
Cognitive: moves from dualism to relativism
Affective: experiences feelings that lead to questioning of own experience
Behavioral: experiences some conflict or meaningful encounter with the "other"

Unawareness or Lack of Exposure
Lack of awareness of the "other"
Cognitive: unaware that the "other" exists
Affective: no feelings for the "other"
Behavioral: does not recognize the "other"

Risk-Taking/Other Exploration
Confront own perception about the "other"
Cognitive: self-reflection paramount
Affective: finds courage to take risk and change behavior toward the "other"
Behavioral: confrontation manifests itself in ways external to the individual

Awareness
Awareness of the "other"
Cognitive: dualism —"I am good; the 'other' is bad, wrong, or unnatural"
Affective: egocentric or feels superior to the "other"; sees self as individual, not connected to anything
Behavioral: aware that the "other" exists but does not validate, affirm, or become involved with

ethnicity, gender, and sexual orientation to understanding learning in adulthood (Hawkesworth, 1997; Hayes and Colin, 1994a; Maher and Tetreault, 1994; Resides, 1996; Ross-Gordon, Martin, and Briscoe, 1990a, 1990b; Tennant and Pogson, 1995; Tisdell, 1995). Not everyone wants to admit that the issues of race, ethnicity, gender, and sexual orientation have or should have any educational relevance, either in relationship to the content being taught or the instructional techniques being used. Some learners become uncomfortable, angry, or just plain turned off when these issues are brought forward. Some have never considered the idea that some of these groups (for example, women and Native Americans) may have different views on how adults learn or how organizations should be managed and led. They instead want context-free ideas of adult learning and leadership, free from social or political orientations, including the socially constructed notions of race, ethnicity, gender, or sexual orientation.

Tisdell (1995), among others (Ellsworth, 1989; Hayes and Colin, 1994a; Maher and Tetreault, 1994), has pointed out the important role that power plays when introducing socially constructed notions of race, ethnicity, gender, and sexual orientation into formal and even nonformal programs of adult learning. Tisdell observes that "what counts as knowledge in a particular learning context—and decisions about what gets included in the curriculum for a given learning activity—are decisions made with attention to the politics of this particular educational context and to what is seen as 'real' knowledge relevant to this educational context" (p. 11). Teaching strategies that allow participants to connect the material to their own life experiences, allow for reflective time, confront differences, and bring together theory and practice seem to provide useful starting points for doing this (Caffarella, 1992; Mezirow and Associates, 1990; Wlodkowski and Ginsberg, 1995). Storytelling, critical incident techniques, role plays, small group work, case studies, and problem-posing strategies seem especially appropriate for promoting different voices, self-disclosure, and alternative ways of looking at these issues.

Other authors have depicted what effective adult education programs might look like that serve people from diverse backgrounds. Ross-Gordon, Martin, and Briscoe (1990a), for example, outline nine characteristics that they found were associated with effective programs that serve minority populations. Among these nine are preserving the cultural distinctness of groups, accommodating preferred learning strategies or learning environments, reaching out to the most disenfranchised, and sponsoring activities that increase the level of intercultural sensitivity of staff (pp. 103–104). These authors also suggest that we "improve our own knowledge and understanding of other cultural groups, particularly those within our respective service areas" (p. 106), and ensure that they have access to all programs of adult education, even if this means changing the way we practice. Tisdell (1995) also speaks eloquently to this issue in her description of what she terms "inclusive learning environments for all adults": environments that take into account the atmosphere of both "the specific learning context of the classroom or learning activity and the organizational context in which one is working" (p. 83).

Cross-Cultural Studies of Development

Although a vast number of cross-cultural studies have been completed in the anthropological tradition, this material has rarely been incorporated into the adult development literature. The lack of cross-cultural material is especially evident when development is viewed from the sociocultural versus psychological paradigm. There are, however, some notable exceptions. Erikson (1978), for example, has provided an excellent sampling of adulthood in other cultures. His essays, primarily linked to the religious orientation of each cultural grouping, give a diverse picture of how the life cycle is depicted according to religious traditions. More recent examples include an edited book by Valsiner (1995), which contains two essays about adult life in India, and the work of Pratt (1991), which focuses on the different conceptions of self within China and the United States. These three studies provide helpful illustrations of how culture is often one of the defining factors in the way that adults develop and change.

In the Valsiner volume, Ullrich (1995) describes a co-constructivist perspective of life course changes among Havik Brahmins in a South India village. She vividly portrays how men and women of this culture, over a sixteen-year period, negotiated and accommodated to new situations, which resulted in changes in many of the ways they carried out their roles in life. She describes J.A., for example, who opened the way for women in her village to pursue careers by being the first woman to take a salaried teaching position at a nursery school prior to her marriage: "At that time a salary provided a person with economic resources to spend as desired. Women had traditionally been dependent on men for every cent, just as sons and younger brothers were dependent on fathers and older brothers. . . . After J.A.'s marriage, nursery school teaching became an option for women awaiting marriage [and] was reserved for unmarried women. . . . Now there are [even] Havik Brahmin women employed elsewhere as nursery school teachers who have decided against marriage" (pp. 183–184). J.A.'s story was an exemplar for unmarried women to have more choices in their developmental journeys.

Verma (1995) also analyzed the changes that have taken place in the social roles of women over the past three generations in India. Using a cultural-historic paradigm, she describes how the roles of rural, middle-class, and higher-upper-class affluent women have been altered over time. More specifically Verma depicts changes in the relationship between the mother-in-law and the daughter-in-law, the *purdah* (or veiling), and women as home managers. For example, the

> change in the *purdah* system across generations in India has been quite notable. . . . *Purdah* did not mean just veiling, but some strict rules that forbade women to go outside their homes for visiting relatives and friends, for shopping or entertainment, or even for getting an education. . . . *Purdah* meant almost total seclusion of women from the outside world, and it was a manmade rule for safeguarding women's chastity and modesty from outsiders and the "evil eyes." [p. 148]

The changes in the *purdah* system have allowed women to obtain a higher educational level and employment outside the home, which have expanded their developmental potential and options. Verma concludes "that the transformation in women's social role in India has been gradual but surely taking place at a number of manifest levels. However, the pace of the transformation has been relatively 'fast' or 'slow' for different categories of women, depending on their socioeconomic status, education, and place of habitation" (p. 161).

And finally, Pratt (1991) and Pratt, Kelly, and Wong (1998) have challenged us to look at the conceptions of self from two different cultural perspectives, that of China and the United States. He stresses that definitions of the self in China are tied to family continuity, socially prescribed roles, the acceptance of hierarchical relationships as supreme, compliance with authority, a value on stability versus change, and the current political ideology. "The resulting self," he writes, "finds an identity that is externally ascribed, subordinated to the collective, seeks fulfillment through the performance of duty, and would have little meaningful existence apart from ordained roles and patterns of affiliations. If this is true, the Chinese self is, largely, an externally ascribed, highly malleable, and socially constructed entity" (Pratt, 1991, p. 302). In contrast, Pratt views the self as defined by cultural tradition in the United States as driven "primarily by individual autonomy and the right to choose as central values to be protected and promoted" (Pratt, 1991, p. 303). Although this way of viewing the self is often equated with the masculine view of self versus the more feminine connected self, these different ways of conceptualizing the self lead to important implications for the practice of adult education.

Pratt (1991) and Pratt, Kelly, and Wong (1998) go on to provide a link between how these different views of the idealized self, and thus the end point of development, need to be considered when designing learning situations for adults. More specifically, Pratt questions whether we can impose as part of our practice of adult education our Westernized assumptions about adult development on people who have a very different sense of what characterizes how mature adults should function. "For example [in China], attempting to get adult students to express their opinions and feelings, choose among learning assignments, participate in self-evaluation, or challenge the stated positions of those in authority, for example, the instructor's opinions, usually meets with some resistance. . . . What lies beneath these patterns is far more than simple reticence or courtesy. These behaviors are deeply rooted in a culture and society that is profoundly different than those that expect students to be outspoken and autonomous" (Pratt, 1991, p. 305). We have made similar observations in working with adult learners from other parts of Asia, such as Taiwan and Indonesia. Pratt concludes that "adult education within any country is not simply a neutral body of knowledge and procedures. . . . There are significant cultural and ideological differences [in how adulthood is defined] . . . which must be considered when exporting (or importing) educational practices and procedures" (Pratt, 1991, p. 307).

One other example of the importance of cross-cultural studies of adult development and learning is the recognition of the value and worth of indigenous ways of learning (see Chapter Two). In a provocative book, Cajete (1994) advocates that Indian educators develop "a contemporary, culturally based, educational process founded upon traditional Tribal values, orientations and principles, while *simultaneously* using the most appropriate concepts, technologies, and content of modern education" (p. 17). In making this statement he assumes that "Indians view life through a different cultural metaphor than mainstream America" and therefore have been "forced to adapt to an educational process not of their making" (p. 19). Greater opportunities for learning could be developed for Indians if the foundations of education are "indigenously inspired and ecologically based" (p. 21). Cajete outlines a number of elements that characterize indigenous educational processes. These elements are grounded in the beliefs that "environmental relationships, myths, visionary tradition, traditional arts, Tribal community, and Nature centered spirituality have traditionally formed the foundations in American Indian life for discovering one's true face (character, potential, identity), one's heart (soul, creative self, true passion), and one's foundation (true work, vocation), all of which lead to the expression of a complete life" (p. 23).

Other scholars who have spoken to the importance of acknowledging indigenous culture in adult learning include Brennan (1997) and Kidd and Coletta (1980).

INTEGRATIVE PERSPECTIVES ON DEVELOPMENT

The challenge to create integrative perspectives of adult development that reflect a more holistic picture of adult life has received attention in the literature over the past two decades. Observations by long-term scholars of development (Levinson, 1986, Levinson and Levinson, 1996; Moen, Elder, and Luscher, 1995; Rodin, Schooler, and Schaie, 1990; Tennant and Pogson, 1995) and those who have studied adulthood for the first time (Bryant, 1989) make us cognizant of the incompleteness of our narrow definitions of adulthood, whether from the psychological, the biological, or the sociocultural perspective. As Bryant (1989, pp. 3–4) put it so eloquently, "One need only look at the plights of those in even very recent history who were out of sync with their time, the forerunners of new criteria for normal adult development—the women who could not be patently subservient to men, the men who could not be independent of emotions, the oldsters who persist in physical and sexual vigor. . . . It seems virtually impossible that psychologists and sociologists could concurrently accommodate the change that these individuals represent. What they can do is only observe, compute and rhapsodize over statistics, and inject some of their own thought and personal dispositions." There have been attempts to respond to the call for a more integrated theory of adult development, through combining two or more of the perspectives reviewed in this chapter (Baltes, 1982; Bronfenbrenner, 1995; Kahana and Kahana, 1996; Levenson and Crumpler, 1996; Magnusson, 1995; Peck, 1986; Perun and Bielby, 1980; Peters, 1989). Four models of adult development—those proposed by Baltes (1982), Magnusson (1995), Perun and Bielby (1980), and Peters (1989)—are illustrative of this new wave of theory building.

Baltes (1982, p. 18) introduced one of the earlier comprehensive models that emphasized a "multicausal and interactive view" of adult development. Drawing on the work of Havighurst, Neugarten, and others, he hypothesized that biological and environmental forces constitute the basic determinants of development. These are then influenced by three major sets of factors: normative age-graded influences (forces normally correlated with age), normative history-graded influences (events that are widely experienced by one age group of people), and nonnormative influences (factors significant to one particular person). The interaction of these influences results in developmental changes over the life span. Baltes hypothesizes that the relative significance of the three developmental influences may vary at different points in the life span—"for example, age-graded influences may be especially important . . . in old age, whereas history-graded nonnormative influences may predominate in early and middle adulthood" (Schaie and Willis, 1986, p. 22).

These three developmental influences (age graded, history graded, and nonnormative) have been subsumed in a later work by Baltes (1987) under the concept of contextualism as one of six theoretical propositions he proposed to guide the thinking and research in the life span perspective of development. In addition to the concept of contextualism, his other propositions are that there is no single direction for change in adulthood (multidirectionality), development consists of the joint occurrences of both growth and decline (development as gain or loss), development can take many forms (plasticity), development varies substantially in accordance with historical and cultural conditions (historical embeddedness), and further understanding of development will come from collaborative work among several disciplines, including psychology, anthropology, biology, and sociology (multidisciplinary approach). Within this life span perspective, Baltes and others (Baltes, 1982, 1987; Baltes and Reese, 1984) assume "there is *lawfulness* to the changes we see in adult life. . . . Our task . . . is to uncover and understand the nature of that lawfulness. They do *not* assume that the specific pathways followed by adults will necessarily all be the same; they do not assume that all pathways lead toward either decline or toward higher efficacy. They do assume that the underlying lawfulness will create many surface patterns" (Bee, 1996, p. 74). Baltes has also stressed the need for new "development-specific" research methodologies to address the more interactive and complex models of adult development.

One response to Baltes's concern related to methodology is a recent integrative model proposed by Magnusson (1995). Grounded in four basic assumptions, Magnusson argues that his model "can serve as a general theoretical framework for planning, implementation, and interpretation of empirical research on specific aspects of individual development" (p. 19). His four assumptions are as follows (pp. 25–29):

1. The individual functions and develops as a total integrated organism. Development does not take place in single aspects, taken out of context.

2. The individual functions and develops in a continuously ongoing, reciprocal process of interaction with his or her environment.

3. At each specific moment, individual functioning is determined in a process of continuous, reciprocal interaction between mental factors, biological factors, and behavior—on the individual side—and situational factors.

4. The individual develops in a process of continuous reciprocal interaction among psychological, biological, and environmental factors.

What is key to this model is that "individuals do not develop in terms of single variables but as total integrated systems. In this perspective, all changes during the life span of a person are characterized by lawful continuity" (p. 39). Magnusson emphasizes that his model "does not imply that the whole system of an individual must be studied at the same time. The essential function of the model is that it enables us to formulate problems at different levels of the functioning of the total organism, to implement empirical studies, and to interpret the results in a common, theoretical framework" (p. 50).

The third model we discuss is not widely known, but we have found it useful in framing development from the integrative perspective.

Perun and Bielby (1980) view adulthood as "consisting of a large number of *temporal progressions*—sequences of experiences or internal changes each of which follow some timetable" (Bee, 1996, p. 75). Pictured as a set of disks, similar to machine gears rotating on a central rod, each disk represents a part of the developmental picture: physical changes, changes in nuclear family roles (like marrying and having children), changes in other family roles (such as death of a parent), changes in work roles, and changes in emotional and personal tasks of adulthood (Perun and Bielby, 1980). Each of these gears or disks moves at different rates for different people, "thus creating a unique pattern for each adult" (Bee, 1996, p. 76). For example, one person may delay having children until her early forties so she can establish herself in a career, while another may start a family in her teens and then start a career once her children are grown. The first person would have speeded up her career or work progression, while slowing down her family life cycle, while the second person would be doing just the opposite. In addition, the entire developmental process is embedded in historical time, which also affects the developmental progression in each of the major areas.

Developmental changes come from two sources within this model. The first is the basic changes that happen within each of the temporal progressions, some of them inevitable and others chosen. Second, asynchrony, which "occurs when one or more dimensions is off-time in relation to others" (Perun and Bielby, 1980, p. 105), triggers other changes. For example, when a person's spouse or partner dies in early adulthood, the nuclear family roles and possibly the work roles often change dramatically, especially if there are minor children involved. Bee (1996, p. 77) has outlined a number of "intriguing and potentially useful implications or expansions of this model." Among these are that the rate of movement along any of the temporal dimensions may be influenced by gender, race, class, ethnicity, and sexual orientation.

The final illustrative model, that of Peters (1989), is more practical in nature. Peters, as part of a framework for extension education programming through the adult life span and similar to the other models discussed, brings together the biological, psychological, and sociological aspects of adult development. The model's first key element is the changing nature of the life structure, consisting of three task-related subsystems—work, other, and self. Work consists of the job-related activities in which the person engages; other consists of the many relationships adults have, such as family, friends, and social acquaintances; and self is the individualized nature of each person. It is the interrelationship of these subsystems that depicts "who the person is" at a particular time in his or her life (p. 86). Internal forces (psychological, biological) and external forces (social expectations, economic conditions) make up the second major element in the model. These forces influence the choices people make about their work, their relationships with others, and how they see themselves as individuals. Young adults, for example, often concern themselves with building and maintaining a job or career; therefore, the work subsystem predominates, with lesser attention paid to the other aspects of life. A person's life structure does not remain stable but changes as a result of both the internal and external forces and the individual's choices. It is the reconfiguration of this life structure that is assumed to be the "essence of development" (p. 86). In addition to mapping out the model itself, Peters has outlined specific implications for educational programming in terms of both the needs assessment process and the educational strategies for learning.

Although application of these integrated models to learning in adulthood has been limited, the message conveyed by the theorists is clear: to understand development in adulthood fully, one must move beyond explanations fostered only by one or two perspectives. Educators of adults must be mindful of the impact of single-perspective theories "on shaping and maintaining conventionally held views about what it means to be a mature and healthy adult" (Tennant, 1988, p. 65). The psychological perspective, which has been used as the major lens through which educators of adults have viewed development, can be widened to include the other lens of biological, sociocultural, and integrated perspectives. Tennant and Pogson (1995) observe that "the raw material in the process of development are the organism, with its constitutionally endowed equipment; and the social environment, with its historical and cultural formations. Development thus proceeds through a constant interaction between the person and the environment. [Further], because development is contested, and because different versions of development serve the interests of different groups, it is as much a political as it is a psychological construct" (p. 199). Therefore, it is important to foster a multiperspective focus in our study and practice of how adult development theory is linked to learning in adulthood.

SUMMARY

We have reviewed in this chapter adult development from two perspectives: the influence of sociocultural factors on development and the integrative paradigm of development. From the sociocultural perspective, change in adulthood is determined more by sociocultural factors, such as social roles, race, and gender, than by individual maturation. Three strands of work from the sociocultural perspective were described, and implications for this work for adult learning were addressed. Discussed first was the importance of social roles, such as parent, worker, or friend. Social roles are determined primarily by societal expectations and change over time. Adult educators have often designed programs tied to social roles, such as parenting classes or workshops on retirement. Society still determines at what age we ought to be engaged in which life events.

Addressed next was the socially constructed nature of the concepts of race, gender, ethnicity, and sexual orientation and how defining these concepts as social constructions versus individual traits has affected the way we think about adult development. Representative developmental theories of Cross, Helms, Bem, and D'Augelli were reviewed, with the caveat that understanding development through their lens is difficult because scholars have given different meanings to each of these concepts. In addition, most adults rarely represent just one of these categories. For this reason, other scholars, like Wilson and Chávez, Guido-DiBrito, and Mallory, have posited developmental ideas and models that address multiple social categories. Educators of adults have more recently been interested in how race, gender, ethnicity, and sexual orientation might be linked to learning. Mention was also made of cross-cultural studies of adult development, although these types of studies are scarce. Pratt, through his work in China, and Cajete, who studied indigenous Indian education, have contributed a great deal to our understanding of how cross-cultural studies can add to our knowledge of learning in adulthood.

The chapter concluded with a description of integrated perspectives on development with salient examples of theorists who have included the biological, psychological, and sociological perspectives in their models of adult development (for example, Baltes and Magnusson). To understand fully how adult development is linked to adult learning, we suggested that educators of adults move to multiple explanations of what adulthood is all about, rather than rely on just one or two paradigms. We especially need to acknowledge perspectives beyond the psychological lens that has driven our research and practice on learning in adulthood for the past three decades. The more we know about adult learners, the changes they go through, and how these changes motivate and interact with learning, the better we can structure learning experiences that both respond to and stimulate development.

CHAPTER SEVEN

Cognitive Development in Adulthood

That other people can think so differently from us about the same things comes as no surprise. We all know people who think in absolutes; it is either right or it is wrong, good or bad. Witness some of the talk show hosts who make it clear to their listeners that their opinions are the only way to think. They voice their sentiments in many arenas, from how to bring up the kids to who not to vote for in the upcoming elections. For others, everything is relative to everything else. It seems as if these people not only change their minds a lot, but it takes them forever to get closure. And then we have all found ourselves in situations where we really do not know what to think; there is no one right answer, however long we puzzle over the question or problem. Should we quit a job because those in power act in ways we find offensive when our family depends on our salary to survive? Should we speak up in public forums about issues of race, gender, and class, if in speaking we cause enormous pain to ourselves and those closest to us? Should we be allowed to help someone we love die more peacefully, even if it means using illegal methods? Examining the myriad ways that adults think has intrigued scholars throughout the ages, from philosophers to poets and, more recently, developmental psychologists and educators. More specifically, researchers have raised questions about whether adults can change their thinking patterns, and if so what might these changing patterns of thinking look like over the adult life span.

The study of the pathways of adult cognitive development, that is, how thinking patterns change over time, is often linked to a combination of factors, primarily the interaction of maturational and environmental variables. As in other research traditions on learning, the major studies on cognitive development have been predominantly carried out with children and adolescents. When this research is extended to adulthood, the underlying assumption has often been that adults move toward a final stage of cognitive development, however that is defined, or if that stage has been attained, work at maintaining that stage. Still other theorists have posited models of cognitive development that may be unique to adulthood.

Explored first in this chapter is the foundational work of Piaget and how scholars have used and extended this work. We then discuss alternative conceptualizations of cognitive development that are linear or categorical in nature (for example, Belenky, Clinchy, Goldberger, and Tarule, 1986; Perry, 1981). This discussion is followed by an exploration of dialectic thinking and models that are representative of this form of thinking. The contextual perspective on cognitive development and key theorists who represent this perspective are presented next. We conclude the chapter with an overview on the concept of wisdom, which is often posited as the pinnacle of cognitive development.

FOUNDATIONAL WORK

When we speak of cognitive development, Jean Piaget immediately comes to mind. Although Piaget's work is entirely focused on childhood cognitive development, his theory has provided the foundation for work completed with adults. Piaget proposed four invariant stages of cognitive development that are age related. These stages represent "qualitatively different ways of making sense, understanding, and constructing a knowledge of the world" (Tennant, 1988, p. 68). In Piaget's view, children's thought processes move from innate reflex actions (sensory-motor stage), to being able to represent concrete objects in symbols and words (preoperational stage), to an understanding of concepts and relationships of ideas (concrete operational stage), to an ability to reason hypothetically, logically, and systematically (formal operational stage). Piaget contended that normal children have the capacity to reach this final stage of formal operations between the ages of twelve and fifteen, which he later revised upward to ages fifteen to twenty (Piaget, 1972). It is this final stage, characterized by the ability to think abstractly, that characterized the apex of mature adult thought for Piaget.

Tennant (1988, p. 77) has noted a number of ways in which Piaget's work laid the foundation for our understanding of cognitive development in adulthood. Piaget's most salient contributions in this respect are as follows:

- The emphasis on qualitative rather than quantitative developmental changes in cognition (and his related "structuralist" approach to cognitive development)

- The importance attached to the active role of the person in constructing his or her knowledge (with the implication that learning through activity is more meaningful [than passive learning])

- A conception of mature adult thought (that is, formal operations)

In extending Piaget's theory to the study of adult learners, research has mainly focused on studies of concrete tasks (the concrete operational stage), with only a few studies of formal operational thought (Blackburn and Papalia, 1992). Another line of research has explored why many adults never reach (or perhaps never seem to use) the formal operations stage. For example, it is estimated that "in Western culture, virtually all adults think easily at the concrete operational level, and perhaps half of adults think at the formal operations level at least some of the time" (Bee, 1996, p. 168). Summaries of the application of Piaget's theory to adulthood have been completed by a number of authors (Papalia and Bielby, 1974; Long, McCrary, and Ackerman, 1979; Denney, 1982; Blackburn and Papalia, 1992). The essence of these summaries is threefold. First, within the Piagetian framework, there are diverse explanations for how adult cognition develops and possibly regresses over the life span. Second, there appears to be sufficient evidence to question the traditional view that cognitive development ends with the formal operations stage. Rather, a number of scholars have proposed stages beyond or different from formal operations. And third, "although formal operations generates solutions using logical analysis . . . , Piaget's model provides few useful insights into how adults solve 'real life' personal problems" (Blackburn and Papalia, 1992, p. 157).

In line with the second observation, that cognitive development does not end with the formal operations stage, a number of scholars have proposed new structures or patterns of thinking that are seen as developmentally beyond Piaget's stage of formal operations (for example, Arlin, 1975, 1984; Benack and Basseches, 1989; Kegan, 1994; Labouvie-Vief, 1992; Richards and Commons, 1990; Sinnott, 1984, 1994). The emphasis in this work is that changes in cognition extend beyond or differ from the level of formal operations he proposed. We discuss Arlin's work as representative of theorists who have hypothesized stages beyond Piaget's formal operations.

Arlin (1975, 1984), drawing on the work of Gruber (1973) on the development of creative thought in adults, has sought to identify a fifth stage of development, beyond that of Piaget's formal operations. She contends that formal thought actually consists of two distinct stages, not one, as Piaget proposed. In her framework, Piaget's formal operations stage is renamed the problem-solving stage; the focus of this stage is on "the process of seeking a solution of a specific presented task" (Arlin, 1975, p. 603). Arlin then hypothesizes a new fifth stage, the problem-finding stage, characterized by "creative thought vis-à-vis 'discovered' problems" (p. 603) and the ability to generate and respond to important new questions and problems. In postulating these newly organized stages of development, she fully accepts the commonly recognized criteria for a stage model of development with the notions of sequential and hierarchical ordering of development. Therefore, "the relationship between formal operational thinking in the Piagetian sense (problem-solving stage) and the new stage of problem finding should also be characterized as formal operational thinkers in the Piagetian sense" (p. 603).

Arlin (1975) tested her proposed framework by studying the problem-solving and problem-finding behavior of sixty female college seniors. Although her findings generally support the existence of a distinct fifth stage (at least for some people), the study produced more questions than answers. For example, in further conceptualizing these fourth and fifth stages, it is not clear how the patterns of thinking within each stage relate to one another. Nor is it clear what operations in the problem-solving stage might assist a person in moving into the fifth state of problem finding.

LINEAR AND CATEGORICAL MODELS OF ADULT COGNITIVE DEVELOPMENT

There are other models of cognitive development that differ from Piaget's, and yet are also linear or categorical in nature. These writers come from a variety of disciplines and interests (for example, college student development, women's development, psychology), but all have the same interest in exploring how adult thinking changes over time. Although some of these writers have used Piaget's work as part of their foundational thinking (for example, King and Kitchener, 1994; Perry, 1970), others have moved "beyond the boundaries of Piagetian formality" (Kincheloe and Steinberg, 1993, p. 297) and posed very different assumptions on which to base the research on adult cognitive development (Miller and Cook-Greuter, 1994). A discussion of a range of these linear or categorical models of cognitive development follows.

Perry's Developmental Scheme

Perry's (1970, 1981) map of cognitive development is perhaps the best known and has been used the most often in the study of young adults, most of whom have been college students. Based on a study of the thinking patterns of male college students, Perry proposed a model of cognitive development consisting of nine positions, each position representing a qualitatively different way of interpreting learning experiences. Perry purposely chose the word *position* over *stage* for several reasons, one being that he "considers 'position' to be consistent with the image of a point of view with which one looks at the world" (Evans, Forney, and Guido-DiBrito, 1998, p. 228). As in Piaget's work, each position is conceptualized as hierarchical and sequential and moves from relatively simple thinking patterns to highly complex ways of perceiving and evaluating knowledge. People move from viewing knowledge in "dualistic" terms, as either right or wrong, to an acceptance of knowledge and values as "relativistic"—that is, the context of the knowledge is as important as the knowledge itself. Perry places as much emphasis on the transitions between each position as on the positions themselves and observes: "Perhaps development is all transitions and 'stages' [are] only resting points along the way" (1981, p. 78). Some examples of Perry's proposed positions and the transitions between them are outlined below (see Perry, 1970, 1981, for a complete description):

Position 1: Authorities know, and if we work hard, read every word, and learn Right answers, all will be well.

Transition between positions 1 and 2: But what about those Others I hear about? And different opinions? And uncertainties? Some of our own Authorities disagree with each other or don't seem to know, and some give us problems instead of answers.

Position 2: True Authorities must be Right, the Others are frauds. We remain Right. Others must be different and wrong. . . .

Transition between positions 5 and 6: But if everything is relative, am I relative too? How can I know I'm making the Right Choice?

Position 6: I see I'm going to have to make my own decisions in an uncertain world with no one to tell me I'm Right. . . .

Transition between positions 8 and 9: Things are getting contradictory. I can't make logical sense out of life's dilemmas.

Position 9: This is how life will be. I must be wholehearted while tentative, fight for my values, yet respect others, believe my deepest values right yet be ready to learn. I see that I shall be retracing this whole journey over and over—but, I hope, more wisely. [Perry, 1981, p. 79]

Within this schema one can see shades of the conceptually complex notions of dialectic thinking, which is discussed later in this chapter, as well as the major theme of becoming more relativistic in one's thought patterns as one matures.

Not only is each position descriptive of individual cognitive growth, but Perry's positions have also been used to describe how people view instructors' roles and their own roles as learners. Learners at the lowest positions, for example, tend to view instructors as authority figures; their job as learners is to filter out the right answers from the material presented. Those at the higher end of the continuum view knowledge in a contextual sense and search for relationships between ideas; they see instructors more as guides.

Although most of the work using Perry's schema has been completed with young college students, a few studies have been constructed with nontraditional or older adult students (Cameron, 1983; Lavallee, Gourde, and Rodier, 1990) or with adults who are not students (for example, Wilson, 1996). The findings from these three studies on adult learners were contradictory at best. Lavallee, Gourde, and Rodier

(1990) and Wilson (1996) found that the majority of their respondents were at positions three or four (multiplicity) on Perry's scheme, while Cameron's subjects were primarily at position two (dualist). In addition, the findings of Wilson and Lavallee, Gourde, and Rodier (1990) differed on the importance of the level of education in terms of reaching higher levels of cognitive development. Wilson (1996) found that those with "master's degrees scored significantly higher in intellectual development than did those . . . either with a baccalaureate or less than a baccalaureate degree" (p. 1), while Lavallee, Gourde, and Rodier (1990) concluded that level of education had little effect on the cognitive development of their subjects.

Another use of this work has been an attempt to integrate Perry's work into other areas of study, as Kasworm (1983) has done on self-directed learning. Kasworm, using Perry's framework among others, proposes that self-directed learning "represents a qualitative evolvement of a person's sense of cognitive definition and developmental readiness for ambiguous and nondefined actions" (p. 8). From Kasworm's work and observations made by Perry (1970, 1981) and others, it appears that Perry's work could have implications across a wider spectrum of learners, but this line of thinking has yet to be extended to adults in any systematic or concerted fashion.

The Reflective Judgment Model

King and Kitchener, like Perry, have also constructed a stage model; they term theirs the development of "epistemic cognition" (Kitchener and King, 1981; King and others, 1983; King and Kitchener, 1994). Also like Perry, the majority of the research subjects in their original ten-year longitudinal study were college students, although both male and female students were included, as well as undergraduate and graduate students. Following this group of academically bright white adults (a fourth of whom were seventeen years old when the study began), King and Kitchener (1994) found that "to think reflectively does not emerge fully formed but develops in a sequential fashion, with earlier stages building on prior stages and laying the foundation for subsequent stages" (p. 152). Based on their findings, and also influenced primarily by the work of Piaget (1972) and Dewey (1933), they constructed the reflective judgment model. This model outlines a "developmental progression that occurs between childhood and adulthood in the way people understand the process of knowing and in the corresponding ways that they justify their beliefs about ill-structured problems" (King and Kitchener, 1994, p. 13).

According to this model, people move through seven stages, with the final two stages encompassing the more mature thinking patterns of what King and Kitchener term *reflective thinking*. In Stages One, Two, and Three (termed *prereflective thinking*), people assume that knowledge comes from authority figures or is gained through personal experience. Individuals in these stages do not see problems as ill structured, but rather view all problems as having complete and right answers. In Stages Four and Five, the middle stages, people define knowledge in terms of uncertainty and are more subjective in their thinking. Although they understand that ill-defined problems exist, they have trouble dealing with the ambiguity of those problems and tend to respond in very individualistic ways. In the final two stages of thinking (Stages Seven and Eight), knowledge is no longer a given. Rather, knowledge, especially knowledge used to solve life's ill-structured problems, may have to be constructed by the person, and this knowledge must be understood within the context in which it was generated. Decisions and judgments people make, although they must be grounded in relevant data, should remain open to evaluation and reevaluation. As we shall see in Chapter Ten, King and Kitchener's work is similar to authors who discuss reflective practice in terms of the importance of the context of that practice.

There appear to be many similarities between the Perry scheme and that developed by King and Kitchener. For example, both start with the assumption that people at earlier levels of thinking are more absolute in their thinking and depend primarily on outside authority for their knowledge, while later in the thinking hierarchy, the ideas of relativistic thinking becomes predominant. What is different about the King and Kitchener model is that in their final higher stages of development, they describe a further development of cognitive thinking, that of knowledge construction, while Perry focuses on expanding his ideas of using relativistic thinking in a responsible way. Although a great deal of research has been completed using the reflective judgment model (see King and Kitchener, 1994), few studies, as with the Perry schema, have been completed with adults outside the higher education setting. As with the Perry model, this model holds promise in discovering more about adult cognitive development, provided that the populations are expanded to include adults from all walks of life.

Women's Ways of Knowing

In reaction to the work of Perry (1970) and Kohlberg (1973), among others, in which only male samples were used, researchers have become more interested in hearing the voices of women on developmental issues. The most prominent and often quoted study on cognitive development using a sample of women is the work of Belenky, Clinchy, Goldberger, and Tarule, *Women's Ways of Knowing* (1986). These researchers interviewed women from diverse social and ethnic backgrounds from two major settings: different types of academic institutions and parenting classes. From their in-depth interviews of 135 women, "based on the theoretical and empirical work of Perry, Kohlberg, and Gilligan" (p. 14), Belenky, Clinchy, Goldberger, and Tarule (1986, p. 15) grouped women's perspectives on knowing into five major categories:

1. Silence—a position in which women experience themselves as mindless and voiceless and subject to the whims of external authority. [They are passive, feel incompetent, and are defined by others.]

2. Received knowledge—a perspective from which women conceive of themselves as capable of receiving, even reproducing, knowledge from the all-knowing external authorities but not capable of creating knowledge on their own. [They listen to the voices of others; their world is literal and concrete, good or bad.]

3. Subjective knowledge—a perspective from which truth and knowledge are conceived of as personal, private, and subjectively known or intuited. [The locus of truth shifts to the self; intuition is valued over logic and abstraction; here women begin to gain a voice. Half the women in the study were in this category.]

4. Procedural knowledge—a position in which women are invested in learning and applying objective procedures for obtaining and communicating knowledge. [This position takes two forms: *separate knowing*—the self is separate from the object of discourse, making it possible to doubt and reason; and *connected knowing*—there is intimacy and equality between the self and the object of discourse, based on empathetic understanding.]

5. Constructed knowledge—a position in which women view all knowledge as contextual, experience themselves as creators of knowledge, and value both subjective and objective strategies for knowing. [This stage is characterized by the development of an authentic voice.]

These categories, which are not necessarily fixed or universal, move from the simple to the complex—from having no voice, to being able to value and create different ways of knowing, which are contextual in nature. Although these authors do not assert that the categories constitute specific stages of cognitive development, they appear to present them as such (Clark, 1990), and some people continue to interpret them in this way (Goldberger, 1996b).

Clark (1990, pp. 22–23) also noted significant parallels between the findings of Belenky, Clinchy, Goldberger, and Tarule and those of Perry: "Received knowledge parallels the dualistic position; subjective knowledge correlates with multiplicity; and procedural and constructed knowledge has elements of relativism." In addition, the final category of constructed knowing seems comparable with the more recent findings of King and Kitchener (1994) and Baxter Magolda (1992) (Baxter Magolda's work is reviewed later in this section.) For example, King and Kitchener (1994) speak to the importance of contextual knowing and constructing one's own knowledge as characteristic of their final two stages, and Baxter Magolda (1992) stresses the integration of relational (subjective) and impersonal (objective) knowing as key to what she terms *contextual knowing.* These apparent similarities add confirmation to the work of Belenky and her colleagues and are in line with their original interpretations about their research. Although all of the subjects in their 1986 study were women, Belenky, Clinchy, Goldberger, and Tarule have never claimed that these ways of knowing are distinctively female, even though their work has often been interpreted as such. Rather, they believe that these categories "might be expanded or modified with the inclusion of a more culturally and socioeconomically diverse sample of women and men" (Goldberger, 1996b, p. 7). However, their work, which has provided a significant contribution to understanding adult cognitive development, did uncover salient themes that were either missing or deemphasized in earlier work on cognitive development, themes "related to the experience of silencing and disempowerment, lack of voice, the importance of personal experience in knowing, connected strategies in knowing, and resistance to disempassioned knowing" (Goldberger, 1996b, p. 7).

The work of Belenky, Clinchy, Goldberger, and Tarule has provided both lively debate about their findings and new ways of thinking about how to design educational programs for both women and men (for example, Caffarella, 1996; Taylor and Marienau, 1995; Goldberger, Tarule, Clinchy, and Belenky, 1996; Belenky, Bond, and Weinstock, 1997). Goldberger, Tarule, Clinchy, and Belenky (1996) have compiled the most comprehensive set of materials on how their women's ways of knowing scheme "was taken up, used, evaluated and criticized, extended and elaborated, to accommodate new data and new thinking" (Goldberger, 1996b, p. 2). Criticisms of their theory range from their theory being a women-only model, and more specifically a white women's scheme, to the mistaken argument by some that they are endorsing the superiority of antirational ways of thinking. In their most recent work, however, they have "listened to and learned from women of color and other culture theorists . . . , [and] have become much more alert to the situational and cultural determinants of knowing and to the relationship of power and knowledge" (Goldberger, 1996a, p. 8). The work of Goldberger, Tarule, Clinchy, and Belenky (1996) related to the cultural or contextual significance in cognitive development is reviewed in more depth later in this chapter.

Epistemological Reflection Model

Baxter Magolda (1992) originally developed the epistemological reflection model as a model of knowing and reasoning in college. She has recently extended her work to young adults beyond their college experience. Like others who have studied cognitive development, Baxter Magolda's work is grounded in the assumption that ways of knowing are socially constructed and context bound.

Baxter Magolda (1992, p. 29) followed a group of seventy predominantly white male and female college students over five years, interviewing them yearly, and discovered "four qualitatively different ways of knowing, each characterized by a core set of epistemic assumptions": absolute knowing, transitional knowing, independent knowing, and contextual knowing. Student voices told stories of moving from being certain about what they knew, to uncertainty, and finally to being able to integrate information from diverse points of views in order to apply that knowledge within a particular context. Baxter Magolda noted that only a small percentage of students used contextual knowing while in college. Like Perry's (1981) and King and Kitchener's (1994) work, Baxter Magolda provides excellent descriptions of what this work means for practice in higher education.

Unlike the work on the Perry (1981) and King and Kitchener (1994) schemes, Baxter Magolda found patterns of thinking within each of the ways of knowing that were gender related, that is, "related to, but not dictated by, gender"(p. 22). For example, in the independent knowing category, two patterns emerged: interindividual and individual. Those exhibiting the interindividual pattern, which women used more than men did, were characterized by their "dual focus on thinking for themselves and engaging the views of others" (Baxter Magolda, 1992, p. 56). The individual-pattern students, although also valuing interchange of ideas, still had their primary focus on their own independent thinking and also expected peers to think in the same way. More men than women exhibited this individual pattern. Magolda notes that none of the patterns was employed exclusively by men or women and that these differing patterns "led to equally complex ways of viewing the world" (p. 13). Baxter Magolda's gender-related patterns of how women know bear some similarity to those discovered by Belenky, Clinchy, Goldberger, and Tarule (1986) in their study of just women.

Baxter Magolda (1995) extended her study to follow these students for another two years, after they graduated from college. What she found was that when her subjects exhibited her fourth category of knowing (contextual knowing), their ways of knowing were no longer gender related. Rather, as they took on different adult roles, their patterns of thinking within this contextual framework became more integrated. More specifically, the patterns of relational and impersonal modes of knowing, which characterize contextual knowing, were used in an integrative fashion: "Participants recognized that connecting to their emotions was essential in deciding what to believe, yet they were aware that this had to be balanced with rational reflection. Contextual knowers emphasized that dialogue, or access to other's perspectives and experiences, was required for developing beliefs" (Baxter Magolda, 1995, p. 66). Her more recent descriptions of contextual knowing echo somewhat the descriptions of "constructed knowledge" described by Belenky, Clinchy, Goldberger, and Tarule (1986).

The Transcendence View

A very different view of cognitive development has emerged from scholars writing from the perspective of transpersonal psychology. Wilber (1982, 1983, 1990) and Thomas (1994) are among those researchers who have extended models of cognitive development beyond the rational level by identifying deeper structures in the mind that undergird higher or transpersonal levels of consciousness. An important component of these theories is Consciousness of human beings with a capital C, which denotes "the unlimited reservoir from which we draw personal, ego-centered awareness. Our individual Consciousness is an infinitesimal spark within the eternal flame of Universal Consciousness" (Nuernberger, 1994, p. 96). When we allow ourselves to move beyond our own individual limits of time and space, our individual Consciousness, a whole new world of expanded Consciousness with limitless boundaries, almost mystical in nature, is open to us. "The great spiritual leaders and mystics of all cultures and time . . . all speak of the power of direct knowledge, of reality beyond the capacity of the logic and rationality of the mind" (Nuernberger, 1994, p. 96).

Wilber's (1982, 1983, 1990) model of transpersonal cognitive development allows these spiritual and mystical dimensions to emerge, and it recognizes "cross-cultural differences in values and assumptions that are glossed over by much of our Western psychological theory" (Thomas, 1994, p. 72). To move to these transpersonal levels of development, one must move beyond "the conventional levels of culture and hence beyond normal societal support and structures" (Thomas, 1994, p. 74). More specifically, Wilber has posited eight levels of movement toward the highest level of transpersonal cognitive development. The last two levels illustrate well the transpersonal nature of Wilber's theory. The *subtle* level, level seven, is based on "a truly trans-rational structure . . . not emotionalism or merely felt meaning . . . or hunch" (Wilber, 1982, p. 30). Rather, phrases such as illumination of the spirit, intuition as an elemental sense, and mystical awareness characterize the thinking of this developmental level. The eighth level, the *causal* state, indisputably moves individuals beyond themselves. As described by Wilber (1983, p. 97): "This is total and utter transcendence and release into Formless Consciousness, Boundless Radiance. There is here no self, no God, no final-God, no subjects, no thingness, apart or other than consciousness as such." This final developmental state closely resembles Nuernberger's (1994) notion of the Universal Consciousness.

In reviewing these and other theoretical models of adult cognitive development, what becomes apparent is there are two themes that many of these theories address: that higher stages of cognitive development in some models suggest the presence of dialectical thinking in adulthood, that is, the acceptance of the inherent contradictions and alternative truths; and that context, including the acceptance of cultural differences, is critical in determining what thinking patterns in adulthood really mean. The discussions of dialectical thinking have a long history in adult cognitive development, beginning with the work of Riegel (1973) and others. In contrast, viewing the contextual dimensions of development is more recent. Each of these themes and representative work illustrating the themes is discussed in the next two sections.

DIALECTICAL THINKING

Our modern world is rife with contradictions and paradoxes. We have the capability to clone cells, with the possibility for great advances in medicine and many other areas, yet we fear what might be constructed with this technology. We eradicate one dreaded disease (such as smallpox), and other vicious diseases take its place. We can replace most body parts at will, but ethically cannot decide who should get the limited supply of these parts. We downsize workforces to respond to short-term demands, only to find out that the cost of doing business for some groups actually rises in the long run. And the list keeps expanding to the point where Kegan (1994), among others, views us literally "in over our heads" in responding to a world of continuous change and disparities.

A number of writers point to the fact that conflict and contradictions in adult life are not new phenomena (Phelan and Garrison, 1994); rather, they may just be more apparent now in that we can often see and hear them up close through television and other technological formats. In addition, what used to be intensely personal, such as the beginning and the end of life, has also become public knowledge. How many babies should a women be allowed to carry? Should we continue to support the children of welfare mothers? Who has the right to end someone's life? These are just a few of the questions debated in the public forum. In responding to life's inherent contradictions and complexities, a number of authors have posited that dialectical ways of thinking must become part of the ways adults think. In essence, thinking in a dialectic sense allows for the acceptance of alternative truths or ways of thinking about similar phenomena that abound in everyday adult life. One might abhor killing, for example, and yet silently applaud the gentle person who switches off the life-support system of her spouse who is suffering beyond relief from a terminal illness.

One of the earliest and most thoughtful theorists to describe dialectic thinking was Riegel (1973, 1975, 1976). According to Riegel (1973, p. 350), "dialectic conceptualization characterizes the origin of thought in the individual and in society [and] represents a necessary synthesis in the development of thought toward maturity." In describing the dialectic thought process, Riegel (1973, 1975) proposed a corresponding mode of dialectic operations to stand beside Piaget's formal system (see Figure 7.1). The key to this alternative system is the inclusion of the dialectic, or the acceptance of inherent contradictions and ambiguities in thought processes, at all developmental levels and not just as part of the more mature thought of adulthood. "The skills and competence in one area of concern, for instance in sciences, might be of the type of formal dialectic operations, while in everyday business transactions, might be of the type of concrete dialectic operations," and so on (Riegel, 1973, p. 365). Riegel's basic assumptions are that people do not have to pass through any of the Piagetian levels to reach the higher levels of thinking within the dialectic framework and that people can operate simultaneously on all levels. In proposing this system, Riegel (1973, p. 366) argued that people are not only ready to live with life's inherent contradictions and ambiguities but will accept "these contradictions as a basic property of thought and creativity."

A number of other writers have incorporated the notion of dialectic thinking into their work on adult cognitive development. Kramer (1983, 1989) is representative of theorists who appear to follow the thinking of Riegel (1973) in that she postulates a series of cognitive developmental stages separate from those of Piaget. Kramer's theory is grounded in the assumption that adult thought centers on both relativistic and dialectical operations, with the acceptance of contradiction and different worldviews as hallmarks of adult thinking. She posits a sequence of seven levels of development, with the last four stages representing adolescent and adult thought processes. (See Kramer, 1989, for a complete description of these stages.)

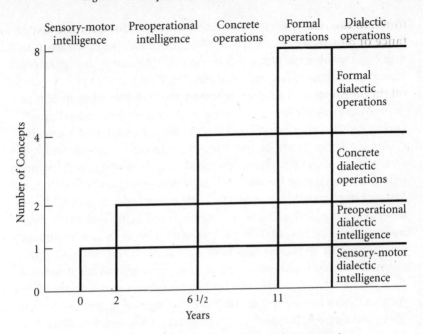

Figure 7.1.   Schematic Representation of Piaget's
Extended Theory of Cognitive Development.
Source: Riegel, 1973, p. 365. Reprinted with permission of S. Karger AG, Basel.

Like Riegel, Kramer (1989, p. 151) observes that rudimentary dialectic thinking begins in childhood, but she hypothesizes that mature dialectic thought (termed the *stage of dynamic dialecticism*) "rarely appears before middle age." This mature dialectic thought is characterized by an awareness that all thought processes are culturally and historically bound and therefore dynamic and constantly evolving. An acceptance of this premise allows people to categorize ways of thinking and yet also accept the inherent contradictions that these different ways of thinking represent. Ways of thinking then become neither inherently good nor bad but rather are seen as unique for different groups of people at specified points in time. Although Kramer's model of cognitive development is not built on Piaget's stages, she does see each adult stage of the model as "characterized by some degree of abstract thought" (1989, p. 155). Thus "a minimal Piagetian competence of formal operativity" (p. 157) is necessary for fully developed adult thinking. Continuing work is being done on this model, such as the effects of the role of gender and role conflict on the development of dialectical thinking (Kramer and Melchior, 1990) and how dialectic thinking can be incorporated into the teaching and learning process in higher education (Kramer and Bacelar, 1994).

Unlike Riegel and Kramer, however, some writers view dialectical thought as evolving from the formal stages Piaget proposed (Pascual-Leone, 1983; Benack and Basseches, 1989). Benack and Basseches (1989, p. 98), for example, in exploring dialectical thinking as a post-formal stage of thought, have developed a "dialectical schemata framework" consisting of twenty-four schemata representing different "moves in thought that dialectical thinkers tend to make." These schemata were abstracted from "writings reflecting dialectic world-outlooks" (Basseches, 1984, p. 72) and interviews with college students and professors about the nature of education. Basseches claims that "some of the dialectical schemata describe ways of introducing dialectical perspectives on existence and knowledge into processes of inquiry. Others describe ways of maintaining dialectical movement within one's own thought" (p. 73). Based on his research, Basseches has suggested that there are actually four phases to the development of mature dialectic thinking. (See Basseches, 1984, and Benack and Basseches, 1989, for a full description of these phases.)

Kegan (1994), framing his work from both a psychological and contextual approach, proposes a level-of-consciousness model that incorporates dialectical thinking as part of the highest level of consciousness. His assumption in proposing this model is that the "hidden curriculum" of modern life necessitates different ways of thinking and "a new conception of *consciousness thresholds* individuals may have to reach in order to satisfy contemporary expectations of love and work" (p. 11). Through examples of real-world demands on our private lives (parenting and partnering) and our public lives (work, dealing with differences, healing, and learning), Kegan (1994) explains how our thinking must continue to evolve through five levels of consciousness in order to navigate our complex lives. First, adults need to discern how to use their mental capacities inherent in social situations. This form of thinking moves adults from the concrete world (having a point of view) to abstractions (being able to build inferences and hypotheses), to abstract systems (conceiving relations between abstractions), and finally to dialectical thinking (testing of paradoxical and contradictory formulations). Dialectical thinking thus becomes the hallmark of mature adult thinking.

Kegan argues that this pressing demand for dialectic thinking comes from our need as adults to respond to what he terms "culture's curriculum"—that is, the mental demands the postmodern world places on us. Kegan, like Riegel and Kramer, also views contradictions and paradoxes as inevitable and at the heart of the dialectical process. He then adds a new framework to this process: trans-systems thinking. What is key in this trans-systems way of thinking is that the parties or systems in conflict move beyond trying to "win" for their position, even the most desired of outcomes—the "win-win" position. Rather what is needed is the recognition that "the other side will not go away, [and] probably *should* not. . . . The conflict is potentially a reminder of our tendency to pretend to completeness when we are in fact incomplete" (Kegan, 1994, p. 319). Therefore, we must acknowledge and value the thought processes that brought about these conflictual relationships, knowing they are often based in fundamental ideological differences. We need to work within these relationships, miserable as that might be, to advance our ways of thinking and working.

In working together, the parties or systems in these conflictual relationships must then focus on transforming who they are versus trying to solve the conflict. As Kegan goes on to observe:

> This view does not mean that the challengers are coopted into the status quo. It means that the old status quo is replaced by a new status quo. It does not mean that blacks can come into the office only if they act white. It does not mean that women's experience is included in the curriculum simply by changing pronouns and making a "Michael" example into a "Mary" example. It means that formally marginalized people will come into the office, and they will have their own distinctive way of seeing things, setting the agenda, getting the goals accomplished; and it means that these ways will be recognized, acknowledged, and respected, provided that some common ground can be found where all contending "cultures" in their wholeness and distinctness can stand. This common ground becomes, in effect, a new status quo and a new ideology, but a much more wholesome one. [p. 345]

From his longitudinal work, Kegan has found that most people do not even enter the fourth level of consciousness until their forties. Kegan sees our expanded life span as a wonderful opportunity to expand our consciousness to this fifth level. From Kegan's perspective, "Highly evolved people do not mate and create highly evolved children.

The evolution of human consciousness requires long preparation. We may gradually become ever more ready to engage the curriculum of the fifth order because we have found ways to increase the number of years we live" (p. 352). In some ways Kegan's thesis is similar to that of Kramer, in that both acknowledge the importance of culture and time in developing truly mature ways of adult thinking.

CONTEXTUAL PERSPECTIVE ON COGNITIVE DEVELOPMENT

When we read through the many theories of cognitive development, some of us might resonate better than other people with many of these theories. Those of us who are white, college educated, and middle class may even have memories of how our thinking has changed over time, which matches at least in part some of these theories. For example, when we introduce the work of Belenky, Clinchy, Goldberger, and Tarule (1986) on women's ways of knowing to graduate students, the white women students latch onto this work, while some of our male students are puzzled, especially about the notions of connected knowing. Inevitably a number of students, both male and female, wonder about the "silence category." Or when we introduce writers like bell hooks (1989, 1994) or P. Collins (1990) to a group of predominantly white middle-class students, or even black males, the material often first makes them angry, as these authors vividly display their emotions and thoughts about how people are racist, demonstrate gender bias, and ignore issues of class. They do not want to be spoken to in this way; they do not deserve this treatment. In essence, they neither want to admit these voices are legitimate, nor do they want to deal with them. As these same students wrestle with this material more and come to grips with its message, most reflect later in the course as to how powerful "being forced" to hear different ways of thinking has been. Acknowledging the contextual factors of cognitive development, that is, taking into account how social, cultural, economic, and political forces shape the development of adult thinking, completes the picture. Our theories and models need to be altered and perhaps totally revamped when these contextual aspects are seriously considered by scholars studying adult cognitive development (Goldberger, Tarule, Clinchy, and Belenky, 1996; Goldberger, 1996a; Hurtado, 1996; Kegan, 1994; Kincheloe and Steinberg, 1993; Labouvie-Vief, 1980, 1984, 1990, 1992, 1994). The work of Labouvie-Vief and Goldberger is used to illustrate the work of scholars who consider context as central to cognitive development.

Labouvie-Vief (1980, 1984) was one of the earlier scholars to acknowledge the importance of contextual factors in cognitive development. Observing that "one feature of development which has become so bothersome to life-span psychologists [is] the contextual embeddedness" (1980, p. 142) of the developmental process, Labouvie-Vief challenged the more accepted notion at that time that the perfection of formal logic was the ultimate goal of adult thinking. Rather, Labouvie-Vief contends that a different form of thinking must be integrated into one's model of adult cognitive development: "While the theme of youth is flexibility, the hallmark of adulthood is commitment and responsibility. Careers must be started, intimacy bonds formed, children raised. In short, in a world of a multitude of logical possibilities, one course of action must be adopted. This conscious commitment to one pathway and the deliberate disregard of other logical choices may mark the onset of adult maturity" (1980, p. 153). In essence, this new form of thinking is "characterized by the ability to fit abstract thinking into the concrete limitations of life" (Tennant, 1988, p. 79). Therefore, what may have been conceived of as a regression in later life to Piaget's notion of concrete thought patterns is, rather, a positive adaptation to the realities of adult life. One key factor in being able to adapt to these new ways of thinking is the ability to accept and even thrive on contradiction. This in turns leads to acceptance of the notion of inherent relativity of knowledge and the ability to be self-regulating in choosing one's worldview.

Labouvie-Vief (1990, p. 256), expanding on her earlier work, postulates that "it may be variables related [more] to one's social context than to one's age that account for particular developmental gradients" in cognition. Therefore, if one wishes to discover changes and patterns in cognitive development, it might be more fruitful to examine groups of people who share pertinent life events and experiences versus people of a certain chronological age group. For example, age has been most often cited as the marker by which cognitive declines are measured. Labouvie-Vief (1990) instead asks the question of whether a major life event, such as retirement, "could be the cause of the ubiquitous decline in cognitive functioning" (p. 263). In posing this framework, Labouvie-Vief is echoing the sentiments of those studying personal and intellectual development from a sociocultural or contextual perspective. (See Chapters Six and Eight.)

More recently, Labouvie-Vief (1994) has explored the role of the mind and gender in the life course. In a fascinating book, *Psyche and Eros*, she brings together her empirical work and her exploration into mythology. Using the classical Greek myth of Psyche and Eros, she examines both historical and current concepts of what is viewed as masculine and feminine qualities. Labouvie-Vief suggests that we need to confront the traditional polarity of masculine and feminine, and thus "restructure the traditional imagery of gender. Such a restructuring involves deidealizing the traditional notion of the masculine and grounding it in the material and concrete [versus the abstract and logical], while elevating the feminine [that of emotion and imagination] and enriching it with mind and spirit" (p. 217). Her work in this arena echoes other scholars, like Bem (1993), who are interested in reconstructing what we mean by gender.

Goldberger (1996a), from interviews with approximately sixty bicultural individuals, primarily women, living in the United States, has added different dimensions of meanings to all of the original categories of knowing that she and Belenky, Clinchy, Goldberger, and Tarule (1986) had described. Goldberger found that the position of "not knowing," that of silence, for example, is a much more complicated phenomenon than was described in *Women's Ways of Knowing*. Rather, how silence is defined can be culturally determined and is actually a positive way of knowing for some. In American Indian cultures, "silence is taught [as something to be respected] within their tribal groups. . . . Allaq [a member of the Inuit nation] remembers the 'nice silence' of many children in a room, listening as the elders told stories. . . . Hard Rider [a member of the Canadian West Coast Dtidahy band], struggling to learn from his grandfather how to be a tribal leader, had already recognized the advantages of silent and respectful listening" (Goldberger, 1996a, p. 343). Goldberger also highlights the importance of silence for others, such as African American women, as a tactical strategy for "negotiating life in white communities or workplaces" (p. 345). This distinction of types of silence has led Goldberger to differentiate between those who are truly silenced "by oppressive and demeaning life conditions who feel powerless, mindless, and truly without words . . . from individuals who resort to strategic or culturally and ritually endorsed silence, but who may have other well-developed ways of acquiring, even constructing knowledge" (p. 346). In reframing the original categories from a contextual perspective, Goldberger views them more as strategies for knowing than as "person types" to which individuals are assigned based on their response patterns. In conceptualizing these categories as knowing strategies, one can then explore how contextual factors limit or expand our ways of knowing and allow us to speak of different uses or even meanings of each of the ways of knowing.

In this review of the work of Labouvie-Vief, Goldberger, and others on the contextual perspective of cognitive development, two major points become apparent. First, the majority of the mainstream theory in adult cognitive development is "based largely on the findings from a mainly White, well educated U.S. population" (Hofer and Pintrich, 1997, p. 89). There is a paucity of studies that incorporate people of color or different social classes or that examine cross-cultural differences. It appears from studies where the contextual aspect is acknowledged that people from varying backgrounds may define and value knowledge quite differently. Goldberger (1996a), for example, shares three stories from bicultural women living in the United States: Kat, a South American–born woman from a mestize background who is a counselor; Allaq, a Native Alaskan of the Inuit people and a health worker; and Toshi, an African American professor recently granted tenure:

KAT: My grandmother [who is a shaman] would teach me the difference between thinking that you know something and knowing it. She would take me out into the woods and have me sense becoming things. Not just looking and describing what I saw. I had to be the tree, I had to be the rock, I was the bird. Some of that [kind of knowing] is helped with the sacred medicine plants. They allow one to open up many different channels and get all the information possible. Whereas [simply] thinking about something feels like it is a very narrow band, a very narrow channel.

ALLAQ: As a child, I learned a lot just listening to the elders. They talked about the way of living of the Yupik people. . . . Knowledge is part of the soul. You have to learn it spiritually in every aspect of life— spiritually, mentally, emotionally, physically, socially, as a whole person. Yugarag is passed through generations. . . . In my world everything is interrelated. Everything interrelates.

TOSHI: Black people have a different way of relating to the world. Even intellectually active black people. And that way is more experientially related than cognitively related. We think less about something but react more. I like being able to go from my experience, rather than having to think about it. As a black person, I don't have to hold it in. I can express it. [pp. 336–337]

What is evident in these stories, and those from other writers (for example, Goldberger, Tarule, Clinchy, and Belenky, 1996; Reybold, 1997), is that culture and personal experience shape what and how people develop their distinctive ways of knowing.

The second point regarding the contextual perspective, as observed by Goodnow (1990, p. 82), is that social context is not, as it is often presented, "a relatively benign, neutral, or free market" commodity. Rather, the social world in which we live "takes an active and managing interest in the ideas people acquire" (p. 93). This active and managing interest manifests itself in two ways related to adult cognitive development. The first is that the dominant culture may subvert ways of knowing it does not value. We return to the stories of Kat, the South American–born woman; Allaq, the Native Alaskan Inuit; and Toshi, the African American woman (Goldberger, 1996a):

KAT: When I came to [the United States], I became very quiet. The silence became almost like this cage that I could not get out of. . . . In this culture, there are certain ways of knowing that are much more valued than others. So unless one can quantify, qualify, and prove and have backup and example, then any knowledge that doesn't fit is just not valid—or society doesn't see it as valid.

ALLAQ: The white society has tried to assimilate and acculturate us through education. We had to hang up our nativeness outside the door and come in and think like white people in the classroom . . . I became very, very angry. And when I was real angry I couldn't listen and I couldn't learn. . . . You know in the Caucasian world, everything is systematic, everything is categorized. Where in my world, everything is interrelated.

TOSHI: But if you want to be successful in this country, the United States of America, you have to be able to function in a white world. You have to give up a lot of who you are [and how you think] to make it through the system. It makes you crazy to do it in a way that's not natural to you. You do it "their way," which is not a bad way, it's just a different way. [pp. 336–337]

Because these ways of knowing may not be valued by the dominant culture, they may be hidden or lost and, worse, viewed as illegitimate or not needed in our modern world. And second, scholars themselves may choose to study only the development of the ways of knowing that they are familiar with and value. This bias will continue to block the construction of alternative models and theories that acknowledge contextual factors as a critical aspect of adult cognitive development.

WISDOM: THE HALLMARK OF ADULT THINKING

Wisdom is often seen as the pinnacle or hallmark of adult thinking. It is something we all speak about and sometimes yearn for as we face the many challenges of adult life. Should we tell our teenage grandchildren they are making horrendous decisions? Should we make a major career change, especially if it means losing our financial security? Can we take a chance on building new relationships when old ones fade? What ethical stands are we willing to "lay down our keys for" (that is, resign) at work? Questions like these haunt many of us, and we wish we had the wisdom of the elders to make the "right" decisions. Yet this wisdom of the ages continues to be a fluid and elusive idea, which is most often characterized by the acceptance of ambiguity, as one of its many virtues.

Wisdom is not a new concept; it has been discussed through the ages by great philosophers and theologians of all backgrounds and persuasions. As Joan Erikson (1988) has observed:

> Throughout time and everywhere on the globe, people have earnestly and with great labor undertaken to pass on, to store, to preserve their nugget of truth, of wisdom. They remain embedded in myth, legend, song, and poetry, carved in hieroglyphs and in cave paintings. In some written form they have been enshrined as "sacred writ" and "relic" housed in such edifices as tombs, temples, mosques, monasteries, cathedrals, and churches. . . . We can find documentation of these records in our great libraries and now in smaller ones, too, as all the verbal knowledge becomes translated and disseminated. Computers and microfilm also increase our capacities to store and make available great riches previously unavailable. [pp. 156–157]

Erikson goes on to point out that "wisdom remains an elusive word because it encompasses an attitude, a disposition toward life, past, present, and future, only occasionally recognized in rare individuals" (p. 177).

Psychologists and educators have defined and studied wisdom from a variety of perspectives. Robinson (1990) noted that the definition of wisdom has changed over time, differing in ancient Greek, traditional Christian, and contemporary conceptions. Sternberg (1990a) defines wisdom as a metacognitive style and Baltes and Smith (1990) as expertise in everyday life. Kramer and Bacelar (1994) link wisdom to being able to think in a dialectic way, while Macdonald (1996, p. 1) states that wisdom is "a whole array of better-than-ordinary ways of being, and living and dealing with the world." And Sternberg (1996b, p. 276) has noted the importance of the social-interaction nature of wisdom, which stresses "that wisdom by definition will hardly ever be found in an individual, but rather in cultural or social interactive products." These and other definitions point to the complexity of the concept. Most researchers do agree, however, that wisdom is the province of adulthood, although older is not always equated with wiser.

Researchers and writers on wisdom have attempted to delineate its major components and its relationship to the aging process. Holliday and Chandler (1986), for example, have sought to provide empirical parameters for the term *wisdom* in three interlocking studies. They first collected general descriptions of wise people from which they formulated the basic description of wisdom in a second study. In the third phase of their research, they "examined the influence of the wise prototype on people's information processing strategies" (p. 44). The 458 subjects in their study represented all age cohorts of adults: young, middle aged, and older. They concluded that wisdom is a multidimensional construct consisting of more than objective and context-free aspects of thought. Using Habermas's (1970) framework, Holiday and Chandler propose a tripartite model of wisdom that consists of technical, practical, and emancipatory elements. In their view, "Wise people must be able to solve problems— but not in an abstract sense. The type of problems that wise people presumably deal with appear to have strong practical and emancipatory components. That is, wisdom problems are problems endemic to life and to the human condition. . . . Consequently, the problems typically involve or center on values" (p. 90). (See Chapter Fourteen for more on Habermas's framework.)

In a somewhat different way, Sternberg (1986b, pp. 177–178) sought to discover people's conceptions or implicit theories of wisdom by exploring "the nature and the interrelationships of intelligence, wisdom, and creativity." Through a series of studies with both laypersons (community volunteers and students) and specialists (college professors from a variety of disciplines), Sternberg found that people not only have implicit theories about intelligence, wisdom, and creativity, but use them to evaluate others. Moreover, he found differences in the way laypersons and specialists perceived each of the three constructs, including the notion of wisdom.

Laypersons perceived the wise individual to have much the same analytic reasoning ability one finds in the intelligent person. "But the wise person has a certain sagacity that is not necessarily found in the intelligent person. He or she listens to others, knows how to weigh advice, and can deal with a variety of different kinds of people. . . . The wise individual is especially well able to make clear, sensible, and fair judgments and is perceived to profit from the experiences of others and . . . learn from others' mistakes, as well as from his or her own" (p. 186). The specialists, on the other hand, tend to emphasize certain aspects of wisdom as more critical than others. The art professors, for example, "emphasize insight, knowing how to balance logic and instinct . . . and sensitivity," while the business professors emphasize such things as "maturity of judgment, understanding of the limitations of one's own actions . . . and appreciation of the ideologies of others" (pp. 186–187). Sternberg concludes that the three major constructs of intelligence, wisdom, and creativity are indeed distinct and yet interrelated and, moreover, that we must pay as much attention to wisdom and creativity as we do to intelligence.

Joan Erikson (1988), also connecting creativity to wisdom, delineated ten attributes of wisdom, including the following:

- *Interdependence and interrelatedness.* In her mind, the "wise elder has learned to understand *interdependence,* the ecology of living with others. Early training and much of adult life stress independence, which if pressed to absurdity leads one to isolation and emotional stagnation. Human beings need one another, and their vital involvement in relationships nourishes and sustains the whole cycle of life" (p. 178).

- *Humor.* It is humor—"healing, enlivening laughter that keeps human feet firmly on the ground (humus). The world being full of incongruities, perplexity would surely be overwhelming if humor abandoned us. . . . When we can even see ourselves as funny, it eases this daily living in such close proximity with ourselves" (p. 182).

• *A sense of the complexity of living.* A wise person embraces the "sense *of the complexity of living,* of relationships, of all negotiations. There is certainly no immediate, discernible, and absolute right and wrong, just as light and dark are separated by innumerable shadings. . . . [The] interweaving of time and space, light and dark, and the complexity of human nature suggests that . . . this wholeness of perception to be even partially realized, must of necessity be made up of a *merging* of the *sensual,* the *logical,* and the *aesthetic* perceptions of the individual" (p. 184).

• *Caritas.* There is "an attitude of wisdom that seems of great importance which can be described as nonpossessive attachment. It is possible to care for and about things, and of course individuals as well as this green earth, without dominating anything. 'Let it be,' the [Beatles] song repeats. 'Let it be'. The wise old man or woman learns to go lightly, receive gratefully, release easily, in order to feel as unfettered as possible. Loss is inevitable, so holding on is defeating" (p. 186).

In discussing each of the ten attributes, Erikson places them within the framework of life cycle development and speaks to how they are nurtured throughout the life span. Erikson closes her discussion by observing that all of these attributes of wisdom should be considered "universal age-old survival skills" (p. 188).

In contrast to the work of Sternberg and Erikson, other writers have framed their work from the perspective that wisdom is a part of intelligence, that is, the "pragmatics of intelligence" (Smith, Dixon, and Baltes, 1989; Dittmann-Kohli and Baltes, 1990). Smith, Dixon, and Baltes, for example (1989, p. 311), view wisdom as cognitive expertise in the fundamental pragmatics of life that are "visible in situations related to life planning, life management, and life review. This expertise is reflected in individuals' definition of, judgments about, and solutions to life problems" and is built on a person's store of factual knowledge and experience. In the most global sense, they see wisdom as "good judgment about important but uncertain matters" (p. 312). The basis of this wise judgment "is both specialized knowledge about life in general and a repertoire of efficient strategies for applying and adapting that knowledge to many contexts, interpersonal situations, and life tasks" (p. 326).

Macdonald (1996) reflects a few of the same sentiments of the scholars we have just reviewed. Writing from a lay-oriented exploration of wisdom, Macdonald, like Erikson, has outlined attributes of people who are wise, although these attributes are mostly different from Erikson's. These attributes include "seeing things clearly; seeing things as they are; acting in prudent and effective ways; acting with the well-being of the whole in mind; deeply understanding the human/cosmos situation; knowing when to act and when not to act; being able to handle whatever arises with peace of mind and an effective, compassionate, holistic response; and being able to anticipate potential problems and avoid them" (p. 1). In addition, Macdonald connects his foundation for wisdom to Maslow's concept of self-actualization and the values espoused as part of that concept: "wholeness, perfection, completion, justice, aliveness, richness, simplicity, beauty, goodness, uniqueness, effortlessness, playfulness, truth, honesty, reality, self-sufficiency" (p. 2). Although Macdonald uses values like reality and playfulness as part of the foundation of wisdom, his sense of wisdom seems very rationalistic and almost otherworldly.

Despite the different perspectives from which wisdom has been studied and the lack of consensus on its precise dimensions, several points of agreement have emerged (Holliday and Chandler, 1986; Erikson, 1988; Sternberg, 1990b; Jarvis, 1992; Kramer and Bacelar, 1994; Bennett-Woods, 1997). Wisdom is grounded in life's rich experiences and therefore is developed though the process of aging. Although book learning may be a part of developing wisdom, it is not a requirement. Rather, being able to respond well to the pragmatics of life seems to form the core of being wise. Moreover, wisdom seems to consist of the ability to move away from absolute truths, to be reflective, and to make sound judgments related to our daily existence, whatever our circumstances.

In reflecting on this study of wisdom and how it might enrich learning in adulthood, we are struck by observations made by Dychtwald and Flower (1989) about "the third age"—that part of life beyond age sixty, a time of life that more and more people are experiencing as healthy and vital individuals. Dychtwald and Flower contend that this third age allows for the "further development of the interior life of the intellect, memory, and imagination, of emotional maturity, and of one's personal sense of spiritual identity" (p. 53). It is a time for people to give back to society through their wisdom, power, and spirituality "the lessons, resources, and experiences accumulated over a lifetime" (p. 53). They then quote Monsignor Fahey, the director of Fordham University's Third Age Center: "People in the third age should be the glue of society, not its ashes" (p. 53). Their conclusion is clear and dramatic: "Think about it. We know even with the best care overall fitness will decline gradually over the years. While the strength of the senses is weakening, what if the powers of the mind, heart, and the spirit are rising? If life offers the on-going opportunity for increased awareness and personal growth, think how far we could evolve, given the advantage of extra decades of life!" (p. 52). Their observations of using our later years to develop our cognitive thinking abilities further are similar to Kegan's (1994), discussed earlier. In incorporating the concept of wisdom in our thinking about cognitive development, mature adult cognition is more than just abstract logic, complex reasoning, and dialectical thinking; it also encompasses the ability to think, feel, and act "wisely" in life.

SUMMARY

Cognitive development refers to the change in thinking patterns as one grows older. Much of the earlier work on cognitive development in adulthood has been grounded primarily in the work of Piaget. One line of research has focused on how Piaget's stages play out in adulthood. A more fruitful research tradition, grounded in Piaget's work, has been the conceptualization of adult stages of cognition beyond that of formal operations, such as the work of Arlin (1975). Other researchers have posited entirely new schemes of adult cognitive development. These alternative theories range from the traditional stage theories of development, such as the work of Perry (1970, 1981) and King and Kitchener (1994), to those theories that bring in new voices (Belenky, Clinchy, Goldberger, and Tarule, 1986; Goldberger, Tarule, Clinchy, and Belenky, 1996) and different ways of framing development, represented by Baxter Magolda (1992) and Labouvie-Vief, 1980, 1990).

In the review of the many theories of adult cognitive development, two major themes became apparent: the importance of dialectical thinking and that contextual factors are critical in determining how we develop our thinking patterns as adults. Dialectical thinking, as represented by the work of Riegel (1973), Kramer (1983, 1989), and

Kegan (1994), allows for the acceptance of alternative truths or ways of thinking about the many contradictions and paradoxes that we face in everyday life. To be able to engage in dialectic thinking is viewed by some as the only way to navigate our postmodern world successfully. Bringing in the contextual perspective on adult cognitive development acknowledges that the world around the thinker makes a difference in how adults develop their thinking patterns. Social, cultural, economic, and political forces help shape both how we think and what kind of knowledge we value. The contextual perspective was illustrated by later work of Labouvie-Vief (1990, 1992, 1994) and Goldberger (1996a).

The chapter concluded with a brief overview of the concept of wisdom, often regarded as the hallmark of mature adult thinking. Although it has been discussed over the ages by the great philosophers and theologians, this area of study has received little attention in the literature on cognitive development and learning in general. Representative conceptions of wisdom, such as those of Holliday and Chandler (1986), Sternberg (1986b), Erikson (1988), and Macdonald (1996), were reviewed. Despite the different perspectives from which wisdom is viewed, scholars seem to agree that wisdom involves special types of experience-based knowledge and is characterized by the ability to move away from absolute truth, to be reflective, and to make sound judgments related to everyday life.

CHAPTER EIGHT

Intelligence and Aging

T he adage that "you can't teach an old dog new tricks" haunts both instructors of adults and adult learners themselves as they set forth on new learning ventures. The image of staff members who refuse to use the office e-mail system because "it just takes too long to learn" is still a reality. So too is the existence of the young trainer, fresh out of graduate school, who secretly believes she will never be able to teach her entrenched training staff anything, let alone to work as a team. This powerful myth—that adults lose their ability to learn as they age—prevails, although for the most part it has not been substantiated in the literature.

Intelligence is defined in a number of ways. From the perspective of the casual observer, intelligence is often equated with "being smart"—that is, being able to act intelligently when dealing with everyday life. But there is another definition of intelligence that many adults have carried with them since their elementary school days: intelligence is a specific measurement of their ability to learn. While not actually knowing their IQ scores, many adults have vague recollections of being labeled an "average," "above-average," or "below-average" student. Worse still are the memories of using IQ tests to be placed in a "slow" reading or math group or of watching one's best friend be put in the "high group." Beginning with the early work of Spearman (1904), Binet (1916), Thorndike, Bregman, Tilton, and Woodyard (1928), and others, researchers have sought to understand the nature of intelligence and whether it changes with age.

In the chapter, we first explore the concept of intelligence and how it has been measured. Next, we present several theories of intelligence developed since the 1960s that inform our practice as educators of adults. We follow with a review of how age affects intellectual abilities. The chapter concludes with an exploration of three ideas about intellectual functioning in adulthood that are particularly intriguing and useful for educators of adults.

CONCEPT OF INTELLIGENCE AND ITS MEASUREMENT

The concept of intelligence has become much more complex and multifaceted over the last two decades, often causing confusion to casual readers. Different words describing the same concept have been interchanged or slightly modified, adding to the complexity of understanding the vast array of work on adult intelligence. For example, some authors use the terms *intellectual development* and *cognitive development* interchangeably, whereas other authors using these terms are exploring very different phenomena. Schaie (1996) and Berg (1992) have sought to add clarity to discussions of what the term *intelligence* means. Berg (1992) highlights several perspectives that dominate current research in intelligence. Among these are the psychometric tradition, the process orientation of Piagetian and neo-Piagetian thought, information processing, and the contextual perspective. Schaie (1996) agrees that at least two of these theoretical perspectives—those of information processing and the psychometric tradition—have driven the study of intelligence, but adds a third, that of practical intelligence. More specifically, Schaie purports that "there is a natural hierarchy in the study of intelligence leading from information processing, through the products measured in tests of intelligence, to practical and everyday intelligence" (p. 266). The Piagetian and neo-Piagetian traditions were discussed in Chapter Seven and the information processing perspective is discussed in Chapter Nine. In this chapter we use work from the psychometric tradition, practical intelligence, and the contextual perspective to illustrate important ideas related to intelligence and aging.

Intelligence has been most often studied from the psychometric tradition (J. Anderson, 1996; Schaie and Willis, 1986; Sternberg, 1996b), which assumes that it is a measurable construct. Those who have studied intelligence from this perspective, as echoed in the words of Schaie (1996, p. 267), assert that "the products or intellectual skills that characterize psychometric intelligence are likely to represent the most appropriate label for the direct prediction of many socially desirable outcomes." Some who have studied intelligence from the psychometric perspective, such as Binet and Spearman (Schaie and Willis, 1986; Schaie, 1996), describe it as a single factor termed the "general ability" or "g" factor. This means that a person's "performance on many different types of tests (vocabulary, arithmetic, object assembly, block design) can be explained in terms of a *single* underlying ability" (Hayslip and Panek, 1989, p. 197). Therefore, scores from diverse tests or subscales can be combined to form an overall general score or index of intelligence quotient (IQ). The g factor is most often viewed as an innate capacity that is genetically determined.

Schaie (1996) views this single concept of intelligence as appropriate for childhood but not as useful beyond adolescence "because of the lack of a unidimensional criterion in adults and because convincing empirical evidence supports the presence of multiple dimensions of intelligence displaying a different life course" (p. 267). "The 'purest' tests of these multiple dimensions [grounded in the psychometric tradition] are sometimes administered as tests of the 'primary mental abilities'" (Schaie and Willis, 1986, p. 290) consisting of spatial ability, perceptual speed, numerical ability, verbal relations, words, memory, and induction.

Intelligence Testing with Adults

The first widespread use of intelligence testing with adults was by the army in World War I, with the administration of the Army Alpha Tests of Intelligence. Thorndike, Bregman, Tilton, and Woodyard (1928) followed closely behind with their pioneering work that challenged the fundamental notion that learning ability peaks very early in life. Using primarily laboratory or schoolroom tasks, Thorndike measured the speed of the performance of people from ages fourteen to fifty on a variety of tasks, from memorizing poetry to acquiring an artificial language (Kidd, 1973). Thorndike, Bregman, Tilton, and Woodyard (1928, pp. 178–179) concluded from their many studies that, "in general, teachers of adults of age twenty-five to forty-five should expect them to learn at nearly the same rate and in nearly the same manner as they would have learned the same thing at twenty." In reflecting on Thorndike's work, Kidd (1973) noted two major contributions. The first was to raise the age of onset of the downhill slide of a person's ability to learn from twenty years of age to forty-five. Second, and even more important, Thorndike "helped to stimulate colleagues to reject traditional views and formulas" (Kidd, 1973, p. 79) about learning in adulthood. Other noted studies of intelligence (Jones and Conrad, 1933; Miles and Miles, 1932) of that same era reached similar conclusions, "although they found that the decline begins at a later age and the rate of that decline is not as sharp as in 'Thorndike's curve'" (Cross, 1981, p. 158).

Overall, the use of psychometric intelligence tests with adults has not been as prevalent as the testing of children. The predominant uses of intelligence tests with adults include assessing people in the workplace for job placement and in clinical settings for appropriate treatment plans. In addition, intelligence tests have been used in research to determine how intellectual abilities change as people age. The two tests of adult intelligence most often used in both research and practice are the Wechsler Adult Intelligence Scale–Revised (WAIS-R) (Thomas, 1992; Sternberg, 1996b) and the Primary Mental Abilities (PMA) test. The most recent version of the PMA is the Schaie-Thurston Adult Mental Abilities Test (STAMAT) (Schaie, 1985, 1987).

The WAIS-R (and its predecessor, the WAIS) consists of eleven subtests grouped into verbal and performance scales. This test provides three scores: a verbal, a performance, and an overall score. The verbal portion of the test relies heavily on language skills, such as word definitions and general information items, although two subtests of this scale also address basic numerical abilities. Responses to the performance scales are primarily based on nonverbal skills such as locating missing parts of a picture or reconstructing block designs. The majority of the verbal tests are not timed; all those in the performance category are timed. Several of the WAIS-R and WAIS subtests are often grouped together for measuring Cattell's (1987) constructs of fluid and crystallized intelligence, which are discussed later in this chapter. Wechsler himself believed early on in his career that mental ability as a whole declines with age in a similar fashion to the rest of one's body (Kidd, 1973; Schaie and Willis, 1986).

On closer examination on both earlier and later WAIS test results, however, it became apparent to both Wechsler and others that the decline in intellectual functions was not equal for all tasks: "In general, scores on performance tests [did] show a loss, but not on the verbal tests" (Kidd, 1973, p. 81). "One key was that the subtests in which older subjects do poorly are all 'speeded' tests" (Schaie and Willis, 1986, pp. 294–295). These conflicting results raised numerous questions about the true nature of adult intelligence that are still being debated (Goleman, 1995; Sternberg, 1996a, 1996b). For example, are verbal tests more appropriate measures of intelligence in adulthood than performance tests? Is a timed task as valid as an untimed task? Is adult intelligence more than what can be measured by conventional measures of intelligence?

The second test of adult intelligence, the PMA test, is often associated with the work of Schaie and colleagues on intelligence and aging (Schaie, 1979, 1994, 1996). The underlying assumption of the PMA, grounded in the work of Thurstone and Thurstone (1941), is that intelligence is actually several distinct abilities and not a single general trait. Purported to measure five relatively independent factors, the PMA test battery consists of five subtests: (1) verbal meaning, which is the ability to understand ideas expressed in words; (2) space, describing the ability to think about an object in two or three dimensions; (3) reasoning, involving the ability to solve logical problems; (4) number, the ability to handle arithmetic problems; and (5) word fluency, concerning the speed and ease with which words are used (Schaie, 1979). The PMA subtests, all of them timed, can be reported as a composite score that constitutes an overall index of intellectual ability. Like the WAIS-R, the PMA appears to assess academic abilities (such as verbal and reasoning ability) related to formal schooling. In a challenge to this idea, Schaie and others (Schaie, 1996; Willis and Schaie, 1986) found that at least in later adulthood, certain primary mental abilities do predict competent behavior in specific situations— for example, "competence in active situations was predicted by spatial ability and inductive reasoning, and competence in passive situations was predicted by verbal abilities" (Schaie and Willis, 1986, p. 290). Active situations included traveling around a city looking for a new residence or preparing large meals for friends, while more passive ones were attending an art exhibit or worrying about the ability to pay a debt. To these researchers, the findings suggest "a strong relationship between the 'building blocks' of intelligence and abilities on real life tasks" (p. 290). Only further research will tell whether the PMA and other intelligence tests of this nature can actually be used as adequate predictors of everyday intelligence.

Major Issues and Future Concerns in Assessing Adult Intelligence

In using the traditional psychometric measures of intelligence with adults, there are two cogent issues: the tests themselves and the social and policy implications of IQ scores. As Tennant and Pogson (1995) have observed, these tests "are too culture-specific; . . . [and] they are constructed from problems and tasks derived from the context or 'culture' of schooling rather than everyday life" (p. 17). In other words, in using these tests, we perpetuate the notion of intelligence as being more "academic" in nature and culture free. In addition, Thomas (1992) has pointed out that the timed nature of some of these tests is biased against older adults, in that the reaction time of many older adults is slower (see Chapter Four).

The second issue, that of how scholars have used the results from IQ tests to make statements about groups of people in society and then propose policy initiatives related to the statements, has been the most controversial and possibly the most perilous of the two problems cited. *The Bell Curve,* by Herrnstein and Murray (1994), represents the most recent iteration of this problem. These authors assert that intelligence, as measured by traditional IQ tests, "has a powerful bearing on how people do in life . . . [and] that people differ in intelligence for reasons that are not their fault" (p. 535), meaning that intelligence is substantially inheritable. They recommend sweeping and often repressive policy changes grounded in simplification of the rules for living so that persons of "low cognitive ability" (who are most often poor and/or of color) can function better in society. Rebuttals and challenges to Herrnstein and Murray's work have come from many quarters, from scholars who study intelligence to historians and social scientists (Fraser, 1995; Jacoby and Glauberman, 1995; Kincheloe, Steinberg, and Gresson, 1996). As Jacoby and Glauberman (1995, p. xi) have observed, "The extraordinary response to *The Bell Curve* suggests it touches an open nerve. The book bespeaks to a society that is losing confidence in its own egalitarian and democratic process."

In thinking about future means of assessing intelligence in adulthood, two major concerns have surfaced. First, we must develop assessment tools that can measure both academic and practical notions of intelligence, including emotional intelligence. This effort would include further study of existing measures, such as that undertaken by Willis and Schaie (1985), as well as the development of new assessment tools (Baltes, Dittmann-Kohli, and Dixon, 1984; Gardner, 1995). Second, we must pay more attention to revising and designing assessments that are "age fair." These measures would take into account "tests of adult intelligence relevant to competence at different points in the lifespan" (Schaie and Willis, 1986, p. 292), unlike current measures, which assess primarily competencies needed for academic activities. Research in this arena has just begun. The development of alternative assessments of intelligence suitable for adult learners will require much time and effort.

REPRESENTATIVE THEORIES OF INTELLIGENCE

Two theories of intelligence grounded in the psychometric tradition of measurement, those of Horn and Cattell and of Guilford, which are useful in helping us understand more clearly the connection between intelligence and aging, are described first in this section. These descriptions are followed by a review of the work of scholars who have challenged traditional theories, such as Gardner and Sternberg, who believe that these traditional models have little, if any, relationship to what they term "real-world" or "practical" intelligence. Theorists who advocate practical intelligence most often view intelligence as a combination of biological and environmental factors and stress genetic and environmental interactions.

Although this interactionist perspective of intelligence is not a new idea (for example, Piaget, 1952, and Vygotsky, 1978, were interactionists), only relatively recently have theories of intelligence emphasized the importance of this interaction to both the continued development and assessment of adult intelligence. Tennant and Pogson (1995) have provided a thoughtful treatise on why practical intelligence has been overlooked for so long, especially by scholars representing Western culture. They assert that "historically, Western culture has taken a lower view of manual work than of cognitive activity [which has led to] the exaltation of the theoretical or contemplative over the practical" (pp. 37, 39). More specifically, they cite the attributes of verbal, abstract, and complex thinking as being far more valued than either those of concrete and sensual thought or the active use of knowledge.

Theory of Fluid and Crystallized Intelligence

One of the major conceptualizations of adult intelligence was popularized by the work of Cattell (1963, 1987) and Horn (Horn 1976, 1982, 1985). They viewed intelligence as consisting of two primary factors: fluid intelligence (Gf) and crystallized intelligence (Gc). Fluid intelligence, or the ability to perceive complex relations and engage in short-term memory, concept formation, reasoning, and abstraction, is measured by tests for rote memory, basic reasoning, figural relations, and memory span. In contrast, crystallized intelligence is normally associated with acculturated information—those "sets of skills and bits of knowledge that we each learn as part of growing up in any given culture, such as verbal comprehension, vocabulary, [and] the ability to evaluate experience" (Bee, 1996, pp. 155–156). Examples of measures of crystallized intelligence include vocabulary and verbal comprehension, numerical reasoning, and an individual's ability to extract information from the environment. Tests of fluid intelligence are primarily speeded and are viewed as "culture fair," while crystallized intelligence is more likely to be assessed by nonspeeded measures. There is no single test that researchers can use to measure both factors of intelligence; rather, researchers often label tests as measures of either fluid or crystallized intelligence (see, for example, Christensen, 1994; Kaufman, Kaufman, Chen, and Kaufman, 1996).

Although the popular understanding is that fluid intelligence is more innate and therefore dependent on a neurophysiological base, Horn (1985, p. 289) now does not hold to this notion: "There are good reasons to believe that Gf is learned as much as Gc, and that Gc is inherited as much as Gf." Rather, he believes that both types of intelligence can be nurtured, at least until very old age. This has led researchers to study whether fluid intelligence, which was thought to be primarily innate, can be either restored (if loss has been shown) or strengthened as people age (Baltes and Willis, 1982; Lohman and Scheurman, 1992; Schaie and Willis, 1986; Willis and Schaie, 1994). Schaie (1996) provides a concise summary of this work.

Overall, even with studies showing that the loss of fluid intelligence is remediable, there is still consensus that fluid intelligence begins to decline much earlier, perhaps at age thirty-five or forty (Horn and

Donaldson, 1980), than crystallized intelligence. Again, challenges to the exact time frame of decline and what that decline means have been made on a number of fronts, including the ways in which fluid intelligence has conventionally been measured. Some researchers (for example, Lohman, 1989; Schaie, 1996) would like to see more useful and realistic tests of fluid intelligence for adults based on the underlying premise that "fluid and crystallized general abilities can be placed along a continuum" throughout the life span (Lohman and Scheurman, 1992, p. 78). Lohman and Scheurman go on to argue that educators must "encourage fluidization, not merely crystallization of knowledge and skills" (p. 81), because both types of intelligences are needed as we grow older.

Guilford's Structure of Intellect Model

In contrast to the two-factor model of fluid and crystallized intelligence proposed by Cattell, Guilford's model (1967, 1985) consists of 120 theoretical factors clustered into three major categories that are independent of each other: (1) contents, referring to the type of verbal, numerical, or behavioral material being tested; (2) operations, which are the basic mental processes such as memory, reasoning, and creative thinking; and (3) product, referring to the form of information that results from the interactions of the other two categories (from a single unit to complex patterns of information). A key assumption underlying the model is that the mental operations used on a particular task area are as important as the nature of the task itself. Guilford's model offers researchers an alternative frame of reference about the human intellect on which hypotheses about new factors of intelligence can be generated (Guilford, 1967, 1985; Huyck and Hoyer, 1982). Therefore, the model continues to provide a major building block for expanding our thinking about the fundamental nature of human intelligence.

Some have expressed reservations about the theory's utility: "While Guilford's theory of intelligence has generated a great deal of research, the structure of intellect model has for the most part yet to be integrated into adult developmental research on intelligence" (Hayslip and Panek, 1989, p. 198). The noted exception has been the studies on divergent thinking: the ability to produce alternative ideas or solutions. For example, in cross-sectional comparisons of the creative process and products of younger versus older women, Alpaugh, Parham, Cole, and Birren (1982) found a decline in divergent thinking abilities with age. They hypothesized that the older creative person may rely "more on previous experience than on present divergent thinking abilities, whereas younger creators draw more heavily on divergent thinking" (p. 112). Although Guilford's model has not been used often by researchers of intelligence in adulthood, we believe his model, especially the notion of both multiple and interacting factors of intelligence, may prove useful in future research and theory building on adult learning.

Gardner's Theory of Multiple Intelligences

Gardner is representative of theorists who broke away from the psychometric tradition of intelligence during the early 1980s. From Gardner's perspective, the concept of intelligence has been too narrowly limited to the realm of logical and linguistic abilities, primarily by the way intelligence has been measured. Rather, he argues, "there is persuasive evidence for the existence of several relatively autonomous human intellectual competencies . . . that can be fashioned and combined in a multiplicity of adaptive ways by individuals and cultures" (Gardner, 1983, pp. 8–9). From a number of unrelated sources, such as studies of prodigies, brain-damaged patients, and normal children and adults, Gardner originally identified seven different forms of intelligence, with an eighth recently added. His first seven forms include "not only the standard academic ones of linguistic, logical-mathematical, and spatial (the visual skills exhibited by a painter or architect) but also musical, 'bodily-kinesthetic,' and two 'personal' intelligences involving a fine-tuned understanding of oneself and others" (Levine, 1987, p. 54). (See Gardner, 1983, for a complete description of his seven original intelligences.) Gardner calls his newest form of intelligence the "naturalist" intelligence: "The intelligence of the naturalist involves the ability to recognize important distinctions in the natural world (among flora, fauna). It can also be applied to man-made objects in our consumer society (cars, sneakers). Obviously this skill is crucial in hunting or farming cultures, and it is at a premium among biologists and others who work with nature in our own society" (Shores, 1995, p. 5).

In introducing this new theory, Gardner (1983, p. 280) stressed that "the idea of multiple intelligences is an old one" recognized even in early Greek times. In Gardner's framework, our tendency to label people as being generally bright, average, or dull just does not seem to fit. Rather, a person may exhibit high intelligence in one or two areas, such as music and math, and yet demonstrate only average intelligence in other respects. In other words, you can be very talented in one or two areas and have little or no capacity in other areas. Gardner views his theory of multiple intelligences as presenting a critique of the predominant model of "psychometrics-as-usual" in measuring intelligence. Therefore, although scholars have made some attempts to develop and use traditional paper-and-pencil tests to measure multiple intelligences (for example, Shearer and Jones, 1994; Rosnow, Skleder, Jaeger, and Rind, 1994), Gardner (1995) himself argues that any assessments of multiple intelligences must be "intelligent fair"; that is, the assessments must "examine the intelligence directly rather than through the lens of linguistic or logical intelligence (as ordinary paper-and-pencil tests do)" (p. 202).

When Gardner proposed his theory of multiple intelligences, he was interested in both promoting theory building on the nature of intelligence with his fellow psychologists and having scholars examine the educational implications of his theory. His work has stirred a great deal of theoretical debate among scholars, but what Gardner was unprepared for was the almost overwhelming positive response among educators of preschool and school-age children (Gardner and Hatch 1989; Gardner, 1993, 1995). The theory of multiple intelligences was almost immediately put into practice, and whole curricula have been developed using this conceptualization of intelligence. We even found one article that described using his theory as the basis for graduate study (Brougher, 1997). Although almost all of the published work we could locate described applications with children, as in the case of Guilford's theory, we see significant value in integrating Gardner's ideas into our study and practice of learning in adulthood. We recommend paying heed to Gardner's (1995, p. 206) position that there is no "single educational approach based on the MI [multiple intelligences] theory . . ., [and] that educators are in the best position to determine the uses to which MI theory can and should be used."

Sternberg's Theories of Intelligence

Sternberg too has broken from the tradition of framing intelligence as primarily a measure of formal testlike problem solving to one that includes problem solving for everyday life. Unlike the "schooling world," where problems are usually highly definitive and structured, real-world issues tend to be both ill defined and contexualized. Therefore, Sternberg contends that most theories, especially the measures of intelligence, address only the "schooling" kind of intelligence and almost totally ignore the notion of practical intelligence. Sternberg has proposed an important theory of human intelligence, the triarchic theory, and a layperson's version of theory that he terms "successful intelligence."

According to Sternberg (1985, 1986a, 1988), the triarchic theory is composed of three subtheories: a componential subtheory, describing the internal analytical mental mechanisms and processes involved in intelligence; an experiential subtheory focusing on how a person's experience combined with insight and creativity affects how she thinks; and a contextual subtheory, emphasizing the role of the external environment in determining what constitutes intelligent behavior in a situation. The first part of the subtheory, the mental mechanisms of intelligence, is posited as universal: "Although individuals may differ in what mental mechanisms they apply to a given task or situation, the potential set of mental mechanisms underlying intelligence is claimed to be the same across all individuals, social classes, and cultural groups" (Sternberg, 1986a, pp. 23–24). The other two parts of Sternberg's theory, which emphasize the experience of the learner and the real-world context, are seen as having both universal and relativistic components. The universal aspect has to do with areas being studied within each of these subparts of the theory (such as the processes of automation, environmental adaption, and shaping). These processes are seen as important no matter what the cultural milieu or the person's experience with the tasks or situations chosen to measure these aspects. The relativistic nature of these parts of the theory comes from the recognition that what constitutes intelligent behavior is not the same for all groups of people. As Sternberg puts it, "Parts of the theory are culturally universal, and parts are culturally relative" (1986a, p. 24).

Sisco (1989) offers an excellent overview of how Sternberg's triarchic theory may apply to adult learning. From Sisco's perspective, "one of the most significant implications would appear to be something that many adult educators have believed, at least implicitly, for a long time now: that human intelligence is much more than performance on standardized tests and achievement in schools" (p. 287). In taking this view, Sternberg (1985, 1988) and Gardner (1983) offer similar observations: that intelligence consists of not only the academic abilities, such as verbal and logical-mathematical skills, but also the capacity to perform in the everyday world. Sternberg's notion of practical intelligence—"intelligence as it operates in real-world contexts" (1986a, p. 301)—seems especially useful in gaining a clearer picture of adult intelligence.

A second major application from Sternberg's work, cited by Sisco (1989), is the notion that intelligence can be taught. Although others have investigated this idea (for example, Schaie, 1996), Sternberg has offered a comprehensive blueprint of a practical training program for enhancing intellectual skills (see Sternberg, 1986a, 1988). In this program Sternberg offers applied examples of each subtheory along with practical exercises. According to Sisco, the main strengths of this program are that "it is based on a theory that has been subjected to fairly extensive and rigorous empirical testing . . . , focusing on academic as well as practical intelligence . . . , [and] has assessment tools for measuring training effects" (p. 287).

Sternberg (1996b) has carried his work further into what he calls "successful intelligence." His view of successful intelligence is grounded in the same basic components as those in his triarchic theory: "To be successfully intelligent is to think well in three different ways: analytically [componential subtheory], creatively [experiential subtheory], and practically [contextual subtheory]. . . . Analytical thinking is required to solve problems and to judge the quality of ideas. Creative intelligence is required to formulate good problems and ideas in the first place. Practical intelligence is needed to use the ideas and their analysis in an effective way in one's everyday life" (Sternberg, 1996b, pp. 127–128). All three intelligences are interrelated and therefore are needed in adult life. Sternberg stresses that it is not enough just to have these three abilities; rather, people are successfully intelligent when they are able to choose how and when to use these abilities effectively. For example, students in graduate programs often develop research studies that meet the test of being highly analytical in nature. Nonetheless, the problems they choose to study may not be important to their fields (lack of creative intelligence) or have little practical significance (something valued in educational research). Sternberg goes on to outline twenty characteristics and attributes of people who are successfully intelligent, with the assertion that "their presence can serve as self-activators and can lead, ultimately, to success . . . , [while] their absence [results in] self-sabotage and failure" (p. 251). Successfully intelligent people motivate themselves, know how to make the most of their abilities, translate thought into action, have a product orientation, complete tasks and follow through, and are not afraid to risk failure. In summary, Sternberg's work on intelligence, like that of Gardner, is very useful in informing both the theory and practice of learning in adulthood.

Goleman's Theory of Emotional Intelligence

Goleman (1995) too has challenged our traditional views of intelligence. By expanding what we mean by intelligence, Goleman (1995, p. 9), grounding his work in the new discoveries of the emotional architecture of the brain, asserts that we have two very different ways of knowing—the rational and the emotional—which are, for the most part, intertwined and "exquisitely coordinated; feelings are essential to thought, thought to feelings." Yet, in Goleman's beliefs, it is the emotional mind—in his terms, emotional intelligence—that is the major determiner of success in life. Building on the work of Salovey and Mayer (1990), Goleman describes five major domains of emotional intelligence: knowing one's emotions, managing emotions, motivating oneself, recognizing emotions in others, and handling relationships. He believes self-awareness of one's feelings is the key to emotional intelligence, but one must also be attuned to the emotions of others. His descriptions of how adults might display their emotional intelligences are similar to Gardner's concepts of personal intelligences. For example, both authors speak to the need for people to make personal connections and be empathetic as well as to have access to their own internal feelings. In addition, Goleman's ideas about emotional intelligence are echoed in Sternberg's list of the characteristics and attributes of people who display successful intelligence.

As with Gardner's theory of multiple intelligences, educators of children have gravitated to Goleman's ideas. And Goleman himself has outlined a number of ways that schools could change their practices to encourage the development of emotional intelligence. In addition, Goleman has addressed how emotional intelligence can assist in our lives as adults, in both home and work situations. Other authors too have addressed the concept of emotional intelligence in adulthood (Simmons and Simmons, 1997; Weisinger, 1998). Weisinger (1998), for example, has explored the application of emotional intelligence in the workplace. Based on his work with a variety of businesses and other organizations, he gives helpful practical examples and exercises on how to develop one's own emotional intelligence and then use that intelligence in relating to others effectively in work situations. Weisinger's hope is that people who have developed their own emotional intelligence can build emotionally intelligent organizations.

We move next in the chapter to a discussion of the contextual perspective of intelligence. As will become apparent, there is some overlap among researchers who highlight the importance of context as a critical component of adult intelligence and those who stress the concepts of practical and emotional intelligence.

THE CONTEXTUAL PERSPECTIVE OF INTELLIGENCE

Acknowledging the contextual dimension of intelligence in adulthood has moved thinking about intelligence beyond individual learners. Within the broad framework of the contextual perspective, two major threads are important in gaining a clearer understanding of adult intelligence: intellectual abilities lie at the intersection between mind and context, and intelligence is defined differently by different social classes and cultural groups.

We all have wondered why some people can be successful in more than one setting, even when those settings are radically different, while others fail miserably when they move, even when they are doing the same job. One explanation is that people who succeed across settings have the internal capacity and are able to scan and adapt to new environments. Without the ability to understand and actively participate in new situations, a contextual theorist would observe that being cognitively competent internally makes little, if any, difference. In essence, the contextual perspective captures the adaptive functions of intelligence—being able to act intellectually within a number of different contexts, based on accumulation of both generalized and specialized knowledge and abilities (Baltes, Dittmann-Kohli, and Dixon, 1984; Dixon, 1992; Sternberg, 1985, 1994b, 1996b).

Also within the contextual framework, we have come to understand that intelligence is not defined the same way by different cultural groups and social classes (Berry, 1996; Keats, 1995; Kohl de Oliveira, 1995; Luttrell, 1989; Sternberg, 1996b). As Kohl de Oliveira (1995, p. 245) has observed, "Individuals, growing up in their cultural settings, develop their own conceptions about intellectual competence, acquisition and use of cognitive abilities, and organization of these abilities within different situations." For example, respondents in Luttrell's study (1989, p. 37) of working-class black and white women judged people as intelligent by their ability "to cope with everyday problems in an everyday world." In other words, they saw using common sense as an important intellectual skill. But even in their definitions of common sense, each group described the formulation and value of this commonsense know-how very differently. White women valued working-class men's commonsense knowledge, such as manual and craft knowledge, more highly than their own intuitive knowledge springing from their domestic responsibilities. In contrast, black women viewed as important the knowledge and abilities they gained through caretaking and domestic work. In addition, working-class black women also considered their racial identity and relationships with "extended kin" and the black community as critical to both what they know and how they used this knowledge.

Kohl de Oliveira (1995, p. 262), in her longitudinal study of how adults in a *favela* (squatter settlement) in the city of São Paulo, Brazil, understand intelligence, found that her respondents "characterized intelligent people as those who are able, basically, to 'make things,' to create concrete products with their own hands: build houses, do woodwork, do mechanical work, paint, make objects in straw, ceramics, and so on." These people, who were living in a squatter settlement, defined intelligence as the ability to cope with their everyday lives, which in essence meant possessing the skills to make things with their own hands and having the ability to learn easily and quickly things that could assist them in their daily survival.

Although the concept of practical intelligence could be used to describe how both the Luttrell and Kohl de Oliveira respondents characterized intelligence, the concrete descriptions their subjects used are different from those given by the populations often used in studies of intelligence: those with middle-class backgrounds. For example, in a study by Berg and Sternberg (1992), subjects from membership lists of large Protestant churches in the New Haven, Connecticut, and Salt Lake City, Utah, areas used phrases like "is able to analyze topics in new and original ways," "is open-minded to new ideas and trends," "displays good common sense," "acts in a mature manner," "acts responsibly," and "is interested in home and family life" as important behaviors characterizing adults with practical intelligence.

AGE AND INTELLECTUAL ABILITIES

Does intelligence decline with age? Responses to this question are mixed and often controversial. The classic school of thought contends that intelligence enters a process of irreversible decline in the adult years, although the hypothesized onset of that decline has been extended from the early twenties to at least the age of fifty or sixty. Others say that intelligence is relatively stable through the adult years, with substantial intellectual changes occurring only very late in life, and then primarily "in abilities that were less central to the individual's life experience and thus perhaps less practiced" (Schaie, 1996, p. 2). In essence, we have enough brain capacity to do almost anything we choose, until serious illness sets in. Still others argue that intelligence declines in some respects, remains stable in others, and may even increase in some functions (Baltes, Dittmann-Kohli, and Dixon, 1984; Kaufman, Kaufman, Chen, and Kaufman, 1996; Raykov, 1995).

What creates this confusing picture of adult intellectual abilities? Botwinick (1977) has provided a helpful framework, citing four key factors on which the controversies rest: definitions of age or aging, definitions of intelligence, types of tests used to measure intelligence, and research methods and their pitfalls. All of these factors are discussed in this section, using current ideas from research and practice. Underlying most of this discussion is that we are addressing the issue of age and intellectual abilities primarily from the perspective of the psychometric framework.

What Is Meant by Age and Aging

Whether or not one believes intelligence declines with age depends on "where in the age spectrum one chooses to look" (Botwinick, 1977, p. 580). Are we talking about adults in early, middle, or later adulthood? In reviewing data on early and middle adulthood, our response would be that intelligence does not decline with age. (See Baltes, Dittmann-Kohli, and Dixon, 1984; Schaie, 1994, 1996; Schaie and Hertzog, 1983.) In fact, some intellectual functions, no matter what testing procedures are employed, seem to increase over the course of the years. Our response to whether intelligence declines in later adulthood is not as clear-cut. (See Baltes, 1993; Baltes, Dittmann-Kohli, and Dixon, 1984; Horn and Donaldson, 1976; Schaie, 1996.) Most agree that some decline in functioning occurs between age sixty and the early seventies, but the precise nature of decline and, more important, its practical effect on learning ability are still unknown. For example, intelligence does appear to drop within a few years of death. This phenomenon, labeled the *terminal drop*, might account at least in part for the decrease in the intellectual functioning of older adults. This explanation contrasts with the traditional view that intellectual impairment is a universal condition of advancing age (Labouvie-Vief, 1990; Troll, 1982). In line with this observation, only a few studies have addressed the intellectual abilities of healthy adults beyond the age of seventy. In one longitudinal comparison of subjects ranging in age from seventy-three to ninety-nine, researchers found that although many of the subjects showed some decline in abilities, more than half displayed no such changes, even at the older ages (Field, Schaie, and Leino, 1988). In a more recent study of eighteen people between the ages of 100 and 106, these "centenarians reported rich late-life learning experiences, . . . the majority of [which] occurred through social interactions" (Fenimore, 1997, p. 57).

Definitions of Intelligence

There is no universal agreement as to what constitutes intelligence. Therefore, when we speak about changes in intellectual ability as we age, a key question must be answered: What do we mean by intelligence? When intelligence is defined as a unitary property, the research tends to confirm that intelligence does indeed decline with age, although again the point of the departure for that decline often varies (Schaie and Willis, 1986). Yet when intelligence is defined as a multifaceted entity, the response tends to be that some of our abilities decline, while others remain stable or even increase (Baltes, 1993; Baltes, Dittmann-Kohli, and Dixon, 1984; Schaie, 1979, 1987, 1996; Sternberg and Berg, 1987).

The best example of this kind of thinking is seen in the study of fluid and crystallized intelligence, where it is hypothesized that fluid intelligence decreases with age whereas crystallized intelligence first increases and then remains relatively stable (Horn, 1982). Intertwined with this idea of multidimensional intelligence is an even more fundamental question: Are the primary factors that have been identified as the building blocks of intelligence, such as verbal and numerical abilities, the foundations on which all intellectual skills are developed for a lifetime? Or are different kinds of intellectual abilities, such as those needed for everyday learning, of greater importance for learning in adulthood? (See Gardner, 1983, 1995; Labouvie-Vief, 1990; Schaie, 1987, 1996; Scribner, 1984; Sternberg, 1986b, 1996b; Sternberg and Wagner, 1986.) These are questions for which no clear answers are yet forthcoming, but common sense would tell us must be addressed more fully.

Types of Tests

Behind every intelligence test is a definition of intelligence, whether given directly or implied by the test's author. Thus, it is apparent that generalizations about intelligence and about the aging process are also affected by the tests used.

Most research on the effects of intelligence and aging has been conducted using either the WAIS-R or the PMA. The question then arises as to whether either of these two measures captures a holistic picture of adult intelligence. Some would say that they do (for example, Schaie, 1979, 1987), while others have raised serious questions about their validity for adult learners (Sternberg, 1986a, 1996b; Sternberg and Wagner, 1986). Another criticism of both of these tests, and others like them, has been their inclusion of timed items. All of the PMA subtests are timed, and about half of the subtests in the WAIS-R are timed. Is a timed test, particularly one involving perceptual motor function, a valid measure of intelligence, especially for older adults? Some would choose to eliminate this factor of speed in assessing intelligence. Moreover, questions have been raised about the language of the test items, which may be biased toward a younger age cohort.

Research Methods

The research designs employed in investigations of changes in intelligence over the life span have also generated much discussion in the literature. Results of cross-sectional studies, those that compare one-time test scores of different age groups (twenty, forty, and sixty years old, for example), have been misinterpreted to show that as we age, our intelligence declines. (See Botwinick, 1977; Knox, 1977; Schaie and Willis, 1986.) Findings from longitudinal studies, however, usually support a very different conclusion. Based primarily on re-administration of intelligence tests over time and to the same group of people, various longitudinal investigations demonstrate that intellectual abilities of groups of older people are remarkably stable over time (Ivnik and others, 1995; Rabbitt and others, 1993; Schaie, 1994, 1996). However, the group data appear to mask individual changes within each of the cohort groups. Botwinick (1977, p. 582), reflecting on this problem of research designs, has observed that "the cross-sectional method may spuriously magnify age decline, and the longitudinal method may minimize it." In cross-sectional investigations, the background and experiences of the different cohorts being studied may cloud the results due to such factors as formal educational attainment and health. Moreover younger cohorts, especially those of college students in their twenties, may be more "testwise" than those comprising people in their sixties and seventies. In longitudinal studies, on the other hand, there are problems of selective attrition and dropout.

In response to this problem, researchers have adopted alternative designs to control some of the biases inherent when only a simple cross-sectional or longitudinal design is used. (See Bee, 1996, and Schaie and Willis, 1986, for a description of these designs). Schaie and his associates, as part of the Seattle Longitudinal Study, provide the best example of the work using these alternative designs (Schaie, 1979, 1994, 1996; Schaie and Hertzog, 1983; Schaie and Labouvie-Vief, 1974; Schaie and Parham, 1977; Schaie, Willis, and O'Hanlon, 1994). The primary variables for this study were the five measures of psychological competence from the PMA tests described in the previous section. The data for the study were collected from more than five thousand subjects over a thirty-five-year period in six testing cycles. With six cross-sectional studies, in addition to longitudinal data, the researchers were able to do a number of different forms of analysis, such as cross-sequential and cohort sequential. In essence, the cross-sectional data showed a typical pattern of intellectual decline, while the longitudinal data suggested little if any decline of any practical consequence until after the mid- to late sixties. Even "this decrement is modest until the 80s are reached, and for most individuals it is not a linear phenomenon but occurs in stair-step fashion" (Schaie, 1994, p. 308). Schaie and others attributed the differences in findings between the two research designs to cohort variation—differences between the generations versus differences in the ages of subjects. These cohort variations are, in turn, attributed to higher educational levels of succeeding generations and overall better nutrition and health care that may have resulted in superior physiological brain functioning.

Schaie's (1996) overarching conclusion from this vast array of data is that any significant reductions in intelligence do not occur in most persons until their eighties or nineties and then not in all abilities or for all individuals. "Even at such advanced ages, competent behavior can be expected by many persons in familiar circumstances. Much of the observed loss occurs in highly challenging, complex, or stressful situations" (Schaie, 1996, p. 273), versus the everyday tasks of life. Schaie (1994) and his colleagues have also isolated variables that reduce the risk of cognitive decline in old age, among them, absence of cardiovascular and other chronic diseases, living in favorable environmental circumstances, substantial involvement in activities, maintenance of high levels of perceptual processing speed into old age, being married to a spouse of high cognitive status, and rating one's self as satisfied with one's life.

INTELLIGENCE, AGING, AND ADULT LEARNING

Among the many new ideas about intellectual functioning in adulthood, three ideas surface as the most intriguing and useful to educators. The first is the framing of more holistic conceptions of adult intelligence that are grounded in the real lives of adults of all colors, races, and ethnic backgrounds. Theorists such as Gardner (1983, 1995) and Sternberg (1996a, 1996b) have moved the boundaries of intelligence beyond just the minds of individuals and have challenged researchers and practitioners to consider how the individual and the context interact to shape intellectual functioning in adulthood. They have also moved intelligence out of the hallowed hallways of schools and universities, which have always placed more value on academic skills and abilities, into how people function in all aspects of life. Sternberg (1994b) has added a further idea to understanding of the mind in context: that of the "luck" or "whoops" factor. Each of us is born with different gifts and into different circumstances. Some of us are lucky enough to find places where our gifts have been prized and nurtured (luck factor), while others, no matter what the individual effort, are never recognized or are blocked by circumstances beyond their control (whoops factor).

Second, researchers such as Schaie (1994, 1996) are creating a greater understanding of the internal and external factors that can strengthen intellectual abilities. This is especially important as life expectancy has increased dramatically, especially in developed nations. We may not have control over all of these factors, such as disease or high levels of perceptual processing speed; however, individuals can control other variables such as maintaining activity levels and effecting public policy decisions benefiting older adults (Peterson and Masunaga, 1998). With further exploration of both mainstream and alternative theories of intelligence, our sense is that other controllable factors will be isolated as well.

Third, educators of adults have tremendous opportunities to help ensure that adult learners, especially older adults, are provided a variety of educational opportunities to inhibit decline and expand our intellectual capacity. This assertion is premised on the assumptions that adult intelligence encompasses far more than results on traditional IQ tests and that researchers have identified, and will continue to isolate, numerous other factors on which intelligence depends (for example, Herasymowych, 1997; Schaie, 1996; Schaie and Willis, 1986; Sternberg, 1996a). We need to think through carefully what intellectual abilities and skills are the most useful for adults, both young and old, and could be amenable to educational interventions. Good models of such materials are Perkins's (1995) book on the science of the learnable intelligence, Weisinger's (1998) work on emotional intelligence at work, and Herasymowych's (1997) ideas on increasing intelligence through action learning. Herasymowych (1997), for example, developed and successfully tested a practical model for increasing managers' capacity for reflecting on their experience critically, using the literature on the learning cycle, action learning, and learnable intelligence. And Perkins (1995) describes a number of programs in which the teaching of intelligence, and more specifically what he terms reflective intelligence, was effectively taught. Perkins views reflective intelligence in adults as being particularly supportive of "coping with novelty . . . [and] thinking contrary to certain natural trends" (pp. 112–113).

SUMMARY

In this chapter we discussed the concept of intelligence and how different ways of viewing intelligence can better help us understand learning in adulthood. The most often used paradigm of intelligence is the psychometric tradition, which assumes that intelligence is a measurable quantity. First conceptualized from this tradition as a single factor of general ability, the construct has broadened to include the notion that there are multiple forms of intellectual ability, such as those proposed by Horn (1976), Cattell (1963), and Guilford (1967). Commonly used tests of adult intelligence that fit within this psychometric tradition include the Wechsler Adult Intelligence Scale–Revised and the Primary Mental Abilities Test. Two issues that have surfaced with the use of these types of tests are the test items and the social and policy implications of IQ scores.

Challenges to the psychometric tradition have come primarily from scholars who question whether what is measured as intelligence through this tradition has any relationship to what these scholars have termed real-world or practical intelligence and how context affects development. Three of the most prominent theorists who represent this alternative view of intelligence are Gardner (1983), Sternberg (1985, 1996b), and Goleman (1995). The contextual perspective of intelligence, which often includes the notion of practical and emotional intelligence, acknowledges the importance of the intersection of the mind and the outside world as critical in gaining a clearer understanding of intelligence. What this acknowledgment means is that intelligence has been defined differently by people of varying cultural backgrounds and social classes.

The question of whether adults retain their intellectual abilities as they age has not been definitively answered. Four key factors on which the age and intelligence controversies center are the definition of age or aging, definitions of intelligence, types of tests used to measure intelligence, and research methods and their pitfalls. The consensus is that significant reductions in intelligence do not occur in most people until their eighties or nineties, and then not in all abilities or for all individuals. In addition, a number of variables reducing the risk of intellectual decline in old age have been isolated, such as living in favorable circumstances and maintaining substantial involvement in activities. What this means is that we need to replace the stereotype of the old dog and new tricks with a somewhat different adage: "And so we come to the general conclusion the old dog can learn new tricks, but the answer is not a direct and simple one. . . . He is less likely to gamble on the results, particularly when he is not convinced that the new trick is any better than the old tricks which served him so well in the past. He may not learn the new trick as rapidly as he did in the past, but learn it he does. Further, the best evidence seems to indicate that, if he starts out as a clever young pup, he is very likely to end up as a wise old hound" (Bischof, 1969, p. 224).

The chapter concludes with an exploration of three ideas about intellectual functioning in adulthood that are particularly intriguing and useful for educators of adults: alternative conceptions of adult intelligence that do not rely on psychometric measurement as their foundation, factors that have been isolated as either halting any decrement or even increasing adults' intellectual capacities, and the tremendous potential that educators of adults have for providing learning opportunities that can strengthen adults' intellectual abilities.

PART THREE

The Learning Process

Understanding learning in adulthood is like piecing together a puzzle; there are many parts that must be fitted together before the total picture emerges. The individual learner and the context in which the learning takes place are key pieces of this puzzle. A third piece is the learning process. To be better learners ourselves, and to be better facilitators of other people's learning, we need to understand how learning occurs and whether adults learn differently than children do. Do adults have different capabilities and ways of processing material? If so, how do these differences affect their ability to learn? What role does experience play in adult learning? And how does traditional learning theory inform our understanding about learning in adulthood? These crucial questions are addressed in the following chapters.

Chapter Nine focuses on memory and cognition and how brain structures and functioning affect learning. After reviewing how memory works, we turn to the different components of memory—sensory, working, and long-term memory—and how age may or may not affect an adult's ability to remember. Other important aspects of cognition that we discuss are the concepts of schemas, how prior knowledge and experience affect learning, and the differences between cognitive style and learning style. Although the major work in cognition has been done primarily with children and computer modeling, many educators have generalized the findings to include learning in adulthood but without the necessary verification studies. Therefore, the focus of this chapter is on work oriented toward adult learning. The final area we explore in Chapter Nine is one of the most fascinating frontiers in the study of learning, the neurobiological basis of learning. Although neurobiologists have provided captivating descriptions of how the human brain is organized and functions, making any direct connections between what we have learned about the brain and specific learning interventions is yet to come (Bruer, 1997). Rather, what we have are tentative and often tantalizing hypotheses about the neurobiology of learning.

In Chapter Ten we explore the role of experience and learning, which has a long legacy in the writings on adult learning. Discussed first in the chapter are representative theories that offer varying conceptual views of the process of learning from experience, including the seminal work of Dewey (1938) and the more recent work of such scholars as Jarvis (1987a), Boud and Walker (1990), Bateson (1994), and Usher, Bryant, and Johnston (1997). Although the focus of this work has been on individual learners, in recent years there has been a shift to understanding how the context affects learning and how it is an integral component of the learning process. We then describe reflective practice, one of the major ways that educators have structured learning from experience. We conclude the chapter with an overview of situated cognition and descriptions of two instructional approaches—cognitive apprenticeship and anchored instruction—that are based in situated cognition, stressing how "authentic experiences" grounded in real-life situations are viewed as one of the key components in operationalizing this concept.

Part Three closes with a chapter reviewing five traditional theories of learning. Beginning with the earliest developed orientation to learning, behaviorism, the chapter goes on to review cognitivism, humanism, social learning theory, and constructivism. Each of these orientations, which offer very different explanations of learning, has something to contribute to the understanding of the learning process. We examine each theory in terms of its major proponents, its explanation of the learning process, the purpose of education, the role of the learner, and the influence each has had on adult education.

CHAPTER NINE

Memory, Cognition, and the Brain

O ne of the predominant views about adult learning is that learning is an internal process; it involves something happening inside our heads. Cognitive scientists, primarily from the discipline of psychology, have had the longest history of research in this arena. What cognitive scientists do is "attempt to discover the mental functions and processes that underlie observed behavior" (Bruer, 1997, p. 10). These mental functions and processes include, but are not limited to, the study of how people receive, store, retrieve, transform, and transmit information. Neurobiologists, on the other hand, "study the anatomy, physiology, and pathology of the nervous system" (Taylor, 1996, p. 301), including the brain and related systems. They are primarily interested in the structures of the brain and how the brain actually works, including its electrical and chemical systems. With more recent technological advances, like magnetic resonance imaging (MRI) and positron emission tomography (PET), neurobiologists have begun to generate actual pictures of how the brain operates.

In using work from both the cognitive and neurobiological sciences to talk about learning in adulthood, care must be taken because the majority of studies in these two areas have been done with children (for the cognitive sciences) or with animals (in the neurosciences). Still, there are some intriguing ideas that have informed the study of adult learning from both perspectives. The work with adult populations related to cognition has been primarily in the area of memory and aging. This chapter first highlights that work, presenting an overview of the information processing framework. Next, we explore the concept of knowledge structures or schemas, the effect of prior knowledge and experience on learning, and cognitive and learning styles. These three topics, which are grounded in the cognitive sciences, are important for educators of adults to understand. Key ideas relating to neurobiology and learning are then reviewed. These include how the brain is organized and functions, and the limitations we currently have in connecting this knowledge about the brain to learning and education. The chapter concludes with a short discussion of the promises of merging the current research in the cognitive and neurobiological sciences for gaining a clearer picture of adult learning.

HUMAN MEMORY

Fear of memory loss is a common concern of people as they age. Parents often observe how much more easily their children can remember such simple things as telephone numbers and computer access codes, while many older adults seem to remember childhood events vividly but sometimes have difficulty remembering the names of people they just met. These observations and images foster the idea that memory loss is a normal result of aging and thus is something we all must accept. Are these perceptions of memory loss accurate, and, if so, what effects do they have on learning in adulthood? Often memory functions are equated with learning or are seen as one of the primary mental processes associated with learning (Huber, 1993). If adults do suffer major changes, especially decline, in their memory functions, it follows that the learning process may also be impaired. To understand how memory can be affected by the aging process, we first need to examine how the process of memory from the cognitive framework is conceptualized.

Since the 1960s, human memory has been studied primarily from the information processing approach (J. Anderson, 1996; Kausler, 1994; Ormrod, 1995; Salthouse, 1992b). The mind is visualized as a computer, with information being entered, stored, and then retrieved as needed. Conceptualizing where people store or file what they learn, termed the *structural aspect of memory,* was the first major focus of study from this perspective. Three categories have been traditionally used to describe the different structures of memory: sensory memory, short-term memory, and long-term memory. More recently there has been a movement away from dividing up the structure of memory in such a definitive manner. This change in thinking has stemmed primarily from the study of working memory, which has been conceptualized in three different ways: as part of long-term memory, as part of or the same as short-term memory, or as the mediator between sensory memory and either long- or short-term memory (J. Anderson, 1996; Kausler, 1994; Ormrod, 1995). For the purposes of our discussion, we discuss human memory within the framework of sensory, working, and long-term memory.

Sensory memory, also called the sensory register, "holds incoming information long enough that it can undergo preliminary cognitive processes" (Ormrod, 1995, p. 218). Primarily through the senses of vision, hearing, and touch, images, sounds, and vibrations are entered into our memory systems. Sensory memory has a very brief storage time of only milliseconds before it either enters our working memory system or is lost. "Working memory is a hypothesized 'entity' or 'process' (the vagueness is deliberate), responsible for preserving information while simultaneously processing the same or other information. . . . The most salient characteristic of working memory is that it has definite limits, a fact made very apparent when one tries to perform a task containing many steps, none of which are difficult to perform in isolation" (Salthouse, 1992a, p. 39). The storage capacity of working memory is estimated to be from 5 to 30 seconds. Long-term memory has an enormous capacity for storage and is that part of the memory structure that retains information for long periods of time. "It includes memory for specific events and general knowledge that has been gleaned from those events over the years" (Ormrod, 1995, p. 225). Long-term memory has been conceptualized as the most complicated component of the memory system, and therefore has received the most attention in the research literature.

In recent years our understanding of long-term memory has moved from viewing it as one monolithic system "to one that is less hierarchical, involving several different kinds of memory, each playing a significant role" (Taylor, 1997b, p. 293). Most of the research on long-term memory has involved explicit (or declarative) memory, "the term used for things which we can consciously recall" (J. Anderson, 1996,

p. 229). "This form of memory is more sensitive and prone to interference, but it is also invaluable, providing the ability for personal autobiography and cultural evolution" (Taylor, 1997b, p. 263). Implicit (or nondeclarative) memory, on the other hand, "concerns itself with memories that we are not conscious we have" (J. Anderson, 1996, p. 229). Although these memories are developed unconsciously and thus form a hidden world we know little about, "people are influenced by [these types of memories] without any awareness they are remembering" (Schacter, 1996, p. 161). Several authors have provided useful descriptions of several forms of implicit memory, including procedural knowledge (skills and habits), category-level knowledge, conditioning, and priming, and they describe practical examples of how these types of implicit memory are used (J. Anderson, 1996; Schacter, 1996; Squire, Knowlton, and Musen, 1993; Taylor, 1997b). Classic examples of implicit memories are riding a bike, which is procedural knowledge, and the "acquisition of rules often found in grammar [involving categorical knowledge]. Grammar is a particularly good example of implicit memory, where people have acquired abstract rules, but are unable to articulate what guides their speech and writing" (Taylor, 1997b, p. 264).

The second major focus of study within the information processing framework has been how we process information. The processing aspect consists of "the mental activities that we perform when we try to put information into memory (learn), or make use of it at some later date (remember)" (Schulz and Ewen, 1988, p. 134). Usually the memory process is divided into three phases (J. Anderson, 1996; Ormrod, 1995; Schacter, 1996). The encoding or acquisition phase is the initial process in which the information is entered into the system. Filing this material for future use is termed the storage or retention phase. The final phase, retrieval, describes how you get material out of storage when needed. Two of the most common methods of retrieval are recall, or bringing forth "to-be-remembered" information, and recognition, which involves choosing from a group of possible answers. As we well remember from our school testing days of essay versus multiple-choice exams, "recall is considered to be a more demanding test of retrieval than is recognition" (Schulz and Ewen, 1988, p. 138).

A number of alternatives have been proposed for how the structural components fit within the process model (J. Anderson, 1996; Ormrod, 1995; Salthouse, 1992a). The most common explanation is that information from our environment is registered within sensory memory through our visual, auditory, and tactile senses. Material is then selectively transferred or encoded into working memory. The control system of selective attention determines what is important enough to be moved into working memory. There is considerable flexibility with what can be done with the information in working memory. It "can be used as a cue to retrieve other information from long-term memory, it can be elaborated, it can be used to form images, it is used in thinking, it can be structured to be placed in long-term or secondary memory, or if nothing is done with it, it can be discarded" (Di Vesta, 1987, p. 211).

Because the functions of working memory are complex and its time and capacity are limited, two major control processes are used to sort and file the data: chunking and automatization. Chunking essentially is organizing the information in groups or patterns (a phone number in three chunks—970–351–2119, for example), while automatization allows for a chunk of information to become so familiar that a person can handle it without recall thinking (Kausler, 1994; Ormrod, 1995). The material structured in working memory for long-term memory is then encoded into that memory bank for permanent storage. The information "is rarely stored in long-term memory exactly as it was received. Individuals tend to remember the 'gist' of what they see and hear rather than word-for-word sentences or precise mental images" (Ormrod, 1995, p. 226). The material is organized "so that related pieces of information tend to be associated together" (Ormrod, 1995, p. 226) by highly organized episodes (by time and place) or by meaningful relations to earlier stored material. This type of processing is sometimes referred to as deep processing versus the shallow processing done at the working memory level. The information is then retrieved as needed from this long-term storage.

MEMORY AND AGING

A great deal of research from the information processing framework has been conducted on the topic of memory and aging (J. Anderson, 1996; Kausler, 1994; Rybash, Hoyer, and Roodin, 1986; Salthouse, 1985, 1992a; Siegler, Poon, Madden, and Welsh, 1996; A. D. Smith, 1996). The general consensus from that work is that certain memory functions do decline with age. Nevertheless, a number of authors have cautioned that because of methodological considerations and the variables being studied, this work must be interpreted with care. The vast majority of it has focused on comparing young adults (usually college students) with older adults by using cross-sectional designs (Bee, 1996). These two factors combined make it difficult to generalize across age groups because of subject and cohort bias. Subject bias comes from using people in a study who do not necessarily represent the general population (such as college students versus the broad population of young adults). Cohort bias or effect "is any difference between groups of adults of varying ages that is due not to age or aging, or to any other developmental process, but simply to the fact that the different age groups have grown up under different historical and cultural circumstances" (Bee, 1996, p. 11). Moreover, most of this research has been conducted primarily in laboratory settings using memory tasks and activities, such as repeating back nonsense words and lists of random numbers. The primary criticism leveled against this type of research on memory is that these tasks and skills are generally artificial and taken out of the context of everyday life. A response to this criticism in recent years has been to design "ecologically valid" research that takes into account the everyday learning demands of adults (Agrawal and Kumar, 1992; N. Anderson, 1996; Knopf, 1995; Langer, 1997; Rybash, Hoyer, and Roodin, 1986). With these limitations in mind, we offer a summary of this research on memory in adulthood.

Sensory and Working Memory

In general, few clearly defined changes have been found in sensory memory as people age. Because there are fairly major changes with age in both vision and hearing, one would expect to see these changes reflected in sensory memory. Yet only minor deficits have been found, although it is often difficult with testing procedures to distinguish between age-related physiological decline in the senses themselves, especially hearing, and actual decrements in the process of sensory memory.

Working memory, on the other hand, with its definite limits, "is considered by many researchers to be a potentially important mediator of the relations between age and cognition" (Salthouse, 1992a, p. 39). More specifically, the processing speed within working memory has been shown to be very important in accounting for differences in the memory performances of older adults (Bors and Forrin, 1995; Salthouse, 1992a, 1992b, 1995; A. D. Smith, 1996). Older adults appear to process materials more slowly, especially ones that are more complex in nature. One of the explanations for this slowing of the processing of information seems to be the "older adults' capacity to simultaneously perform a cognitive task while trying to remember some of the information for a later memory task" (Smith, 1996, p. 241). In other words, it appears to be more difficult for older adults to both respond immediately to whatever stimulus triggered working memory and store pertinent information in long-term memory. Salthouse (1995, p. 124) does caution, however, that this "processing speed interpretation is still at the speculative stage," and much more research needs to be completed on working memory.

Long-Term Memory

As with working memory, age deficits are also more commonly found in long-term memory (Bee, 1996; Rybash, Hoyer, and Roodin, 1986; Smith, 1996). Three major differences have surfaced in long-term memory for older versus younger learners: changes in the encoding or acquisition of material, the retrieval of information, and the speed of processing. Few changes have been noted in the storage or retention capacity of long-term memory over the life span.

The question that often surfaces in reviewing the process related to long-term memory is whether it is more difficult for adults as they age to get information into the system (to encode it) or get it out (to retrieve it). The response to this question appears to be both. It is not yet clear which part of the process creates more difficulty (Bee, 1996; Smith, 1996). Encoding problems are most often associated with the organization of information. Specifically, older adults appear to be less efficient at organizing new material. Possible explanations of why organization is a problem relates to the amount and type of prior knowledge they already possess. According to Ormrod (1995, p. 261), "Storage processes such as meaningful learning and elaboration can occur only to the extent that learners have existing knowledge to which they can connect new material." In addition, "if this new information is clearly viewed by the person as 'wrong' within the context of what they believe about the world, they may sometimes ignore the information altogether" (p. 266). In other words, this type of information may never enter long-term memory because it is incompatible with what the person already knows.

On the retrieval side, changes are most often noted in the recall versus recognition of information. In tests of recall, for example, major differences have been demonstrated for older and younger people, whereas in recognition activities, the differences are small or non-existent, although the retrieval time may be slower (Bee, 1996). Many older adults do "know" things, but "they can not readily or quickly bring [them] to mind. If they are given a hint, or reminded of the item at some later time, the memory [may] come back" (Bee, 1996, p. 162). Another aspect of retrieval that is often taken as a given is that older persons can retrieve "ancient memories" better than younger people, along with the accompanying myth that older people can clearly remember events in their distant past but have trouble recalling recent events. Rather, it appears that this reversal of memory strengths—remote memories are stronger than recent memories—may be a natural phenomenon that occurs at all ages, not just with older people. We all seem better able to recall occurrences that happened to us in the distant or far past than in very recent past.

In terms of the speed of processing, adults do seem to have more difficulty with speeded tasks, especially ones that are complex (as was also noted with working memory). When tests for memory tasks are paced—meaning that the time given per item or between items is fixed—age deficits definitely show an increase (Salthouse, 1985; Smith, 1996). Salthouse (1995) and Smith (1996) account for at least part of these differences in speeded tasks as a slowing of both the encoding and retrieval processes in both long-term and working memory.

In summary, in relation to long-term memory it appears that older adults may not acquire or retrieve information as well as do younger adults, nor do they organize information as effectively. This line of research may have limited generalizability because of the research designs, the subjects, the memory activities tested, and the separation of the research from the real world of the adult learner.

Real-Life Memories

In response to some of the criticisms of memory research just cited, a different approach has been taken by placing memory tasks in the context of everyday adult lives, called functional memory by some researchers (N. Anderson, 1996). This strand of research, which fosters what has been termed ecological validity, has received little attention, primarily because it is affected by so many different variables and is still considered controversial by some researchers (J. Anderson, 1996). The term *ecological validity* assumes that the tasks being studied are meaningful to the person and accurately reflect real-life adult experiences. These studies use a variety of memory tests, from "memory for text" formats, which include reviews of sentences, paragraphs, and stories versus single words and symbols, to memory skills for everyday activities, such as keeping appointments and remembering what items to buy at the grocery store (N. Anderson, 1996; Knopf, 1995; Luszcz, 1992). These studies also address some of the other concerns voiced by scholars of the contextual approach, such as the person's needs and motivation, the specificity of the task, and situational variables. The evidence is mixed as to whether there is less decline when using memories that are grounded in actual situations versus the more artificial tasks used in laboratory studies (Smith, 1996).

Fostering Memory Capacity and Skills

The assumption underlying the research on memory is that memory capacity and skills form one of the keys to how adults learn. Formal memory training, the most structured approach to building memory skills, has been shown to be useful in helping older adults cope with memory deficits (Bee, 1996; Rybash, Hoyer, and Roodin, 1986). This training has most often focused on the teaching of encoding strategies, such as practicing rehearsal information or fostering the use of mnemonics (devices for helping people improve their memory). For example, Yesavage (1983) taught older adults to improve their name and face recall using visual imagery as a mnemonic. Moreover, Perlmutter and Hall (1985) have suggested teaching adults about metamemory—the understanding of the way the memory system works. A number of authors have suggested ways to integrate training in memory skills into formal learning programs for adults: providing both verbal and written cues, such as advance organizers and overheads, when introducing new material to learners; using mnemonics and rehearsal strategies; and giving opportunities to apply the new material as soon after the presentation as possible. (For a thorough discussion of these ideas, see Knox, 1986; Di Vesta, 1987; Ormrod, 1995; West, Farmer, and Wolff, 1991.)

Adults learning on their own may also find it helpful to use memory aids in their learning activities (Rybash, Hoyer, and Roodin, 1986). These can come in many forms, from structured checklists for learning a new skill to personal note taking on items of interest. For example, someone might jot down in a pocket notebook interesting new words she encountered each day. She could then practice using these words until they became a natural part of her vocabulary.

Cognitive psychologists, in addition to their work on memory and aging, have provided us with a number of other important concepts related to learning in adulthood. Three of those concepts—knowledge structures, the role of prior knowledge and experience, and learning and cognitive styles—are discussed next in the chapter.

KNOWLEDGE STRUCTURES

Within the cognitive framework, the emphasis is on what learners know versus how they behave. This knowing involves both the acquisition of knowledge, discussed in the section on human memory, and the actual structure of that knowledge (J. Anderson, 1996; Bruer, 1993; Cervero, 1988; Shuell, 1986). In this perspective, considerable importance is placed on prior knowledge as well as new knowledge being accumulated. Since it is assumed that most adults have a greater store of prior knowledge than children, understanding the role that this knowledge plays in learning is critical. In thinking through the possible connections of prior knowledge to learning in adulthood, the concept of schemas provides a useful framework. (See J. Anderson, 1996; Di Vesta, 1987; Ormrod, 1995; Rumelhart and Norman, 1978.)

Schemas "represent categorical knowledge . . . , [that is] concepts in terms of supersets, parts, and other attribute value pairs" (J. Anderson, 1996, pp. 155–156). "People often form schemas about events as well as objects; such event schemas are often called scripts" (Ormrod, 1995, p. 264). These schemas, which may be embedded within other schemas or may stand alone, are filled with descriptive materials and are seen as the building blocks of the cognitive process. Schemas are not just passive storehouses of experience, however; they are also active processes whose primary function is to facilitate the use of knowledge. "It seems that schemas are a major mechanism for elaborating material . . . , and are also a major mechanism for reconstructing memories" (J. Anderson, 1996, p. 216).

We all carry around with us our own individualized set of schemata that reflect both our experiences and our worldview. Therefore, as adult learners, each of us comes to a learning situation with a somewhat different configuration of knowledge and how it can be used. For example, some participants in a workshop on diversity in the workplace may bring to that experience firm beliefs that diversity is a worthwhile goal based on their positive experiences with women and people of color. Others may not believe in diversity at all, and view it as an easy way for "some people" to get hired. And still others may be downright angry, either because they believe they have been discriminated against or passed over for a promotion because they were of the "wrong color" or gender. Therefore, each learner in the workshop not only comes with different schema sets but also departs having learned very different things—even though all were exposed to basically the same material.

In categorizing schema types, two kinds of knowledge are most often distinguished: declarative knowledge and procedural knowledge. Anderson (1993) describes declarative knowledge as "factual knowledge that people can report or describe"; procedural knowledge, by contrast, "is knowledge people can only manifest in performance" (p. 18). We may be able to describe two or three different models for instruction (declarative knowledge), for example, but when we try to put these models into action (procedural knowledge), we may fail miserably. Because the question is open whether learning facts or knowing how to perform comes first, the scenario just described could also be reversed: a person may be an excellent instructor and yet have no specific knowledge of instructional models.

According to Rumelhart and Norman (1978), three different modes of learning fit the schema framework: *accretion,* meaning the daily accumulation of information that is usually equated with learning facts; *tuning,* which includes slow and gradual changes in current schema; and *restructuring,* involving both the creation of new schema and reorganization of those already stored. Many current models of memory reflect only learning by the accretion or fact-gathering process. Educators, however, are well aware that most learning in adulthood goes far beyond the simple memorization of facts. The expectation is that adults will be able to put those facts to good use in their everyday living, whether as workers, parents, spouses, friends, and so on. Therefore, the processes of tuning and restructuring of information, as well as both declarative and procedural knowledge, become vital in adult learning. The general processes of problem solving and critical thinking are good examples of the importance of these constructs. Specifically, in most problem-solving situations, we are trying to fit new ideas (declarative knowledge) and ways of acting (procedural knowledge) into earlier patterns of thinking and doing (our current schemas). If we are unable to change our earlier thought patterns (that is, fine-tune or restructure them), our chances of being able to frame and act on problems from a different perspective are remote, if not impossible.

In addition to these three different modes of learning (accretion, tuning, and restructuring) cognitive scientists also cite the importance of a fourth process, metacognition, defined as "the ability to think about thinking, to be consciously aware of oneself as a problem solver, and to monitor and control one's mental processing" (Bruer, 1993, p. 67). Metacognition is often viewed as the highest level of mental activity and is especially needed for complex problem solving.

PRIOR KNOWLEDGE AND EXPERIENCE

One key assumption underlying the concept of schemas is that "learning is cumulative in nature—nothing has meaning or is learned in isolation from prior experience. This assumption has a pedigree dating back to Dewey, who said, 'no one can think about anything without experience and information about it'" (Cervero, 1988, p. 41). In addition, many adult educators, such as Knowles (1980), Caffarella (1994), MacKeracher (1996), and Daley (1998), have also spoken to the importance of acknowledging adults' prior knowledge and experience as integral to the learning process. In exploring the role of prior knowledge and experience in learning, two ideas are important: the amount of prior knowledge and experience and its nature.

In terms of the amount of prior knowledge and experience one possesses, the difference between those who know a great deal about what they are experiencing (termed experts) and those who know very little (novices) is key. A person can be an expert in a variety of areas from growing tomatoes to skiing. According to Sternberg (1995, p. 10), "Perhaps the most fundamental difference between experts and novices is that experts bring more knowledge to solving problems . . . and do so more effectively than novices." In addition, experts are able to solve problems faster and in a more economical way, have stronger self-monitoring skills, and are able to view and solve problems at a deeper level than novices (Ferry and Ross-Gordon, 1998; Sternberg, 1995; Tennant and Pogson, 1995). J. Anderson (1996, pp. 283, 292, 294) has observed that experts appear to solve problems more effectively and more quickly because of the following processing changes:

- They switch from explicit use of declarative [factual] knowledge to direct application of procedural [performance] knowledge.

- They learn the sequences of actions required to solve the problem or portions of the problem [known as tactical learning].

- They develop new constructs for representing key aspects of a problem.

- They can recognize chunks in problems which are patterns of elements that repeat over problems.

J. Anderson (1996, p. 273) contends that "no one develops expertise without a great deal of hard work . . . [and] the difference between . . . novices and . . . experts increases as we look at more difficult problems."

In further examination of the issue of a novice versus expert learner, many authors (for example, J. Anderson, 1996; Glaser, 1984, 1987; Glaser and Chi, 1988; Tennant and Pogson, 1995) have noted that being an expert is related to certain domains or subject matter areas. More specifically, experts acquire ways of organizing problems that are "optimally suited to problems in a [specific] domain" (J. Anderson, 1996, p. 289). And "as people become more expert in a domain, they develop a better ability to store problem information in long-term memory and to retrieve it" (p. 296). Educators have often observed that being an expert in one area does not necessarily translate into being an expert in another, no matter what the learner's motivation or background. Many graduate students, for example, although very perceptive and advanced in their own fields of study, may have a great deal of trouble completing statistical and advanced research design courses that are quantitatively based. This is especially true of students who are not mathematically inclined. Moreover, some people become experts in carpentry or tracing genealogy, while others view these tasks as beyond their capabilities.

Therefore, in helping adults connect their current experience to their prior knowledge and experience, we need to be knowledgeable about the amount of prior knowledge they possess in a particular area and design our learning activities accordingly. For example, in teaching a group of expert instructors of adults, it probably does little good to outline just one instructional model, even when this model is the newest and supposedly the most complete model. They can probably think of every exception under the sun as to why this model will not work with all of their students. It would make more sense to ask these instructors to look at alternative models, including this new model, then have them problem-solve which of these models or parts of these models have worked best for them in what type of situations. By following this plan, the participants' level of expertise would be acknowledged, they would be asked to think more deeply about the many situations they have faced in teaching, and they would need to use their problem-solving abilities related to their prior knowledge and experience as instructors.

It would be helpful, in addition, to know how the transition between being a novice and being an expert takes place in order to facilitate learning from prior knowledge and experience. To this end, J. Anderson (1996), Glaser (1987), Chi, Glaser, and Farr (1988), and Sternberg (1995), among others, have provided comprehensive descriptions of the development of expertise that are useful in designing learning activities to assist adults in moving along the continuum from novice to expert.

COGNITIVE STYLE AND LEARNING STYLE

Another important aspect of cognition related to learning in adulthood is the notion of cognitive style. Cognitive styles are characterized as consistencies in information processing that develop in concert with underlying personality traits. They are reflected in "how individuals typically receive and process information" (Joughin, 1992, p. 4) and encompass the ways people see and make sense of their world and attend to different parts of their environment. Some people tend to look at problems from a global perspective, while others are more interested in taking in the detail (Flannery, 1993c). The latter types, which Flannery labels analytical information processors, want information in a step-by-step manner and tend to perceive information in an abstract and objective manner. In contrast "the global learners process information in a simultaneous manner. The ideas or experiences are seen all at once, not in any observable order" (Flannery, 1993c, p. 16). In addition, global learners perceive information in a concrete and subjective manner.

A number of cognitive-style dimensions, including the concepts of global and analytical processing styles, have been identified through research (Bonham, 1987; Joughin, 1992; Kolb, 1984; Messick, 1976, 1984, 1996). The outstanding feature of these varying dimensions is their tendency to be bipolar. In contrasting people's cognitive styles, we tend to label people as being at either end of the continuum, which is "probably not complex enough to capture the essence of individual differences among human beings" (Bonham, 1988, p. 15). For the most part, cognitive styles are considered relatively stable.

Although a great deal of research has been conducted on cognitive styles, much of the research has been done with children, and "no style has led to clear implications with respect to adult learning" (Joughin, 1992, p. 4). Therefore it is still unclear how this work may relate to helping adults learn more effectively. Hiemstra and Sisco (1990) have conjectured that knowledge about cognitive styles might assist instructors in predicting how learners are "likely to form typical learning tasks such as remembering, selecting, comparing, focusing, reflecting, and analyzing" information (p. 241). In addition, Flannery (1993c) has asserted that "teaching, texts and structures can be adapted to teach to different" cognitive styles (p. 19).

A related yet somewhat different phenomenon is the concept of learning style. The literature describing cognitive and learning style is rather confusing; some authors use the two terms interchangeably (see Tennant, 1988; Toye, 1989), others view *cognitive style* as the more encompassing term (Kirby, 1979), and still others see *learning style* as the more inclusive term (Hiemstra and Sisco, 1990; James and others, 1996). Clearly there is no common definition of learning style, nor is there a unified theory on which this work is based (Bonham, 1987, 1988; Claxton and Murrell, 1987; Flannery, 1993a; Sternberg, 1990b). Learning style "attempts to explain learning variation between individuals in the way they approach learning tasks" (Toye, 1989, pp. 226–227). More specifically, James and Blank (1993, pp. 47–48) "define *learning style* as the complex manner in which, and conditions under which, learners most efficiently and most effectively perceive, process, store and recall what they are attempting to learn." Although this definition and other parallel definitions of learning style (for example, Smith, 1982) are quite similar to cognitive style, it appears that the real difference between these two concepts lies in the emphasis placed by learning style researchers on the learning situation versus the more general notion of how people perceive, organize, and process information. Therefore, those who study learning style usually place the emphasis on both the learner and the learning environment (Hiemstra and Sisco, 1990; James and Blank, 1993).

It is also important to acknowledge that learning styles may be in part culturally based (Anderson, 1988; Bell, 1994; Brookfield, 1990; Macias, 1989). Anderson (1988, p. 4), for example, asserts that "it would seem feasible that different ethnic groups, with different cultural histories, different adaptive approaches to reality, and different socialization practices, would differ concerning their respective learning styles." He goes on to observe that "there is no such thing as one style being 'better than another,' although in our country [the United States] the Euro-American style is projected by most institutions as the one which is most valued" (p. 6). Anderson characterizes the Euro-American style as primarily field independent, analytic, and non-affective, which to him reflects primarily male and acculturated minority views. In contrast, he views a non-Western style (meaning such groups as American Indians, African Americans, and many Euro-American females) as field dependent, relational and holistic, and affective. Bell's (1994) research with African Americans confirms some of Anderson's thinking on learning styles. Bell's findings support "a holistic African American learning style . . . which consistently reflects a relational style. . . . The relational style has been defined as a preference for a whole-to-parts (rather than parts-to-whole) analysis of information, a perceptual vigilance for person social cues over object cues, and a preference for contextually 'rich' over contextually 'sterile' (abstract) learning/problem-solving structures" (p. 57).

Despite the lack of uniform agreement about which elements constitute a learning style, it seems apparent that learning-style inventories, unlike most cognitive-style instruments, have proved useful in helping both learners and instructors alike become aware of their personal learning styles and their strengths and weaknesses as learners and teachers. What must be remembered in using these instruments, however, is that each inventory measures different things, depending on how the instrument's author has defined learning style. In using the variety of learning-style inventories available, it is therefore important to help learners understand how the author of the instrument has conceptualized learning style. (For a review of these instruments see Smith, 1982; Bonham, 1987; James and Blank, 1993.) Some of the most popular instruments used with adults have been Kolb's Learning Style Inventory (1984) and Grasha-Riechmann's Student Learning Style Scales (Hruska, Riechmann, and Grasha, 1982). It is also important to remember that "learning style instruments are best used as tools to create awareness that learners differ and as starting points for individual learners' continued investigation of themselves as learners" (Hiemstra and Sisco, 1990, p. 240). This careful use of learning-style inventories, especially in making programming decisions about learners, is especially crucial; James and Blank (1993, p. 55) have observed that "although various authors claim strong reliability and validity for their instruments, a solid research base for many of these claims does not exist."

More recently Sternberg (1994a, 1996c) has proposed a new term, *thinking styles,* which seems very similar, if not identical, to *learning styles.* Sternberg (1994a) defines a thinking style as "a preferred way of using one's abilities. It is not in itself an ability but rather a preference. Hence, various styles are not good or bad" (p. 36). Although Sternberg has described his theory of thinking styles primarily in the context of children, and more specifically childhood education, many components of his theory would also be useful in understanding the thinking patterns of adults. His work on thinking styles is grounded in ten general characteristics of styles, such as "styles can vary across tasks and situations, people differ in strengths of stylistic preferences, styles are socialized, and styles can vary across the life span—they are not fixed" (Sternberg, 1996c, pp. 349–350). Sternberg uses the concept of mental self-government, patterned after the kind of governments and government branches that exist worldwide, to describe his theory of thinking styles. "According to this theory, people can be understood in terms of the functions, forms, levels, scope, and leanings of government" (Sternberg, 1996c, p. 351). Table 9.1 sets out the styles. Sternberg (1994a, p. 39) emphasizes the importance of taking into account people's thinking styles in designing learning programs and cautions that most instructors are best at teaching people "who match their own styles of thinking and learning . . . and tend to overestimate the extent to which their students share their own styles."

In summary, scholars studying learning from a cognitive perspective have added a great deal to our knowledge about learning in adulthood. Some of the major contributions described thus far in this chapter are our understanding of memory and how aging may affect memory processes, how our knowledge is organized in schemas, what effect prior knowledge and experience have on learning, and the concepts of cognitive and learning style. In Chapter Ten we review another view of learning, situated cognition, to which cognitive scientists have also contributed. We now turn to a discussion of one of the newest research arenas related to adult learning, the neurobiology of learning.

Style	Characterization
Functions	
Legislative	Likes to create, invent, design, do things his or her own way, have little assigned structure
Executive	Likes to follow directions, do what he or she is told, be given structure
Judicial	Likes to judge and evaluate people and things
Forms	
Monarchic	Likes to do one thing at a time, devoting to it almost all energy and resources
Hierarchic	Likes to do many things at once, setting priorities for which to do when and how much time and energy to devote to each
Oligarchic	Likes to do many things at once, but has trouble setting priorities
Anarchic	Likes to take a random approach to problems; dislikes systems, guidelines, and practically all constraints
Levels	
Global	Likes to deal with big picture, generalities, abstractions
Local	Likes to deal with details, specifics, concrete examples
Scope	
Internal	Likes to work alone, focus inward, be self-sufficient
External	Likes to work with others, focus outward, be interdependent
Leaning	
Liberal	Likes to do things in new ways, defy conventions
Conservative	Likes to do things in tried-and-true ways, follow conventions

Table 9.1. Styles of Mental Self-Government.

Source: Adapted from Sternberg, Robert J. "Allowing for Thinking Styles." *Educational Leadership*, Volume 52, Number 3, pages 36–40. (Figure 1, page 38). Alexandria, VA: Association for Supervision and Curriculum Development. Copyright © 1994 ASCD. Reprinted by permission. All rights reserved.

NEUROBIOLOGY AND LEARNING

Although the cognitive sciences have contributed a great deal to our knowledge about learning in adulthood, one of the most fascinating frontiers in the study of learning is that of the neurobiological basis of learning. This work is grounded in the study of neurobiology: "the life sciences that involve the anatomy, physiology, and the pathology of the nervous system" (Taylor, 1996). Although most of our knowledge about the linkage of our brains to our minds is currently only in the form of working hypotheses, what we might learn from scientists who study the physical functions of the brain and its related systems has the possibility of moving our understanding of learning significantly forward. Viewing the devastation of the memory and learning capacity of a person with advanced Alzheimer's disease or a massive stroke brings home to each of us the innate and yet almost mystical ways in which the brain functions.

The image of the computer has been the primary way we have pictured how the brain works. But more recently scholars have argued that the computer is "an inappropriate model because a computer is developed, programmed, and run by an external force, and our brain isn't" (Sylwester, 1995, p. 18). Edelman (as cited by Sylwester, 1995) has suggested a better model:

> That the electrochemical dynamics of our brain's development and operation resemble the rich, layered ecology of a jungle environment. A jungle has no external developer, no predetermined goals. Indeed, it's a messy place characterized more by organic excess than by goal-directed economy and efficiency. No one organism or group runs the jungle. . . . So it is with our brain, Edelman argues. Think of the vast number of highly connected neural networks that make up our brains as the neural equivalent of the complex set of jungle organisms that respond variously to environmental challenges. The natural selection processes that shape a jungle over long periods of time also have shaped our brain over an extensive period, and they shape our brain's neural networks over our lifetime. [Sylwester, 1995, pp. 18–19]

Thus, from Sylwester's perspective, "learning becomes a delicate but powerful dialogue between genetics and the environment. . . . Our brain is powerfully shaped by genetics, development, and experience— but it also then actively shapes the nature of our own experiences and the culture in which we live" (p. 21). This image of the brain as a jungle raises in Sylwester's mind, among others (for example, *Scientific American*, 1992), many questions about how we conceptualize learning and what the implications might be in the future for the teaching and learning process. What becomes very clear is that the connections between what we know about how the brain functions and learning are very complex, and therefore the majority of work is still in its infancy in terms of having practical relevance to adult learning.

The way the brain is organized and functions has captured the notice of the general public as well as continued study by the scientific community (Bissette, 1996; Boucouvalas, 1988b; De Beauport, 1996; Lemonick, 1995; Pert, 1997; Restak, 1995; *Scientific American*, 1992; Sylwester, 1995). "For good reason, the brain is sometimes hailed as the most complex object in the universe. It comprises a trillion cells, 100 billion of them neurons linked in networks that give rise to intelligence, creativity, emotion, consciousness and memory" (Fischback, 1992, p. 51). One of the most striking features of the brain "are the large, seemingly symmetric cerebral hemispheres" (p. 48) that sit on a central core or base. The two hemispheres are connected by the corpus callosum, a large band of nerve fibers that provides interactions between the two sides and allows the two hemispheres to collaborate on many tasks. The largest part of the brain, which consists of these two hemispheres, "contains an outer layer of gray matter called the cerebral cortex and underlying white matter that relays information to the cortex" (Lemonick, 1995, p. 46). The cerebral cortex (or cortex), about the size of an office desk when spread out, is made up of "the most evolutionary ancient part of the cortex [the limbic system] . . . and the larger, younger neocortex [which] is divided into frontal, temporal, parietal and occipital lobes" (Fischback, 1992, p. 51).

The limbic system is "our brain's principal regulator of emotions. It also influences the selection and classification of experiences that our brain stores as long-term memory. . . . Because the limbic system plays important roles in processing both emotion and memory, emotion is an important ingredient in processing many memories" (Sylwester, 1995, p. 44). The amygdala appears to be the main structure within the limbic system for processing emotion, while the hippocampus, also part of the limbic system, appears to play an important role in converting short-term memories into long-term ones. Also embedded within the limbic system are other structures, such as the thalamus and hypothalamus, which also assist in regulating our emotional life and physical safety. The thalamus is an especially important part of the system because it is a major relay center for information coming into the brain. The other four lobes have been found to have very specific, but not exclusive, functions, such as the occipital lobe for vision and the frontal lobe for planning, language expression, and speech. The central core or base of the brain on which the major parts of the brain rest consists of "structures such as the medulla, which regulates the autonomic functions (including respiration, circulation, and digestion), and the cerebellum, which coordinates movement (Fischback, 1992, p. 51).

How information is exchanged within the structures of the brain has fascinated neurobiologists and laypeople alike. Although we have a number of newer technologies, such as magnetic resonance imaging and positron-emission tomography, that give us clearer pictures of the way the brain operates, we still do not know for sure how the system truly functions. One of the most popular visions is that "most messages involve neuron-to-neuron communication . . . [whereby] a neuron constantly receives messages from and sends messages to other cells" (Sylwester, 1995, p. 29). "A typical neuron collects signals from others through a host of fine structures called dendrites. The neuron sends out spikes of electrical activity through a long thin strand known as an axon, which splits into thousands of branches" (Hinton, 1992, p. 145). The communication among neurons is mediated by chemical molecules, called neurotransmitters, "that are released at specialized contacts called synapses" (Fischback, 1992, p. 50). These neurotransmitters can be classified into three types, with the peptides, such as endorphin, being the largest and most complex form. It is at these synapses that "the electrical and chemical brain seemed to merge" (Pert, 1997). The neurotransmitters send either "excitatory or inhibitory messages to the receiving neurons. . . . Neural activity in our brain is fortunately much more inhibitory than excitatory. At any moment, we focus our attention, limit our activity, and ignore most of our memories. Imagine life with a principally excitatory brain that continually attended to everything, carried out all possible actions, and had continual open access to all prior experiences!" (Sylwester, 1995, p. 36).

What is critical about this internal transmission process is that "information in our brain flows in multiplex patterns" (Sylwester, 1995, p. 39) and involves parallel processing. "Parallel processing means that many conscious and unconscious actions occur simultaneously within circuitry that includes all sorts of interconnections and feedback loops. . . . At some level, everything seems connected to everything else" (Sylwester, 1995, pp. 39–40). These multiple connections and patterns mean that information moves not in a linear fashion but in highly complex and multilayered ways. In addition, despite the fact that we continue to lose brain cells as we age, it appears that there is also an inherent "plasticity (i.e., modifiability and regenerative capacity) of the neuronal structures" (Boucouvalas, 1988b, p. 16). In fact, "many structures of the brain appear to be modified by enriching *experiences* (particularly exposure to a variety of experiences). . . . In other words, the brain appears to be a plastic organ responding to shaping and modifiability by interaction with the external culture and environment" (Boucouvalas, 1988b, p. 16).

More recently, Pert (1997) has challenged the idea that the brain is the only part of us that can gather, process, and share information, more specifically emotional messages. Based on her findings that the peptides and other informational or chemical substances and their receptors are found in the body's nerves of all kinds, it would then follow that emotions could be stored and mediated by other parts of the body. Therefore, Pert hypothesizes that "we could no longer consider the emotional brain to be confined to the classical locations of the amygdala, hippocampus, and hypothalamus. . . . These recent discoveries are important for appreciating how memories are stored not only in the brain, but in a *psychosomatic network* extending into the body . . . all the way out along pathways to internal organs and the very surface of our skin. I'd say that the fact memory is encoded or stored at the receptor level means that memory processes are emotion-driven and unconscious (but, like other receptor-mediated processes, can sometimes be made conscious)" (pp. 141, 143). According to Pert,

> What this translates into in everyday experiences is that positive emotional experiences are much more likely to be recalled when we're in an upbeat mood, while negative emotional experiences are recalled more easily when we're already in a bad mood. Not only is memory affected by the mood we're in, but so is actual performance. . . . It doesn't take an expert in emotional theory to recognize that there is a very close intertwining of emotions and memory. For most of us, our earliest and oldest memory is an extremely emotion-laden one. [p. 44]

This recognition that emotion and memory are clearly linked, whether these functions are based primarily in the brain or throughout our bodies, could have enormous implications for how we understand learning in adulthood.

CONNECTIONS TO LEARNING

Connecting what we know about the brain and related systems to learning in adulthood is at best a set of working hypotheses. Although some educators have tried to make very direct correlations by devising what they term *brain-based learning programs* (for example, Caine and Caine, 1994), we still have a long way to go before we can make any really useful linkages that will affect large numbers of adults. This gap between the theoretical knowledge of how the brain and related systems work, and practical applications of that knowledge, has created questionable educational practices.

The major issue has been the simplistic applications some educators have made based on supposed factual knowledge about the brain. As Bruer (1997, p. 4) argues, "Currently we do not know enough about brain development and neural function to link that understanding directly, in any meaningful, defensible way to instruction and educational practice." He observes that even neuroscientists, "while interested in how their research might find application outside the laboratory and clinic, are more guarded in their claims, [and] often . . . puzzled by the neuroscientific results educators choose to cite, by the interpretations educators give those results, and by the conclusions educators draw from them." For example, one of the major applications of brain research to learning has been related to brain hemisphere differences and specializations. The idea that our brains are divided into two hemispheres, or halves, has led some educators to design full programs for the left versus the right brain. By the end of these programs, sponsors claim that people have more fully developed their untapped right or left brain potential. Although there are indeed hemispheric specializations, a number of researchers have pointed out that both hemispheres are active and involved in most tasks and situations (Farley, 1988; Restak, 1995; Springer, 1987; Sylwester, 1995). "For example, the left hemisphere (in most people) processes the objective content of the language—*what* was said—while the right hemisphere processes the emotional content of facial expressions, gestures, and language intonation—*how* it was said. By processing related information from different perspectives, the hemispheres collaborate to produce something that becomes a unified mental experience" (Sylwester, 1995, p. 49).

MERGING RESEARCH FROM THE COGNITIVE AND NEUROBIOLOGICAL SCIENCES

Rather than relying on either neurobiology or cognitive sciences, the promise of connecting what we know about how the brain functions and learning comes primarily from the merger of the two sciences (Bruer, 1997; Crick and Koch, 1992; Kandel and Hawkins, 1992; Siegler, Poon, Madden, and Welsh, 1996; Smith, 1996). Bruer (1997) has used the metaphor of the bridge to illustrate this point. On the one hand we have a "well-established bridge" of knowledge about learning from the cognitive sciences. We have a newer bridge between "cognitive psychology and neuroscience. This newer bridge is allowing us to see how mental functions map onto brain structures. When neuroscience does begin to provide useful insights for educators about instruction and educational practice, those insights will be the result of extensive traffic over the second bridge. Cognitive psychology provides the only firm ground we have to anchor these bridges" (Bruer, 1997, p. 4). He goes on to observe that in the future "we should attempt to develop an interactive, recursive relationship among research programs in education, cognitive psychology and systems neuroscience. . . . In the meantime, we should remain skeptical about brain-based educational practice and policy" (p. 15).

Two areas that hold some promise for further investigation within this framework are the emotional and attentional mechanisms of the brain (Pert, 1997; Sylwester, 1995; Taylor, 1996). For example, Taylor (1996) describes "from a physiological perspective, the interdependent relationship that exists between emotion and reason based on a review of the contemporary research in neurobiology" (p. 301). He concludes from this review that "without emotions, rationality cannot work. . . . Without the emotional value that gives salience to positive and negative decisions, people are unable to reason" (p. 303). Pert (1997) goes even further and asserts that "emotions are constantly regulating what we experience as 'reality.' The decision about what sensory information travels to your brain and what gets filtered out depends on what signals the receptors [for emotion] are receiving" (p. 1997). She goes on to state that "fortunately, however, [these] receptors are not stagnant. . . . This means that even when we are 'stuck' emotionally, fixated on a version of reality that does not serve us well, there is always a biochemical potential for change and growth" (p. 146). Those writing about emotional intelligence (for example, Gardner, 1983; Goleman, 1995), as discussed in Chapter Eight, also ground their assertions in this study of the emotional mechanisms and processes of the brain.

Emotion can be seen in addition as part of the attentional mechanism, in both our conscious and unconscious processes of learning. "Our emotions allow us to assemble life-saving information very quickly, and thus to bypass the extended conscious and rational deliberation of a potential threat. . . . Emotion also has an important positive side that can move life beyond mere survival into a much more pleasant sense of joie de vivre. . . . We may accept grief, but we tend to move toward those things that give us joy—music, games, jokes, dances, caresses, sunsets, celebrations, vacations" (Sylwester, 1995, pp. 73, 74). In addition to the emotional component of the attentional mechanism, it is important to investigate other neurobiological elements for such processes as getting and sustaining our attention on important situations and tasks, and knowing when and how to shift our attention quickly when new information arrives. By gaining clearer biological explanations of emotional, attentional, and other physiological mechanisms that facilitate memory and learning, we should gain a better understanding about how the mind works and adults learn.

SUMMARY

Understanding the internal workings of the learning process have fascinated scientists for decades. Researchers from the cognitive sciences have the longest history of research in this important arena, and more recently scholars from the neurobiological sciences are offering new hypotheses about how the brain and related systems are involved in learning. Perhaps the most exciting new arena of study, with the greatest potential for expanding our knowledge base of the internal processes of learning, are the combined efforts of cognitive scientists and neuroscientists working together to address how and where learning happens in the brain.

Cognitive scientists, primarily from the discipline of psychology, describe how people receive, store, retrieve, transform, and transmit information. Most of the work from this framework has focused on memory and aging, with the resulting conclusion that there are some apparent losses as we age in both working and long-term memory. How this loss affects the everyday learning activities of adults is still unanswered, except that we know that most older adults take a longer time to process complex information. Other important aspects of cognition reviewed in this chapter are the concepts of schemas, the effect of prior knowledge and experience on learning, and cognitive and learning-style theories. The concept of schemas has provided a useful framework for thinking about both the forms of knowledge (declarative and procedural) adults have accumulated over time and how that knowledge is transformed and used. In exploring the effects of prior knowledge and experience on learning, the concepts of novice and expert learners were stressed. The differences between cognitive and learning styles were discussed as well, with the resulting observation that learning styles seem to be a more useful concept. The learning-style inventories, although many have questionable reliability and validity from a research standpoint, appear to have proved effective in helping both learners and instructors gain some basic understanding of their strengths and weaknesses as learners and instructors.

Neurobiologists, from fields such as anatomy and physiology, have provided some fascinating descriptions of how the brain is organized and functions. Especially with the newer technologies, such as MRI and PET, we can catch glimpses of how our brain operates during differing types of learning episodes. Direct connections between what we see and have learned about the brain, and learning interventions are still yet to come. What we have now are tentative hypotheses about the neurobiology of learning.

With this caveat in mind, we first described the most current theories of how the brain is organized and how information is exchanged within the structures of the brain. We then commented on how educators have tried to apply this knowledge, with limited, if any, success because of this lack of definitive knowledge about the relationships between brain functioning and learning. We closed with a discussion of two areas, that of the emotional and attentional mechanisms of the brain, that hold the most promise for further collaborative work among cognitive and neuroscientists and could inform our practice as adult educators. It is hoped that we will be able to draw from this work helpful observations and techniques, and possibly even biological interventions, that could assist adults in the learning process.

CHAPTER TEN

Experience and Learning

We vividly remember attending a professional development program where the program presenters spent quite a bit of time at the start gathering information from participants concerning what they already knew about the subject and what they wanted to know. This collection of data was spread out on newsprint on most available wall space. Ah yes, we all thought. These presenters really know how to tune into us as adult learners. They are getting a good sense of our prior knowledge and experience and what our needs as learners are. We assumed they would use the material we had generated, which represented both our individual and collective selves, as both a starting point for our learning and a way to help us connect our new learning to what we already knew. Were we ever wrong! Instead the presenters went on to do their own "show and tell," and never again referred to the materials on the wall. Once again our experiences were seen as inconsequential in the learning process, and as a result the majority of the participants either tuned themselves out or left before the session was over.

Numerous adult educators have underscored the fundamental role that experience plays in learning in adulthood (for example,

Boud and Miller, 1996b; Freire, 1970b; Jackson and Caffarella, 1994; Knowles, 1980; Lindeman, 1961; Mezirow, 1981; Usher, Bryant, and Johnston, 1997). For example, one of Lindeman's (1961, p. 6) four major assumptions about adult learning was that "the resource of highest value in adult education is the learner's experience." Experience then becomes "the adult learner's living textbook . . . already there waiting to be appropriated" (p. 7). Similarly, one of the major assumptions underlying Knowles's (1980, p. 44) work on andragogy is that adults "accumulate an increasing reservoir of experience that becomes an increasingly rich resource for learning." As adults live longer they accumulate both a greater volume and range of experiences. Knowles also observes that adults tend to define themselves by their experiences, describing themselves as parents, spouses, workers, volunteers, community activists, and so on. Boud and Miller (1996b) and Usher, Bryant, and Johnston (1997), also acknowledging that experience is foundational to adult learning, advocate that adults use their experience, but with a clear understanding that this form of knowledge is highly influenced by sociocultural and historical factors.

Although adult educators have accepted for some time the connection between experience and learning, we are still learning about this connection and how to use it most effectively in both formal and nonformal learning situations. A number of questions puzzle us: What leads to learning from experience? Is the context in which the experience happens important? Are there ways we can design learning episodes to capture this experiential component best? In this chapter we explore responses to these and other important questions related to experience and learning. Discussed first are representative scholars who have addressed how we learn from life's experiences. Next is an exploration of how in general we can assist each other in learning from experience. We then describe reflective practice, one of the major ways educators have structured learning from experience. An overview of situated cognition, stressing how authentic experiences are viewed as one of the key assumptions in operationalizing this concept, is then provided. As part of this overview, we also examine how the individual learner and the context of the learning cannot be separated within the situated frame of learning. We conclude the chapter by discussing instructional practices that are grounded in the concept of situated cognition.

LEARNING FROM LIFE EXPERIENCES

John Dewey (1938), in his classic volume *Experience and Education,* made some of the most thoughtful observations about the connections between life experiences and learning. More specifically, Dewey postulates that "all genuine education comes about through experience" (p. 13), although "he is careful to note that *not all experience educates,* by which he means that not all experiences lead to the growth of ever-widening and deeper experiences" (Merriam, 1994, p. 81). In fact, some experiences "mis-educate," in that they actually "distort growth . . . , narrow the field of further experiences . . . , [and land people] in a groove or rut" (Dewey, 1938, p. 13). Judging whether experiences actually produce learning can be difficult because "every experience is a moving force. Its value can be judged only on the ground of what it moves toward and into" (p. 31). For example, being diagnosed as HIV positive may make some people so bitter and angry that any positive or growth-enhancing learning from that life change is almost impossible. On the other hand, others become highly active inquirers and participants in maintaining their health as well as involved in caring for those with full-blown AIDS.

For learning to happen through experience, Dewey (1938, p. 27) argues that the experience must exhibit the two major principles of continuity and interaction: "The principle of the continuity of experience means that every experience both takes up something from those which have gone before and modifies in some way the quality of those which come after." In other words, experiences that provide learning are never just isolated events in time. Rather, learners must connect what they have learned from current experiences to those in the past as well see possible future implications. For example, we can assume that people who are enjoying their retirement have been able to connect their past experiences to those of the present. Glennie, a retired salesperson, who may have always traveled vicariously through the Sunday paper's travel section, has bought a small travel trailer and now spends six months of the year exploring new places.

The second principle, that of interaction, posits that "an experience is always what it is because of a transaction taking place between an individual and what, at the time, constitutes his environment" (Dewey, 1938, p. 41). Going back to the example of Glennie, she is learning about new places firsthand because she now has the time and means to visit them. Through her travels, she has developed an interest in Native American culture and so seeks out new tribal groups to explore. As illustrated through Glennie's interest in Native American culture, the two principles of continuity and interaction are always interconnected and work together to provide the basis for experiential learning. What Glennie has learned in visiting one reservation "becomes an instrument of understanding" for attending the next tribal celebration with a different group of Native Americans. In translating Dewey's ideas into educational practice, what is key is how important the situation becomes in promoting learning. Developing a welcoming and comfortable atmosphere, providing the right materials, and linking these materials to learners' past and future experiences is critical in assisting adults to learn from their experiences.

A number of other writers have also examined how we learn from experience (Bateson, 1994; Boud and Walker, 1990, 1992; Kolb, 1984; Jarvis, 1987a, 1987b; Usher, 1992; Usher, Bryant, and Johnston, 1997). Kolb (1984), building primarily on the work of Dewey, Piaget, and Lewin, conceptualized that learning from experience requires four different kinds of abilities: (1) an openness and willingness to involve oneself in new experiences (concrete experience); (2) observational and reflective skills so these new experiences can be viewed from a variety of perspectives (reflective observation); (3) analytical abilities so integrative ideas and concepts can be created from their observations (abstract conceptualization); and (4) decision-making and problem-solving skills so these new ideas and concepts can be used in actual practice (active experimentation). Kolb pictured these capabilities as interrelated phases within a cyclical process, starting with the concrete experience and then moving through reflective observation and abstract conceptualization to active experimentation. Whatever action is taken in the final phase becomes another set of concrete experiences, which in turn can begin the experiential learning cycle again. "Thus, in the process of learning, one moves in varying degrees from actor to observer, and from specific involvement to general analytic detachment" (Kolb, 1984, p. 31).

In thinking through how to make Kolb's learning cycle more usable by practitioners, Barnett (1989) has added a fifth component to Kolb's model, that of "planning for implementation," which he has inserted between the abstract conceptualization and active experimentation phase (see Figure 10.1). Planning for implementation, which also assumes the ability to problem-solve and make decisions, allows time

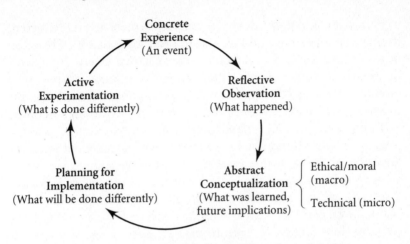

Figure 10.1.　A Model of Reflective Thought and Action.
Source: Barnett, 1989, p. 4.

for people to develop a specific plan for action, which they then carry out in the active experimentation phase. At the very least this plan should include "a rationale for undertaking the plan, specific activities that will occur, other people who will be involved, a time line of events and activities, and types of data to be collected to determine how the plan is working" (Barnett, 1989, p. 6). The active experimentation phase then becomes the time when this plan is actually carried through. Barnett sees this planning phase as important in operationalizing Kolb's cycle for two reasons: it moves people in a concrete way toward a commitment to action, and it provides a mechanism for further learning and subsequent action. Through reflecting on what happened as a result of the plan (which becomes a concrete experience), the experiential learning cycle begins again.

Jarvis (1987a, 1987b) expands on the work of Kolb, seeing Kolb's model as too simplistic for explaining the complex phenomenon of learning from experience. Jarvis (1987a, p. 16) premises his theory on the assumption that "all learning begins with experience." "Like Kolb, he believes that learning involves transforming these experiences into knowledge, and he would add skills and attitudes. Like Dewey, he emphasized the *potential* of learning from experience; not all experience leads to learning" (Merriam, 1994, p. 82).

Jarvis's (1987a) model of the learning process begins with the person's moving into a social situation in which a potential learning experience might occur. From an experience there are nine different routes that a person might choose to take, some of which result in learning and some of which do not (see Chapter Twelve for a complete explanation of Jarvis's theory). Jarvis includes both experimental learning (the result of a person experimenting on the environment) and reflective practice (thinking about and monitoring one's practice as it is happening) with what he conceives as the highest forms of learning. Both experiential learning and reflective practice call for fairly intense involvement of the learner.

Capturing many of the elements proposed by Dewey, Kolb, and Jarvis, Boud and his colleagues (Boud, Keogh, and Walker, 1985, 1996; Boud and Walker, 1990, 1992; Boud and Miller, 1996b) also describe how adults can learn from experience. These scholars, like those we have discussed previously, believe "that learning can only occur if the experience of the learner is engaged at some level" (Miller and Boud, 1996, p. 9). In promoting learning from experience, Boud and his colleagues see a strong link between using the reflective process and actually learning from experience. Boud, Keogh and Walker's (1985, 1996) original model consisted of three stages: (1) returning to and replaying the experience, (2) attending to the feelings that the experience provoked, and (3) reevaluating the experience. In recollecting what took place during the experience, these authors assert that exploring "the feelings evoked during the experience" (Boud, Keogh, and Walker, 1996, p. 43) is of particular importance. More specifically, we need to work through any negative feelings that have arisen and eventually set those aside, while retaining and enhancing the positive feelings. If the negative feelings are not addressed, what commonly happens is that learning becomes blocked. In the reevaluation stage, our aim is to use this experience as a way of getting us ready for new experiences, and thus new learning. Four processes may contribute to this reevaluation stage: "*association,* that is, relating of new data to that which is already known; *integration,* which is seeking relationships among the data; *validation* to determine the authenticity of the ideas and feelings which have resulted; and *appropriation,* that is, making knowledge one's own" (Boud, Keogh, and Walker, 1996, pp. 45–46).

In response to some criticism of this initial model, Boud and Walker (1990, 1992) have recently revised their model to include the totality of life experiences, in which they acknowledge that "each experience is influenced by the unique past of the learner as well as the current context" (Miller and Boud, 1996, p. 9). "Thus their most recent model of learning through experience accounts for the preparation the learner brings to the experience, the experience itself (during which the learner can both 'notice' and 'intervene'), and the two-way process of reflecting back and forward during and subsequent to the experience" (Tennant and Pogson, 1995, p. 161). In revising their model, their current stance is more aligned with the original thinking of Dewey and that of Schön (whose work is discussed later in this chapter).

Like the more recent work of Boud and Walker (1990, 1992) and the earlier work of Dewey (1938), Bateson (1994) and Usher, Bryant, and Johnston (1997) speak to the importance of the situated nature of experience in learning, although in very different ways. Bateson (1994, p. 30), using the metaphor of the double helix, asserts "that lessons too complex to grasp in a single occurrence spiral past again and again, small examples gradually revealing greater and greater implications." In other words, we continually recycle our past experiences, especially those "events that were ambiguous, mysterious, incomplete. . . . What was once barely intelligible may be deeply meaningful a second time. And a third" (pp. 30–31). Bateson goes on to observe that one way to encourage this spiral learning is to encounter familiar issues within an unfamiliar environment. More specifically, she believes that examining our life experiences through the framework of other cultures can provide powerful learning experiences. One example Bateson gives is to look at parenting practices within totally different cultural frames. Through these observations, we learn that parenting and childhood experiences are very much bound by culture. As a result, we can have the opportunity to rethink our own worlds as children, as well as our actions as parents or perhaps grandparents. Our earlier or current experiences about being a child and a parent or grandparent become more accessible to awareness through this spiral learning process, and therefore we may be more open to changing our beliefs and actions related to these experiences.

Usher, Bryant, and Johnston (1997) approach the situated or contextual nature of experience in a very different way from most other scholars who discuss experience as foundational to learning. Although they acknowledge that Jarvis (1987a) and Boud and Walker (1990), among others, use a contextual or sociological frame for learning from experience, they still view the work of these authors as centered on an individualized self who uses experiences as "*raw material*" to be acted upon by the mind through the controlled and self-conscious use of the senses (observations) and the application of reason (reflection)" (Usher, Bryant, and Johnston, 1997, p. 101). Rather, grounded in the assumption that "the self is a culturally and historically variable category," Usher, Bryant, and Johnston (1997, p. 102) view experience as a text to be used in learning—as "something to be 'read' or interpreted, possibly with great effort, and certainly with no final, definitive meaning" (p. 104). Like Bateson (1994), these authors assert that "the meaning of experience is never permanently fixed; thus, the text of experience is always open to reinterpretation" (p. 105). Usher, Bryant, and Johnston have proposed a "map" of experiential learning within the framework of postmodern thought. With this model, "learning does not simplistically derive from experience; rather, experience and learning are mutually positioned in an interactive dynamic" (p. 107). In posing this model, these authors view the use of experience as part of the learning process as "inherently neither emancipatory nor oppressive, neither domesticating nor transformative. Rather, . . . it is perhaps most usefully seen as having a potential for emancipation *and* oppression, domestication *and* transformation, where at any one time and according to context both tendencies can be present and in conflict with one another" (p. 105).

Usher, Bryant, and Johnston's model, shown in Figure 10.2, is structured around two intersecting continua—*Autonomy-Adaptation* (empowerment of individuals to act independently to being able to adapt one's actions in relation to the context) and *Expression-Application* (being able to apply what one knows within real-world contexts)—and four quadrants, referred to as Lifestyle, Confessional, Vocational, and Critical. Learning from experience happens both between and within the quadrants, which represent different types of learning venues.

Lifestyle practices center on the achievement of autonomy through individuality and self-expression, particularly in taste and style (for example, ways of speaking, clothes, leisure pursuits, vacations). Experience is used as a means of defining a lifestyle that is both actively sought by people, but also influenced by socially and culturally defined norms. Instructors become facilitators who assist learners in interpreting their own knowledge and opening up different experiences so these learners can view alternative ways of thinking about lifestyle.

Vocational practices are conveyed through the market. Learners need to be highly motivated in the direction of a personal change linked to the needs of the socioeconomic environment. Vocationalism then is designed to produce flexible competencies and a predisposition to

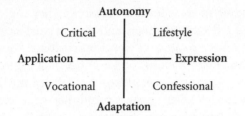

**Figure 10.2.   Map of Experiential Learning in the
Social Practices of Modernity.**

Source: Usher, Bryant, and Johnston, 1997, p. 106.

change. As a result of learning adaptive skills through experiential
means, learners become more empowered to respond to their changing vocational environments.

In *confessional practices* our private, self-regulating capacities become
public. In other words, to realize oneself, to find out the truth about oneself, to accept responsibility for oneself, becomes both personally desirable and economically functional. The emphasis within this process
is on self-improvement, self-development, and self-regulation. Experience is used as enabling access to knowledge and the innermost truths
about self, which in turn creates productive and empowered people in
a number of roles (for example, as active citizen, ardent consumer,
enthusiastic employee).

In *critical practices* there is a recognition that experience is never a
basic given. The focus is on changing particular contexts rather than
adapting to them, and therefore working with learners becomes a
political practice. Experiential learning becomes a strategy designed
to find and exercise one's voice in the service of self and social empowerment and transformation and is not regarded as something that
leads to knowledge, but as knowledge itself.

In constructing this model, Usher, Bryant, and Johnston suggest that
"educators need to help [learners] to problematise and interrogate
experience as much as to access and validate it" (p. 118). In this way,
the model could be used as a heuristic device for learners to "triangu-
late experience through an investigation of personal meanings alongside the meanings of others and the presence and influence of different
contexts" (p. 120). For example, in conducting a workshop on effective ways of relating to a diverse customer base, the workshop facilitators might choose to use the experience of the participants as one

of the major content areas for the workshop. They could first ask the participants to reflect individually and then in small groups on times when they have been treated differently as customers because of their gender, race, disability, or ethnic background. In doing this they would use what Usher, Bryant, and Johnston have called the lifestyle experiences of the learners. Participants could then generate lists in their small groups of how their experiences have been the same or different and share those with the large group. The facilitators could then ask people to reflect critically on what they had learned from each other's experiences, and how they might use this knowledge to improve their own customer service practices (thereby integrating their experiential knowledge from the lifestyle, vocational, and confessional practices arenas). Hopefully by having the participants reflect on their own and others' experiences, the end result might be a positive change in how they think and act with customers from diverse backgrounds or perhaps reinforce the positive methods they were already using.

The end product might be quite different if the instructors or learners also chose to view the issue from a critical practices perspective. By using the lens of critical practices to reflect on their individual and collective experiences, they could, for example, come to the realization that the only way to serve a diverse group of customers effectively would be to change the culture of the organization, and not just their individual practices.

Clearly the role of experience in learning is a highly complex process. Although it is important that individual learners are able to reflect on and revisit their own experiences and learn from them, the importance of assisting learners to recognize the contextual factors and how experiences are defined by those factors can not be left to chance.

ASSISTING OTHERS IN LEARNING FROM EXPERIENCE

Boud and Miller (1996b, 1998) and their colleagues (Miller and others, 1997) have provided one of the most eloquent and useful descriptions of the general roles that adults can play in helping others learn from their experiences, no matter what form this learning takes. Miller and Boud (1996, p. 7) term "the function of working with the experience of others as 'animation' and refer to the person who works to promote others' learning as an 'animator.'" They describe "the function of animators to be that of acting with learners, or others, in situations where learning is an aspect of what is occurring. . . . While teaching or instruction may be an aspect of animation, it is a secondary one which is subordinate to that of fostering learning from experience" (p. 7). Therefore, although animators may be someone with a teaching or instructional role, they also may be friends, co-learners, or supervisors. Key to the influence of animators is the relationship they build with learners. This relationship is influenced by a number of factors, including the political and economic context of their working together. One of the central tasks of animators then becomes to establish "an appropriate micro-culture, climate, and space within which to work" (Boud and Miller, 1996a). This includes acknowledging the power relations in this relationship as well as the broader constraints that are present in most learning settings. Animators also need to take into consideration the feelings and emotions of the learner and construct what they are doing so that the experiences of the learners are the primary source of learning.

Included in the work of Boud and Miller (1996b) are detailed depictions of how instructors and community workers have carried through their role of animator in a variety of settings. Tisdell (1996b), for example, describes how she uses the life experiences of her graduate students and her own developing sense of feminist consciousness to teach feminist theory. Tisdell uses stories to work with her students' individual and collective experiences as a way to "problematise gender relations [and] to demystify [feminist] theory" (p. 120). "Some of the things that typically come up . . . are the significance of gender socialization, of mothers' primary influence in the home and family, of religion, and of a growing awareness in each of our lives over time of the patriarchal nature of most societal institutions" (p. 120). She is also able to bridge to what her students do not know through their experiences to broaden their knowledge of feminist theory. Because most of her students are white and middle class, they typically have little experience with thinking about race and class as a fundamental part of understanding feminist theory. By acknowledging their lack of experience in these areas through their sharing of stories, those students in her class who have experienced poverty or an understanding of themselves as racial beings begin to fill in some of the missing pieces of what it is like to be poor or a person of color.

Ireland (1996) reflects back on his role over twenty-five years as an animator with a group of male construction workers in Brazil. In this role, he worked with these workers to help them get elected to the directorship of their local union chapter. Once they were elected, which took a number of years, his role changed to that of assisting the directors in learning how to administer a complex bureaucracy, which included supervision of staff and the overseeing of work actions, such as strikes. More recently, he has concentrated on formal literacy and postliteracy programs for the rank-and-file members. In thinking back on these learning experiences, Ireland points to three fundamental lessons he has learned. First, "the bonds of friendship and shared political ideals are both necessary ingredients of the learning process" (p. 139). Second, in educational processes of a long-term nature, the context in which that learning process takes place profoundly affects what happens in that process, and the needs of both animators and learners continually evolve and are altered. And third, "the permanent interplay between experiential learning and more systematic learning processes within the perspective of popular education is particularly pertinent for workers with low levels of formal schooling. . . . Experience is an invaluable dimension of informal and formal learning processes in the same way that theory and practice are two sides of the same coin" (pp. 139–140).

Other authors have described very specific processes of how adults learn from experience. In the remaining sections of this chapter we explore two concepts that have influenced greatly how adult educators use learners' experience as a central part of the learning process: reflective practice and situated cognition.

REFLECTIVE PRACTICE

Reflective practice allows one to make judgments in complex and murky situations—judgments based on experience and prior knowledge. Although reflective practice is most often associated with professional practice, this process can be applied to other types of learning situations, both formal and informal. Practice knowledge, the cornerstone of reflective practice, consists of much more than abstract theoretical or technical knowledge (Schön, 1983; Cervero, 1988; Peters, 1991). The knowledge we gain through experience and the way we practice our craft is just as important. The initiation of reflective practice involves using data in some form, which almost always includes our past and current experiences. Our tacit knowledge about practice, that is, knowledge that we use every day, almost without thinking about it, is an important part of these data.

Three major assumptions undergird the process of reflective practice (Cervero, 1988; Osterman and Kottcamp, 1993; Peters, 1991; Schön, 1983, 1987):

Assumption One. Those involved in reflective practice are committed to both problem finding and problem solving as part of that process. In problem finding, the assumption is that often the problems we are presented with in practice are murky and ill defined. Therefore, we need to be open to discovering new problems or different ways of looking at old problems.

Assumption Two. Reflective practice means making judgments about what actions will be taken in a particular situation. Because these actions usually involve seeking changes in ourselves, other people, or in systems, there is an ethical dimension to reflective practice.

Assumption Three. Reflective practice results in some form of action, even if that action is a deliberate choice not to change practice. Without this action phase, the reflective practice process is incomplete. The lack of attention to this phase as a critical part of reflective practice often frustrates practitioners who are committed to reflection, but see it as a dead-end endeavor when nothing tangible results.

Although reflective practice theoretically should result in the most thoughtful and useful solutions to practice problems, this may not be the case depending on the beliefs educators have about this practice. Wellington and Austin (1996) have argued that depending on their beliefs and values, practitioners have very different orientations toward reflective practice. These differing orientations influence both how reflective practice is used, and therefore the possible outcomes of this practice. For example, do those involved believe that education should be a liberating or "domesticating" form of practice? And what is more important to them: system or human concerns? Wellington and Austin have depicted a way of thinking about reflective practice that acknowledges how it could be filtered through the belief and value systems of practitioners, which in their view results in five orientations toward reflective practice: the immediate, the technical, the deliberative, the dialectic, and the transpersonal (see Figure 10.3).

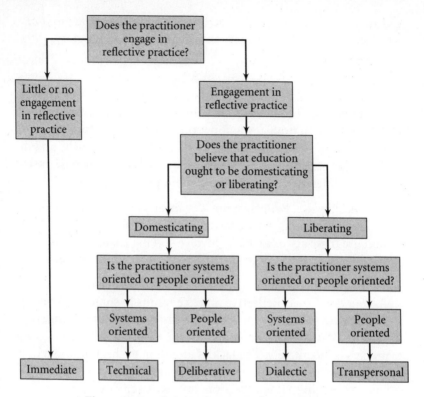

Figure 10.3.   Orientations to Reflective Practice.
Source: Wellington and Austin, 1996, p. 312.

Practitioners who use the immediate orientation, focusing basically on survival, rarely use any form of reflective practice. Those who view practice as more of a domesticating activity, that is, they see societal needs as taking precedence over individual needs, lean toward the technical and deliberative orientations. The technical mode "uses reflection as an instrument to direct practice" (Wellington and Austin, 1996, p. 308), usually within predetermined guidelines and standards. The deliberative orientation "places emphasis on the discovery, assignment and assessment of personal meaning within an educational setting" (p. 310). Those operating from this orientation are typically humanistic, stress communication, and believe that the attitudes and values of learners are important. Although people who use the deliberative orientation sometimes are uncomfortable with the organization in which they work, they nevertheless tend to work within that system. And finally, those who view educational practice as liberating primarily use the dialectic and transpersonal orientation. Practitioners using the dialectical orientation toward reflective practice "reject the limitations of authorized organizational structures and parameters and are uncomfortable working within them. . . . They tend to . . . focus on political and social issues . . . [and] advocate political awareness and activism" (p. 310). On the other hand, the transpersonal orientation "centers on universal personal liberation. . . . They question educational ends, content and means from a personal, inner perspective" (p. 311).

Wellington and Austin cast these orientations not as competing views of what reflective practice should encompass, but as different ways of going about reflective practice. They believe that practitioners need to recognize their own predominant modes, as well as respect the preferred orientations of others. "When practitioners become aware of their own preferences and prejudices across models, they can begin to reflect upon a wider range of questions and develop a wider range of responses" (p. 314). No matter what orientation people have, two basic processes have been identified as central to reflective practice: reflection-on-action and reflection-in-action.

Reflection-on-Action

Reflection-on-action involves thinking through a situation after it has happened. This mode of reflection is presented by most authors as primarily an analytical exercise, which results in new perspectives on experiences, changes in behavior, and commitments to action. In reflection-on-action, we consciously return to the experiences we have had, reevaluate these experiences, decide what we could do differently, and then try out whatever we decided to do differently. Different authors have offered various models of carrying out this reflective cycle. Kolb's (1984) model, or adaptations of his model, is the one most often used in practice (see Figure 10.1). The cyclical nature of the model allows for a process of continued change and growth. Boud, Keogh, and Walker (1985, 1996) have added to Kolb's work on reflection-on-action by stressing we must attend to the feelings created by our experiences in order for the reflective process to be truly effective. In addition, they have added more in-depth descriptions of four cognitive processes (association, integration, validation, and appropriation) that can contribute to the reflective process. And Osterman and

Kottkamp (1993), borrowing from the work of Argyris and Schön (1978), set reflective practice within the framework of espoused theories (beliefs) and theories-in-use (actions). Within this frame, they view the reflective practice cycle as helping practitioners become aware of and act on the discrepancies between their beliefs (their espoused theories) and what they actually do.

Descriptions are plentiful on how to put into practice reflection-on-action (for example, Brookfield, 1996b, Jackson and Caffarella, 1994; Smyth, 1996; Osterman and Kottkamp, 1993). Some of the most popular methods used in education and other fields are portfolio development, journal writing, and critical reflection (see Chapter Fourteen for a more thorough discussion of critical reflection). Key to all of these methods is the framing of critical observations and questions as part of the reflection-on-action process. For example, Smyth (1996), in assisting teachers to uncover the social constraints in which they practice, asks them to respond to four stem questions: (1) Describe (What do I do?), (2) Inform (What does this mean?), (3) Confront (How did I come to be like this?) and (4) Reconstruct (How might I do things differently?). Through this process "teachers begin to link consciousness about the processes that inform the day-to-day aspects of their teaching with the wider political and social realities within which it occurs . . . [and] they are able to challenge the . . . way schools are conceived, organised and enacted" (Smyth, 1996, p. 54).

Reflection-in-Action

In contrast, reflection-in-action reshapes "what we are doing while we are doing it" (Schön, 1987, p. 26). "Thinking on your feet" and "keeping your wits about you" are commonly used phases that describe reflection-in-action. Schön (1983, 1987, 1991, 1996) is perhaps the best-known author who has challenged professionals to incorporate this form of reflective process as an integral part of professional development. In Schön's view, reflection-in-action is triggered by surprise. What we have been thinking and doing all along as professionals no longer works. "We think critically about the thinking that got us into this fix or this opportunity; and we may, in the process, restructure strategies of action, understanding of phenomena, or ways of framing problems. . . . Reflection gives rise to [the] on-the-spot experiment" (Schön, 1987, p. 28).

For example, in running an institute for professionals, the institute staff sense that the sessions on a particular day have not gone well. Over coffee, they ask for feedback from participants, and the general observation is that they are finding the material too esoteric and are tired of being "talked at." The next presenter, who is listening to these conversations, has also planned to lecture. Although Ron knows he is an excellent lecturer, he decides that unless he changes the way he presents the material, he will totally lose the audience. Knowing that many of the people in the audience have experience related to his content area, he asks for volunteers to join him in a panel discussion on the topic, explaining that he is changing his format to respond to their needs as learners. While Ron works with the panel members on their roles, he asks the rest of the participants to generate questions they would like to ask panel members. Although he has never used this format in quite this way before, he believes it might work and is willing to take a chance to recapture the interest of the participants. In this way, Ron is using his expertise as an instructor to change on the spot what he is doing as a presenter as he goes along. Schön goes on to observe that competent and experienced professionals use reflection-in-action as a regular part of their practice, although they may not verbalize they are doing this. This form of reflective practice allows professionals to go beyond the routine application of rules, facts, and procedures and gives them the freedom to practice their craft more as a professional artistry where they create new ways of thinking and acting about problems of practice.

Recently there have been both validation of and criticisms to Schön's model of reflection-in-action. Ferry and Ross-Gordon (1998), for example, in exploring the links between experience and practice, support Schön's theory that "reflection-in-action goes beyond 'stable rules' by devising new methods of reasoning" (p. 107) and fostering new ways of framing and responding to problems. Educators who were reflective in their practice used both reflection-on-action and reflection-in-action to build their expertise. They did not find, however, that the amount of experience a person possessed necessarily had anything to do with that person using reflective practice.

On the other hand, Usher, Bryant, and Johnston (1997) assert that although Schön adequately describes the reflection-in-action process, in his own work he did not use "his own practice as a producer of text . . . [and they view that as] a problem of the *absence of reflexivity* in his own work" (p. 143). By this, Usher, Bryant, and Johnston meant that Schön did not question how the context of his work, being academic in nature, could get in the way of the message. They would have liked to have seen a text that included both the conventional academic type of writing as well as more informal commentary on what was written, including critical comments on what Schön had proposed. Overall Usher, Bryant, and Johnston believe that despite Schön's clear message that reflection-in-action should be implemented in a critical manner, the way in which he conveyed that message makes it easy for practitioners to co-opt the process into one of a technical and rationalistic dialogue.

Boud and Walker (1990, 1992) also have revised their earlier framework of reflective practice to include Schön's idea of reflection-in-action. As pictured in Figure 10.4, Boud and Walker, like Schön, believe that "we experience as we reflect and we reflect as we experience" (Boud and Walker, 1992, p. 168). In other words we cannot, nor should we, separate our past experiences from our current ones. In capturing the reflective element while the experience is happening, Boud and Walker believe it is necessary to use the interaction between the milieu and the learners. They suggest two ways of doing this. The

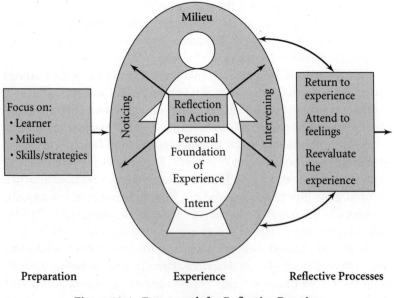

Figure 10.4. Framework for Reflective Practice.
Source: Boud and Walker, 1990, p. 67.

first is "*noticing,* by which the person becomes aware of the milieu, or particular things within it, and uses this for the focus of reflection" (Boud and Walker, 1990, p. 68). The second is "*intervening,* in which the person takes an initiative in the event" (p. 68). Learners may intervene by asking for clarification of what is happening and may even attempt to change the event in some minor or major way. In formal and nonformal settings, learners can often benefit from assistance by facilitators in helping them in the noticing and intervening processes.

Tremmel (1993) also argues that reflection-in-action is critical to professional practice, but from a very different perspective. Grounding his thinking in the Zen Buddhist tradition of "mindfulness," he, like Schön, believes that reflection can best be accomplished in the midst of everyday practice. Mindfulness, a specific Zen practice, "is 'to return,' [that is] . . . to 'return' to mindful awareness of the present moment" (p. 443). Being mindful is to pay attention to the here and now, not in an analytical or evaluative way, but rather to invest oneself in "the present moment with full awareness and concentration" (p. 443). It is to move away from the endless parade of thoughts that go through our minds in any one situation, and instead pay attention to what we are thinking and feeling at that moment; it becomes in essence the study of the self at any one point in time. For example, rather than thinking about what I have written about reflective practice, or how I will edit what I have written, being mindful makes me aware of how my shoulders ache right now sitting at the computer, how difficult mindfulness is for me to explain with my Western ways of thinking, and how I hope that at least a few people will be able to grab this idea and help others understand it. The concept of mindfulness seems important to me, even if I cannot explain it well. Tremmel goes on to suggest that "freewriting," that is, writing everything down that comes to mind without editorializing, might be one way for professionals to pay more attention to the here and now in their work. We have used "stem writing" in this way, where we ask learners to respond to a specific stem (such as "What I am feeling right now is . . ." or "What I wish would happen is . . .") with the first thing that comes to their mind as one way to enter this realm of the present.

Writing in a similar vein to Tremmel, but coming from a very different cultural tradition, Nuernberger (1994) also speaks of the importance of using our powers of attention in reflective practice. Grounded in Tantric thought as expressed through the work of Shankara, "considered to be India's greatest logician and philosopher" (Nuernberger,

1994, p. 90), Nuernberger reminds us that our powers of attention and concentration are crucial to the reflective life. As he observes: "Typically, our mind is scattered. When we pay attention, we focus the mind's energy. The more focused we become, the greater our concentration, the more powerful our mind [and therefore our reflective processes] become" (Nuernberger, 1994, p. 112–113).

Nuernberger asks us to draw on four types of knowledge in our reflective practice: spiritual knowledge, intuitive knowledge, instinctual knowledge, and analytic or sensory knowledge. Spiritual knowledge is almost mystical in quality and allows for what he terms transformational experiences, which alter "the identity of the individual and eventually [lead] to wisdom" (Nuernberger, 1994, p. 109). Intuitive knowledge is what we gain when we have what he terms "insight into the real consequences of our actions . . . [and gives us] the power to discern cause/effect relationships and subtle movements of change" (Nuernberger, 1994, p. 109). Instinctual knowledge is based on subliminal perception, related to the very essence of our own personas or beings. It is the knowledge that we respond to long before we are even aware of any specific sensory information, such as what we see or hear. For example, using our instinctual knowledge is knowing that there is something wrong with a loved one or that we are in danger, but having no specific signs we can point to that tell us that. Nuernberger cautions us that "we can be misled by our instincts when we confuse them with emotional needs, wants, and fears, or through lack of awareness" (p. 110). The knowledge that is most familiar to us is our analytical or sensory knowledge, the knowledge we gain through hearing, seeing, and feeling. "Distorted emotions, poor memory, even faulty sensory mechanisms may limit sensory knowledge" (Nuernberger, 1994, p. 110). In addition, our sensory knowledge is influenced by the conventions of the world around us; it is contextual in nature. Practical consequences of using our attention and concentration skills effectively in reflective practice range from strengthening our perceptual and visionary skills to enhancing our health and well-being.

SITUATED COGNITION

Although reflective practice and situated cognition both involve learning from real-world experiences, how these experiences are interpreted is often vastly different. In most models of reflective practice, learning from experience is still viewed as something that goes on in someone's head. Individuals, whether by themselves or in groups, think through problems presented to them and then act on those problems by changing their practice on the spot or as they encounter similar situations at a later date. Experience provides the catalyst for learning in reflective practice, but most often it is seen as separate from the learning process itself.

In situated cognition, one cannot separate the learning process from the situation in which the learning is presented. Knowledge and the process of learning within this framework are viewed as "a product of the activity, context, and culture in which it is developed and used" (Brown, Collins, and Duguid, 1989, p. 32). The proponents of the situated view of learning argue that learning for everyday living (which includes our practice as professionals) happens only "among people acting in culturally organized settings" (Wilson, 1993c, p. 76). In other words the physical and social experiences and situations in which learners find themselves and the tools they use in that experience are integral to the entire learning process.

Hansman and Wilson (1998), through their study of the teaching of computer-based writing to community college students, provide us with an excellent example of how the major components of situated cognition translate into practice. The students in this study perceived computers to be their major tools for learning. Using computers as tools "gave them 'power' over their writing" (p. 30), and this "power" made writing easier for them than just using pen and paper. "Thus, computers used as tools shaped how students wrote, or at least their perceptions of how they wrote" (p. 30). Students also perceived that using computers allowed them "to construct their own processes for writing, which typically meant that they did not follow prescribed 'how to' methods" (p. 30). And finally, the interactive and relaxed social environment of the class gave students the opportunity to talk with one another about the writing process, which included having students critique each other's work. In essence, the learning experience for these students became a complex social phenomenon, "situated [and] structured by people interacting with each other in tool-dependent environments" (p. 36).

In viewing learning from a situated perspective, two other ideas are key. The first is the emphasis in the learning process changes from being concerned about memory and how we process information internally (discussed in Chapter Nine) to that of perception and the settings in which those perceptions are made (Young, 1993). In essence, according to Clancey (1997), "every human thought and action is adapted to the environment, that is, *situated,* because what people *perceive,* and how they *conceive of their activity,* and what they *physically do* develop together" (pp. 1–2). This situated nature of cognition makes the transfer process from using learning gained from one situation to the next more problematic, which has led some theorists to question whether knowledge, especially practical knowledge, can really transfer across situations (Anderson, Reder, and Simon, 1996; Lave, 1988). Context, then, and how this influences the perceptions learners make, is "the element that makes sense of cognition" (Wilson, 1993a, p. 338) versus a nuisance variable that muddies the waters and gets in the way of "real learning." Of course, not everyone shares this view that the situational aspects of learning are the key to understanding cognition (for example, see Anderson, Reder, and Simon, 1996, 1997).

Second, making the assumption that learning and knowing are primarily a cultural phenomenon moves the study of cognition (and, therefore, learning from experience) into the social and political realm and raises the issue of knowledge and power as a legitimate part of the study of cognition (Kirshner and Whitson, 1997; Wilson, 1993c). Although this issue of power and knowledge is fundamental to the theory of situated cognition, it has often been downplayed or overlooked in favor of how to apply the concept practically. This has also been true until recently in much of the work on learning and experience and reflective practice (Usher, Bryant, and Johnston, 1997; Wellington and Austin, 1996). In acknowledging cognition and learning from experience as a cultural phenomenon, the perspectives of critical, feminist, and postmodern thinkers (see Chapter Fifteen) become crucial. A major result of thinking about cognition from a cultural frame is the critiques that have been fostered about traditional educational theory and practice (Brown, Collins, and Duguid, 1989; Lave, 1988; Wilson, 1993c). Foremost among these critiques is a challenge to the fundamental notion that learning is something that occurs within the individual. Rather, learning encompasses the interaction of learners and the social environments in which they function.

In using experience within the framework of situated cognition, the emphasis is on "providing enabling experiences in authentic versus decontextualized contexts" (Choi and Hannafin, 1995, p. 53). As Greeno (1997) has thoughtfully observed, "When we recognize that all learning involves socially organized activity, the question is not *whether* to give instruction in a 'complex, social environment' but *what kinds* of complex, social activities to arrange, for which aspects of participation, and in what sequence to use them" (p. 10). In this perspective education and training by just abstraction is of little use. Rather, "to meet the test of 'authenticity,' situations must at least have some of the important attributes of real-life problem solving, including ill-structured complex goals, an opportunity for the detection of relevant versus irrelevant information, active/generative engagement in finding and defining problems as well as in solving them, involvement in the student's beliefs and values, and an opportunity to engage in collaborative interpersonal activities" (Young, 1993, p. 45). Cognitive apprenticeships and anchored instruction are two ways in which the concept of authentic experiences has been put into practice by educators.

Cognitive Apprenticeships

Cognitive apprenticeships have received the most attention in the literature. "Cognitive apprenticeship methods try to enculturate [learners] into authentic practices through activity and social interaction in a way similar to that evident—and evidently successful—in craft apprenticeship" (Brown, Collins, and Duguid, 1989, p. 37). The cognitive nature of the apprenticeship places emphasis on teaching learners different ways of thinking about whatever they are learning, as well as any skills associated with the apprenticeship.

Based on a study of different forms of cognitive apprenticeship used in several professions, such as engineering, medicine, and educational administration, Brandt, Farmer, and Buckmaster (1993) have offered one of the clearest descriptions of cognitive apprenticeships as an instructional process. (Also see Farmer, Buckmaster, and LeGrand, 1992; Prestine and LeGrand, 1991.) Their five-phase model (see Table 10.1) "starts with deliberate instruction by someone who acts as a model; it then proceeds to model-guided trials by practitioners who progressively assume more responsibility for their learning" (Farmer, Buckmaster, and LeGrand, 1992, p. 42).

Crucial aspects of implementing successful cognitive apprenticeships are selecting appropriate real-world situations or tasks that are grounded in learner needs, finding the right person or persons to do the modeling, and facilitating the learning process. (See Choi and Hannafin, 1995, for clear and concise descriptions of facilitating skills.)

	Role of Model	Role of Learner	Key Concepts
Phase 1: Modeling	Model real-life activity that learner wants to perform satisfactorily. Model states aloud the essence of the activity. He or she can include tricks of the trade.	Observe performance of total activity, not merely the individual steps. Develop a mental model of what the real thing looks like.	Articulation Domain-specific heuristics
Phase 2: Approximating	Provide coaching to the learner. Provide support when needed.	Approximate doing the real thing and articulate its essence. Reflect on the model's performance. Use self-monitoring and self-correction.	Scaffolding Coaching
Phase 3: Fading	Decrease coaching and scaffolding.	Continue to approximate the real thing. Operate in increasingly complex, risky, or ill-defined situations. Work individually or in groups.	Fading
Phase 4: Self-directed learning	Provide assistance only when requested.	Practice doing the real thing alone. Do so within specified limits acceptable to profession and society.	Self-directed learning
Phase 5: Generalizing	Discuss the generalizability of what has been learned.	Discuss the generalizability of what has been learned.	Generalizability

Table 10.1. Cognitive Apprenticeship Phases.
Source: Brandt, Farmer, and Buckmaster, 1993, p. 71.

In facilitating this process, models "must express the essence of their thoughts, which may otherwise be unspoken, while they demonstrate how to do a particular aspect of the task" or solve a specific problem (Brandt, Farmer, and Buckmaster, 1993, p. 76). Through this articulation, learners are given access not only to what they see, but to what the model is seeing and sensing, plus the model can give further explanations about what she is doing. Coaching learners as they work through the situations or tasks is also a helpful facilitating process, as well as regulating the task difficulty and providing support (scaffolding). The outcomes of cognitive apprenticeships are twofold: (1) internalizing what has been learned so learners can do the task or solve the problem on their own, and (2) generalizing what they have learned as both a way to apply this learning to similar situations and as a starting point for further learning.

Anchored Instruction

Anchored instruction "provides a way to recreate some of the advantages of apprenticeship training in formal educational settings" (Cognition and Technology Group at Vanderbilt, 1990, p. 2). More specifically, the purpose of anchored instruction is to create situations in which learners, through sustained experiences, can grapple with the problems and opportunities that experts encounter. To do this, the instructional process is anchored in what the Cognition and Technology group calls macrocontexts, which are complex problems explored over extended periods of time and through multiple lenses (Cognition and Technology Group at Vanderbilt, 1990, 1992, 1993). These macrocontexts, which in essence become the tools of learning, can take many forms. For example, instructors could provide videodisks containing the problems to be explored, or they could ask learners to prepare problem-based case studies. We have found building macrocontexts to be an especially effective instructional technique with graduate students and professional groups we have worked with over an extended period of time. The goal of anchored instruction is to have learners "experience what it is like to grow from novices who have only rudimentary knowledge . . . to relatively sophisticated experts who have explored an environment from multiple points of view" (Cognition and Technology Group at Vanderbilt, 1990, p. 9).

SUMMARY

The experiences of adults have always been viewed as a critical component of learning in adulthood. Although exploring the role of experience in learning has a long history, we continue to discover more about the connections between learning and experience and how to assist adults in formal and nonformal settings to capture the richness of learning from experience. Discussed in this chapter were the theories of Dewey (1938), Kolb (1984), Jarvis (1987a) Boud and Walker (1990), Bateson (1994), and Usher, Bryant, and Johnston (1997), which offer varying conceptual views of the process of learning from experience. Central to all of these writers is the notion that learning from experience involves adults' connecting what they have learned from current experiences to those in the past as well to possible future situations. Therefore, learning from experience is cyclical in nature; whatever we learn from one experience is then applied to new experiences. Although the focus of the study of the role of experience in learning has been on the individual learner, there has been a shift to understanding how the context of that learning influences both the learning process and the outcomes.

Assisting each other in learning from experience is a critical role adults play as educators in formal settings and as friends, supervisors, and colleagues. Key to this role, which Miller and Boud (1996) have termed being an animator, is the relationships we build with learners. In building these relationships, Miller and Boud point to the importance of understanding the power dynamics in these relationships and emphasize creating supportive climates for learning that acknowledge the contextual nature of knowledge, including the political and social dimensions of that knowledge.

Reflective practice, one of the major ways educators have structured learning from experience, focuses on helping learners make judgments based on experience related to primarily complex and murky problems. One of the fundamental premises underlying reflective practice is that practice knowledge is much more than theoretical and technical knowledge, which is primarily rational in nature. In addition, the knowledge gained through solving the ill-defined problems of practice is just as critical, if not more so. There are many orientations to reflective practice depending on the beliefs and values of the person using this practice. A range of orientations (such as the technical, the deliberate, the dialectical, and the transpersonal) and both reflection-on-action and reflection-in-action should be a regular part of reflective practice.

Experience also plays a critical role in the practice of situated cognition, which acknowledges the importance of the social and cultural context of learning. In other words, the physical and social experiences and situations in which learners find themselves and the tools they use are integral to the learning process. The importance of the authenticity of the experience in which adults learn is stressed within the situated framework. Two ways educators have put this concept of authentic experiences into formal practice are cognitive apprenticeships and anchored instruction. The primary focus of each of these forms of instruction is to help learners develop specific skills and competencies in a particular context of practice.

CHAPTER ELEVEN

Key Theories of Learning

~~~~

Learning, so central to human behavior yet so elusive to understanding, has fascinated thinkers as far back as Plato and Aristotle. Indeed, the views of these two philosophers underpin much modern research on learning conducted by psychologists and educators. The fact that so many people have thought about, investigated, and written about the process of learning over the years suggests the complexity of the topic. Learning defies easy definition and simple theorizing. This chapter reviews some of the major ways that learning has been studied and delineates the contributions these orientations have made to our understanding of learning in adulthood.

Originally, learning was within the purview of philosophical investigations into the nature of knowledge, the human mind, and what it means to know. Plato believed that the physical objects in our everyday world have corresponding abstract forms that we can come to know "by reflecting on the contents of one's mind" (Hergenhahn, 1988, p. 31). Aristotle, on the other hand, believed that all knowledge comes through the senses; these sense impressions can be pondered "to discover the lawfulness that runs through them" (p. 33). Plato's "rationalism" can be seen in Gestalt and cognitive psychology; Aristotle's "empiricism" is particularly evident in early behavioral psychology. Later philosophers presented variations on these two basic positions, ranging from Descartes's separation of mind and body to Kant's notion of innate mental faculties.

It was not until the nineteenth century that the study of the mind, of how people know, and, by extension, of behavior became "scientifically" investigated. Hergenhahn (1988, p. 42) writes that Hermann Ebbinghaus "emancipated psychology from philosophy by demonstrating that the 'higher mental processes' of learning and memory could be studied experimentally" and that many of his findings on learning and memory published in 1885 are still valid. Another pioneer, Wilhelm Wundt, set up the first psychological laboratory in Leipzig in 1879 and investigated how experience is assimilated "into the knowledge structures one already had" (Di Vesta, 1987, p. 206). By the turn of the century, systematic investigations into human learning were well under way in Europe and North America.

In this chapter we first present a brief discussion of learning and learning theories in general, and then we focus on five different learning theories: behaviorist, cognitivist, humanist, social learning, and constructivist. These five theories are attempts to codify much of the information just reported in Chapters Seven through Ten. These theories also present a contrast to the attempts to build theories of *adult* learning that are examined in Part Four.

LEARNING AND LEARNING THEORIES

Although learning has been defined in a variety of ways, most definitions include the concepts of behavioral change and experience. A common definition from psychologists, especially those who were investigating the phenomenon until the 1950s, is that learning is a change in behavior. This definition, however, fails to capture some of the complexities involved—such as whether one needs to perform in order for learning to have occurred or whether all human behavior is learned. The notion of change still underlies most definitions of learning, although it has been modified to include the potential for change. And the idea that having an experience of some sort, rather than learning as a function of maturation, is important. Thus a reasonable definition of learning would be: "Learning is a relatively permanent change in behavior or in behavioral potentiality that results from experience and cannot be attributed to temporary body states such as those induced by illness, fatigue, or drugs" (Hergenhahn, 1988, p. 7). Or as Maples and Webster (1980, p. 1) stated more simply, "Learning can be thought of as a process by which behavior changes as a result of experiences."

Learning as a process (rather than an end product) focuses on what happens when the learning takes place. Explanations of what happens are called learning theories, and it is these theories that are the subject of this chapter. There are, however, many explanations of learning, some more comprehensive than others, that are called theories. How the knowledge base in this area is divided and labeled depends on the writer. Hilgard and Bower (1966), for example, review eleven learning theories and then note that they fall into two major families: stimulus-response theories and cognitive theories. Knowles (1984) uses Reese and Overton's (1970) organization in which learning theories are grouped according to two different worldviews: mechanistic and organismic.

Since there is little consensus on how many learning theories there are or how they should be grouped for discussion, we have organized this chapter according to orientations that present very different assumptions about learning and offer helpful insights into adult learning. With these criteria in mind, five basic orientations have been selected for discussion: behaviorist, cognitivist, humanist, social learning, and constructivist. As Hill (1977, p. 261) has observed, "For most of us, the various learning theories have two chief values. One is in providing us with a vocabulary and a conceptual framework for interpreting the examples of learning that we observe. These are valuable for anyone who is alert to the world. The other, closely related, is in suggesting where to look for solutions to practical problems. The theories do not give us solutions, but they do direct our attention to those variables that are crucial in finding solutions."

For the five orientations examined in this chapter, the following topics are covered: the major proponents, the view of the learning process itself, the purpose of education, the role of the teacher, and the ways in which these theories are manifested in adult learning. A summary of this information can be found in Table 11.1 at the end of the chapter.

BEHAVIORIST ORIENTATION

Behaviorism is a well-known orientation to learning that encompasses a number of individual theories. Developed by John B. Watson in the early decades of the twentieth century, behaviorism loosely encompasses the work of such people as Thorndike, Tolman, Guthrie, Hull, and Skinner (Ormrod, 1995). What characterizes these investigators is their underlying assumptions about the process of learning. In essence, three basic assumptions are held to be true. First, observable behavior rather than internal thought processes is the focus of study; in particular, learning is manifested by a change in behavior. Second, the environment shapes behavior; what one learns is determined by the elements in the environment, not by the individual learner. And third, the principles of contiguity (how close in time two events must be for a bond to be formed) and reinforcement (any means of increasing the likelihood that an event will be repeated) are central to explaining the learning process (Grippin and Peters, 1984).

Edward L. Thorndike, a contemporary of Watson, is "perhaps the greatest learning theorist of all time" (Hergenhahn, 1988, p. 55). A prolific researcher and writer, "he did pioneer work not only in learning theory but also in the areas of educational practices, verbal behavior, comparative psychology, intelligence testing, the nature-nurture problem, transfer of training, and the application of quantitative measures to sociopsychological problems" (p. 55). His major contribution to understanding learning has come to be called connectionism, or the S-R theory of learning. Using animals in controlled experiments, Thorndike noted that through repeated trial-and-error learning, certain connections between sensory impressions, or stimuli (S), and subsequent behavior, or responses (R), are strengthened or weakened by the consequences of behavior. Thorndike formulated three laws of learning to explain his findings: the Law of Effect, which states that learners will acquire and remember responses that lead to satisfying after-effects; the Law of Exercise, which asserts that the repetition of a meaningful connection results in substantial learning; and the Law of Readiness, which notes that if the organism is ready for the connection, learning is enhanced; otherwise learning is inhibited (Ormrod, 1995). Although Thorndike himself and later researchers modified these laws, they are nevertheless still applied widely in educational settings.

Thorndike's connectionism became refined and expanded on by his contemporaries and by those who followed. Pavlov, for example, working in Russia, added concepts of reinforcement, conditioned stimulus, and extinction to the basic notion of the stimulus-response connection. Guthrie stated that one law of learning based on contiguity is all that is needed to make learning comprehensible: "Whatever you do in the presence of a stimulus, you do again when that stimulus is re-presented" (Grippin and Peters, 1984, p. 61). Tolman (1959) introduced the notion that learning occurs in relation to purpose and that there are intervening variables between a stimulus and a response. Hull (1951) expanded Tolman's concept of intervening variables and proposed that a response depends on such factors as habit, strength, drive, and motivation. Important as the work of these researchers was (for a detailed discussion, see Hergenhahn, 1988; Ormrod, 1995; Sahakian, 1984), behaviorism was most developed as a theory of learning by B. F. Skinner.

Skinner's major contribution to understanding learning is known as operant conditioning. Simply stated, operant conditioning means "reinforce what you want the individual to do again; ignore what you want the individual to stop doing" (Grippin and Peters, 1984, p. 65). Reinforcement is essential to understanding operant conditioning. If behavior is reinforced or rewarded, the response is more likely to occur again under similar conditions. Behavior that is not reinforced is likely to become less frequent and may even disappear. Within this framework, even something as complex as personality can be explained by operant conditioning. Personality, according to Skinner (1974, p. 149), is a "repertoire of behavior imported by an organized set of contingencies"—in effect, a personal history of reinforcements. Skinner's research concentrated on positive and negative reinforcement schedules, the timing of reinforcements, and avoidance behavior. In essence, his work indicates that since all behavior is learned, it can be determined by arranging the contingencies of reinforcement in the learner's immediate environment. Behaviorists since Skinner have taken into account certain aspects of the human organism but still emphasize that it is environment that controls behavior, "not some mechanism within the individual" (Grippin and Peters, 1984, p. 71).

The behaviorist orientation has been foundational to much educational practice, including adult learning. Skinner in particular has addressed the application of his theory to educational issues. As he sees it, the ultimate goal of education is to bring about behavior that will ensure survival of the human species, societies, and individuals

(Skinner, 1971). The teacher's role is to design an environment that elicits desired behavior toward meeting these goals and to extinguish undesirable behavior.

Several educational practices can be traced to this type of learning. The systematic design of instruction, behavioral objectives, notions of the instructor's accountability, programmed instruction, computer-assisted instruction, competency-based education, and so on are solidly grounded in behavioral learning theory. Adult vocational and skills training—in which the learning task is broken into segments or tasks—in particular draws from behaviorism, as does technical and skills training within human resource development (HRD). The relatively new field of HRD focuses on adult learning in organizational settings, especially business and industry. Employees attend training sessions to improve performance, with performance usually being objectively and quantitatively measured (Swanson and Arnold, 1996). Some have even conceptualized HRD as human performance technology designed "to change the outcomes of behavior" (Jacobs, 1987, p. 19). Thus, the behavioral orientation to learning has had a profound effect on our educational system. It has also been challenged by theorists from two radically different perspectives: cognitivism and humanism.

COGNITIVE ORIENTATION

The earliest challenge to the behaviorists came in a publication in 1929 by Bode, a Gestalt psychologist. He criticized behaviorists for being too particularistic, too concerned with single events and actions, and too dependent on overt behavior to explain learning. Gestalt (a German word meaning "pattern or shape") psychologists proposed looking at the whole rather than its parts, at patterns rather than isolated events. Through the research of Gestaltists Wertheimer, Kohler, Koffka, and later Lewin (Hergenhahn, 1988; Ormrod, 1995), Gestalt views of learning rivaled behaviorism by the mid-twentieth century. These views have been incorporated into what have come to be labeled as cognitive or information processing learning theories.

Perception, insight, and meaning are key contributions to cognitivism from Gestalt learning theorists. According to cognitivists, "The human mind is not simply a passive exchange-terminal system where the stimuli arrive and the appropriate response leaves. Rather, the thinking person interprets sensations and gives meaning to the events that impinge upon his consciousness" (Grippin and Peters, 1984,

p. 76). Learning involves the reorganization of experiences in order to make sense of stimuli from the environment. Sometimes this sense comes through flashes of insight. Hergenhahn (1988, p. 252) summarizes the learning process according to Gestalt psychology: "Learning, to the Gestaltist, is a cognitive phenomenon. The organism 'comes to see' the solution after pondering a problem. The learner thinks about all the ingredients necessary to solve a problem and puts them together (cognitively) first one way and then another until the problem is solved. When the solution comes, it comes suddenly, that is, the organism gains an *insight* into the solution of a problem. The problem can exist in only two states: (1) unsolved and (2) solved; there is no state of partial solution in between." A major difference between Gestaltists and behaviorists, therefore, is the locus of control over the learning activity. For Gestaltists it lies with the individual learner; for behaviorists it lies with the environment. This shift to the individual—and in particular to the learner's mental processes—is characteristic of cognitivist-oriented learning theories.

A cognitive psychologist who clarified the focus on internal cognitive processes was Jean Piaget (1966). Influenced by both the behaviorist and Gestalt schools of thought, Piaget proposed that one's internal cognitive structure changes partly as a result of maturational changes in the nervous system and partly as a result of the organism's interacting with the environment and being exposed to an increasing number of experiences. His four-stage theory of cognitive development and its implications for adult learning were discussed more fully in Chapter Seven.

Currently, a number of research and theory-building efforts take as their starting point the mental processes involved in learning. These efforts include information processing theories, work on memory and metacognition, theories of transfer, mathematical learning theory models, the study of expertise, computer simulations, and artificial intelligence (see Chapter Nine). Converging with cognitive learning theory are theories of instruction that attempt to unite what is known about learning with the best way to facilitate its occurrence. Ausubel, Bruner, and Gagne provide good examples of how the understanding of mental processes can be linked to instruction.

Ausubel (1967) distinguishes between meaningful learning and rote learning. He suggests that learning is meaningful only when it can be related to concepts that already exist in a person's cognitive structure. Rote learning, on the other hand, does not become linked to a person's cognitive structure and hence is easily forgotten. Also unique is Ausubel's notion of "reception" learning. New knowledge is processed by the learner "only to the extent that more inclusive and appropriately relevant concepts are already available in the cognitive structure to serve a subsuming role or to provide definitional anchorage" (1967, p. 222). He suggests the use of "advance organizers" to prepare a person for new learning (1968). Ausubel's work can be seen as an antecedent to current research on schema theory whereby schemata—structures that organize the learner's worldview—determine how people process new experiences (J. Anderson, 1996; Di Vesta, 1987; Ormrod, 1995).

Ausubel emphasizes the importance of the learner's cognitive structure in new learning. Bruner, whose views are often contrasted with Ausubel's, emphasizes learning through discovery. Discovery is "in its essence a matter of rearranging or transforming evidence in such a way that one is enabled to go beyond the evidence so reassembled to additional new insights" (Bruner, 1965, pp. 607–608). According to Knowles (1984), Bruner's instructional theory is based on a theory about the act of learning that involves "three almost simultaneous processes: (1) acquisition of new information . . . ; (2) transformation, or the process of manipulating knowledge to make it fit new tasks; and (3) evaluation, or checking whether the way we have manipulated information is adequate to the task" (p. 25).

Linking the acquisition and processing of knowledge to instruction has probably been most thoroughly developed by Gagne, Briggs, and Wager (1992). They contend that there are eight different types of knowledge—signal learning, stimulus-response, motor training, verbal association, discrimination learning, concept learning, rule learning, and problem solving—each with appropriate instructional procedures. Kidd (1973, p. 182) points out that the work of Gagne and others has been an important influence on the "learning how to learn" concept, which has been explored in some depth by Smith, who has been particularly interested in applying it to adult learning (Smith, 1982, 1987; Smith and Associates, 1990). According to Smith (1982, p. 19), "Learning how to learn involves possessing, or acquiring, the knowledge and skill to learn effectively in whatever learning situation one encounters." Three subconcepts are involved: the learner's needs, a person's learning style, and training, which is organized activity, or instruction, to increase competence in learning. In addition to Smith's work on learning how to learn, the cognitive orientation can be seen in two other areas that have particular relevance for adult learning. First, interest in cognitive development in adulthood has been the subject of recent research (see Chapter Seven); second, the study of learning processes as a function of age (see Chapters Eight and Nine) draws from the cognitive focus on learning. (See also Tennant and Pogson, 1995.)

In summary, cognitively oriented explanations of learning encompass a wide range of topics with a common focus on internal mental processes that are within the learner's control. Di Vesta (1987, p. 229) has summarized recent directions in cognitive learning: "It is apparent that the current cognitive movement, rather than seeking the general all-encompassing laws for controlling and predicting behavior, as did the earlier grand theories of learning, is directed toward miniature models of specific facets of cognition, such as models of discourse analysis, models of comprehension, ways of aiding understanding and meaningful learning, the nature of the schemata, the memory system, the development of cognitive skills, and the like."

HUMANIST ORIENTATION

Humanist theories consider learning from the perspective of the human potential for growth. This shift to the study of the affective as well as cognitive dimensions of learning was informed in part by Freud's psychoanalytic approach to human behavior. Although most would not label Freud a learning theorist, aspects of his psychology, such as the influence of the subconscious mind on behavior, as well as the concepts of anxiety, repression, defense mechanism, drives, and transference, have found their way into some learning theories. Sahakian (1984), in fact, makes the case for psychoanalytic therapy as a type of learning theory.

Despite Freud's focus on personality, humanists reject the view of human nature implied by both behaviorists and Freudian psychologists. Identifying their orientation as a "third force," humanists refuse to accept the notion that behavior is predetermined by either the environment or one's subconscious. Rather, human beings can control their own destiny; people are inherently good and will strive for a better world; people are free to act, and behavior is the consequence of human choice; people possess unlimited potential for growth and development (Rogers, 1983; Maslow, 1970). From a learning theory perspective, humanism emphasizes that perceptions are centered in experience, as well as the freedom and responsibility to become what one is capable of becoming. These tenets underlie much of adult learning theory that stresses the self-directedness of adults and the value of experience in the learning process. Two psychologists who have contributed the most to our understanding of learning from this perspective are Abraham Maslow and Carl Rogers.

Maslow (1970), considered the founder of humanistic psychology, proposed a theory of human motivation based on a hierarchy of needs. At the lowest level of the hierarchy are physiological needs such as hunger and thirst, which must be attended to before one can deal with safety needs—those dealing with security and protection. The remaining levels are belonging and love, self-esteem, and, finally, the need for self-actualization. This final need can be seen in a person's desire to become all that he or she is capable of becoming. The motivation to learn is intrinsic; it emanates from the learner. For Maslow self-actualization is the goal of learning, and educators should strive to bring this about. As Sahakian (1984) notes, learning from Maslow's point of view is itself "a form of self-actualization. Among the growth motivations was found the need for cognition, the desire to know and to understand. Learning is not only a form of psychotherapy . . . , but learning contributes to psychological health" (p. 438). Although self-actualization is the primary goal of learning, there are other goals (p. 439):

1. The discovery of a vocation or destiny

2. The knowledge or acquisition of a set of values

3. The realization of life as precious

4. The acquisition of peak experiences

5. A sense of accomplishment

6. The satisfaction of psychological needs

7. The refreshing of consciousness to an awareness of the beauty and wonder of life

8. The control of impulses

9. The grappling with the critical existential problems of life

10. Learning to choose discriminatively

Another major figure writing from a humanist orientation is Carl Rogers. His book *Freedom to Learn for the 80s* (1983) lays out his theory of learning, which he sees as a similar process in both therapy and education. In fact, his "client-centered therapy" is often equated with student-centered learning. In both education and therapy, Rogers is concerned with significant learning that leads to personal growth and development. Such learning, according to Rogers, has the following characteristics (p. 20):

1. *Personal involvement:* the affective and cognitive aspects of a person should be involved in the learning event.

2. *Self-initiated:* a sense of discovery must come from within.

3. *Pervasive:* the learning "makes a difference in the behavior, the attitudes, perhaps even the personality of the learner."

4. *Evaluated by the learner:* the learner can best determine whether the experience is meeting a need.

5. *Essence is meaning:* when experiential learning takes place, its meaning to the learner becomes incorporated into the total experience.

Quite clearly, Rogers's principles of significant learning and Maslow's views have been integrated into much of adult learning. Knowles's theory of andragogy, with its assumptions about the adult learner (see Chapter Twelve), and much of the research and writing on self-directed learning (see Chapter Thirteen) are grounded in humanistic learning theories. As Caffarella (1993b, p. 26) observes about self-directed learning, "The focus of learning is on the individual and self-development, with learners expected to assume primary responsibility for their own learning. The process of learning, which is centered on learner need, is seen as more important than the content; therefore, when educators are involved in the learning process, their most important role is to act as facilitators, or guides." Moreover, humanistic theories have the potential for designing a true learning society, since "there is a natural tendency for people to learn and that learning will flourish if nourishing, encouraging environments are provided" (Cross, 1981, p. 228).

SOCIAL LEARNING ORIENTATION

This learning theory, which combines elements from both behaviorist and cognitivist orientations, posits that people learn from observing others. By definition, such observations take place in a social setting—hence the label "observational" or "social" learning (Lefrancois, 1996). Just *how* the learning occurs has been the subject of several investigations.

Miller and Dollard in the 1940s were the first to explore how people learn through observation. Drawing from stimulus-response and reinforcement theory, they argued that people do not learn from observation alone; rather, they must imitate and reinforce what they have observed. "If imitative responses were not made and reinforced, no learning would take place. For them, imitative learning was the result of observation, overt responding, and reinforcement" (Hergenhahn, 1988, p. 321). These ideas are totally congruent with the behaviorist orientation to learning. Miller and Dollard's main contribution was to demonstrate that "social-personality phenomena could be described and explained with the more objective and reliable concepts of a learning theory" (Phares, 1980, p. 412). Not until the 1960s, however, with the work of Bandura, did social learning theory break from a purely behaviorist orientation.

Bandura focused more on the cognitive processes involved in the observation than on the subsequent behavior. Central to his theory is the separation of observation from the act of imitation. One can learn from observation, he maintains, without having to imitate what was observed (Lefrancois, 1996). In fact, the learning can be vicarious: "Virtually all learning phenomena resulting from direct experiences can occur on a vicarious basis through observation of other people's behavior and its consequences for the observer" (Bandura, 1976, p. 392). In addition to being cognitive and vicarious, Bandura's observational learning is characterized by the concept of self-regulation. He contends that "persons can regulate their own behavior to some extent by visualizing self-generated consequences" (p. 392).

Observational learning is influenced by the four processes of attention, retention or memory, behavioral rehearsal, and motivation (Hergenhahn, 1988). Before something can be learned, the model must be attended to; some models are more likely than others to be attended to, such as those thought to be competent, powerful, attractive, and so on. Information from an observation then needs to be retained or stored for future use: "Symbols retained from a modeling experience act as a template with which one's actions are compared. During this rehearsal process individuals observe their own behavior and compare it to their cognitive representation of the modeled experience" (Hergenhahn, 1988, p. 327). Finally, the modeled behavior is stored until a person is motivated to act on it. More recently, Bandura has focused on self-efficacy, that is, our own estimate of how competent we feel we are likely to be in a particular environment. This self-assessment influences how effective we are in interactions with others and with our environment (Lefrancois, 1996).

Bandura's theory has particular relevance to adult learning in that it accounts for both the learner and the environment in which he or she operates. Behavior is a function of the interaction of the person with the environment. This is a reciprocal concept in that people influence their environment, which in turn influences the way they behave. This three-way interactive model is pictured by Bandura as a triangle (Bandura, 1986; Staddon, 1984). Learning is set solidly within a social context.

The importance of the social situation is central to Rotter's (1954) theory, which includes strands from behaviorism, cognitivism, and personality theory. Rotter's theory is framed by seven propositions and attendant corollaries that delineate relationships among the concepts of behavior, personality, experience, and environment. Rotter's theory assumes "that much of human behavior takes place in a meaningful environment and is acquired through social interactions with other people" (Phares, 1980, p. 406). Key to understanding "which behavior (once acquired) in the individual's repertoire will occur in a given situation" (p. 407) are the concepts of expectancy and reinforcement. Expectancy is the likelihood that a particular reinforcement will occur as the result of specific behavior: "The way in which the person construes or psychologically defines the situation will affect the values of both reinforcement and expectancy thereby influencing the potential for any given behavior to occur" (p. 408). Phares notes that research on the ways in which expectancies "generalize and change" has been a major contribution to our understanding of the learning process (p. 426).

Several useful concepts emerge from social learning theory. For example, the motivation to engage in adult learning activities might be partly explained by Rotter's (1954) notion of locus of control. Some people attribute their successes and failures to factors over which they feel they have no control—they exhibit an external locus of control—versus those who attribute successes and failures to personal, internal factors. An example of how this might relate to motivation and participation in adult education would be the case of someone out of work. He might blame his unemployment on factors over which he feels he has no control such as "the economy," or lack of public trans- portation, or his age, gender, or skin color. Another person, whose locus of control is more internal, might decide that his being unemployed is more due to his inability to get along with coworkers, his lack of com- puter skills, and so forth. This person is much more likely to engage in learning activities to make himself more employable. Another con- nection to adult learning is the importance of context and the learner's interaction with the environment to explain behavior. That is, expla- nations of learning may need to focus on more than overt behavior, mental processes, or personality. Studying the interaction of all these factors may result in a more comprehensive explanation of how adults learn. Moreover, Bandura's work on observational learning and mod- eling provides insights into social role acquisition and the nature of mentoring, a topic explored in depth by several adult educators (see Cohen, 1995; Daloz, 1986; Galbraith and Cohen, 1995).

CONSTRUCTIVISM

Like some of the other theories already reviewed, constructivism encompasses a number of related perspectives. Basically, a construc- tivist stance maintains that learning is a process of constructing meaning; it is how people make sense of their experience. Beyond that basic assumption, constructivists differ as to the nature of real- ity, the role of experience, what knowledge is of interest, and whether the process of meaning making is primarily individual or social (Steffe and Gale, 1995).

In an essay underscoring the variety of perspectives that are labeled constructivist, Phillips (1995) identifies six major strands: von Glaser- feld's work in math and science education, Kant's notions of knowledge and experience, feminist theorists' views on knowledge construction, Kuhn's work on scientific paradigms and revolutions, Piaget's theory of cognitive development, and Dewey's assumptions about knowledge and experience. Where these strands seem to converge is in the debate over the individual versus the social. Driver and her colleagues (1994) frame the issue as one of personal versus social constructivism. Draw- ing heavily from Piaget, learning as an individual or personal activity involves a "progressive adaptation of [an] individual's cognitive schemes to the physical environment" (Driver and others, 1994, p. 6). Meaning is made by the individual and is dependent on the individ- ual's previous and current knowledge structure. Learning is thus an internal cognitive activity. Teaching from the personal constructivism perspective involves providing "experiences that induce cognitive conflict and hence encourage learners to develop new knowledge schemes that are better adapted to experience. Practical activities supported by group discussions form the core of such pedagogical practices" (Driver and others, 1994, p. 6).

The social constructivist view, on the other hand, posits that knowledge is "constructed when individuals engage socially in talk and activity about shared problems or tasks. Making meaning is thus a dialogic process involving persons-in-conversation, and learning is seen as the process by which individuals are introduced to a culture by more skilled members" (Driver and others, 1994, p. 7). This approach involves learning the culturally shared ways of understanding and talking about the world and reality.

Phillips (1995) points out that a continuum actually exists between the personal or individual orientation of Piaget and Vygotsky and the social perspective of feminist epistemologists. Some constructivists "believe that their theories throw light on both the question of how individuals build up bodies of knowledge and how human communities have constructed the public bodies of knowledge known as the various disciplines" (p. 7). Cobb (1994, p. 13), for example, suggests viewing mathematical learning as "both a process of active individual construction and a process of enculturation into the mathematical practices of wider society." However, regardless of one's position on the continuum, there are important pedagogical implications to be derived, "each of which has a degree of credibility that is independent of the fate of the respective epistemologies" (p. 10). Candy (1991, p. 275), writing from a predominantly social constructivist perspective, discusses how this view translates to adult education: "Becoming knowledgeable involves acquiring the symbolic meaning structures appropriate to one's society, and, since knowledge is socially constructed, individual members of society may be able to add to or change the general pool of knowledge. Teaching and learning, *especially for adults,* is a process of negotiation, involving the construction and exchange of personally relevant and viable meanings" (emphasis added).

A constructivist perspective is congruent with much of adult learning theory. Candy (1991, p. 278) points out that "the constructivist view of learning is particularly compatible with the notion of self-direction, since it emphasizes the combined characteristics of active inquiry, independence, and individuality in a learning task." Transformational learning theory (see Chapter Fourteen), especially as presented by Mezirow, focuses on both the individual and social construction of meaning. Perspective transformation is a highly cognitive process in which one's meaning schemes and meaning perspectives undergo radical change (Mezirow, 1991). The central role of experience in adult learning is another point of connection. Andragogy and other models of adult learning see life experience as both a resource and a stimulus for learning; so constructivism too begins with the learner's interaction with experience. Finally, much of what the field of adult learning draws from situated cognition is constructivist in nature (see Chapter Ten). Concepts such as cognitive apprenticeship, situated learning, reflective practice, and communities of practice are found in both adult learning and constructivist literature. Two adult education practice arenas in particular where constructivist and situated cognition concepts are having an impact are in continuing professional education (Ferry and Ross-Gordon, 1998) and human resource development (Stamps, 1997). As Wegner (cited by Stamps, 1997, pp. 38–39) explains, "What is shared by a community of practice—what makes it a community—is its practice. The concept of practice connotes doing, but not just doing in and of itself. It is doing in a historical and social context that give structure and meaning to what we do. . . . Learning is the engine of practice, and practice is the history of that learning. . . . Indeed, practice is ultimately produced by its members through the negotiation of meaning."

SUMMARY

Learning, a process central to human behavior, has been of interest to philosophers, psychologists, educators, and politicians for centuries. Since the late nineteenth century, the systematic investigation of this phenomenon has resulted in many explanations of how people learn. This chapter has reviewed some of these theories. Because there are dozens of learning theories and volumes written describing them, we have explored different orientations to learning, any of which might include numerous learning theories. The behaviorist, cognitivist, humanist, social learning, and constructivist orientations were chosen for their diversity and for their insights into learning in adulthood. Table 11.1 summarizes these five orientations. Since each is based on different assumptions about the nature of learning, the strategies one

Aspect	Behaviorist	Cognitivist	Humanist	Social Learning	Constructivist
Learning theorists	Guthrie, Hull, Pavlov, Skinner, Thorndike, Tolman, Watson	Ausubel, Bruner, Gagne, Koffka, Kohler, Lewin, Piaget	Maslow, Rogers	Bandura, Rotter	Candy, Dewey, Lave, Piaget, Rogoff, von Glasersfeld, Vygotsky
View of the learning process	Change in behavior	Internal mental process (including insight, information processing, memory, perception)	A personal act to fulfill potential	Interaction with and observation of others in a social context	Construction of meaning from experience
Locus of learning	Stimuli in external environment	Internal cognitive structuring	Affective and cognitive needs	Interaction of person, behavior, and environment	Internal construction of reality by individual
Purpose of education	Produce behavioral change in desired direction	Develop capacity and skills to learn better	Become self-actualized, autonomous	Model new roles and behavior	Construct knowledge
Teacher's role	Arranges environment to elicit desired response	Structures content of learning activity	Facilitates development of whole person	Models and guides new roles and behavior	Facilitates and negotiates meaning with learner
Manifestation in adult learning	• Behavioral objectives • Competency-based education • Skill development and training	• Cognitive development • Intelligence, learning, and memory as function of age • Learning how to learn	• Andragogy • Self-directed learning	• Socialization • Social roles • Mentoring • Locus of control	• Experiential learning • Self-directed learning • Perspective transformation • Reflective practice

Table 11.1. Five Orientations to Learning.

might use to enhance learning will depend on one's orientation. Instructors and program developers can use this review of major learning theories to identify their own theory of learning and discover the strategies for facilitating learning that are most congruent with their theory.

In brief, behaviorists define learning as a change in behavior. The focus of their research is overt behavior, which is a measurable response to stimuli in the environment. The role of the teacher is to arrange the contingencies of reinforcement in the learning environment so that the desired behavior will occur. Findings from behavioral learning theories can be seen in training and vocational adult education.

In contrast to behaviorists, researchers working from a cognitivist perspective focus not on external behavior but on internal mental processes. Cognitivists are interested in how the mind makes sense out of stimuli in the environment—how information is processed, stored, and retrieved. This orientation is especially evident in the study of adult learning from a developmental perspective. The major concerns are how aging affects an adult's ability to process and retrieve information and how it affects an adult's internal mental structures.

Also in contrast to behaviorism is the humanistic orientation to learning. Here the emphasis is on human nature, human potential, human emotions, and affect. Theorists in this tradition believe that learning involves more than cognitive processes and overt behavior. It is a function of motivation and involves choice and responsibility. Much of adult learning theory, especially the concepts of andragogy and many of the models of self-directed learning, are grounded in humanistic assumptions.

The fourth orientation discussed here is social learning. This perspective differs from the other three in its focus on the social setting in which learning occurs. From this perspective, learning occurs through the observation of people in one's immediate environment. Furthermore, learning is a function of the interaction of the person, the environment, and the behavior. Variations in behavior under the same circumstances can be explained by idiosyncratic personality traits and their unique interaction with environmental stimuli. Social learning theories contribute to adult learning by highlighting the importance of social context and explicating the processes of modeling and mentoring.

Finally, constructivism, representing an array of perspectives, posits that learners construct their own knowledge from their experiences.

The cognitive process of meaning making is emphasized as both an individual mental activity and a socially interactive interchange. Aspects of constructivism can be found in self-directed learning, transformational learning, experiential learning, situated cognition, and reflective practice.

The Learning
Transaction with Adults

The accumulation of information and experiences grounded in practice often leads to thinking about how the parts of what we know might fit together to form some sort of explanatory framework. In Part Four of *Learning in Adulthood*, we review a number of efforts to explain adult learning. Some of these efforts, as in the work on self-directed learning, are in fact tentative frameworks for ordering research—frameworks suggesting future directions for theory. Other efforts can properly be labeled models, if we define model as a visual representation, or theories. A theory is a set of interrelated concepts that explain some aspect of the field in a parsimonious manner.

We begin Chapter Twelve with a discussion of Knowles's (1980) concept of andragogy, which he originally termed a theory of adult learning. Probably the best-known set of principles or assumptions to guide adult learning practice, andragogy actually tells us more about the characteristics of adult learners than about the nature of learning itself. The first half of the chapter is devoted to a thorough review and critique of andragogy. The second half of Chapter Twelve reviews four other models of adult learning: Cross's (1981) characteristics of adult learners (CAL) model, McClusky's (1970a) theory of margin, Knox's

(1980) proficiency theory, and Jarvis's (1987a) model of the learning process.

Since Tough's work on adult learning projects published in 1971, self-directed learning and individual learning projects have captured the imagination of researchers and writers both inside and outside the field of adult education. Although learning on one's own is the way most adults go about acquiring new ideas, skills, and attitudes, this context has often been regarded as less important than learning that takes place in more formal settings. Chapter Thirteen discusses three types of models—linear, interactive, and instructional—developed to describe the process of learning when that learning is primarily managed by the learners themselves. Most adults use more of an interactive model in that they do not necessarily plan what, how, or when they want to learn. Scholars have also focused on studying self-direction as a personal attribute of the learner. Two ideas that have received the most attention in this approach are the notion of readiness for self-directed learning and the concept of autonomy. The chapter concludes with a review of the major issues researchers need to address in building future research agendas in self-directed learning.

Chapters Fourteen and Fifteen are new to this second edition of *Learning in Adulthood*. Changes in cognition and consciousness constitute the focus of transformational learning reviewed in Chapter Fourteen. Mezirow's (1991) perspective transformation and Freire's (1970b) conscientization contend that changes in perspective or consciousness are the defining characteristic of learning in adulthood. Mezirow's theory in particular has stimulated considerable debate and research within the past ten years. Drawing primarily from Freire and Mezirow, the first half of the chapter reviews the theoretical bases for transformational learning by highlighting the concepts of the centrality of life experience, the nature of critical reflection, and the connection between transformative learning and adult development. Also examined in the chapter are the following issues: the extent to which the theory takes context into account, whether the theory relies too heavily on rationality, the place of social action, and the educator's role in facilitating transformative learning.

The last chapter in Part Four is titled "Critical Theory, Postmodern, and Feminist Perspectives." Although none of these approaches would be considered an adult learning theory in and of itself, each is having a significant impact on how educators of adults think about adult learning and the practice of adult education today. Each of these frameworks, to varying degrees, has directed attention to how race, class, and gender shape the learning transaction, how power and oppression are inherent in the process, and how diversity and multiplicity characterize the context of learning as well as how knowledge is constructed in that context. In addition to these general concepts, which cut across several perspectives, we look specifically at the contributions made by each of the three schools of thought: critical theory, postmodernism, and feminist pedagogy.

CHAPTER TWELVE

Andragogy and Other Models of Adult Learning

D o adults learn differently from children? What distinguishes adult learning and adult education from other areas of education? What particular characteristics about the learning transaction with adults can be identified to maximize their learning? Prior to the 1970s, adult educators relied primarily on psychologists' understandings of learning in general to inform their practice (see the chapters in Part Three). With the publication of Houle's *The Design of Education* (1972), Kidd's *How Adults Learn* (1973), and Knowles's *The Adult Learner: A Neglected Species* (1973) and *The Modern Practice of Adult Education* (1970), attention turned to research and theory-building efforts in adult learning. Attempts at codifying differences between adults and children as a set of principles, a model, or even a theory of adult learning have been, and continue to be, pursued by adult educators. However, just as there is no single theory that explains all of human learning, there is no single theory of adult learning. What we do have are a number of frameworks or models, each of which contributes something to our understanding of adults as learners. The best known of these efforts is andragogy, a concept Knowles introduced from Europe in a 1968 article. Andragogy focuses on the adult learner and his or her life situation, as do a number of other models presented in this chapter.

The first part of the chapter is devoted to describing and critiquing andragogy. In the second half of the chapter we review four other models of the adult learning transaction: Cross's CAL model, McCluskey's theory of margin, Knox's proficiency theory, and Jarvis's learning process.

ANDRAGOGY

Over thirty years ago Malcolm Knowles (1968, p. 351) proposed "a new label and a new technology" of adult learning to distinguish it from preadult schooling. The European concept of *andragogy,* meaning "the art and science of helping adults learn," was contrasted with pedagogy, the art and science of helping children learn (Knowles, 1980, p. 43). Andragogy is based on five assumptions about the adult learner:

1. As a person matures, his or her self-concept moves from that of a dependent personality toward one of a self-directing human being.

2. An adult accumulates a growing reservoir of experience, which is a rich resource for learning.

3. The readiness of an adult to learn is closely related to the developmental tasks of his or her social role.

4. There is a change in time perspective as people mature—from future application of knowledge to immediacy of application. Thus an adult is more problem centered than subject centered in learning (Knowles, 1980, pp. 44–45).

5. Adults are motivated to learn by internal factors rather than external ones (Knowles and Associates, 1984, pp. 9–12).

From each of these assumptions (the fifth was added after the original four), Knowles drew numerous implications for the design, implementation, and evaluation of learning activities with adults. For example, with regard to the first assumption that as adults mature they become more independent and self-directing, Knowles suggested that the classroom climate should be one of "adultness," both physically and psychologically. The climate should cause "adults to feel accepted, respected, and supported"; further, there should exist "a spirit of mutuality between teachers and students as joint inquirers" (1980, p. 47). Being self-directing also means that adult students can participate in the diagnosis of their learning needs, the planning and implementation of the learning experiences, and the evaluation of those experiences.

This theory, "model of assumptions" (Knowles, 1980, p. 43), or "system of concepts" (Knowles, 1984, p. 8) as Knowles has also called it, has given adult educators "a badge of identity" that distinguishes the field from other areas of education, especially childhood schooling (Brookfield, 1986, p. 90). Andragogy became a rallying point for those trying to define the field of adult education as separate from other areas of education. However, it also stimulated more controversy, philosophical debate, and critical analysis matched only, perhaps, by the recent discussions on transformational learning (see Chapter Fourteen).

At first the main point of contention was whether andragogy could be considered a "theory" of adult learning (Elias, 1979). Davenport and Davenport (1985, p. 157) chronicle the history of the debate and note that andragogy has been classified "as a theory of adult education, theory of adult learning, theory of technology of adult learning, method of adult education, technique of adult education, and a set of assumptions." They are a bit more optimistic than other critics for andragogy's chances of possessing "the explanatory and predictive functions generally associated with a fully developed theory" (p. 158). For them, the issue can be resolved through empirical studies that test the underlying assumptions.

Hartree (1984) observed that it was not clear whether Knowles had presented a theory of learning or a theory of teaching, whether adult learning was different from child learning, and whether there was a theory at all—perhaps these were just principles of good practice. The assumptions, she noted, "can be read as descriptions of the adult learner . . . or as prescriptive statements about what the adult learner *should* be like" (p. 205). Because the assumptions are "unclear and shaky" on several counts, Hartree (1984) concludes that while "many adult educators might accept that the principles of adult teaching and conditions of learning which he [Knowles] evolves have much to offer, and are in a sense descriptive of what is already recognized as good practice by those in the field, conceptually Knowles has not presented a good case for the validity of such practice. . . . Although he appears to approach his model of teaching from the point of view of a theory of adult learning, he does not establish a unified theory of learning in a systematic way" (pp. 206–207).

Brookfield (1986, p. 98), who also raises the question of whether andragogy is a "proven theory," assesses to what extent a "set of well-grounded principles of good practice" can be derived from andragogy. He argues that three of the assumptions are problematic when drawing inferences for practice: self-direction is more a desired outcome than a given condition, and being problem centered and desiring immediate application can lead to a narrow, reductionist view of learning. Brookfield finds only the experience assumption to be well grounded. However, even it can be questioned. The fact that adults have lived longer than children and thus have a quantity of experience greater than children have does not necessarily translate into quality experience that can become a resource for learning; indeed, certain life experiences can function as barriers to learning (Merriam, Mott, and Lee, 1996). Further, children in certain situations may have a range of experiences qualitatively richer than some adults (Hanson, 1996). As for the more recently added fifth assumption, although adults may be more internally than externally motivated to learn, in much of workplace learning and continuing professional education, not to mention governmental or socially mandated learning (as in the case of driving school, job preparation, and prison education, for example), participation is required.

On the issue of whether andragogy can be considered a theory of adult learning, perhaps Knowles himself put the issue to rest. In his autobiographical work, *The Making of an Adult Educator* (1989, p. 112), he wrote that he "prefers to think of [andragogy] as a model of assumptions about learning or a conceptual framework that serves as a *basis* for an emergent theory" (emphasis added).

A second point of criticism was Knowles's original inference that andragogy, with all its technological implications for instruction, characterized adult learning, while pedagogy, with another set of implications, characterized childhood learning. Close scrutiny of the five assumptions and their implications for practice by educators in and out of adult education led Knowles to back off his original stance that andragogy characterized only adult learning. The clearest indication of this rethinking was the change in the subtitles of the 1970 and 1980 editions of *The Modern Practice of Adult Education*. The 1970 subtitle is *Andragogy Versus Pedagogy,* whereas the 1980 subtitle is *From Pedagogy to Andragogy.* Knowles's later position, as reflected in the 1980 subtitle, is that pedagogy-andragogy represents a continuum ranging from teacher-directed to student-directed learning and that both approaches are appropriate with children and adults, depending on the situation. For example, an adult who knows little or nothing about a topic will be more dependent on the teacher for direction; at the other extreme, children who are naturally curious and who are "very self-directing in their learning *outside of school* . . . could also be more self-directed in school" (Knowles, 1984, p. 13). Andragogy now appears to be situation specific and not unique to adults.

There are also some inconsistencies in Knowles's reconstruction of andragogy-pedagogy into a continuum. As Brookfield (1986) points out, his reformulation from a dichotomy to a continuum only added to the conceptual confusion, for, as Cross (1981, p. 225) observes, "a continuum from pedagogy to andragogy really does not exist. Although some andragogical assumptions (such as experience) lie on a continuum, others (such as problem-centered versus subject-centered learning) appear more dichotomous in nature." In support of Cross's critique, a study by Delahaye, Limerick, and Hearn (1994) testing the notion of a continuum between andragogy and pedagogy found the relationship to be more complex than the one-dimensional line of a continuum: "An individual can be located within a two dimensional space that is bounded on one side by andragogy and on the adjoining side by pedagogy. For example, a learner could be considered to be high on pedagogy and high on andragogy, or low on pedagogy and low on andragogy" (p. 195).

More recent critiques of andragogy have pointed out that in its slavish focus on the individual learner, the sociohistorical context in which learning takes place is virtually ignored (Grace, 1996b; Little, 1994; Pearson and Podeschi, 1997; Pratt, 1993). Knowles's reliance on humanistic psychology results in a picture of the individual learner as one who is autonomous, free, and growth oriented. There is little or no awareness that the person is socially situated and, to some extent, the product of the sociohistorical and cultural context of the times; nor is there any awareness that social institutions and structures may be defining the learning transaction irrespective of the individual participant. Pratt (1993, p. 22) summarizes these two tensions as "likely to characterize further debate about andragogy. First, there is a tension between freedom and authority, especially regarding the management and evaluation of learning. Andragogy leans heavily toward learner freedom (versus teacher authority) on this issue, promoting self-direction and personal autonomy. Second, there is a tension between human agency and social structures as the most potent influences on adult learning. Here, andragogy is unconditionally on the side of human agency and the power of the individual to shed the shackles of history and circumstance in pursuit of learning."

Grace (1996b, p. 383) points out how Knowles himself and his theory of andragogy were logical products of the 1960s, "a period of rapid change; action-oriented curricula that valued individual experience were advocated. The individual had to keep up and self-improvement was in *vogue*. The andragogical model in the face of pedagogy was welcomed by many adult educators as revolutionary" (p. 383). But although its influence on adult learning has been substantial over the past thirty years, "Knowles never proceeded to an in-depth consideration of the organizational and social impediments to adult learning; he never painted the 'big picture.' He chose the mechanistic over the meaningful" (Grace, 1996b, p. 386). Pratt (1993), Grace (1986b), and others (Collins, 1992; Jarvis, 1987a) see andragogy's hold on the field subsiding as more sophisticated analyses of the adult learner as a social being living and learning in a social context take center stage. In the words of Grace (1996b, p. 391), because "Knowles has reduced the adult learner to a technically proficient droid, operating in a world where formulaic social planning and self-directed learning mantras are the order of the day," he "is in danger of being left behind. The adult learning pendulum is slowly swinging away from him."

Considering that andragogy has been the primary model of adult learning for nearly thirty years, relatively little empirical work has been done to test the validity of its assumptions or its usefulness in predicting adult learning behavior. A few studies have focused on the relationship between andragogical assumptions and instruction. Beder and Darkenwald (1982) asked teachers who taught both adults and preadults if their teaching behavior differed according to the age of the students. Teachers reported viewing adult students differently and using more andragogical techniques. Gorham (1985), however, actually observed teachers of adults and preadults. She found no differences in how a particular teacher instructed adults or preadults, although teachers claimed that they did treat the two age groups differently. Beder and Carrea (1988) found that training teachers in andragogical methods had a positive and significant effect on attendance but no effect on how teachers were evaluated by the students. Yet another study draws from Knowles's assumption that adults are self-directing and thus like to plan their own learning experiences. Rosenblum and Darkenwald (1983) compared achievement and satisfaction measures between groups who had planned their course and those who had it planned for them. No differences were found in either achievement or satisfaction. Courtenay, Arnold, and Kim (1994) reviewed all previous literature and research *and* conducted their own quasi-experimental study of learner involvement in planning. They found previous research results to be inconclusive (indeed, "capricious"); from their own study, which attempted to address some of the shortcomings of previous studies, they found that "participation in planning does not appear to affect learning gain or satisfaction, even when the amount of participant input in planning is increased; the relationship between classroom environment and achievement or satisfaction is inconsequential; and classroom environment . . . may simply be a function of the satisfaction of the learner" (p. 297). They recommend more thought be given to both the independent variable (that is, just what constitutes learner participation in planning) and the dependent variables (for example, perhaps unintended learning is as important as achievement).

Although there has not been much direct testing of the validity of andragogy, one could consider the extent to which a broader range of research in adult learning may or may not support the assumptions underlying andragogy. For example, some of the research on self-directed learning (see Chapter Thirteen) would tend to support the assumption that as adults mature, they move toward self-direction. Many studies on participation (see Chapter Three) indicate that participation is clearly linked to adult roles of worker, family member, and so on, lending support to the assumption that the readiness of an adult to learn is closely linked to the developmental tasks of his or her social roles. That the developmental issues of adulthood lead to learning was also underscored in Aslanian and Brickell's (1980) findings that 83 percent of adult learners were engaged in learning activities because of some transition in their lives. On the other hand, the growing prevalence of mandated continuing education could be cited to argue against the assumption that adults are internally motivated.

Despite these rather grim predictions of andragogy's demise, practitioners who work with adult learners continue to find Knowles's andragogy, with its characteristics of adult learners, to be a helpful rubric for better understanding adults as learners. The implications for practice that Knowles draws for each of the assumptions are also considered to be good instructional practice for all ages, especially adults. Thus, we see andragogy as an enduring model for understanding certain aspects of adult learning. It does not give us the total picture, nor is it a panacea for fixing adult learning practices. Rather, it constitutes one piece of the rich mosaic of adult learning.

OTHER MODELS OF ADULT LEARNING

Although andragogy remains the best-known model of adult learning, there are a number of other models that offer us some insights into adult learning. The following four models will be discussed: Cross's CAL model, McClusky's theory of margin, Knox's proficiency model, and Jarvis's learning process. Like andragogy, these models have a common focus on the characteristics and life situation of the adult learner.

Cross's CAL Model

The characteristics of adults as learners (CAL) model offered by Cross (1981, p. 234) is "a tentative framework to accommodate current knowledge about what we know about adults as learners in the hope that it may suggest ideas for further research and for implementation." Cross points out that some of the assumptions of andragogy such as readiness and self-concept can be readily "incorporated into [the] CAL construct" (p. 238).

Based on differences between children and adults, the model consists of two classes of variables: personal characteristics and situational characteristics (see Figure 12.1). Personal characteristics comprise physical, psychological, and sociocultural dimensions. These are continua and reflect growth and development from childhood into adult life. Situational characteristics focus on variables unique to adult participants—for example, part-time versus full-time learning and voluntary versus compulsory participation.

Cross (1981) believes her model incorporates completed research on aging, stage and phase developmental studies, participation, learning projects, motivation, and so on. The model can also be used to stimulate research by thinking across and between categories. It might be asked, for example, whether there is a "relationship between stage

Personal Characteristics
$- - - - - - - - - - - - - - - \rightarrow$ Physiological/Aging $- - - - - - - - - - - - - - \rightarrow$
$- - - - - - - - - - - - - \rightarrow$ Sociocultural/Life phases $- - - - - - - - - - - - - \rightarrow$
$- - - - - - - - - - \rightarrow$ Physiological/Developmental stages $- - - - - - - - - - - \rightarrow$

Situational Characteristics
Part-time learning versus full-time learning
Voluntary learning versus compulsory learning

Figure 12.1.   Characteristics of Adults as Learners:
A Conceptual Framework.
Source: Cross, 1981, p. 235.

of ego development and voluntary participation in learning" or whether transition points in development "generate extra amounts of volunteer learning" (p. 248). Rather than suggesting implications for practice, as Knowles's andragogy does, Cross's model offers a "framework for thinking about *what* and *how* adults learn" (p. 248).

Although the CAL model is intended to be a comprehensive explanation of adult learning, the variables may be too broadly defined. What situational characteristics when combined with which personal characteristics lead to explaining different types of learning, for example? Probably a more serious problem with the model is its focus on the characteristics of adults, which tells us little about how adults actually learn or if they learn differently than children do. Furthermore, the personal characteristics can apply to children as well as adults since they are on continua reflective of growth from childhood into adulthood. Nor do the situational characteristics neatly divide between children and adults. Some adult learners are full time, and some participate because of mandatory continuing education requirements; some preadults are part-time learners, and some learning is done on a voluntary basis. Perhaps because of some of these weaknesses, the CAL model has yet to be empirically tested.

McClusky's Theory of Margin

McClusky first presented his theory of margin in a 1963 publication, followed by discussions of application in 1970 and 1971. His theory is grounded in the notion that adulthood is a time of growth, change, and integration in which one constantly seeks balance between the amount of energy needed and the amount available. This balance is conceptualized as a ratio between the "load" (L) of life, which dissipates energy, and the "power" (P) of life, which allows one to deal with the load. The energy left over when one divides load by power McClusky called "margin in life" ($M = L/P$).

Both load and power comprise external and internal factors. Hiemstra (1993, p. 42) explains: "The external load consists of tasks involved in normal life requirements (such as family, work, and community responsibilities). Internal load consists of life expectancies developed by people (such as aspirations, desires, and future expectations). Power consists of a combination of such external resources . . . as family support, social abilities, and economic abilities. It also includes various internally acquired or accumulated skills and experiences contributing to effective performance, such as resilience, coping skills, and personality."

Taking both power and load into consideration, McClusky (1970a) explains how the theory works:

> Margin may be increased by reducing Load or increasing Power, or it may be decreased by increasing Load and/or reducing Power. We can control both by modifying either Power or Load. When Load continually matches or exceeds Power and if both are fixed and/or out of control, or irreversible, the situation becomes highly vulnerable and susceptible to breakdown. If, however, Load and Power can be controlled, and, better yet, if a person is able to lay hold of a reserve (Margin) of Power, he [sic] is better equipped to meet unforeseen emergencies, is better positioned to take risks, can engage in exploratory, creative activities, is more likely to learn, etc. [p. 83]

To engage in learning, then, an adult must have some margin of power "available for application to the processes which the learning situation requires" (McClusky, 1970a, p. 84). Adult students in particular have to be adept at juggling multiple responsibilities and demands on their time. McClusky gives two examples of how his theory might be applied to an adult's situation:

> First, I have an image of Mrs. A, a mother and the only adult in a poorly furnished home with four children at school and two at home, barely holding the line against family breakdown. Fighting a contin-

ual battle for survival, she has *no margin* for the P.T.A., night school
..., or the inner-city neighborhood committee organized to cooperate with local programs of urban renewal.

For our second example let us sketch a more optimistic picture. Mr.
C is in the prime of his middle years. In good physical condition, with
competence in his profession, with substantial influence in the community, and with access to ample financial resources, Mr. C carries a
large *load* which is a reflection of his *powers*. If his load is just a notch
under his capacity, it might appear that his margin is small, but at any
time and at his own discretion, Mr. C can reduce his *load* and hence
his *margin* may be regarded as ample. [p. 28]

Maintaining some margin of power in order to engage in learning
is a concept adults readily relate to. As Hiemstra (1993, p. 42) observes,
an adult student's first encounter with McClusky's theory is often "an
epiphany in terms of their own life circumstances."

McClusky (1970a) also saw his theory as helpful in explaining the
developmental changes characteristic of adult life (see Chapter Five).
Changes adults undergo as they age could be translated into adjustments of load and power. These adjustments are made "as a person
accumulates and later relinquishes adult responsibilities and modifies
the varying roles which the successive stages of the life cycle require"
(p. 84). Since learning in adulthood is often a function of changing
roles and responsibilities and physical and mental development,
McClusky's theory can be used in understanding this link between
development and learning. Several studies have in fact investigated
this link. Baum (1980) used the theory as a framework for exploring
the power and load of one hundred randomly selected widows. Self-
identified problems encountered in widowhood were viewed as load
factors, and services and resources available to widows were categorized as power factors. She found that negative attitudes toward
widowhood predicted more problems (load), but that it also led to
finding more resources (power). As load increased, power increased,
resulting in a fairly stable margin in life. Using an instrument developed to measure margin in life, Stevenson (1980) compared the load,
power, and margin patterns of independent older adults, nursing
home residents, and young and middle-aged adults. She found that
the two groups of older adults perceived themselves as having slightly
more power (and less load) than the young and middle-aged adults.
Finally, a number of studies have used McClusky's theory to study

adult student needs, performance, and participation in continuing education (Demko, 1982; Garrison, 1986; Hansen, 1988; James, 1986; Mikolaj, 1983; Walker, 1996; Weiman, 1987). The findings of all of these studies were mixed, so no clear-cut generalizations can be drawn regarding the validity of McClusky's theory.

McClusky's theory has appeal in that it speaks to the everyday events and life transitions that all adults encounter. It is perhaps a better counseling tool than it is an explanation of adult learning, however. In fact, there is a striking similarity between McClusky's power, load, and margin concepts and the components of Schlossberg's model for counseling adults in transition. In her model, one determines the ability to work through a transition by assessing the relative strength of four factors: the situation, the self (internal strengths), external supports, and strategies one has developed to handle stress (Schlossberg, 1984, 1987). Although life events and transitions certainly precipitate many (and some would say the most potent) learning experiences, McClusky's model does not directly address learning itself but rather *when* it is most likely to occur. One might also question whether a reserve of energy or margin of power is necessary for learning to occur. Learning can occur under conditions of stress or, in McClusky's terms, when load is greater than power. In addition, the fact that learning itself has the potential to increase one's power is not addressed by McClusky.

Knox's Proficiency Theory

Knox's (1980) proficiency theory also speaks to an adult's life situation. Adult learning, he writes, is distinctive on at least two counts: "the centrality of concurrent adult role performance" (p. 383) and the "close correspondence between learning and action beyond the educational program" (p. 384). Proficiency, as defined by Knox, is "the capability to perform satisfactorily if given the opportunity" (p. 378), and this performance involves some combination of attitude, knowledge, and skill. At the core of his theory is the notion of a discrepancy between the current and the desired level of proficiency. This concept of proficiency helps explain "adult motivation and achievement in both learning activities and life roles. Adults and society expect that individual adults will be proficient in major life roles and as persons generally" (1985, p. 252). A model representation of the theory contains the following interactive components: the general environment, past and current characteristics, performance, aspiration, self, discrepancies, specific environments, learning activity, and the teacher's role.

This set of interrelated concepts hinges on what Knox (1980, p. 99) defines as being the purpose of adult learning (whether self-directed or in organized programs): "to enhance proficiency to improve performance." Both teachers and learners can benefit from an analysis of the discrepancy between current and desired levels of proficiency: "An understanding of discrepancies between current and desired proficiencies helps to explain motives of adult learners and enables those who help adults learn to do so responsively and effectively" (Knox, 1986, p. 16). Knox (1986, p. 16) is careful to distinguish between his notion of proficiency and competency-based learning: "Whereas competency-based preparatory education emphasizes the achievement of minimal standards of performance in educational tasks, proficiency-oriented continuing education emphasizes achievement of optimal standards of proficiency related to adult life roles."

Knox's theory is not well known by adult educators, perhaps because its publication has been in sources outside the field. Its emphasis on performance would also appear to limit its application to learning that can be demonstrated by better performance. More problematic is the model's mixture of learning, teaching, and motivation. Knox (1985, p. 252) writes that the theory "suggests fundamental relationships among essential aspects of adult learning and teaching which constitute an interrelated set of guidelines for helping adults learn, with an emphasis on motivation." How one tracks the interaction of numerous components (or "essential aspects of adult learning and teaching") to arrive at an explanation of how adults learn is far from clear. And perhaps because of the complexity of the model and difficulty operationalizing the interrelationships of the variables, no reports of empirical use of the model could be found.

Jarvis's Learning Process

Jarvis's (1987a, p. 16) model begins with an adult's life situation or, more correctly, an adult's experience: "Even miseducative experiences may be regarded as learning experiences. . . . *All* learning begins with experience." Some experiences, however, are repeated with such frequency that they are taken for granted and do not lead to learning, such as driving a car or household routines. At the start of the learning process are experiences that "call for a response" (p. 63). Like

Knox's and McClusky's theories, Jarvis's model is based on a discrepancy between biography (all that a person is at a particular point in time) and experience—an incident that a person is unprepared to handle. This "inability to cope with the situation unthinkingly, instinctively, is at the heart of all learning" (1987a, p. 35).

For Jarvis (1987a, p. 64), all experience occurs within a social situation, a kind of objective context within which one experiences life: "Life may be conceptualized as an ongoing phenomenon located within a sociocultural milieu which is bounded by the temporality of birth and death. Throughout life, people are moving from social situation to social situation; sometimes in conscious awareness but in other occasions in a taken-for-granted manner." Jarvis's model of the learning process begins with a person moving into a social situation in which a potential learning experience occurs. From an experience, there are nine different routes that a person might take, some of which result in learning and some of which do not. Presumption, nonconsideration, and rejection do not result in learning. The six other responses (preconscious, practice, memorization, contemplation, reflective practice, and experimental learning) represent six different types of learning. The nine responses form a hierarchy. The first three are nonlearning responses, the second three are nonreflective learning, and the final three are reflective learning. These last three, Jarvis (1987a, p. 27) says, are the "higher forms of learning." Of the nonlearning responses, one can respond in a mechanical way (that is, presume that what has worked before will work again), one can be too preoccupied to consider a response, or one can reject the opportunity to learn. The nonreflective learning responses can be preconscious (that is, a person unconsciously internalizes something); one can practice a new skill until it is learned; or learners can acquire information "with which they have been presented and learn it, so that they can reproduce it at a later stage" (p. 33). The three higher forms of learning call for more involvement. Contemplation is thinking about what is being learned and does not require a behavioral outcome; reflective practice is akin to problem solving; experimental learning is the result of a person's experimenting on the environment.

In his book on the model, Jarvis (1987a) explains how each of the nine responses coincides with the visual representation of the learning process (see Figure 12.2). A person enters a social situation, has an experience, and can exit (box 4) unchanged because he or she ignored the event or took it for granted. One might also go from the experience (box 3) to memorization (box 6) and exit either unchanged (box 4) or changed (box 9). For a higher type of learning, a person might go from the experience to reasoning and reflecting (box 7) to practice and experimentation (box 5) to evaluation (box 8) to memorization (box 6) and to being changed (box 9).

More than the other theories discussed in this chapter, Jarvis's model does deal with learning itself. The thoroughness of his discussion, which concentrates on explaining the responses one can have to an experience, is a strength of the model. These responses encompass multiple types of learning and their different outcomes, a refreshingly comprehensive view of learning. Furthermore, his model situates learning within a social context; learning is an interactive phenomenon, not an isolated internal process. There is some question, however, as to whether his model is unique to adults. Although it was constructed from research with adult learners and has been used by Jarvis with adults in various settings, he himself suspects that "it is as valid for children as it is with adults. . . . There may be a relationship between the frequency of use of these different types of learning and the age of the learner, [but] no evidence exists at present that might verify this" (Jarvis, 1987a, pp. 35–36).

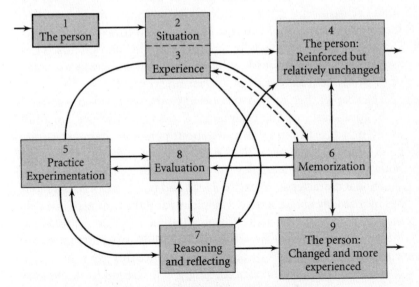

Figure 12.2.   A Model of the Learning Process.
Source: Jarvis, 1987a, p. 25. Reprinted by permission.

SUMMARY

Although there was sporadic attention given to adult learning in the early decades of the twentieth century, it was not until the 1970s that adult educators themselves began to focus systematically on some of the distinguishing characteristics of adult learning as separate from the body of information from psychologists' and educational psychologists' investigations of learning in general. This shift in focus was part of the field's efforts to differentiate itself from other areas of education. It also led to the search for a single theory of adult learning, one that would differentiate adults from children, include all types of learning, and was at once elegant and simple. But just as there is no single theory that explains human learning in general, no single theory of adult learning has emerged to unify the field. Rather, there are a number of theories, models, and frameworks, each of which illuminates some aspect of adult learning. The ones reviewed in this chapter all focus on adult learner characteristics of the adult's life situation, or both.

The best-known theory of adult learning is Knowles's andragogy. Nevertheless, it is less of a theory and more of a set of assumptions about adult learners that learners and educators alike can use to strengthen the learning transaction. The assumptions regarding an adult's self-concept, experience, readiness to learn, problem-centered focus, and internal motivation all have some intuitive validity, making andragogy popular with practitioners in many fields. These assumptions were critiqued in this chapter, as was Knowles's isolation of the individual learner from the learning context.

The chapter then turned to reviewing other less well-known models of adult learning. Like andragogy, Cross's characteristics of adults as learners (CAL) model is more about personal characteristics of adults than learning per se. McClusky's theory of margin emphasizes both personal characteristics (internal load and power factors) and situational characteristics (external load and power factors). His model has more to say about adult development and the timing of learning, though, than about the actual learning transaction. Knox's proficiency theory centers on the gap between what adults currently know and what they want to know or be able to do. Once this gap is identified, instruction can be planned accordingly. The last model discussed is Jarvis's model of the learning process. All life experiences hold the potential for learning to occur. Some experiences result in learning, and some do not. Jarvis's model distinguishes among nine responses, six of which involve learning (three nonreflective learning and three reflective learning). Although the model is derived from research with adult learners, Jarvis does not claim that it is limited to adults.

All of the models discussed in this chapter contribute in their own ways to advancing our understanding of adult learners, but with the possible exception of Jarvis's, none tells us much about the learning process itself. Furthermore, there has been little research testing the power of the models to explain or predict adult learning behavior. The process of model and theory building does, however, stimulate inquiry and reflection, all of which may eventually provide some of the answers to our questions about adult learning.

CHAPTER THIRTEEN

Self-Directed Learning

S ince Tough's work on adult learning projects published in 1971, self-directed learning has captured the imagination of researchers and writers both inside and outside the field of adult education. Many public schools and colleges and universities have used this concept to describe one of the major goals of their institutions: to enable their students to be lifelong, self-directed learners. Although learning on one's own has been the primary mode of learning in adulthood throughout the ages, serious study of this phenomenon is relatively recent in comparison to other aspects of learning in adulthood, such as intelligence and participation. Why is there this apparent dichotomy between the prevalence of this learning mode and the lack of serious study for so long? One response has been that only learning that takes place in formal institutions is relevant to adult educators (Houle, 1988; Verner, 1964). As Houle (1988, p. 89) observed, reflecting back on his seminal work, *The Inquiring Mind* (1961), "When some people began to think that it might be interesting or significant to deal directly with the learning desires or processes of the individual, the idea was greeted with apathy or scorn, particularly so far as self-directed learning was concerned." Therefore, studying learning within the natural environment of adults' everyday life had not been considered worthwhile or even possible. Tied in with this perspective is the role of educators of adults. Should we be working with learners outside the formal institutional environment? And might we be cutting into our own "business" as educators if we acknowledge that many adults can learn very effectively without our assistance? Despite these concerns, the study of self-directed learning has emerged as one the major thrusts of adult education research over the past three decades.

Tough (1967, 1971), building on the work of Houle (1961) and others, provided the first comprehensive description of self-directed learning as a form of study, including the key elements of self-directed learning, which he termed *self-planned learning*. Drawing on a study of the learning projects of sixty-six people from Ontario, Canada, he found that "highly deliberate efforts to learn take place all around you. The members of your family, your neighbors, colleagues, and acquaintances probably initiate and complete several learning efforts, though you may not be aware of it" (Tough, 1971, p. 3). Writing about the same time as Tough, Knowles proposed that one of the hallmark assumptions of adult learning is that learners become increasingly self-directed as they mature (Knowles, 1970, 1980). Knowles's thinking about self-directed learning is grounded in his concept of andragogy, discussed in Chapter Twelve. Although there have been challenges to his assumption that adult learners strive toward greater self-direction, there are many who treat it as fact and structure their practice accordingly.

Building on the pioneering work of Houle (1961), Tough (1978, 1979), and Knowles (1970), the earlier research in this arena was primarily descriptive in nature (Brockett, 1985b; Caffarella and O'Donnell, 1987, 1989). The emphasis in this early work was on verifying that adults do deliberately learn on their own and discovering how they go about doing this. Following these descriptive studies, researchers began providing more in-depth conceptual models (for example, Brockett and Hiemstra, 1991; Candy, 1991; Garrison, 1997; Long, 1991b; Spear, 1988). Scholars also initiated a debate about what the goals of self-directed learning should be (Brockett and Hiemstra, 1991; Brookfield, 1986; Collins, 1988; Mezirow, 1985b) and started exploring the personal characteristics and attributes of those who were self-directed in their learning (Candy, 1991; Chene, 1983; Oddi, 1986). In addition, a number of writers sought to bring greater clarity and precision to the term and the many related terms that have been used to describe this phenomenon (for example, Bouchard, 1994; Confessore and Confessore, 1992; Gerstner, 1992; Hiemstra, 1996; Kenney, 1996; Long and others, 1989, 1990).

What became clear from our review of this rich array of research is the recognition that self-directed learning has a number of different facets and that conceptions differ with which aspect is studied (Carre, 1997; Rowland and Volet, 1996). Therefore, in discussing this research, we have grouped these many studies into three broad categories, each outlining a major facet of self-directed learning. Literature that explores the goals of self-directed learning is reported first. We then examine research that describes self-directed learning as a process or form of study. Third, we review self-directedness as a personal attribute of the learner. We conclude the chapter with a discussion of the major challenges that must be considered in building future research and theory in self-directed learning.

GOALS OF SELF-DIRECTED LEARNING

Often defined by the underlying philosophical position of the writer, the goals of self-directed learning can be grouped into three major aims: (1) to enhance the ability of adult learners to be self-directed in their learning, (2) to foster transformational learning as central to self-directed learning, and (3) to promote emancipatory learning and social action as an integral part of self-directed learning. The first goal, that of enhancing the ability of adults to be self-directed in their learning, has stemmed primarily from the work of Knowles (1980) and Tough (1979). This ability to be self-directed in one's learning is conceived as both a set of personal attributes and specific skills (Brockett and Hiemstra, 1991; Caffarella and O'Donnell, 1989). Within this goal, the assumption is that part of the job of educators of adults is to help learners, whether they are learning on their own or in formal learning programs, to be able to plan, carry out, and evaluate their own learning. For example, in the independent pursuit of learning, educators might provide assistance to individuals or groups of learners in locating resources or mastering alternative learning strategies. The learners themselves would seek out this assistance, perhaps in community learning centers or through learning technologies. This first goal has spawned the majority of research in self-directed learning.

Goal One is grounded primarily in the assumptions of humanistic philosophy, which posits personal growth as the goal of adult learning. Brockett and Hiemstra (1991, pp. 26–27), for example, have stated that their model of self-directed learning, the Personal Responsibility Orientation (PRO), is based on three fundamental ideas espoused by this philosophy: "that human nature is basically good, . . . that individuals possess virtually unlimited potential for growth . . . [and] that only by accepting responsibility for one's own learning is it possible to take a proactive approach to the learning process." Accepting responsibility and being proactive take into account two other tenets of humanistic philosophy: personal autonomy and free will to make individual choices. So, too, is the earlier work of Knowles (1975, 1980) largely influenced by this philosophical stance. The most often quoted sources of this orientation toward self-directed learning and learning in general are Maslow (1970) and Rogers (1969, 1983). (See Chapter Eleven for a more complete description of the humanistic orientation to learning.)

Goal Two, that of fostering transformational learning as central to self-directed learning, is found primarily in the work of Mezirow (1985b) and Brookfield (1985, 1986). Mezirow (1985b, p. 27) suggests that "there is probably no such thing as a self-directed learner, except in the sense that there is a learner who can participate fully and freely in the dialogue through which we test our interests and perspectives against those of others and accordingly modify them and our learning goals" (p. 27). In essence, adults need to reflect critically and have an "understanding of the historical, cultural, and biographical reasons for one's needs, wants, and interests. . . . Such self-knowledge is a prerequisite for autonomy in self-directed learning" (Mezirow, 1985b, p. 27). Brookfield (1985, 1986) echoes Mezirow's ideas by calling on adult educators to distinguish clearly between the techniques of self-directed learning and the internal change in consciousness. More specifically, Brookfield (1986, p. 38) asserted that "the most complete form of self-directed learning occurs when process and reflection are married in the adult's pursuit of meaning." Although neither writer took this work further, this goal of self-directed learning became the foundation for the third goal of self-directed learning: promoting emancipatory learning and social action.

Writers advancing Goal Three have been some of the strongest critics of the first goal of self-directed learning: enhancing the ability of individual learners to be more self-directed in their learning. The heart of their criticism is that this first goal is too narrow, with the focus of that goal being primarily instrumental learning and assisting individual learners. In contrast, authors who support the goal of promoting emancipatory learning and social action want included not only the examination by learners of the sociopolitical assumptions under which they learn and function, but the incorporation of collective action as an outcome. Unless the definition of self-directed learning is broadened to include these components, these proponents view self-directed learning as merely a technique "to condition the individual into taken-for-granted acceptance of what is offered" (Collins, 1996, p. 115). Collins (1988, 1991, 1994, 1995a, 1996) has been the most persistent and eloquent in echoing these concerns about how self-directed learning has been conceptualized and practiced. In his most recent work, Collins (1996, p. 119) emphasizes the importance of having an "unequivocal focus of emancipation as a core concern" in the study of self-directed learning and adult learning in general. By this Collins means that participatory research methods should be used to foster democratic and open dialogue about self-directed learning, and ethical and political concerns about self-directed learning should be a part of this dialogue. To foster the study of this critical practice of self-directed learning, Collins suggests that researchers use critical theory and interpretive and participatory research approaches.

In this same vein, Brookfield (1993b, p. 227) asserts "that any authentic exercise of self-directedness requires that certain political conditions be in place." More specifically, Brookfield argues first that having learners exercise control over all educational decisions needs to be a consistent element of self-directed learning. As such, educators of adults in formal and nonformal settings need to shift to learners as much control as possible in the learning process. Brookfield views this shift as difficult to accomplish in settings where the culture itself is highly controlling, such as some higher education institutions or corporate environments. Therefore, he asserts that educators "might decide to work collectively at changing the political culture of institutions. . . . Control from this perspective would be seen in our coming to understand the origins, functioning and contradictions of the system and in our working to change or replace it with one that honors our daily activities as educators." Second, Brookfield calls for more easily accessible and adequate resources so that learners can more readily exercise control over their learning, especially learners who have been denied access to resources because of cost or preferential treatment for privileged groups.

How authors view the process of self-directed learning is often the driving force behind the conceptualization of the process models they develop, although this may not be explicitly stated. Our observation is that the majority of process models of self-directed learning reflect Goal One, enhancing the ability of adult learners to be self-directed in their learning, and sometimes Goal Two, fostering transformational learning.

SELF-DIRECTED LEARNING AS A PROCESS

Self-directed learning as a process of learning, in which people take the primary initiative for planning, carrying out, and evaluating their own learning experiences, has received a great deal of attention in the literature. We contend, as described in Chapter Two, that this form of learning can take place both inside and outside institutionally based learning programs. For the most part, however, being self-directed in one's learning is a natural part of adult life. Within this category of self-directed learning as a process, three types of models—linear, interactive, and instructional—have been extensively discussed in the literature. In the next three subsections we set out descriptions and critiques of the most prominent and the most promising models of self-directed learning. These models represent a mixture of conceptual, empirical, and experientially derived views of the process of self-directed learning.

Linear Models

The early models of self-directed learning, those proposed by Tough (1971) and Knowles (1975), were linear in nature. Learners moved through a series of steps to reach their learning goals in a self-directed manner. The resulting frameworks of the learning process for these models included many elements of the traditional teaching process. In reference to Tough's work, Gerstner (1987) and Caffarella (1994) have observed that this type of work may have developed from Tough's dissertation on adult self-teachers (Tough, 1966, 1967), which was grounded in the literature addressing teaching and curriculum planning.

Tough (1967, 1971, 1979) proposed the first comprehensive description of self-directed learning, which he termed *self-planned learning*. Drawing on a study of the learning projects of sixty-six people from

Ontario, Canada, he found that 70 percent of all learning projects were planned by the learners themselves. He defined a learning project as "a highly deliberate effort to gain and retain certain definite knowledge and skill, or to change in some other way. To be included, a series of related learning sessions (episodes in which the person's primary intention was to learn) must add up to at least seven hours" (Tough, 1978, p. 250). Tough found that learners used thirteen steps in self-planned learning projects, representing key decision-making points about choosing what, where, and how to learn (Tough, 1971, pp. 94–95):

1. Deciding what detailed knowledge and skill to learn. . . .

2. Deciding the specific activities, methods, resources, or equipment for learning. . . .

3. Deciding where to learn. . . .

4. Setting specific deadlines or intermediate targets.

5. Deciding when to begin a learning episode.

6. Deciding the pace at which to proceed during a learning episode.

7. Estimating the current level of his knowledge and skill or his progress in gaining the desired knowledge and skill.

8. Detecting any factor that has been hindering learning or discovering inefficient aspects of the current procedures.

9. Obtaining the desired resources or equipment or reaching the desired place or resource. . . .

10. Preparing or adapting a room (or certain resources, furniture or equipment) for learning or arranging certain other physical conditions in preparation for learning. . . .

11. Saving or obtaining the money necessary for the use of certain human or nonhuman resources. . . .

12. Finding time for the learning. . . .

13. Taking steps to increase the motivation for certain learning episodes. . . .

Tough's model of self-directed learning became the basis for numerous dissertations and research studies around the world. A range of specific populations have been studied using Tough's original or modified interview schedule: pharmacists (Johns, 1973), urban and rural populations (Peters and Gordon, 1974), extension agents (Bejot, 1981), nurses (Kathrein, 1981), farmers (Bayha, 1983), students at all levels (Geisler, 1984; Kratz, 1978), older adults (Hiemstra, 1976), clergy (Morris, 1977), and physicians (Richards, 1986). The most comprehensive study to date, grounded in Tough's work, was that of Penland (1977) in which he completed a national study in the United States of self-planned learning. Although there is disagreement on the amount and type of self-directed learning that goes on in the general population, we can say without reservation that the existence of the independent pursuit of learning in natural settings has been established (Brookfield, 1984; Caffarella and O'Donnell, 1987, 1988).

Knowles's (1975) description of self-directed learning consists of six major steps: (1) climate setting, (2) diagnosing learning needs, (3) formulating learning goals, (4) identifying human and material resources for learning, (5) choosing and implementing appropriate learning strategies, and (6) evaluating learning outcomes. His steps are somewhat similar to those proposed by Tough (1979). Knowles includes numerous resources for both learners and teachers for completing each of these tasks. Among the materials he describes, we have found the ones on learning contracts and evaluation to be the most useful. Although the work of Tough and Knowles "has provided the language, the concepts, and more importantly the descriptive terms for key elements and processes of self-planned learning" (Kasworm, 1992, p. 56), other scholars have conceptualized different pictures.

Interactive Models

A second portrait of self-directed learning is that this learning process is not so well planned or linear in nature. Rather, there is an emphasis on two or more factors, such as opportunities people find in their own environments, the personality characteristics of learners, cognitive processes, and the context of learning, which collectively interact to form episodes of self-directed learning. Five such models are discussed as illustrative of the work in this arena: the models of Spear (1988), Cavaliere (1992), Brockett and Hiemstra (1991), Danis (1992), and Garrison (1997).

SPEAR'S MODEL. Spear (1988), building on his earlier work with Mocker (Spear and Mocker, 1984), has presented a model that rests on three major elements: the opportunities people find in their own environments, past or new knowledge, and chance occurrences. He found, through an exploratory study of ten training and development personnel, that the process of self-directed learning could be reduced to seven principal components (Spear, 1988, pp. 212–213):

Knowledge
1. Residual knowledge: knowledge the learner brings to the project as a residue from prior knowledge

2. Acquired knowledge: knowledge acquired as part of the learning project

Action
1. Directed action: action directed toward a known or specific end

2. Exploratory: action that the learner chooses without knowing what the outcomes may be or with certainty that any useful outcome will ensure

3. Fortuitous action: action that the learner takes for reasons not related to the learning project

Environment
1. Consistent environment: includes both human and material elements that are regularly in place and generally accessible

2. Fortuitous environment: provides for chance encounters that could not be expected or foreseen and yet affect the learner and the project

After further analysis of the data, Spear proposed that each self-directed learning project is composed of sets or clusters of those elements. For example, one learning cluster could be described as follows. Susan, who is part of an informal study group on adult development (a consistent environment), has decided that she would like to learn more about the work on women's development, a subject she has become familiar with through graduate study and independent readings (residual knowledge). She decides to attend a series of discussions offered by the local women's center (directed action) on the topic and finds most of these discussions to be useful (acquired knowledge). At the end of one discussion, she decides some refreshment might be appropriate and stops at a nearby coffee shop with a friend (fortuitous action). By chance, they encounter that evening's resource person discussing her session with two staff members from the center, and they are invited to join their lively exchange (exploratory action).

Spear concluded from this analysis that self-directed learning projects do not generally occur in a linear fashion—that is, one cluster does not necessarily bear any relation to the next cluster. Rather, information gathered through one set of activities (one cluster) is stored until it fits in with other ideas and resources on the same topic gleaned from one or more additional clusters of activities. A successful self-directed learning project is one in which a person can engage in a sufficient number of relevant clusters of learning activities and then assemble these clusters into a coherent whole. Spear (1988, p. 217) concludes, "The learner is perhaps in greatest control when the assembling of the clusters begins and decisions are made regarding what knowledge is of most and least importance."

Although only a few studies have been conducted using all or parts of Spear's framework (for example, Berger, 1990; Padberg, 1994), other researchers have come to similar conclusions in their work (Berger, 1990; Candy, 1991; Danis and Tremblay, 1987, 1988; Tremblay and Thiel, 1991). Danis and Tremblay (1987, 1988), for example, who studied ten long-term adult learners, found that their respondents were able to specify learning goals only when they had mastered certain knowledge or skills, and that in general these learners went about learning on their own using multiple approaches as opposed to using only one approach. In addition, they noted that the impact of random events stood out in that these learners took advantage of any opportunities offered to them. Berger (1990), in her study of twenty white males with no formal degrees beyond high school, found little evidence that her subjects did any preplanning in their self-directed learning activities. Her subjects "constantly redefined their projects, changed course, and followed new paths of interest as they proceeded" (p. 176). In essence, the majority of her respondents adopted a trial-and-error approach, with an emphasis on hands-on experience and practice, guiding themselves by both their successes and their mistakes as they moved on to new levels of learning.

CAVALIERE'S MODEL. The interactive model that Cavaliere (1992) proposed captures some of the elements and observations made by Berger (1990) and others, but in more depth. Cavaliere, as a result of her case study of how the Wright brothers learned to fly, identified five specific stages of their learning project: (1) inquiring (a need to solve a problem), (2) modeling (observing similar phenomena and developing a prototype model), (3) experimenting and practicing (continuous refinement and practice with the model), (4) theorizing and perfecting (perfection of their skills and product), and (5) actualizing (receiving recognition for the product of their learning efforts). Within each of these five steps, four "repetitive cognitive processes (goal setting, focusing, persevering and reformulation) occurred . . . with a clearly identifiable breakpoint [between stages], preceded by frustration and confusion on the part of the Wright Brothers" (p. 53). Similar to Spear's (1988) observations, the importance of a set of specific opportunities and resources within the Wright brothers' own environment was critical to the success of their learning endeavor. Cavaliere's sophisticated model is especially useful in that it describes both the stages of the learning process and the cognitive processes used throughout a major learning endeavor. We have not found any studies to this point that have tested this model, although some of the ideas presented by Cavaliere are similar to the Danis model, which is presented later in this section.

BROCKETT AND HIEMSTRA'S MODEL. In their Personal Responsibility Orientation (PRO) model, Brockett and Hiemstra (1991, p. 26) provide a new framework for what they term *self-direction in learning,* which comprises "both instructional method processes (self-directed learning) and personality characteristics of the individual learner (learner self-direction)." In the instructional processes dimension, learners assume primary responsibility for planning, implementing, and evaluating their learning experiences. The authors note that "an educational agent or resource often plays a facilitating role in this process" (p. 24). In this facilitation role, instructors must possess skills in helping learners do needs assessments, locate learning resources, and choose instructional methods and evaluation strategies. Many of these skills have been discussed in previous literature on self-directed learning (for example, Knowles, 1975, and Tough, 1979) and are stressed in their model, with an emphasis on the interactive nature of the teaching and learning process.

Their second dimension, related to the personality characteristics of individual learners, "centers on a learner's desire or preference for assuming responsibility for learning" (p. 24). The notion of personal responsibility, which they define as "individuals assuming ownership for their own thoughts and actions" (p. 26), is the point of departure for understanding their concept of self-direction in adult learning. Their concept of personal responsibility is grounded in the concepts of humanism and human potential. Although they agree that individual learners are central to the idea of self-direction, they also regard the context, or social milieu, in which that learning activity transpires as important. In acknowledging these contextual factors, they recognize the importance of situational factors in the self-directed learning process, which mirrors others' descriptions of the process of self-directed learning (for example, Danis, 1992; Grow, 1991; Spear, 1988). Hiemstra (1992) and Hiemstra and Brockett (1994) have further described various aspects of using self-directed learning as an instructional method, but we found no studies that have tested the PRO model of self-direction.

The only critical discussion of the PRO model that we could locate was a review of the book by Flannery (1993c). Although Flannery believed the PRO model was well supported by the literature, and the suggestions made for practice from a "how-to sense" were useful, she did cite some problems she had with the conception of the model as presented. First, because she viewed the model as primarily humanistic in orientation and driven by the psychological perspective of learning, she believed Brockett and Hiemstra paid only "lip service to the contributions of sociology" (p. 110). Although these authors had acknowledged the importance of the social milieu in which self-directed learning takes place, she saw their discussion as inadequate, because the sociological and cultural issues related to self-direction in learning received only cursory examination. For example, Flannery viewed the authors as extending "their humanistic values across the globe by seeking examples of self-directed learning in countries outside of North America . . . [while ignoring] the cultural context of [these] other countries and the possibility that self-directed learning may mitigate against the cultural communication patterns and actual learning values of these countries" (p. 110). Although she did see weaknesses in the PRO model, she still believed it offers "a contribution to adult education [by organizing] the disparate literature into a model which integrates particular elements of self-directed learning" (p. 110).

DANIS'S FRAMEWORK. Danis (1992) has proposed a "map of the territory" that researchers could use to study the major components of self-directed learning and explain how the various components of the model interact. This model is grounded in the notion of what she terms self-regulated learning, referring to the various process components of the learning cycle and not to the internal cognitive aspects. The components and subcomponents of this model, summarized in Table 13.1, are based on a synthesis of relevant data from research in self-directed learning, self-instruction, and learning and study strategies.

Because Danis used a comprehensive literature base in building this model, it is not surprising that some of the components appear in other models that have already been discussed (for example, the environmental factors). Although no studies could be found using the Danis model, the richness of the model and its interactive nature should challenge researchers to develop a more in-depth understanding of self-directed learning.

GARRISON'S MODEL. Garrison (1997) is the most recent scholar to propose a multidimensional and interactive model of self-directed learning. His model (see Figure 13.1), grounded in a "collaborative constructivist" perspective, "integrates self-management (contextual control), self-monitoring (cognitive responsibility) and motivational (entering and task) dimensions to reflect a meaningful and worthwhile approach to self-directed learning" (p. 18).

The first dimension, self-management, acknowledges the social milieu in which learners are interacting, whether they are in formal or informal settings. It involves learners' taking control of and shaping the contextual conditions such that they can reach their stated goals and objectives. "Control," says Garrison, "does not translate into social independence or freedom from influence. Educational self-management concerns the use of learning materials within a context where there is opportunity for sustained communication. Self-management of learning in an educational context must consider the opportunity to test and confirm understanding collaboratively" (p. 23), which translates into increased responsibilities for the learner.

"The next two dimensions of the model—self-monitoring and motivation—represent the cognitive dimensions of self-directed learning" (p. 24), which Garrison believes have been given little attention in the literature on self-directed learning. Self-monitoring describes the ability of learners to be able to monitor both their cognitive and metacognitive processes, which includes learners' being able to use a repertoire of learning strategies and the ability to think about their thinking. "Self-monitoring is synonymous with responsibility to con-

Components/Subcomponents	Description of Components/Subcomponents
Strategies	Ways used by learners to acquire or apply new knowledge and learners' awareness of their own use of these methods.
Phases	Stages of learning activities, which are interrelated and may be recursive: (1) reacting to a triggering event or situation, (2) seeking and selecting specific knowledge to be acquired and available resources, (3) organizing and structuring both the knowledge to be acquired and the strategies, (4) acquiring and integrating the new knowledge, (5) assessing the quality of the learning outcome and learning strategies used, and (6) applying the new knowledge.
Learning content	Any new knowledge that is acquired by the learner. The focus is on the types and levels of complexity of the learning outcomes, and the link between the new knowledge and relevant prior experience.
The learner	Any individual learner or collective group of learners, such as self-taught groups or associations, that acquires new knowledge. Learning abilities, identity, developmental factors, cultural factors, and social factors are taken into consideration for individual and collective groups of learners.
Context	The external factors within the environment that facilitate, inhibit, or modify the acquisition or application of new knowledge. These factors include the conditions or circumstances that influence the time or place of learning; the resources used by learners with regard to assessment, handling, and exchange; and social and organization structures that intervene at higher hierarchical levels.

Table 13.1. Components and Selected Subcomponents of the Danis Framework.

Source: Adapted from Danis, 1992, pp. 56–59.

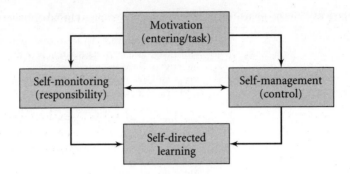

Figure 13.1. Dimensions of Self-Directed Learning.
Source: Garrison, 1997, p. 22.

struct meaning . . . [and] is very much associated with the ability to be reflective and think critically" (pp. 24, 25). The motivational dimension involves what influences people to participate or enter into a self-directed learning activity and what keeps them participating in the activity or task: "Motivation and responsibility are reciprocally related and both are facilitated by collaborative control of the educational transaction" (p. 29). Garrison observes that self-monitoring and motivation need to be explored in much greater detail by those studying self-directed learning. Because this model is so recent, we found no further research or discussion of it.

Instructional Models

The third category of self-directed learning models represents frameworks that instructors in formal settings could use to integrate self-directed methods of learning into their programs and activities. This way of organizing instruction, as noted in Chapter Two, allows for more learner control and independence within these settings. Two models are highlighted that were designed with formal settings in mind: those of Grow (1991) and Hammond and Collins (1991).

Grow's (1991) Staged Self-Directed Learning (SSDL) model outlines how teachers can assist students to become more self-directed in their learning. Grow, who grounded his model in the situational leadership model of Hersey and Blanchard (1988), describes four distinct stages of learners:

Stage 1: Learners of low self-direction who need an authority figure (a teacher) to tell them what to do

Stage 2: Learners of moderate self-direction who are motivated and confident but largely ignorant of the subject matter to be learned

Stage 3: Learners of intermediate self-direction who have both the skill and the basic knowledge and view themselves as being both ready and able to explore a specific subject area with a good guide

Stage 4: Learners of high self-direction who are both willing and able to plan, execute, and evaluate their own learning with or without the help of an expert

Within each of these stages, Grow outlines possible roles for the teacher or facilitator, depending on the learner's stage. He goes on to explore the problems that may arise when there is a mismatch between the role or style of the teacher and the learning stage of the participants. Grow emphasizes that good teachers individualize their teaching strategies to match the learner's stage of self-direction and allow the students to become more self-directed in their learning. Therefore, integrating self-directed learning as a way to organize learning experiences is situational in nature. Grow's thoughts on integrating the notion of self-direction into formal instruction are very similar to those of Pratt (1988), Long (1989), and Hiemstra and Sisco (1990). In support of his work, Grow (1994) noted that he had found two other groups that have also used the situational leadership framework, developing models similar to his (Ames and Ames; and Baker, Roueche, and Gillett-Karam, as cited by Grow, 1994).

Responding to Grow's request for an ongoing conversation on his model, Tennant (1992) offered a number of observations and questions about the utility and explanatory power of the model. Among Tennant's questions, the following seem to be the most substantial: Who is the best person, the teacher or student, to judge which stage a student is within, and how should this be done? What if there is a mismatch between the learner's ability and willingness to use self-directed methods of the instructional process? At what point in the learning process should teachers change from one stage to another, and who should take the lead in this change: the teacher or the student? And finally, how would Grow respond to conceptualizing self-direction as a generic quality as opposed to a situation-specific ability, especially when Grow appeared to equate stages 3 and 4 as synonymous with being more autonomous and psychologically mature?

Grow (1994) has given thoughtful responses to three of these four questions. First, Grow states that the teacher should be responsible for estimating a student's learning stage from classroom behavior and work submitted. He is suspicious of quantifiable measures for doing this task and recommends that teachers rely on their observational skills. Second, Grow refers readers to Hersey and Blanchard's (1988) book for a more detailed discussion of the mismatches between the ability and willingness of a student to use self-directed learning methods in formal classroom situations. And third, Grow views Tennant's question about the tension between conceptualizing self-direction as a generic quality, versus a situation-specific ability, as "a genuinely useful clarification. . . . Tennant rightly says we should not be 'too eager to consider self-directed learning to be synonymous with autonomy, psychological growth and maturity, at least without considerable qualification.' . . . It is painfully clear that certain individuals can be intensely self-directed learners without being mature, wise, or even sane" (pp. 112–113). The question that Grow does not address and needs further clarification is at what point teachers should change styles and who should take the lead in this change process. In addition, Grow raises two other provocative questions in his response: How should teachers work with students who are resistant to any facilitative form of learning (stages 3 and 4)? And when is it effective for teachers to use a style that is mismatched with students' learning stages? What is clear in Grow's response to Tennant is that one size does not fit all students when integrating self-directed learning modes into instructional processes. Rather, the degree of learner control depends on the situation and learner skills, which is similar to Pratt's observations (Pratt, 1988).

The final model to be reviewed, proposed by Hammond and Collins (1991), is the only model that explicitly addresses the goal of promoting emancipatory learning and social action as a central tenet of self-directed learning. Grounding their work in studies of critical pedagogy, popular education, and participatory research, these authors have outlined a seven-component framework for assisting learners in formal settings to engage in the critical practice of adult education. In their model, learners take the initiative for

1. Building a cooperative learning climate

2. Analyzing and critically reflecting on themselves and the social, economic, and political contexts in which they are situated

3. Generating competency profiles for themselves

4. Diagnosing their learning needs within the framework of both the personal and social context

5. Formulating socially and personally relevant learning goals that result in learning agreements

6. Implementing and managing their learning

7. Reflecting on and evaluating their learning

What makes their model different from Knowles's and other process models is the purposeful inclusion of the critical perspective through the examination of the social, political, and environmental contexts that affect their learning, and the stress on developing both personal and social learning goals.

Although greater control of the learning process is what Hammond and Collins see as the immediate goal for learners using their model of critical self-directed learning, their "ultimate goal is to empower learners to use their learning to improve the conditions under which they and those around them live and work" (p. 14). As with the PRO model, we found no research studies where the authors used Hammond and Collins's model as their conceptual framework.

SELF-DIRECTION AS A PERSONAL ATTRIBUTE OF LEARNERS

A second major focus in the research literature on self-directed learning has been self-directedness as a personal attribute or characteristic of the learner. The assumption underlying much of this work is that learning in adulthood means becoming more self-directed and autonomous (Brockett and Hiemstra, 1991; Candy, 1991; Knowles, 1980; MacKeracher, 1996; Percy, Burton, and Whitnall, 1994; Tennant and Pogson, 1995). Recall that one of Knowles's (1980, p. 43) four major tenets of andragogy is that mature "adults have a deep psychological need to be generally self-directing." Brockett and Hiemstra (1991) echo Knowles's assumption in that they see a link between learner self-direction, which they define as characteristics of learners that predispose them toward taking primary responsibility for their own learning, and a positive self-concept. Brockett (personal correspondence, 1998) even argues, based on strong research support (Brockett and Hiemstra, 1991; Sabbaghian, 1979), that this link between learner self-direction and a positive self-concept is one of the two or three major findings that we can glean from this literature. More recently, Tennant and Pogson (1995) have asserted that "the idea of autonomous or self-directed learning is firmly entrenched in contemporary thinking about adult education and there has been a great deal of scholarly interest in the subject" (1995, p. 121).

Research into the nature of the self-directed learner asks the who and what questions: Are these learners introverts or extroverts? What is their learning style? What level of education have they achieved, and does this affect their ability to be self-directed? Are they more autonomous than other learners? How do we know if learners are ready for self-directed ways of learning? Basically researchers are trying to gain an understanding of the typical self-directed learner's characteristics or attributes. More specifically, researchers have tried to link a number of different variables with being self-directed in one's learning—for example, readiness for self-directed learning (Guglielmino, 1977, 1997a; Long and others, 1996), educational level (Bejot, 1981; Savicevic, 1985; Confessore and Confessore, 1994), personality factors (Fox and West, 1983; Oddi, 1984, 1986), learning style (Adenuga, 1991; Deroos, 1982; Theil, 1984), field independence and field dependence (Brookfield, 1986; Pratt, 1984), creativity (Torrance and Mourad, 1978), life satisfaction (Brockett, 1985b), health promotion and wellness (Leeb, 1983; Owen, 1996), and autonomy (Candy 1991; Chene, 1983).

These researchers' findings and observations for the most part, however, are confusing and contradictory. Deroos (1982), for example, whose participants consisted of 175 men and women enrolled in a three-year independent study program for health care professionals, found that an abstract learning style, based on the Kolb (1984) classification, was related to a person's persistence in self-directed learning. Theil (1984), whose subjects included thirty men and women from French-speaking associations, concluded that the accommodator style, which combines both active and intuitive components, was related to success in self-directed learning. And Adengua (1991) discovered, through studying 178 male and female U.S.-born and foreign graduate students, that a balance of preference for both active and abstract learning styles increases learners' self-directedness. From a more conceptual perspective, Pratt (1984) states that people with tendencies toward field independence are more capable of self-directed learning, and Brookfield (1986) expresses the opposite view—that field dependence is more characteristic of self-directed learners. Brookfield's view, which is contrary to what most other theorists have expressed, is grounded in the idea that "self-directed learning is equated with the exhibition of critical reflection on the part of adults" (p. 42) and that the beliefs (such as the contextuality and relativity of knowledge) needed for this kind of thinking are most often seen in field-dependent versus field-independent learners. The notion of readiness and the concept of autonomy have been studied and discussed most often in the literature on self-directedness in learning as a personal attribute.

Self-Directed Learning Readiness

Readiness, which implies an internal state of psychological readiness to undertake self-directed learning, has received the most attention in the study of self-directed learning in terms of data-based studies (Guglielmino, 1997a). Guglielmino (1977) has provided the most-used operational definition for self-directed learning. She states that it consists of a complex of attitudes, values, and abilities that create the likelihood that an individual is capable of self-directed learning. She identifies the psychological qualities involved in readiness for self-directed learning as initiative, independence, and persistence in learning; acceptance of responsibility for one's own learning; self-discipline; a high degree of curiosity; a strong ability to learn independently; enjoyment of learning; a tendency to be goal oriented; and a tendency to view problems as challenges rather than obstacles. These qualities undergird her Self-Directed Learning Readiness Scale (SDLRS), of which there are two major versions, one of them a self-scoring version (the Learning Preference Assessment).

The SDLRS is the most often used quantitative measure in studies of self-directed learning. Examined in studies using the SDLRS are a wide range of issues from relating readiness for self-directed learning with creativity (Torrance and Mourad, 1978), numbers of learning projects undertaken (Hassan, 1981), and life satisfaction (Brockett, 1985b) to self-directed learning readiness as it relates to success in job performance (Durr, Guglielmino, and Guglielmino, 1996; Guglielmino, 1996; Guglielmino and Guglielmino, 1988; Guglielmino and Roberts,

1992), to professional development (Guglielmino and Nowocien, 1997) and in college level programs (Long, 1991b; Long and Morris, 1996). Examples of the most far-reaching implications, based on studies using readiness as a major variable, are that "individual readiness for self-directed learning could be an important factor in matching certain types of jobs with applicants seeking those jobs" (Guglielmino and Roberts, 1992, p. 271) and that "employees who score lower in readiness for self-directed learning should be given opportunities to become effective self-directed learners" (Durr, Guglielmino, and Guglielmino, 1996, p. 355).

Although the results of the majority of these studies have found some relationship among readiness for self-directed learning and the various variables that have been studied, caution must be used in interpreting results. Claims and counterclaims have been made related to the basic reliability and validity of the SDLRS. The earliest concerns about the SDLRS were raised by Brockett (1985a, 1985b) and Caffarella and Caffarella (1986). Brockett observed that the test may not be valid for adults with low-level literacy, and Caffarella and Caffarella questioned using the scale with adults possessing higher levels of education (beyond the bachelor's degree) because their scores were all significantly above the mean prior to any intervention being done to increase their readiness for self-direction. The most significant criticisms of the SDLRS have come from analyses completed by Field (1989, 1991), West and Bentley (1991), Straka (1996), and Straka and Hinz (1996). West and Bentley concluded that the SDLRS should not be used as a screening tool for self-directed learning programs, and Field (1989, p. 138) contends from his analysis that "the problems inherent in the scale are so substantial that it should not continue to be used." Straka and Hinz (1996) raise an even more fundamental issue: whether the SDLRS fits the parameters of a true psychometric scale. (It should be noted that Straka and Hinz used the original scale from Guglielmino's dissertation, whereas most of the research and use of the SDLRS has been on a subsequent version of that scale.)

On the other side, in a tripartite response to Field's work, Guglielmino, Long, and McCune (1989) dismiss most of Field's arguments due to "errors of omission and commission" in Field's research. Specifically, they have criticized Field's analysis of the SDLRS on three major grounds: incorrect interpretation of sources cited, the limited nature of his subject pool for a study of this type, and the statistical procedures used. There have been no formal responses to the critiques by West and Bentley and Straka. In addition, other studies and reviews have also been offered as support for the validity or reliability of the SDLRS (for example, Delahaye and Smith, 1995; Guglielmino, 1997b; Long and Walsh, 1992; McCune and Guglielmino, 1991; Morris, 1997).

Brockett and Hiemstra (1991) have provided one of the most thoughtful commentaries on the use of the SDLRS:

> We believe that despite several apparent substantive and methodological concerns, the SDLRS has made a most important contribution to the present understanding of the self-directed learning phenomenon by generating considerable research, controversy and dialogue. We think that this contribution ultimately outweighs the limitations that seem to be inherent within the instrument. . . . At the same time, we believe that the criticisms raised cannot be overlooked. There remains too many questions, particularly relative to the validity of the scale. . . . We are unwilling to dismiss the scale [like Field and Straka]. . . . However, we do recommend that the SDLRS be used with the same discretion as any other standardized instrument. [pp. 74–75]

Autonomy and Self-Directedness in Learning

The relationship of autonomy and self-directness in learning has been discussed primarily at the conceptual level. Chene (1983), for example, defines three major elements that describe an autonomous learner: independence, the ability to make choices and critical judgments, and the capacity to articulate the norms and limits of a learning society. Candy (1991) adds to Chene's notion of the autonomous learner by characterizing autonomous people as those with a strong sense of personal values and beliefs. These values and beliefs give them a solid foundation for conceiving goals and plans, exercising free choice, using rational reflection, having the willpower to follow through, and exercising self-restraint and self-discipline. The same overarching concepts of independent thinking, self-responsibility, and control over actions of learning are also highlighted by Brockett and Hiemstra (1991), Garrison (1992), and Tennant and Pogson (1995).

Autonomy, however, is not necessarily context free; there is a relationship between the personal and situational variables that must come into play for a person to be autonomous in certain learning situations. Knowles (1975, 1980) was the first to express the importance of context in his descriptions of andragogy. He qualified his assertion that adults are naturally self-directing when he observed that people move toward self-directedness at differing rates and not necessarily in all dimensions of life, and that in some situations adults may need to be at least "temporarily dependent" in learning situations. For example, when coping with a crisis, such as a flood or an earthquake, people may need or want to rely on the information and direction of others, both during the event itself and at least for a time in the aftermath of the event. This same sentiment, that even those adults who can and want to be self-directed in their learning may choose not to exhibit or pursue this characteristic at certain times, has been expressed by a number of authors (Brockett and Hiemstra, 1991; Candy, 1987, 1991; Pratt, 1988; Tenant and Pogson, 1995).

Four major variables appear to have the most influence on whether individual adult learners exhibit autonomous behavior in learning situations: their technical skills related to the learning process, their familiarity with the subject matter, their sense of personal competence as learners, and their commitment to learning at this point in time. "Since this combination will vary from situation to situation, a learner's autonomy is also likely to vary from one context to another, and educators must avoid the automatic assumption that simply because a person has successfully learned something in the past either in an instructional setting or outside it, he or she will be able to succeed in a new area: Orientation, support and guidance may all be required in the first stages of a learning project" (Candy, 1991, p. 309). In addition, moving from an individual to more of a collective context, Candy (1991) and Tennant and Pogson (1995) posit that the socially constructed nature of the self and knowledge may also limit adults' capacity for autonomy or self-directedness in learning. Adults, in part, are their historical and cultural selves and often find themselves in learning situations where others around them determine what is worth knowing and how that knowledge should be used.

In a similar vein, Boucouvalas (1988a) has challenged the exclusive emphasis on the autonomous self as only a partial explanation of what selfhood is all about. She turns to the concept of homonomy in conjunction with autonomy as complementary dimensions of the growth of self. While autonomy reflects independence and uniqueness, homonomy is "the experience of being part of meaningful wholes and in harmony with superindividual units such as family, social group, culture, and cosmic order" (p. 58). The prime motivations for the autonomous self are achievement and conquest, whereas participation in something beyond the individual self is the motivation for the homonomous (connected) self. Other more recent writers in self-directed learning agree with Boucouvalas's observation and call for further exploration of the social aspects of self-directedness and the concept of interdependence in the learning process (Ahteenmaki-Pelkonen, 1994; Rowland and Volet, 1996). Giving wider recognition to this connected or interdependent part of the self may allow for a fuller explanation of the collaborative aspects of self-directed learning referred to by Tough (1978, 1979), Knowles (1975), and Caffarella (1993b) in activities such as teamwork, shared resources, and peer networks.

BUILDING FUTURE RESEARCH AND THEORY

Although there continues to be a vast array of studies on self-directed learning, we believe, as do Candy (1991) and others, that the development of a richer research agenda in self-directed learning has been slow to evolve. We attribute this lack of new direction to three causes: insufficient critical dialogue and use of the theory and models that have been developed, continual disregard of the observations of previous researchers about recommendations for future research, and predominant use of the quantitative or positivist paradigm in data-based studies.

Insufficient critical dialogue and use of the theory and models that have been developed is a major stumbling block in moving the research agenda in self-directed learning forward. Over the past decade, a number of authors have derived sophisticated conceptual models (for example, Brockett and Hiemstra, 1991; Candy, 1991; Cavaliere, 1992; Danis, 1992; Garrison, 1997; Grow, 1991; Metzger, 1997) that have challenged us to think more clearly about what constitutes self-direction in learning. Yet critical discussion of these models has been scarce, and data-based studies grounded in these models are almost nonexistent. The major exceptions to this lack of critical conversation have been the observations of authors advocating a more critical practice of self-directed learning (for example, Brookfield, 1993b; Collins, 1991, 1996) and the dialogue on the Grow model (Grow, 1994; Tennant, 1992). Instead, we continue to have discussion about how one conceptual definition is needed versus accepting the premise that self-directed learning is a multifaceted concept. As Rowland and Volet (1996, p. 99) have concluded, based on a case study of self-direction in community learning, "there is no composite list of what constitutes self-directed learning, and . . . in discussing the concept we need to keep in mind multiplicity and diversity." Keeping this notion of multiplicity in mind, we need to revisit the many models that have been developed and reuse, merge, or disregard those that are not useful.

The second reason the research agenda is not as rich as it could be—the continual disregard of previous researchers' observations about directions for research—is at least tangentially related to the first. Just as researchers rarely use the more recent conceptual models that have been developed, so too do they seldom choose topics to study that have been raised by previous scholars as important questions for further research. The one major exception has been the work generated on self-directed learning readiness (for example, see Long and others, 1996, 1997). The authors who have generated especially provocative questions and observations about self-directed learning in general include Tough (1978, 1979), Spear and Mocker (1984), Brookfield (1984, 1986, 1993b), Caffarella and O'Donnell (1987), Long and others (1988, 1992, 1997), Brockett and Hiemstra (1991), Candy (1991), and Collins (1991, 1996). Following are some of the research questions that have been raised and would generate an expanded knowledge base about self-directed learning:

- *How do adults in natural settings who are self-directed in their learning learn over long periods of time?* These studies could be accomplished in a number of ways, from following a specific group of learners over time to completing content analyses of autobiographies and biographies. A few studies of this nature have been completed (for example, Danis and Tremblay, 1987; Houle, 1984), but more work is needed.

- *How does the process of self-directed learning change as learners move from being novices to experts in subject matter and learning strategies?* A group of learners could be followed over time, in natural, formal, or nonformal settings, or learners could be asked to reflect back on specific learning experiences they have had when they moved from being novices to experts. Studies of this nature could also add to the general knowledge base about cognition in adulthood.

- *How, in formal learning settings, do the issues of power and control affect introducing and sustaining the use of self-directed learning methodologies in instruction?* In framing these studies, researchers could explore the perceptions of power and control issues that are held by instructors, students, and administrators. Qualitative methodologies, such as observations and interviews, would probably be the most useful in this type of research.

- *Does having learners use self-directed learning approaches in formal and nonformal settings affect the practice of these learners as instructors and program planners?* These data could be gathered in a number of ways, from written questionnaires to observations and interviews. Some information has been gathered related to this question (for example, Caffarella and Caffarella, 1986), but further data could prove useful in understanding how we learn our own practices as educators.

- *Should public policy be formulated related to self-directed learning in formal settings, and if so, what should be the nature of this policy?* Tough (1978), Brockett and Hiemstra (1991), and Brookfield (1993b) have been the strongest voices in raising public policy issues related to self-directed learning. What is currently needed is systematic study of these policy issues, especially with the increased use of technology in the learning process.

- *What constitutes the critical practice of self-directed learning from the perspective of those who are actively involved in this practice? Are educators of adults willing to expand the critical practice of self-directed learning, especially in formal programs of learning, and if so, what are the most effective ways to incorporate this framework into our work as educators?* Because the knowledge base of the critical practice of self-directed learning is limited, studies need to be completed to see if this practice is carried out, and if so how. Studies of this practice could be done through case studies and other qualitative methods.

- *Is there a set of definitive personal attributes or characteristics that typify learners who are self-directed? If so, how do contextual factors affect how these learners carry through their self-directed learning ventures?* Although research has been conducted on the question of what personal attributes characterize learner self-directedness, the debate continues over what these attributes are and if the instruments we have adequately measure these attributes. Both quantitative and qualitative work needs to be completed to explore these questions further.

The predominant use of the quantitative or positivist paradigm, the third cause, "has inhibited the emergence of valuable research findings with respect to self-directed learning" (Candy, 1991, p. 437). Candy argues that the unique features of self-direction in learning call for research orientations that allow for the voices of learners to be prominent and to take into consideration the important contextual dimensions of self-directed learning. The interpretive or qualitative and critical approaches have and continue to offer such orientations. Yet despite Candy's and others' (for example, Brockett and Hiemstra, 1991; Collins, 1991, 1996; Pilling-Cormick, 1996) recognition that a broader array of research orientations is needed, the data-based studies that have been published in the past decade are still primarily quantitative in nature. For example, of the twenty-five data-based studies in the 1996 and 1997 volumes by Long and others on self-directed learning, seventeen were quantitative, six were qualitative, and two were a mixed design. We hypothesize that one of the reasons that the quantitative paradigm still predominates is the availability of the SDLRS, which has been used in the majority of the quantitative studies in the past decade (Guglielmino, 1997a) and other quantitative measures (for example, Confessore and Confessore, 1994; Oddi, 1986). Researchers, especially novices, sometimes design studies around the availability of instrumentation rather than tackling the more difficult task of identifying critical problems to be studied to advance an area of study. We believe the study of self-directed learning has suffered from this phenomenon of available instrumentation more than once over the past three decades (for example, the number of studies completed in the Tough tradition).

Pilling-Cormick (1996) has offered a thoughtful essay on using a variety of paradigms for studying self-directed learning, including the positivist, constructivist, and critical paradigms (and we would add feminist approaches). She sees difficulties with adopting only one approach and argues that an integrative approach to studying self-directed learning should be encouraged, including studies that combine both qualitative and quantitative approaches. We agree with the caveat that it is not the approach that should determine what should be studied in self-directed learning, but the importance of the problem or questions to be addressed. In addition, we must continue to be vigilant as researchers in choosing groups to study that represent a wide spectrum of learners. This includes purposefully including people of color, of different socioeconomic classes, and of different cultural backgrounds as study participants.

Although we see the building of a richer and wider research agenda in self-directed learning as critical for expanding the knowledge base about self-direction in learning, we also view this work as fundamental for the continued recognition of the importance of this form of learning in our everyday lives. The ability to be self-directed in one's learning is critical to our individual and collective survival and prosperity in a world of continuous personal, community, and societal changes. The example of Brenda, a woman who had been diagnosed with breast cancer, which we used in Chapter Three to illustrate self-directed learning in natural settings, warrants mention here again.

Little did one of us know (Rosemary Caffarella) that she would become like Brenda just shortly before the first edition of this book (1991) was published. Like Brenda, Rosemary became, after much anguish and soul searching, highly directed in her learning so she could be an active member in her treatment and now wellness activities. "So, too, in communities and in society in general, as with personal life events, there is a continuous need for people to be active and informed learners" (Caffarella, 1993b, p. 32). If we are to cope with issues such as AIDS, poverty, prejudice, and social injustice, all learners need to be encouraged and allowed to develop the ability to be self-directed in their learning throughout their lives.

SUMMARY

This chapter has explored the research and theory-building efforts in self-directed learning. Although learning on one's own has been the principal model of learning throughout the ages, serious studies of this subject did not become prevalent until the 1970s and 1980s. In reviewing this research, what became clear is that self-directed learning is a multifaceted concept. Therefore, we grouped the work that we reviewed into three broad categories: the goals of self-directed learning, self-directed learning as a process, and self-direction as a personal attribute of learners.

In discussing the goals of self-directed learning, three major ones were identified. The first goal, that of enhancing the ability of adults to be self-directed in their learning, has generated the most research in self-directed learning. The fostering of transformational learning as central to self-directed learning, the second goal, is foundational to the third goal, that of promoting emancipatory learning and social action. Our assumption is that each of these goals is of equal importance in capturing the essence of self-directed learning.

Within the broad category of self-directed learning as a process, three types of models have been extensively discussed in the literature: linear, interactive, and instructional. The linear models often reflect more traditional ways of thinking about teaching, although they could be applied in learners' natural as well as formal and nonformal settings. The interactive models more closely resemble how learners go about learning primarily on their own, and the instructional models are specifically designed to be used as ways to organize instruction in formal and nonformal settings. Although a rich array of models is now available, little data-based research has been conducted using these models as frameworks, except for studies using Tough's (1979) work.

The notion of readiness and the concept of autonomy have received the greatest attention from scholars who are studying self-direction as a personal attribute of learners. Readiness, which implies an internal state of psychological readiness to undertake self-directed learning, has generated the majority of the data-based studies. This large volume of research is due in part to the availability of the Self-Directed Learning Readiness Scale (SDLRS). Because of the controversy that surrounds the measurement properties of the SDLRS, caution needs to be used in interpreting the results of these studies. The relationship of autonomy and self-directedness in learning has been discussed primarily at the conceptual level. Two major questions have been raised concerning autonomy and self-directed learning: Should autonomy be the hallmark attribute of learners who are self-directed? and How does the context of the learning situation affect learner autonomy?

The chapter concluded with a review of the major issues that researchers must address in building future research agendas in self-directed learning. We contend that the development of a richer research tradition has stagnated, and therefore three major challenges need to be addressed to move this agenda in new directions. The first is that we need more critical dialogue about the models that have been developed; in addition, those models should be tested in future studies. Second, we must listen to the voices of past researchers about recommendations for future studies, because they have posed many important questions. And third, because self-directed learning is a multifaceted concept, we need to use a variety of research paradigms in our work. More specifically, we need to move beyond framing our studies primarily in the positivistic or quantitative paradigm and make a concerted effort to use more interpretive, critical, and feminist approaches.

CHAPTER FOURTEEN

Transformational Learning

ndragogy and self-directed learning (see Chapters Twelve and Thirteen) are two distinct lines of inquiry into aspects of the learning transaction with adults. A third line of inquiry, which has taken center stage since the late 1980s, is transformative or transformational (terms used interchangeably in the literature) learning theory. First articulated by Mezirow in 1978, transformational learning theory is about change—dramatic, fundamental change in the way we see ourselves and the world in which we live. This kind of learning is more than merely adding to what we already know: "Transformational learning *shapes* people; they are different afterward, in ways both they and others can recognize" (Clark, 1993b, p. 47). Rather than focusing on adult learner characteristics as andragogy and self-directed learning tend to do, transformational learning centers more on the cognitive process of learning. The mental construction of experience, inner meaning, and reflection are common components of this approach.

This chapter first examines transformational learning theory as developed by two of its major theoreticians, Jack Mezirow and Paulo Freire. It then draws from a broad range of literature to discuss three important components of transformational learning: experience, critical reflection, and development. Finally, it highlights several key issues in the ongoing debate surrounding transformational learning theory.

THE THEORISTS: MEZIROW AND FREIRE

There is always some danger in singling out particular writers as *the* major theorists of a particular line of inquiry. In the case of transformational learning, Mezirow has been the primary architect and spokesperson, having written a book (1991) and dozens of articles and chapters on the topic over the past twenty years. Although others have expanded components of the theory, focused on the process, or considered applications to practice, Mezirow has evolved a fully developed theory of transformative learning. Freire's (1970b) philosophy of education also signifies adult learning as a transformative process, although he focuses on its social change outcomes more so than Mezirow does. Parallels between these two influential theories can be drawn, and indeed, Mezirow (1991, 1995) has acknowledged the influence of Freire on his own thinking.

Mezirow's Transformation Theory

Although Mezirow first proposed his theory in 1978, more than a decade later, Long (1991a, p. 82) observed that "perspective transformation theory has yet to stimulate a copious body of research or philosophically based literature." The 1990s, however, have witnessed a burgeoning of both empirical research and philosophical critique on Mezirow's theory. In a recent article, for example, Taylor (1997a) reviewed thirty-nine empirical studies using Mezirow's transformative learning as the theoretical framework. Numerous other articles, books, and conference proceedings have built an impressive body of literature around this theory.

Mezirow's theory is about how adults interpret their life experiences, how they make meaning. He in fact defines learning as a meaning-making activity: "Learning is understood as the process of using a prior interpretation to construe a new or a revised interpretation of the meaning of one's experience in order to guide future action" (1996, p. 162). He differentiates between meaning schemes, which are "specific beliefs, feelings, attitudes, and value judgments," and meaning perspectives, which are "broad, generalized, orienting predispositions"

(p. 163). Meaning perspectives are the lens through which each person filters, engages, and interprets the world. Learning can consist of a change in one of our beliefs or attitudes (a meaning scheme), or it can be a change in our entire perspective. A change in perspective is personally emancipating in that one is freed from previously held beliefs, attitudes, values, and feelings that have constricted and distorted one's life. Perspective transformation, key to transformative learning, is thus defined as "the process of becoming critically aware of how and why our presuppositions have come to constrain the way we perceive, understand, and feel about our world; of reformulating these assumptions to permit a more inclusive, discriminating, permeable, and integrative perspective; and of making decisions or otherwise acting on these new understandings. *More inclusive, discriminating, permeable, and integrative perspectives are superior perspectives* that adults choose if they can because they are motivated to better understand the meaning of their experience" (Mezirow, 1990b, p. 14).

The process of transformative learning is firmly anchored in life experience. All human beings have a need to understand their experiences, to make sense of what is happening in their lives. As Mezirow (1990b, p. 11) observes, "No need is more fundamentally human than our need to understand the meaning of our experience." In trying to understand our experiences, we first use all of the usual ways of thinking that have worked in the past. When the old ways of thinking—of making meaning—do not work, we can either deny or postpone grappling with the problem, or we can confront it head on. It is through engaging with the life experience to make meaning that there is an opportunity for a change in perspective. The learner must critically self-examine the assumptions and beliefs that have structured how the experience has been interpreted. This sets in motion a revision of "specific assumptions about oneself and others until the very structure of assumptions becomes transformed" (1981, p. 8). Mezirow believes that adult educators have a responsibility to promote this kind of critical reflection. It is not enough to help learners perform, achieve, and produce. The one significant commitment of adult education is "to help learners make explicit, elaborate, and act upon the assumptions and premises . . . upon which their performance, achievement, and productivity are based" (1985a, p. 148).

Mezirow (1991, p. 223) acknowledges that not all learning in adulthood is transformative: "We can learn simply by adding knowledge to our meaning schemes or learning new meaning schemes . . . and it can be a crucially important experience for the learner." Significant transformational learning involves three phases: "critical reflection on one's assumptions, discourse to validate the critically reflective insight, and action" (1997b, p. 60). According to Mezirow, the process is most often set in motion by a *disorienting dilemma,* that is, a particular life event or life experience such as the death of a loved one, a job change, or an illness that a person experiences as a crisis. This crisis cannot be resolved through the application of previous problem-solving strategies. Next, the learner engages in *self-examination,* which is often accompanied by "feelings of guilt or shame, sometimes turning to religion for support" (1991, p. 168). Self-examination includes the third step of *a critical assessment of assumptions.* Such an assessment leads to the fourth phase of *recognizing that others have gone through a similar process,* painful as it is. Step Five consists of *exploring options* for forming new roles, relationships, or actions, which leads to formulating a *plan of action.* This plan has four steps: acquiring knowledge and skills, trying out new roles, renegotiating relationships and negotiating new relationships, and building competence and self-confidence. The final step or phase of the process is a *reintegration* back into one's life based on the new, transformed perspective (1991). Mezirow (1995, p. 50) comments that although "a perspective transformation appears to follow" the process of creating meaning, it is not necessarily "in this exact sequence."

Empirical studies of transformative learning reviewed by Taylor (1997a), although generally supportive of this process, have also revealed a number of other factors inherent in the process of transformative learning. With regard to the disorienting dilemma, for example, Clark (1993a, p. 81) found that an "integrating circumstance" could also initiate a perspective transformation: "In contrast to the abrupt and dramatic appearance of the disorienting dilemma, the integrating circumstance occurs after and seems to be the culmination of an earlier stage of exploration and searching. . . . This is an indefinite period in which the person consciously or unconsciously searches for something which is missing in their life; when they find this 'missing piece,' the transformational learning process is catalyzed." As another example of how research has expanded the process, Courtenay, Merriam, and Reeves (1998) found that the disorienting dilemma of an HIV-positive diagnosis for their subjects was followed by an initial reaction phase lasting six months to five years. In this period, participants used old, dysfunctional behavior patterns such as excessive drinking to cope with the diagnosis. It was not until some sort of "catalytic experience" occurred that they were able to break free from and examine underlying assumptions about self and the world, setting the transformational learning process into motion.

The new meaning that people create as the result of a perspective transformation is highly subjective, personal, and changeable. "Meaning," Mezirow (1991, p. xiv) writes, "exists within ourselves rather than in external forms such as books," and "our present interpretations of reality are always subject to revision or replacement." To test whether our new meanings are true or authentic, Mezirow (1995, p. 53) says we must "seek the best judgment of the most informed, objective, and rational persons we can find" and enter into "a special form of dialogue." Drawing from the German philosopher Jürgen Habermas, this special form of dialogue is called "discourse": "Discourse involves an effort to set aside bias, prejudice, and personal concerns and to do our best to be open and objective in presenting and assessing reasons and reviewing the evidence and arguments for and against the problematic assertion to arrive at a consensus" (Mezirow, 1995, p. 53).

Drawing from Habermas, there are, according to Mezirow, "ideal" conditions for discourse: having complete information, being free from self-deception, being able to evaluate arguments objectively, having an "equal opportunity to participate in the various roles of discourse," and so on (1995, p. 54). Mezirow is well aware that these are ideal conditions that no interaction can actually effect; however, "dialogue and discourse can proceed in a critically self-reflective manner that aims toward more sensitive, respectful, non-dominating, and non-distorting communication. Facilitating the kind of learning which views difference as an opportunity, a challenge to our abilities to communicate, understand, and learn, is precisely what adult education is about" (1995, p. 55). "Discourse is not a war or a debate; it is a conscientious effort to find agreement, to build a new understanding" (1996, p. 170).

Discourse can occur in one-to-one relationships, in groups, and in formal educational settings; in fact, the educational setting is precisely where adult educators support and facilitate transformational learning through discourse and critical reflection. Several publications have focused on applications, experiences, and suggestions for educators interested in facilitating this type of learning (Cranton, 1994b, 1996, 1997; Mezirow, 1997a; Mezirow and Associates, 1990).

The third phase of Mezirow's process, following critical reflection and discourse, is action: "an integral and indispensable component of transformative learning" (1991, p. 209). The type of action one takes "depends upon the nature of the [disorienting] dilemma" (1997b, p. 60) and can range from making a decision to radical political protest. For critics who see the goal of adult education as social action, Mezirow's theory, with its emphasis on individual transformation, is too egocentric (Taylor, 1997a). He does speak to social action in certain circumstances, however: "When the disorienting dilemma is the result of oppressive action by a partner, employer, landlord, or anyone else, the transformation process *requires* that the learner take action against her oppressor, and when appropriate, collective social action" (1997b, p. 60). From Mezirow's perspective, social change can come about only through individuals' changing: "Personal transformation leads to alliances with others of like mind to work toward effecting necessary changes in relationships, organizations, and systems, each of which requires a different mode of praxis" (1992, p. 252). A three-step process for social action begins with becoming aware of a need to change (Mezirow, 1993). This need arises through critically reflecting on assumptions and biases. Next, "a feeling of solidarity with others committed to change" (p. 189) needs to be established. And finally, one has to learn what actions are appropriate in particular situations to implement change.

To illustrate this three-step process, let us take the case of Karen, who returns to college as an adult. She has always had trouble with certain subjects in school and had assumed she was not that capable or academically inclined. Nevertheless, she decides to try again to get her college degree. She encounters problems, particularly in math courses. Since she assumes she is not smart enough to do college work, she considers withdrawing. However, she has done exceptionally well in other courses, and one of her instructors suggests she be tested for a learning disability. This suggestion causes her to question assumptions about her academic ability, and when a learning disability is confirmed, Karen seeks accommodations that allow her to stay in school. In the process, her image of herself changes. She locates others with learning disabilities, and they form a support and advocacy group. The group works toward raising awareness and changing attitudes on campus regarding learning disabilities.

Freire's Emancipatory Philosophy

Freire was a Brazilian educator whose writings in the 1970s struck a responsive chord worldwide with educators, social workers, clergy, community leaders, and others. As Schugurensky (1996, p. 344) observes, "There is 'before' and 'after' Freire, both in the philosophical approach to adult education, as well as in its practice." While Mezirow focuses on personal transformation, Freire's theory is set within a larger framework of radical social change. In Freire's approach, personal empowerment and social transformation are intertwined and inseparable processes. His conceptions of conscientization (consciousness-raising) and empowerment have contributed significantly to the underlying theoretical framework of transformational learning.

Within Freire's theory of education for social change are components relevant to adult learning situations. He distinguishes between "banking" and "problem-posing" education. In traditional banking education, deposits of knowledge are made into student receptacles; in problem posing, teachers and students cooperate in a dialogue that seeks to humanize and liberate. Central to the learning is a changed relationship between teacher and student. They are coinvestigators into their common reality, the sociocultural situation in which they live. Like Mezirow's notion of discourse, dialogue is the method by which this sharing takes place and by which consciousness is raised. Generative themes, concerns that are posed by the learners themselves, become the content of a learning situation. For example, in asking learners for some words that capture their everyday experience, the word for "slum" or "land" or "taxes" or "illness" or "government" might come up. These words are then broken down into syllables and used in various contexts in learning how to read. At the same time, participants engage in discussions about these concepts. These discussions raise their awareness about their life situations (Freire, 1973). The ultimate goal is liberation, or praxis, "the action and reflection of men [sic] upon their world in order to transform it" (1970b, p. 66).

Freire's ideas emerged out of a context of poverty, illiteracy, and oppression. His analysis thus takes into account forms of oppression, power, and control that pervade all aspects of society, including the teaching-learning transaction. Education for Freire is never neutral: it either domesticates by imparting the values of the dominant group, so that learners assume things are right the way they are, or it liberates, allowing people to reflect critically on their world and take action to move society toward a more equitable and just vision. Like Mezirow, a key component of his philosophy is critical reflection. Critical reflection occurs through problem posing and dialogue with other learners.

For education to be liberating, one's consciousness must be transformed. This process Freire calls conscientization, "in which men, not as recipients, but as knowing subjects, achieve a deepening awareness both of the sociocultural reality which shapes their lives and of their capacity to transform that reality" (1970a, p. 27). There are stages in this process. At the least-aware levels is a magical, fatalistic consciousness in which nothing about one's world is questioned; external forces are in charge, and there is nothing that can be done to change things as they are. Midway between being totally unaware and critical consciousness, people begin to sense that they may have some control over their lives and turn to questioning things as they are. The most sophisticated stage of consciousness is critical consciousness. Here one achieves an in-depth understanding of the forces that shape one's life space, and becomes an active agent in constructing a different, more just reality. Increasing awareness of one's situation involves moving from the lowest level of consciousness, where there is no comprehension of how forces shape one's life, to the highest level of critical consciousness. In the transformation process, one becomes "aware of both the structures that oppress us in society and of the internal structures or myths that direct our behavior" (Scott, 1996, p. 345).

Freire has operationalized his theory of education with techniques that have demonstrated success in combating illiteracy, especially in the Third World. Its application in North America has been limited, owing perhaps to the necessary corollary of social change. Although conscientization is always a political act in Freire's theory, it can be seen as similar to perspective transformation in its characterization of adult learning as the process of becoming aware of one's assumptions, beliefs, and values and then transforming those assumptions into a new perspective or level of consciousness. With regard to learning, Mezirow (1995, p. 44) underscores this comparison: "The process of transformation is the same as that which Paulo Freire has called 'conscientization.' It is a generic process of adult learning."

In summary, Mezirow's and Freire's approaches to adult learning emphasize the importance of inner meaning and mental constructs in defining the nature of learning in adult life. Key to both of their theories is change—change brought about by critical reflection on the origin and nature of our submerged assumptions, biases, beliefs, and values. Tentative new understandings and new meanings are tested out in discourse with others. The process does not end there, however. Our new meanings, perspectives, or consciousness need to be acted on. For Mezirow (1995) this can mean making a decision as well as a change in behavior; personal transformation occurs, and people can choose to act in a socially emancipatory way. For Freire, social action is inherent in critical reflection and emancipation. This ongoing cycle of reflecting, acting in the world on one's new understanding, and then critically reflecting on those actions, is what Freire (1970b) called praxis.

KEY CONCEPTS IN TRANSFORMATIONAL LEARNING

While Mezirow and Freire have given the most robust formulations of transformational learning, others have elaborated on and expanded our understanding of various components of the theory. In our exploration of three of the key concepts of transformational learning—the centrality of life experience, the nature of critical reflection, and the connection between transformational learning and development in adulthood—we draw from several authors in addition to Mezirow and Freire.

Experience

One of the assumptions of andragogy is that adults bring with them a depth and breadth of experience that can be used as a resource for theirs and others' learning (Knowles, 1980). And as Mezirow (1995, p. 58) states, "The subject matter of transformative adult education is the learner's experience." But there are different types of experiences, some of which are more useful to learning than others (see Chapter Ten). Michelson (1996, p. 439) observes that experience can be conceived of as "the shapeless, pre-linguistic product of unmediated sensory input" or "as socially constructed rather than as unmediated." It is the latter conception that provides the basis for transformative learning, for if experience is seen as socially constructed, it can be deconstructed, acted on, and reconstructed.

However experience is construed, the ways in which it can be used in learning differs according to one's theoretical orientation. Tennant (1991) delineates several uses:

First, at the most basic or superficial level, teachers can link their explanations and illustrations to the prior experiences of learners. . . . Second, teachers can attempt to link learning activities to learners' current experiences at work, home, or in the community. . . . Third, teachers can create experiences from which learning will flow. In other words, they can design learning experiences that require the active participation of learners, such as simulations, games, and role plays. These learning experiences establish a common base from which each learner constructs meaning through personal reflection and group discussion. Fourth, the meanings that learners attach to their experiences may be subjected to critical scrutiny. The teacher may consciously try to disrupt the learner's world view and stimulate uncertainty, ambiguity, and doubt in learners about previously taken-for-granted interpretations of experience. [pp. 196–197]

Clearly, Tennant's fourth level is most congruent with the use of experience in transformative learning. Equally obvious is the fact that not all experiences trigger learning—whether the learning is a simple addition to our prior knowledge or a fundamental change in our perspective. Further, the identical experience, a job change or a divorce, for example, can trigger learning for some people but not others. Jarvis (1992, p. 15) explains how experience stimulates learning. "While all learning begins with experience," he writes, "this is not experience for which the learners already have a solution or response." Adults "with all their memories of previous experiences and their store of knowledge, are unable to respond [to the new experience]. . . . There is a disjuncture at a particular point in time between people's biographies—that is, their internalized cultural patterns of social living—and their experience." It is "at this point of disjuncture" that "individuals are forced to ask why this has occurred to them or what it means. These questions are located at the start and at the core of human learning" (p. 15).

Critical Reflection

With an experience that one cannot accommodate into the prior life structure, the transformative learning process can begin. Necessary to the process is critical reflection, the second key concept. Experience itself is not enough to effect a transformation. As Criticos (1993, p. 162) points out, "Was the experience itself valuable? Not at all—what was valuable was the intellectual growth that follows the process of reflecting on experience. Effective learning does not follow from a positive experience but from effective reflection." Reflection is a cognitive process. We can think about our experience—muse, review, and so on—but to reflect critically, we must also examine the underlying beliefs and assumptions that affect how we make sense of the experience.

Mezirow (1991) differentiates among three types of reflection, only one of which can lead to transformative learning. Content reflection, the first type, is thinking about the actual experience itself. Process reflection is thinking about ways to deal with the experience, that is, problem-solving strategies. Premise reflection involves examining long-held, socially constructed assumptions, beliefs, and values about the experience or problem.

Much has been written about critical reflection, especially under the more common topic of critical thinking and reflective practice (see Chapter Ten). Psychologists and educators from kindergarten to higher education have been promoting the acquisition of critical thinking skills for all learners. There are also a number of adult educators in addition to Mezirow who have focused on critical thinking, especially as it relates to transformative learning. Garrison (1991), for example, proposes that critical thinking consists of the five stages of identifying the problem, defining the problem, exploring ways of dealing with it, applying one of the strategies to the problem, and integrating the new perspective. He maintains that this process is congruent with Mezirow's perspective transformation.

The most prominent adult educator writing about critical thinking is Brookfield (1987, 1994). His book on critical thinking, *Developing Critical Thinkers* (1987), presents a rationale as to why critical thinking is important and how adults can become critical thinkers in their family, work, and personal lives and in relation to mass media. Especially relevant to the link between critical thinking or critical reflection and transformative learning is his model of critical thinking. The model consists of five "commonly experienced phases" (p. 25).

First is what he calls a *trigger event,* "some unexpected happening [that] prompts a sense of inner discomfort and perplexity." The next stage, *appraisal,* captures several of the steps in Mezirow's process, including a self-examination of the situation, "brooding" about our discomfort, and finding others who are experiencing a similar problem. In the third phase of *exploration,* we examine new and different ways of explaining or accommodating the experience that has led to our discomfort. The fourth phase is one of *developing alternative perspectives.* Basically we try on a new role, a new way of behaving, a new way of thinking about the problem or experience, and simultaneously gain confidence in the new perspective. Finally, we are able to *integrate* these new ways of thinking or living "into the fabric of our lives" (p. 27). Brookfield has thus delineated a model of critical thinking that is identical to the ten- or eleven-step process of transformative learning presented by Mezirow (1991, 1995).

In subsequent writing (1993b, 1994, 1996a), Brookfield has clarified and expanded his notion of critical thinking. He now sees it as a questioning of and replacement of commonly held assumptions about the self and group, social and political structures. The process of critical thinking becomes politicized when one takes a perspective "which is strongly alternative to that held by a majority" (1996a, p. 59). His mission is to move critical reflection toward an examination of the majority-held assumptions. Such assumptions are hegemonic; that is, people accept things as they are, as "the 'natural' state of affairs. Applied to the field of adult education, this means that critical reflection analyzes commonly held ideas regarding learning and educational practice for the extent to which they perpetuate economic inequity, deny compassion, foster a culture of silence and prevent adults from realizing a sense of common connectedness" (p. 59). In this formulation of critical reflection, Brookfield echoes a more radical political stance.

In an interesting critique of the way critical reflection and experience are related in most of the transformational learning literature, Michelson (1996) points out the particularly Western bias of separating the two. Experience is "immediate but messy. . . . That messiness can be transcended only through . . . the application of sustained and self-conscious rational thought that, by encouraging distance and objectivity, will allow us to identify our prior assumptions, use our minds to critique them for validity and serviceability, and reconstruct them to make them more accurate, inclusive and empowering" (p. 439). In separating ourselves from our experiences in order to reflect critically on them, Michelson suggests that "a rhetoric of order and control undergirds these approaches to adult learning" (p. 444). Furthermore, the assumptions underlying this type of adult learning are themselves unexamined and "deeply complicitous with power differentials of gender, class and race" (p. 439).

The fact that at least two studies have found that some transformations in perspective were effected *without* conscious critical reflection raises questions about the necessity of critical reflection for a transformation to take place. Both Taylor (1994), who studied adults who had lived and worked in another country, and McDonald (1997), who investigated how people became ethical vegans, found some who had transformed their perspective without being aware of the change process. Recently, Mezirow (1998, p. 191) has suggested that transformations may occur through the process of assimilative learning. By this he means that when "our situation changes, and, beyond our scope of awareness, we make a tacit judgment to move toward a way of thinking or behaving that we deem more appropriate to our new situation." Mezirow concedes that "dramatic changes in orientation based upon assimilation rather than critical reflection on assumptions" are possible.

Development

In addition to the centrality of experience and critical reflection, there is in transformational learning theory the notion of individual development. Individual development is both inherent in and an outcome of the process. The ability to think critically, which is mandatory to effecting a transformation, is itself developmental; that is, we can become better, more critical thinkers. Elias (1997) explains how individual and cognitive development are intertwined:

> What are transformed through the processes of transformative learning are several capacities of mind or consciousness. First is the development of a "conscious I" capable of exercising critical reflection. Second is a transformed capacity for thinking, transformed to be more dialectical or systemic, thinking (for example) that perceives polarities as mutually creative resources rather than as exclusive and competitive options and that perceives archetypes as partners for inner dialogue. Third is the capacity to be a conscious creative force in the world, as expressed, for example, as the capacity to intervene in and transform the quality of discourse in a group or learning community. [pp. 3–4]

Mezirow and Associates' 1990 book includes a chapter on Kitchener and King's reflective judgment model, and Mezirow (1995) acknowledges their and others' work as important contributions to understanding adult critical reflection. King and Kitchener's (1994) model, which draws on the earlier work of Perry (1970), consists of seven stages, of which only the last two are characteristic of critical reflection: "People who reason with the assumptions of these stages argue that knowledge is not a 'given' but must be actively constructed and that claims of knowledge must be understood in relation to the context in which they are generated" (King and Kitchener, 1994, p. 66). Mezirow (1998, p. 189) notes that King and Kitchener's model is "consistent with Transformation Theory" in that a person moves through developmental stages, with the last two representing reflective judgment: "It seems clear that movement through these ways of knowing, related to age and education, is toward a more inclusive, differentiating, permeable, critically reflective, and integrative frame of reference."

King and Kitchener's model is reminiscent of women's ways of knowing, delineated by Belenky, Clinchy, Goldberger, and Tarule (1986) and Goldberger, Tarule, Clinchy, and Belenky (1996). In their model, one can "know" in various ways, the most critically reflective being knowledge that the woman herself constructs. Kegan (1994) also sees the development of greater cognitive complexity to be imperative in handling "the mental demands of modern life." Adults need to move toward a fourth order of consciousness, where they are capable of doing more than thinking across and among categories and concepts; the fourth level involves questioning the categories, values, and beliefs themselves and in so doing creating new forms of knowledge, ones that better address the gap between demands made on us and our capacity to meet them. (See Chapter Seven for a discussion of cognitive development.)

Development is also the outcome of transformative learning. Mezirow (1991, p. 155) states clearly that the process of perspective transformation is "the central process of adult development." And "meaning perspectives that permit us to deal with a broader range of experience, to be more discriminating, to be more open to other perspectives, and to better integrate our experiences are superior perspectives" (1990b, p. 14).

That the outcome of transformational learning is development is congruent with the growth orientation of much of adult learning literature generally. Underpinning this orientation is humanist psychology. Maslow (1968, p. 117), for example, stated that "there is a basic human impulse to grow toward health, full humanness, self-actualization, or perfection." Rogers (1961, p. 115) contended that "significant learning" results in a more mature self who is open to experience, to "new people, new situations, new problems." Knowles's (1980) model of andragogy is written quite explicitly from this humanistic perspective, defining adult learning as "a process that is used by adults for their self-development" (p. 25) and "to mature" (p. 28). Similarly, Kegan (1994, p. 287) wrote that higher and adult education's "mission" is to "assist adults in creating the order of consciousness the modern world demands."

Perhaps the most eloquent spokesperson for expressing the link between transformative learning and growth and development in adulthood is Daloz (1986, 1988a). His focus is on adults who are returning to higher education. In an atmosphere of care and support, the role of teacher-mentor is to challenge students to examine their conceptions of self and the world and to formulate new, more developed perspectives. This, he feels, is the "proper aim of education." Education should in fact "promote development. . . . To imagine otherwise, to act as though learning were simply a matter of stacking facts on top of one another makes as much sense as thinking one can learn a language by memorizing a dictionary" (p. 236). Although Daloz (1986) offers "three useful maps" of adult development, he does not prescribe an end point to this transformational journey. This fact raises yet another dimension to the link between transformation and development. Tennant (1993) argues that what constitutes psychological development is itself a social construction; that is, in any society at any particular point in time, there are normative expectations about "what it means to be enlightened or developmentally more mature" (p. 41). He warns that changes that are part of the expected life course (instances of normative development) should not be confused with actual changes in perspective.

Although there are certainly other factors important to transformational learning, we have discussed three that are central to the process. First, transformative learning posits experience as its starting point and as its content for reflection. Engaging the life experience in a critically reflective manner is a necessary condition for transformation. Finally, the entire process is about change—change that is growth enhancing and developmental.

UNRESOLVED ISSUES IN TRANSFORMATIONAL THEORY

The growing prominence of transformational learning theory has generated closer scrutiny of several aspects of the theory. Discussions and critiques of transformative learning center on four issues: the extent to which the theory takes context into account; whether the theory relies too heavily on rationality; the place of social action; and the educator's role in facilitating transformative learning. In fact, these four issues are interrelated and interdependent concerns.

Context

Clark and Wilson (1991) were the first to point out that Mezirow's theory appeared to be acontextual. Derived as it was from research on women returning to school, they note that the women's experiences "were studied as if they stood apart from their historical and sociocultural context, thereby limiting our understanding of the full meaning of those experiences" (p. 78). Further, they contend, Mezirow's own orientation toward autonomy uncritically reflects the values of the dominant culture in our society—masculine, white, and middle class. Stroobants and Wildemeersch (1997) also consider the failure to explore the tension between the individual and the sociocultural, political, and historical contexts to be a limitation of the theory. Additionally, Taylor's (1997a) review of the empirical research on Mezirow's theory revealed a number of studies that found that aspects of the individual's biographical history and sociocultural factors shaped the nature of the transformative learning. Taylor points out that more attention to such factors can help explain, for example, why a disorienting dilemma might lead to a perspective transformation for one person but not another. Indeed, studies accounting for individual biography and context are beginning to give a richer picture of transformative learning.

Recently Mezirow (1996) has attempted to explain better how context fits into his theory. He maintains that certain sociocultural factors at any particular point in history may impede or encourage critical reflection and rational discourse. North American culture, for example, "is fraught with obvious obstacles to learning through discourse. We are painfully familiar with the inequities associated with class, race, and gender. The hegemony of instrumental rationality is another principal distortion," as is "argumentative discourse" (1996, p. 169). "Transformation Theory," Mezirow (1996, p. 169) writes, "does not suggest a disengaged image of the individual learner, but of a learning process characterized by dialogical voices. The social dimension is central, but so are the historical and cultural dimensions of the process." Nevertheless, he maintains that his theory and in particular the conditions of ideal discourse can be used to respond in a constructive way to sociocultural realities that threaten to distort "communication and the adult learning process" (p. 171).

Rationality

The second major issue of transformational learning theory is what appears to be an excessive dependence on rationality as the means of effecting a perspective transformation; other forms of knowing are secondary at best. A number of writers (Boucouvalas, 1997; Hemphill, 1994; Hanson, 1996; Michelson, 1996) have pointed out that rational thinking is a particularly Western concept, a product of the Enlightenment and Descartes' mind-body split. Even in the West, rationality, and in particular its separation from experience, is also gender specific, privileging men, those of the middle and upper classes, and whites. Michelson (1996, p. 445) points out that even Freire is guilty of this bias; his "male-normed language is notorious, as is his failure to treat gender as a category of difference"; also, "his treatment of the colonized mentality of the oppressed raises issues of its own." She notes that "the erasure of non-rational sites of knowledge-production such as emotion, the body and material labour is re-enacted in the draining of knowledge from the shop floor, the home and the native village in favour of professionalized expertise" (p. 446). Hanson (1996) suggests that "for some cultures and situations conformity to the group may be more important than critical autonomy. Critical self-reflection is not always beneficial, as self-awareness and criticism are often the characteristics of seriously depressed people. Self-reflection and critical thinking may be reputed to be universal 'goods,' but we need to be aware of their cultural specificity and power" (p. 105). Hemphill's (1994) study of critical rationality among Chinese immigrants confirmed the importance of the collective, of a group-oriented way of thinking over an individual focus. Michelson (1996, p. 450) notes also that "Afrocentric approaches tend to value knowledge claims that are rooted in personal testimony and constructed through dialogue with others." Mezirow (1998, pp. 187–188) has recently responded to these charges, noting that rationality is not in itself an ideology; rather, "the justification for embracing an ideology depends upon advancing and supporting reasons for doing so. . . . Arguments against the universality of rationality and critical reflection themselves demonstrate the necessity of assessing reasons and becoming critical of assumptions. Once these critics enter into rational discourse, they have no choice but to agree to observe universal principles of rationality."

The Western bias toward rationality seems to preclude other ways of effecting a perspective transformation. Taylor (1997a, p. 48) notes that "multiple studies refer to the significance of intuition (Brooks), affective learning (Clark, Scott, Sveinunggaard), extrarational influences (Vogelsang), and the guiding force of feelings (Hunter, Taylor). The Group for Collaborative Inquiry (1994), in a recent study reconceptualizing the transformative learning process, identified the significance of whole person learning—'awareness and use of all the functions we have available for knowing, including our cognitive, affective, somatic, intuitive, and spiritual dimensions'" (p. 171). Taylor (1996) himself has sought to bring a consideration of emotion into transformational learning by offering a physiological exploration of the interdependence of emotion and reason. Other discussions suggest the importance of learning through emotion and intuition (Brookfield, 1987), "soul learning" (Dirkx, 1997, 1998), levels of consciousness (Boucouvalas, 1993, 1997), imaging in autobiographical learning (Nelson, 1997), the physical body (Chapman, 1998; Schlattner, 1994), and the subconscious (Scott, 1997). Taylor (1997a, p. 49) also notes that a prevalent finding across most of the empirical studies was that knowing occurred in connection with other people, that is, learning through relationships: "It is important to note that connected knowing, often thought [of] as gender based, was also found to be significant among working class men returning to community college."

In reviewing the contributions to Cranton's (1997) recent volume on transformative learning in practice, Grabove (1997, p. 90) concludes "from the authors' stories that there is no single model of transformative learning." Although Mezirow's theory is rather rational, perspective transformations can occur that rely "on internal images, dreams, and fantasies that are 'related to' rather than rationally interpreted," and "soul, imagery, pain, and mythical journeys also surface in the writings [on transformational learning]" (Grabove, 1997, pp. 91, 92).

Social Action

The place of social action in transformational learning theory remains controversial. Mezirow in particular has been criticized for focusing too much on individual transformation at the expense of social change. This criticism is in the light of the fact that he draws heavily from the critical theorist Habermas, for whom radical social change is a central concept (Collard and Law, 1989; Cunningham, 1992; Griffin, 1987; Hart, 1990). Mezirow (1990a, p. 363) indeed states that "we must begin with individual perspective transformations before social transformations can succeed." Action or praxis is, however, a key component of his theory, although "action can mean making a decision, being critically reflective or transforming a meaning structure as well as a change in behavior" (1995, pp. 58–59). Perspective transformation may also result in social action. For Mezirow, though, the role of adult education is to promote and facilitate individual critical reflection in which "the only anticipated learning outcome . . . is a more rational and objective assessment of assumptions" (1995, p. 59). To assume that the outcome is social action is to require "the learner to share the convictions of the educator's own view of social reality [which] would be tantamount to indoctrination" (p. 59).

Both Freire and Mezirow have been criticized for romanticizing the social change process (Newman, 1994a, 1994b). Both educators "start with the oppressed or the person trapped within a culturally induced dependency role, and both require these victims to liberate themselves, albeit with the help of the dialogic or transformative educator" (Newman, 1994a, p. 241). Newman believes this offers little help to those who are oppressed: "How will self-reflection help these kinds of learners when they are next moved on, thrown in jail, sacked, discriminated against, or hurt?" What should be studied, he believes, is "oppression, not the oppressed" (p. 241); adult teaching and learning should focus on identifying strategies to deal with oppression at the same time that we "encourage learners to examine themselves in order to build up their skills, increase or regenerate their knowledge, and rework their meaning perspectives in order to be better able to carry out those strategies" (p. 241). Baptiste (1998) concurs, calling for a pedagogy of disempowerment of our oppressors. Mezirow (1997b, p. 62) has responded to Newman's critique, arguing that "often learners are unaware of being oppressed; they internalize the values of the oppressors." In these situations, it may be necessary to engage in the "'deconstruction' of reified frames of reference" before action can be taken "on one's own behalf" (p. 62).

Educator's Role

There is yet another dimension to this issue of the place of social action in transformational learning theory. The ethical issues involved have been little addressed. For example, what right do adult educators have to tamper with the worldview (mental set, perspective, paradigm, or state of consciousness) of the learner? How invasive is it to study adults in the process of transformation (see Ziegahn, 1998)? How is the goal of educational intervention, whether it is social or personal change or something else, to be determined? What is the educator's responsibility for the action component of praxis? (These questions are addressed in more depth in Chapter Sixteen.)

The educator who supports personal and social transformation as the goal of adult education is confronted by a more practical issue: how exactly to facilitate such learning. Mezirow (1995) lays out the "ideal conditions" of discourse for fostering transformative learning, but to date there is little verification of these conditions in the empirical research (Taylor, 1997a). Brookfield (1987, 1990, 1996a) offers some help through his critical questioning techniques and through a critical incident activity. Daloz (1986) suggests the strategies of challenging, supporting, and visioning that mentors can use to facilitate the learner's personal journey of transformation. Freire (1970b) and Hart (1990) discuss techniques for consciousness raising in groups. Vella (1994) presents twelve principles of adult learning with specific case examples of their implementation in popular education sites around the world. The most extensive discussions of techniques for fostering transformational learning can be found in Mezirow and Associates (1990) and Cranton (1994b, 1996). Recognizing individual differences and learning preferences, Cranton suggests drawing from a repertoire of strategies, including critical questioning and experiential techniques such as role plays and simulations, journal writing, and life histories.

That transformational learning can be an intensely emotional, even painful activity concerns Robertson (1996), who observes that adult educators need better preparation to effect this kind of learning. In transformative learning, "the dynamics of the helping relationship are complex and often involve professional challenges such as transference, countertransference, confidentiality, sexual attraction, supervision, and burnout, each with attendant ethical, legal, and efficacy considerations (Corey, Corey, and Callahan). By and large, the field of adult education has not embraced the challenge of preparing and supporting adult educators to deal with these issues" (Robertson, 1996, p. 44). Robertson goes on to make several recommendations to address this lack of information, including fostering contributions to the scholarly literature, preparing practitioners as part of their academic training, developing an ethical code, and providing consultative support.

To summarize this section on some of the unresolved issues surrounding transformative learning, it is clear that questions of context, rationality, social action, and implementation are not as discrete as presented. To understand the biographical and sociocultural context of the individual learner is to consider other equally if not more powerful ways of knowing than pure rationality. It also means to consider what the appropriate action might be as a result of personal transformation; clearly such action may reside with the person or may be mobilized for some form of collective, social action. Ethical and professional considerations pervade the process, a process that most adult educators are little prepared to handle.

SUMMARY

This chapter has presented a discussion of transformational learning theory. Probably more than any other approach, this theory has captured the attention of adult educators within the past decade, so much so that Hanson (1996) feels that its dominance has replaced andragogy as the primary learning theory of the moment. Whether transformational learning will remain a centerpiece of adult learning theory is, of course, not predictable. It would seem, however, that the theoretical foundations articulated in detail by Mezirow and to some extent Freire are sufficiently robust to foster continued debate, discussion, and research.

In addition to reviewing the major tenets of the theory as laid out by Mezirow and Freire, drawing from a wide range of literature on transformational learning, this chapter also included a more detailed discussion of three of its key components: the centrality of experience, the process of critical reflection, and transformative learning's link to adult development. In the final section of the chapter, we explored four unresolved issues surrounding transformational learning: the extent to which context has been neglected, the overreliance on rational forms of knowing, the nature of the relationship between individual and social change, and questions regarding preparation for and implementation of this type of learning.

CHAPTER FIFTEEN

Critical Theory, Postmodern, and Feminist Perspectives

dult learning in North America has been most influenced by psychology. The focus of most of the approaches to adult learning covered in the previous three chapters is on individual learners: their growth and development and their learning in and out of formal settings. Even transformational learning, especially as conceptualized by Mezirow, appears primarily concerned with personal change. Only within the past decade or so has adult learning been discussed from other than a psychological perspective (see Chapters Four and Six).

In this chapter, where we approach adult learning from a power relations framework, the camera moves from the individual learner to an analysis of the context where learning takes place: the larger systems in society, the culture and institutions that shape learning, the structural and historical conditions framing, indeed defining, the learning event. Questions are raised regarding whose interests are being served by the programs offered, who really has access to these programs, who holds the power to make changes, and what are the intended and unintended outcomes of the way in which adult education and learning opportunities are structured (see Chapter Four). Further, our assumptions about the nature of knowledge—including what counts as knowledge, where it is located (in the individual or in society), and how it is acquired—are also challenged. These questions about knowledge are particularly important for adult educators because presumably the construction and acquisition of knowledge are inherent in the teaching-learning transaction. Because this stance critiques and raises questions about the assumptions we make about the world around us, including those underlying the practice of adult education, it has also been called "critical," as in "critical adult education." However, because *critical* in the sense of questioning and assessing assumptions and becoming empowered in the process can be easily confused with the school of thought known as critical theory, we have opted instead to use the concept of power relations in referring to a group of theoretical orientations having similar agendas.

Adult learning from this perspective, then, is informed by a number of specific philosophical and theoretical orientations, including Marxism, critical theory, multiculturalism, postmodernism, and feminist theory. Although some adult educators are clearly identified with a specific orientation, a number of others draw from several theoretical perspectives. Hart's (1992) analysis of work and learning, for example, is anchored in Marxism, critical theory, and feminist theory. Tisdell (1998) draws from multiculturalism, feminist theory, and poststructuralism in proposing a model of feminist pedagogy for adult education classrooms. Grace (1996a, 1997) maintains that critical theory, feminism, and postmodernism inform one another to the extent that common themes or assumptions can be derived to guide adult learning practices. Further, many educators writing from several of these perspectives claim an indebtedness to Paulo Freire's (1970b) work. The noted black feminist scholar bell hooks (1994, p. 46), for example, speaks of coming to Freire's work "just at that moment in my life when I was beginning to question deeply and profoundly the politics of domination, the impact of racism, sexism, class exploitation, and the kind of domestic colonization that takes place in the United States. . . . Paulo was one of the thinkers whose work gave me a language. He made me think deeply about the construction of an identity in resistance."

This chapter first provides a brief overview of some of the major themes, concepts, and terms that characterize what we are calling contemporary perspectives, derived from Marxist theory, critical theory, multiculturalism, postmodernism, and feminist theory. The chapter then focuses on critical theory, postmodernism, and feminist pedagogy's contributions to adult learning.

COMMON THEMES

An understanding of adult learning and adult education from the perspective of power mandates some familiarity with basic concepts and terminology. In this section, we discuss three themes that characterize this perspective: race, class, and gender, which figure prominently in a critical analysis of adult learning; power and oppression, both key concepts; and knowledge and truth, which are construed in different ways depending on the school of thought. These themes are, of course, highly interrelated; it is not possible to talk about racism, classism, sexism, and other "isms" without reference to power and oppression; nor can power be considered apart from issues surrounding knowledge construction. These themes are brought together later in the chapter in the discussions of critical theory, postmodernism, and feminist theory's contributions to adult learning.

Race, Class, and Gender

Among the characteristics of people that engender prejudice and oppression in American society, race, class, and gender are three of the most powerful and pervasive. The theoretical orientations discussed in this chapter place race, class, and gender and their interactions at center stage in analyzing the power dynamics and the distribution of resources in a particular context. The context can be defined as broadly as society, an institution in society, or even a specific adult education setting. The purpose in moving these issues to the foreground and analyzing systems of power and oppression, especially as they manifest themselves in adult education, is to effect a more informed and democratic practice.

RACE. People of various ethnic groups and other people of color are marginalized in our society, but this discussion of race will primarily be in reference to African Americans, who have experienced the most acute discrimination and oppression in the United States (Hacker, 1992). Colin and Preciphs (1991, p. 62) define racism as "conscious or unconscious, and expressed in actions or attitudes initiated by individuals, groups, or institutions that treat human beings unjustly because of their skin pigmentation. . . . Racism is expressed in attitudes, behaviors, and institutions." Hayes and Colin (1994b) trace the social impact of racism (and sexism) in America. In terms of economics, "about one in three African Americans lives in poverty, compared to about one in ten whites"; in terms of median income, black men make less than white men, and black women make less than white women; occupations are segregated, with "women of color overrepresented in low-skill, low-paid jobs, such as health aide and private household worker. Jobs that had the highest concentration of black men include stevedore, garbage collector, longshore equipment operator, and baggage porter"; in terms of education, "there continue to be significant disparities in educational achievement," and the economic returns "for comparable levels of educational attainment" favor white males in particular (pp. 8–10).

That these disparities based on race exist in the practice of adult education is no surprise. Participation patterns alone have consistently borne out the fact that blacks and other people of color are underrepresented in all types of adult education (see Chapter Three). Amstutz (1994) has suggested three reasons that racism (and sexism) persist in adult education despite well-intentioned efforts. First, she sees a discrepancy between the rhetoric of adult education that speaks of empowerment and equal access, and actual behaviors that more often than not are "unempowering" and "traditional." Second, most adult educators are themselves white and middle class, have had little interaction with minorities of any kind, and have failed to examine their own beliefs, assumptions, prejudices, and biases. Third, she thinks that most adult educators have an unwarranted faith in institutions, believing "that institutional practices are well meaning and that the policies under which their institutions operate are not biased" (p. 43).

The literature on multiculturalism has helped to bring the issues of race and cultural diversity to the attention of educators at all levels of education. Although as Tisdell (1995, p. 26) points out, "the terms of the discourse in the field of adult education tend to be 'power relations' between dominant and oppressed groups, rather than the term 'multicultural education,' . . . some more recent writers are using this term as well." Tisdell (1995) and Ross-Gordon (1994) in particular have synthesized this literature and suggested applications to practice. Tisdell (1995, p. 13) considers the multicultural literature in terms of inclusivity: "Inclusivity in the curriculum requires dealing with at least some of the differences among people based on the factors of race, ethnicity, economic class, gender, age, ability/disability, sexual orientation, and so on." After a comparison of approaches to incorporating multiculturalism into formal educational settings, Tisdell uses the models to evaluate efforts at establishing more inclusive environments in adult basic education, popular education, and higher education.

Ross-Gordon (1994) focuses on the intersections of race, class, and gender in reviewing the multicultural and critical pedagogy literature in order to extract elements of a multicultural pedagogy for adults. What this wide range of literature has in common, Ross-Gordon (1994, p. 315) believes, is "an emphasis on deconstruction of hegemonic knowledge and structures, goals for emancipation of learners, and denial of claims to political neutrality for . . . any form of education" (p. 315). Finally, she develops a composite of ten principles for teaching and learning, including sharing power with learners, fostering collaboration, challenging all forms of oppression, and placing the culture of the student in a central rather than a marginal position. With regard to racism in particular, she finds the "Afrocentric/anti-racist discourse . . . unique in its concern with two concepts. One is the notion of centricity, that the student must find his or her culture to be central (not marginal) within the knowledge shared. Second is the emphasis on learning by teachers (or un-learning) through . . . programs that educate them to recognize and challenge racism, including their own" (p. 316). Similar observations could be made about people of color who are Hispanic in origin.

CLASS. In an analysis in which class is the focus, the aim of the analysis and subsequent action is to bring about a change from a capitalistic political economy to a classless socialist form of government. Drawing largely from Marxism, a class-based analysis emphasizes class struggle, alienation, and revolutionary activity. Workers find no connection or fulfillment through work; "rather, the individual becomes a mere object for production" (Elias and Merriam, 1995, p. 155), alienated from the self as well as others and society in general. It will be only through a revolutionary movement that this relationship between the person and his or her world can be changed. Freire (1970b, p. 61) points out that those who are alienated are considered "marginal," "a pathology of the healthy society. . . . The truth is, however, that the oppressed are not 'marginals,' are not men [sic] living 'outside' society. They have always been 'inside'—inside the structure which made them 'beings for others.' The solution is not to 'integrate' them into the structure of oppression, but to transform that structure so that they can become 'beings for themselves.'" Thus a socialist Marxist framework for adult education would have, Youngman (1986, p. 197) suggests, the dual aims of challenging "the ideology and culture of capitalism" and developing "the general knowledge and technical expertise necessary to reorganise production and society in a fully democratic way."

Perhaps due in part to the collapse of Eastern European communist and socialist states, a strict Marxist analysis is no longer in fashion. Nevertheless, some adult educators argue for its continued relevance (Collins and Collard, 1995; Schied, 1993, 1994; Youngman, 1996). Schied (1994, pp. 445–446) acknowledges that feminist and postmodern thought have questioned making the working class "the privileged agent of change"; indeed, "the primacy of social class has been strongly challenged by notions of gender, race, and colonialism." In spite of this, "the economic dislocation and the exploitation of working people by international corporations is a reality. It is not merely constructed or read or produced by our theoretical perspective. This exploitation is real" (p. 446). Marxist analysis, if "conceived as a moral stance . . . provides adult educators a way to place their practice in some kind of social context" (p. 446). Collins and Collard (1995) concur with Schied. A class-based economic analysis is particularly relevant in today's world, they say, with the "re-emergence of what amounts to class warfare in connection with global economic restructuring" (p. 75). It is time "to make connections between the home, the workplace, and the community—between class and concerns around culture, gender and race" (p. 75). This is in fact what Hart (1992, 1995) does in her Marxist-feminist analysis of work, gender, and class. Youngman (1996, p. 7) agrees, calling for a robust political-economic analysis: "The central issue for a transformative political economy of adult education is how to adequately conceptualize the interconnections between the four main systems of domination in society, namely, those deriving from imperialism, class, gender, and race-ethnicity. It is clear that while none of these systems is reducible to another (for example, the basis of women's oppression is different from that of class oppression), they do affect each other (so that, for example, women's oppression has a class dimension)."

GENDER. While multiculturalists, Marxists, and critical theorists have brought inequities based on economics and class to adult educators' attention, feminist scholars have placed gender, and gender as it intersects with race and class, in the forefront of a critical analysis. Although all versions of feminist theory are concerned with the status of women worldwide, theorists differ among themselves on two counts: how the problem is framed and what needs to be done to change the status of women. Tisdell's (1995) categorization of feminist theories into individually focused theories, structural theories, and postmodern theories offers a useful framework for reviewing these theories.

As the category suggests, individually focused feminist theories are concerned with women as individuals, with how they have come to internalize patriarchy as the norm, and what needs to be done to obtain equal access, rights, and opportunities. Psychoanalytic feminists, for example, maintain that the male domination of women (patriarchy) is deeply rooted in men's and women's subconscious and is perpetuated through gender socialization. Change cannot come about unless people "deal with the patriarchy in their unconscious" (Tisdell, 1995, p. 59).

In contrast to an individual focus, structural feminist theories frame the problem in terms of societal structures and institutions that oppress women. Marxist feminists argue that the two systems of capitalism and patriarchy, in conjunction with each other, oppress women. "Socialist feminists," Tisdell (1995, p. 60) explains, "would agree that two significant and interrelated systems of oppression to women are capitalism and patriarchy. But most socialist feminists also discuss the importance of examining other systems of oppression such as racial oppression and the intersections of the factors gender, race, and class."

Postmodern or poststructural theorists take issue with the unit of analysis, or how the problem is framed by structuralists. One or even two systems of power and oppression do not adequately capture the reality of women's experience and oppression because "some groups are more privileged than others within the particular structural unit or units of analysis. Thus Marxism does not account for the fact that men are more privileged than women; Marxist feminism does not account for the fact that white women have more privilege than women of color" (Tisdell, 1995, p. 61). Postmodernists also take issue with the structuralists' overemphasis on locating power outside the individual. In a postmodern perspective, individuals have some power also—power to affect or resist the status quo. Postmodern feminist theories thus "tend to account for multiple systems of privilege and oppression and their intersections, along with people's capacity for agency or resistance" (p. 61).

Power and Oppression

A second theme underlying this approach is that social inequities, including those found in education, stem from power-based relationships: "Those wielding power can control others in varying ways, getting them to engage in activities not in the powerless' best interest" (Hansen, 1993, p. 2). One of the major tasks of a critical analysis is to uncover and expose these power relationships wherein the domination of one group's interests results in the oppression of other groups. Power and oppression are concepts that permeate the thinking and writing of radical adult educators. As Nesbit (1998, p. 174) explains, "Radical educators regard the world and its constituent societies as full of contradictions and marked by imbalances of power and privilege. Hence, they regard such problems as poverty or illiteracy neither as isolated incidents nor as manifestations of individual inadequacy, but as results of larger social issues. Furthermore, individuals, as social actors, both create and are created by their social worlds." Freire, for example, concluded that the Third World was "characterized by social, political, and economic oppression. . . . The various forms of oppression constitute the concrete problems or contradictions that are the task of [a] revolutionary pedagogy" (Elias and Merriam, 1995, p. 150).

The identification of systems of power and oppression as a lens through which to analyze society is a key component of critical theory. Critical theory originated in the 1940s with the German philosopher Jürgen Habermas and the Frankfurt school. With the advent of World War II, Habermas became disillusioned with Marxism, offering instead a view of society that is more optimistic, one that puts faith in the rationality of human beings to engage in critique and action to bring about a more just, free, and equitable society. The aim of critical theory, Welton (1995a, p. 37) writes, is "to help people to stop being passive victims who collude, at least partly, in their domination by external forces. Critical theory's liberating project is to name the enemies of human freedom, and to point to the possibility of freedom's enlargement." Inglis (1997, p. 4) goes a step further in suggesting that an analysis of power leads to empowerment or emancipation:

"Empowerment involves people developing capacities to act success-fully within the existing system and structures of power, while eman-cipation concerns critically analyzing, resisting and challenging structures of power."

Of concern to those writing from this perspective is the appropri-ation of the "lifeworld"—our everyday personal interactions in home, family, and community—by the "system." The system is conceived of as structures of power (institutions and organizations such as gov-ernment) or the means to power (such as money in a capitalist econ-omy, or knowledge in the information age). These systems have not only "colonized" the lifeworld; they are oppressive (Welton, 1993). "Human beings as childrearers, partners, workers, clients, citizens, and consumers struggle against the process of being turned into objects of corporate and state management. Systemic imperatives, then, threaten to disempower men and women who have the capacity to be empowered, reflective actors" (Welton, 1993, p. 88). To fight the hege-mony of the system (which includes corporate, government, legal, and media dimensions), citizens must engage in rational discourse about sources of power, knowledge, and oppression in the hope of redressing the current imbalance between the power of the lifeworld versus the system. Adult education can be a site for addressing power and op-pression (Baptiste, 1998; Collins, 1991; Griffin, 1987; Newman, 1994a; Rocco and West, 1998; Welton, 1995b; Wilson, 1993b).

Knowledge and Truth

The various schools of thought that make up what we call the power relations perspective all address, to some extent, the nature of truth and the construction of knowledge. Each of the three major orienta-tions discussed in the next section—critical theory, postmodernism, and feminist pedagogy—has a somewhat different notion of knowl-edge and truth.

The major spokesperson for critical theory, Jürgen Habermas, has proposed that there are three types of knowledge: technical, practical, and emancipatory. *Technical knowledge* has to do with the world of facts, of material things that structure our world. This knowledge can be easily verified through checking with documents, authorities, and so on. A statement such as "An adult can obtain a high school diploma through making an acceptable score on the GED" is technical knowl-edge. To say, however, that "a GED diploma is just as good as a high school diploma" moves us into the *practical* realm of knowledge, where communication with others—dialogue—is necessary to establish validity. "Human interchange creates a *practical* interest in the understanding of meaning" (Welton, 1993, p. 83). The validity or truth of the claim is arrived at through dialogical consensus; interpretation, judgment, and sincerity are important here. Finally, a question such as, "Why doesn't the GED diploma have the same status in our society as a high school diploma?" is *emancipatory* in nature because it addresses the forces of society that empower or disempower "some individuals or groups over others" (Welton, 1993, p. 83). That is, one would ask who has determined that a GED diploma has less status. Whose interests does it serve to maintain this status differential? Not all knowledge, then, serves the same interests, nor does all knowledge construction hold the same potential for challenging the status quo or emancipating the individual. Clearly emancipatory knowledge has the most power to address the oppressive forces in society.

From postmodernism comes the notion that there is no single truth or reality independent of the knower. Postmodernism criticizes the modern conception of knowledge as a set of underlying principles that can explain behavior or phenomena across individuals or settings. In the modern world, what constitutes and what is accepted as knowledge is determined by power: "Modernism privileges some ideas and people(s); it marginalizes others" (Cunningham and Fitzgerald, 1996, p. 49). Since "the goal of postmodernism is diversity/pluralism and its ethic is tolerance," knowledge "is either nonexistent or relative, and contradictory notions can all be considered equally true if locally held" (p. 49). Knowledge, then, is something that is part of the social and cultural context in which it occurs; how an individual or a community constructs knowledge and the type of knowledge constructed are socioculturally dependent. This view of knowledge goes hand in hand with how postmodernists view truth. As Cunningham and Fitzgerald (1996, p. 49) explain: "When it comes to truth, there is either no truth, many truths, or truth for a particular culture. In other words, if truth is possible, it is relative. Many poststructuralists/postmodernists deny what they call 'truth with a capital 'T', but allow what they refer to as 'many truths with a small t.' All claims to Truth are seen as arbitrary acts of power that include and exclude individuals and groups."

Feminists who write from a poststructuralist or postmodern perspective hold the same view about knowledge and truth. That is, they assume there is no one Truth, and each woman's truth or knowledge is relative to the sociocultural context of which she is part. Feminist theory encompasses two other views of knowledge construction, however. The psychologically oriented feminist literature has been heavily influenced by Belenky, Clinchy, Goldberger's, and Tarule's *Women's Ways of Knowing* (1986). From their interviews of 135 women, they identified five different ways women construct knowledge, ranging from silence to constructed knowing (see Chapter Seven). Their work suggests that knowledge is something that each individual constructs; the result of this process is a sense of individual empowerment, of gaining a voice along with the ability to effect change in their personal lives. In emancipatory feminist models, on the other hand, knowledge is less personal. Drawing more from critical theory than psychology, these models "examine the political and social mechanisms that have controlled the knowledge production process and marginalized (or left out) the contributions of women and people of color" (Tisdell, 1995, p. 70).

In summary, assumptions underlying a power relations perspective on adult learning draw from a wide range of literature in Marxist and feminist theory, multiculturalism, critical theory, and postmodernism. Any number of concepts and assumptions inform this perspective, but we chose three common themes to set the stage for a discussion of contributions to adult learning from critical theory, postmodernism, and feminist pedagogy. At the heart of all of these orientations is a critical assessment of the forces of economics, class, race, and gender that lead to systems of power and oppression. All also consider how knowledge is constructed and how the nature of its construction can liberate or dominate. We now turn to a more detailed discussion of critical theory, postmodernism, and feminist pedagogy, three of the contemporary perspectives that have had the most impact to date on adult learning.

CRITICAL THEORY AND ADULT LEARNING

In contrast to andragogy and even transformational learning, most practitioners in adult education are unaware of critical theory's potential for examining practice or illuminating the nature of adult learning. This is in part due to the fact that the writing in this area is dense (Brookfield, 1996c) and grasping and operationalizing the concepts involved are difficult. Critical theory itself has been criticized for "asserting domination and reproducing a culture of silence in educational settings" due to its "technical jargon, obscure references, and ambiguous phrasing" (Pietrykowski, 1996, p. 84). In fact we found only one article on critical theory in a practice-oriented publication. In "John's Story: An Exploration into Critical Theory in Education, deMarrais (1991) demonstrates how John's failure to learn to read can be understood as a systemic social problem rather than one of individual failure. The "system" in a critical theory analysis is an institution (such as government or education) that functions to reproduce the status quo, in particular the existing social class structure. Awareness of this oppression can lead to resistance and possibly change. Critical theory's strength lies in its critique of existing economic and social structures and resultant power dynamics. Its weakness, until very recently, is in suggesting workable strategies for effecting change.

A number of adult education intellectuals have brought critical theory, and in particular Habermas's version, to adult education. Welton (1993, 1995b) has articulated the ways in which critical theory can inform adult education theory and practice. He identifies several concepts from critical theory that have affected and can continue to affect adult education: three types of knowledge, ideal conditions for reflective discourse, institutions as learning communities, and the interplay of the system and the lifeworld.

The three types of knowledge discussed earlier in this chapter—technical, practical, and emancipatory—is a framework for understanding and critiquing adult education as a discipline and as a field of practice. Collins (1991, 1995a, 1995b), for example, finds the field of adult education to be overly concerned with technical knowledge (with the least attention to emancipatory) at the expense of social action designed to bring about a more just and equal society. According to Collins, the field is too preoccupied with "professionalizing," with "the cult of efficiency," and with "an eagerness to serve the conventional professions" (1995a, p. 79). This preoccupation with the technical has both distorted learning and diverted adult educators from providing a "context where shared commitments [practical knowledge] towards a socially more free, just, and rational society will coalesce" (1991, p. 119). By this, Collins means that adult educators are too concerned with how to plan programs or arrange a classroom at the expense of considering why some adults do not have access to education, for example.

In a similar approach, Wilson (1993b) uses the tools of critical theory to trace the rise of technical rationality and professionalism represented in the field's handbooks. These handbooks, which are published approximately every ten years, are encyclopedic compilations of essays describing the field of adult education. For the field to become professionalized, a body of knowledge needed to be compiled with which to train adult educators. "This is what the discourse in the handbooks represents. Without this basis in a scientifically-derived body of knowledge, there would be no professional activity to transact in a service economy" (p. 14). Wilson suggests that this critique is important because "it helps in understanding how the field has arrived at its present configuration" (p. 14). Both Collins and Wilson fear that the grip of professionalism and technical rationality prevents the field of adult education from attending to social action and emancipatory interests.

Closely related to forms of knowledge is Habermas's ideal conditions for reflective discourse. Habermas has identified four criteria or conditions that, if applied to interactions among adults, should result in mature, rational, candid, "authentic" discussions: comprehensibility, sincerity, truth, and legitimacy. Mezirow (1995), who has adopted these conditions as central to his transformative learning theory, explains how these conditions work in discussions:

> When we communicate or have doubts about the truth or authenticity of the assertion, the truthfulness of the speaker, or the appropriateness of what is asserted in light of relevant norms, we often seek the best judgment of the most informed, objective, and rational persons we can find. We engage them in a special form of dialogue which Habermas refers to as "discourse." Discourse involves an effort to set aside bias, prejudice, and personal concerns and to do our best to be open and objective in presenting and assessing reasons and reviewing the evidence and arguments for and against the problematic assertion to arrive at a consensus. [pp. 52–53]

These criteria can form a basis for identifying the skills that learners need to engage in more authentic discussions. Mezirow and others realize that these are ideal conditions; nevertheless, they give us a standard to work toward in adult learning transactions.

Critical theory has also contributed to adult education in considering how institutions themselves can become learning communities. According to Welton (1993, p. 89), "Habermas believes that while all institutions are educative, not all are true learning communities. An institution, whether family, corporation, or state agency, may be organized to block free and noncoerced learning processes. Habermas encourages us to ask whether our institutions, large and small, truly enable human beings to unfold their potentials (cognitive, oral, technical, aesthetic) in their daily routine interactions." Strategies to build learning organizations are efforts in this direction, as is the literature on classroom practices that stress emancipatory pedagogies (see Ellsworth, 1989; Schied, Carter, Preston, and Howell, 1997; Tisdell and Perry, 1997; Watkins, 1996; Wilson and Cervero, 1997). In view of this thinking, Welton (1995b, p. 151) even argues that the workplace has potential "as a site for emancipatory learning." Critical adult educators have a "mandate . . . to argue and struggle for workplaces that open up space for non-coerced, free communication pertaining to the organization, control and purposes of work" (p. 152).

Another contribution of critical theory to adult education, identified by Welton (1993), is the notion of the interplay between the lifeworld and the system. The lifeworld is the informal, everyday interactions of daily life, and the system consists of those structures based on money and power (corporations, government, education, and so on) that have an impact on the lifeworld. These systems do more than intrude into the lifeworld; they oppress. Collins (1991, 1995a) is particularly articulate about how forces from the system, such as expertise, competency-based curricula, and much of workplace learning, have disempowered adults in their lifeworlds. In his opinion, spaces in our everyday world where discussions of social and political issues and what can be done about them *could* occur have been taken over by systems that promote technical learning. Self-directed learning, for example, has been touted for its value in creating "professionals." But "the idea of 'facilitating' self-directed learning which Knowles recognized ordinary wide-awake adults already possess ('to be adult means to be self-directing') makes no more sense than comfortable pedagogical chatter about empowering people. For a critical perspective on adult education the initial task is to identify social structures and practices which (mis)shape social learning processes and undermine capacities adults already possess to control their own education" (Collins, 1994, p. 100). For Collins (1991, p. 119), critical practice means being engaged in "definable concrete projects for social change without which talk of justice, emancipation, and equality becomes hollow rhetoric."

Several writers have suggested that popular social movements are the most fruitful sites for this kind of critical pedagogy. Welton (1995c) explains how these sites can be liberating: "The emergence of the well-informed or activated citizen, whose education through participation spirals outward, reaching to new levels of political knowledge and competency, has emerged most decisively in our time on the terrain of civil society in *defense of the threatened lifeworld*. The new social movements (ecology, peace, women, local and personal autonomy) are privileged sites for the rebellious speech of citizens" (p. 154). While agreeing that social movements are "important sources of knowledge as well as profound sites of learning," Holford (1995, p. 104) warns that reactionary forces such as racism may also be categorized as social movements. Adult educators can thus learn much about critical practice from an examination of social movements of all types. In addition to critiquing movements themselves, the role of adult educators in nonformal settings such as these begs investigation, as do their formal educational activities.

Spencer (1995) makes a case for studying old social movements such as labor unions, as well as new social movements. Using the case example of Canadian labor unions' education for environmental concerns, Spencer points out that the old and new can learn from one another. Further, labor unions represent the lifeworld interests of the working class; new social movements are too often dominated by the middle class. Cunningham and Curry's (1997) case study of a grassroots urban development movement in Chicago is an excellent example of what Holford (1995), Spencer (1995), Welton (1995c), and others are recommending. Cunningham and Curry investigated the learning in this movement and came up with a model of learning in community. They discovered that "poor people can reinvent cities"; they "construct their learning by taking advantage of their own cultural tools" (p. 78). In another study, Cain (1998) analyzed how class, race, and gender shaped the learning of community residents in their struggle to deal with a toxic waste dump.

Since the lifeworld and the system are interrelated, there is some merit in focusing on the interaction of the two, from a popular movement standpoint or a systems perspective. "The juxtaposition of lifeworld and system concepts is clearly significant in enabling us to 'think deeply and realistically about the systemic blockages to the achievement of a more fully democratized society'" (Collins, 1995b, p. 198).

Hart's (1995) analysis of the workplace and the lifeworld of the family does just this, as does Hill's (1995, 1998) study of Pennsylvania citizens' groups engaged in environmental conflicts. The citizens' groups and the government regulatory agency "were both instrumental in community learning" and community conflict (1995, p. 163).

Using Welton's framework, we have illustrated how critical theory can inform both adult education theory and practice. However, as with any other theory, there are points of debate and critique. The notion that critical theory is a useful framework for better understanding adult learning has itself been critiqued. Ellsworth (1989), in her now-classic article on problems with applying an emancipatory, dialogic approach to the classroom, found "that key assumptions, goals, and pedagogical practices fundamental to the literature on critical pedagogy—namely, 'empowerment,' 'student voice,' 'dialogue,' and even the term 'critical'—are repressive myths that perpetuate relations of domination" (p. 298). In experimenting with a college class on racism, Ellsworth discovered that she and the students were ill equipped to handle the unequal power relations *in their own classroom*. She writes, "Our classroom was not in fact a safe space for students to speak out or talk back about their experiences of oppression both inside and outside of the classroom. . . . Things were not being said for a number of reasons. These included fear of being misunderstood and/or disclosing too much and becoming too vulnerable; . . . resentment that other oppressions (sexism, heterosexism, fat oppression, classism, anti-Semitism) were being marginalized in the name of addressing racism; . . . [and] confusion about levels of trust and commitment surrounding those who were allies to another groups' struggles" (1989, pp. 315–316). Collard (1995) concurs with Ellsworth, arguing that the conditions of ideal speech (discourse) "merely reintroduces an old elitism under the guise of a communicative ethic" (p. 68). Further, the ideal speech situation "tends to disregard difference and exclude those who have no voice—i.e. it is implicitly hierarchical" (p. 65).

Despite these criticisms, critical theory remains a particularly important underpinning to theory building in adult learning. Mezirow's theory of perspective transformation, discussed in Chapter Fourteen, draws heavily from Habermas. Critical theory has also informed analyses of professionalization, power and oppression, and the dynamics of the teaching and learning transaction.

POSTMODERNISM AND ADULT LEARNING

Uncertainty characterizes today's postmodern world. As Giroux (1992, p. 39) observes, "We have entered an age that is marked by a crisis of power, patriarchy, authority, identity, and ethics. This new age has been described, for better or worse, by many theorists in a variety of disciplines as the age of postmodernism." Unlike the *modern* world, which is characterized by "the scientific, industrial, and social programs, institutions, actions, and artifacts generated by the humanistic and Enlightenment search for the universal foundations of truth, morality, and aesthetics" (Bagnall, 1995, p. 81), in the *postmodern* era, things are much more diverse, fluid, illusionary, and contested, including the reality of the world itself. Identifying oppression, "defining the enemy" (Newman, 1994a), and taking right forms of action are not so easy in a postmodern world. As Plumb (1995b, p. 188) observes, adult education from a "modern" world perspective "is poorly equipped to articulate how it can persist as a meaningful emancipatory practice without reinscribing itself as an institution that suppresses heterogeneity and difference."

In a postmodern world, everything is "contested," up for grabs. What has been or is considered true, real, or right can be questioned; there are multiple interpretations depending on where one is standing and what factors are in juxtaposition with one another. There are no absolutes, no single theoretical framework for examining social and political issues. Hence, critical theory's goal of emancipation and overcoming oppression can itself be questioned because it represents a "logic" that "does not tolerate difference" (Pietrykowski, 1996, p. 90). At the same time, as Collins (1994, pp. 99–100) points out, postmodernism, in contrast to Habermasian critical theory, leaves us with no means of choosing "sensibly between one course of action and another. There is no truth to be found, only a plurality of signs, styles, interpretations, and meaningless process." Therefore, postmodernism can leave us with two almost diametrically opposed views. It can be seen as "offering a pessimistic, negative, gloomy assessment . . . of fragmentation, disintegration, malaise, meaninglessness" (Rosenau, 1992, p. 15). Or it can be seen as hopeful—a world that is "nondogmatic, tentative, and nonideological" (p. 16), one in which adult education can play a major role (Finger, 1995; Usher and Edwards, 1994).

Important for adult learning is the postmodern notion of the self.

The self in postmodern thought is not the unified, integrated, authentic self of modern times. Rather, the self is multiple, ever changing, and, some say, fragmented. As Gergen (1991, p. 7) argues, "Under postmodern conditions, persons exist in a state of continuous construction and reconstruction. . . . Each reality of the self gives way to reflexive questioning, irony, and ultimately the playful probing of yet another reality." Such a notion of self has implications for adult learning and development. In an exploration of this question, Clark (1997, p. 111) argues that "learning from the assumption of a unified self privileges the rational, agenic self and thereby fails to recognize and to give voice to other dimensions of the self." Exploring her own learning from a modernist perspective would have missed "the complex relational quality" of her learning. McLaren (1997, p. 25) writes that "educators as cultural workers" need to assist students in dealing with the following questions of identity:

> How has the social order fashioned me in ways with which I no longer desire to identify? In what directions do I desire and why? To what extent are my dreams and my desires my own? What will likely be the consequences for me and others both like me and different from me? To what extent is society inventing me and by what moral, epistemological, political, or transcendental authority is this taking place? How am I to judge the world that made me and on what basis can I unmake myself in order to remake the world? [p. 25]

Because of this fragmentation, relationships, connectedness, and interdependence are the constants that hold us together. Finger (1995, p. 116) is explicit about moving to a collective action agenda to respond to "the new challenges. . . . Experts must join groups of learners working collectively with real people on concrete problems. . . . Teaching and preaching ready-made solutions to individuals must be replaced with collaborative, vertical, horizontal, and cross-disciplinary learning. Such learning must be recognized as probably the only 'resource' still available to us to get through and out of the ever accelerating vicious circle. This, of course, must be a collective and collaborative effort, because there is no individual way out."

Postmodernists celebrate diversity, among people, ideas, and institutions. By accepting the diversity and plurality of the world, no one element is privileged or more powerful than another. Usher, Bryant, and Johnston (1997, p. 22) speak of the advantages of this perspective:

> Postmodernity has provided spaces for rising social groups such as the new middle classes, for new postmodern social movements and for hitherto oppressed and marginalised groups such as women, blacks, gays, and ethnic minorities to find a voice, to articulate their own "subjugated" knowledges and to empower themselves in a variety of different ways and according to their own specific agendas. In this situation, education stops being a univocal, predictable reality and consequently it makes no sense to speak of it simply as either functioning to reproduce the social order or as implicit social engineering, whether this be for domestication or liberation. . . . Linked with this is the impact of a reconfiguration of education away from its institutional and provider-led location. [p. 22]

Plumb (1995a, p. 246) observes that although so much fragmentation and diversity can be disempowering, it is also what is needed to challenge the equally disparate forces of oppression: "No longer is it sufficient to foster the emergence of a particular kind of identity sufficiently strong to overcome the inequitable norms of capitalism"; rather, "critical adult education must investigate new ways that identity can still productively be mobilized in the fragmenting environment of postmodernity."

Postmodernism has been criticized for its pessimism, its extreme relativism, its lack of a moral center. Furthermore, with few exceptions (see Brookfield, 1995; Kegan, 1994; Tisdell, 1995), it comes up lacking on specific techniques or strategies for dealing with the postmodern classroom or adult education program. What postmodernism does offer adult education is a respect for diversity, a moving of previously marginalized groups into a position of equal value to other groups, and a critique of (or deconstruction, some would say) the categories by which we have labeled aspects of our practice. What does it mean to be categorized as illiterate in our society, for example? The marginalized groups identified by Usher, Bryant, and Johnston—women, blacks, gays, and ethnic minorities—have not found an advocate until very recently in critical theory, which is focused primarily on rationality, economics, class, and power. From postmodernity's challenges to modern, rational thought and society comes a valuing of diversity and opportunities inherent in uncertainty and nondogmatic practices.

FEMINIST PEDAGOGY AND ADULT LEARNING

As the name implies, feminist *pedagogy* focuses on the concerns of women in the teaching-learning transaction. Feminist pedagogy is derived from feminist theory or, more accurately, feminist theories. There are, for example, liberal, radical, psychoanalytic, black, Marxist, and postmodern versions of feminist theory. Based in feminist theory, feminist pedagogy focuses on the experiences, and in particular the oppression, of women in the context of education. However, just as there are many feminisms, there are also numerous strands of feminist pedagogy. Maher (1987) has placed the various perspectives into one of two major categories: liberation models and gender models. Both perspectives address oppression and empowerment—the liberatory from a collective, systemic perspective and the gender model from a personal perspective.

Liberatory models draw from the structuralist and postmodern and poststructural feminist theories reviewed earlier in this chapter, as well as Marxist and critical theory. From this perspective, the structures of society, the systems that intrude on our lifeworlds, oppress through their power and control. The structured nature of power relations and interlocking systems of oppression based on gender, race, and class are seen as being reinforced through education; that is, institutions of learning and the classroom itself reproduce the power structures found in society at large. Liberatory pedagogy examines how these systems of oppression are reproduced and resisted in education. We ask, for example, why white males tend to dominate a classroom discussion (reproduction), or why black working-class women shun formal education (resistance). Liberatory feminist educators attempt to recover women's voices, experiences, and viewpoints and use these to make systems of privilege, power, and oppression visible. Although influenced by Freire's emancipatory praxis and Marxist theory, liberatory feminists are critical of the lack of attention in these approaches to gender and to interlocking systems of oppression based on gender, race, and class.

In the gender model of feminist pedagogy, the focus is on how female identity has been socially constructed to be one of nurturer and how the individual woman can find her voice, becoming emancipated in the personal psychological sense. Drawing from psychoanalytic and humanistic psychology, educators from this stance look to how the educational environment and the learning transaction can be constructed so as to foster women's learning. In this model, a connected approach to learning is advocated, where life experiences are valued, where a woman can come to have a voice and, hence, an identity. "If a woman is to consider herself a real knower, she must find acceptance for her ideas in the public world" (Belenky, Clinchy, Goldberger, and Tarule, 1986, p. 220). The public world begins with a safe classroom where members can support and nurture each other. This connected environment will help women develop their own voices and see themselves as capable of being constructors of knowledge rather than just recipients. In their recent book, *Knowledge, Difference, and Power: Essays Inspired by Women's Ways of Knowing* (1996), Goldberger, Tarule, Clinchy, and Belenky consider how to wed connected and separate knowing, what collaborative knowing might look like, and how color, class, and diversity affect women's learning.

Recently Tisdell (1995, 1996a, 1998) has taken up Maher's challenge to forge a synthesis of the liberatory and gender models that promotes both personal emancipation and public action. Tisdell first identifies four recurring themes in feminist pedagogy: how knowledge is constructed, the development of voice, the authority of the teacher and students, and dealing with differences. She finds the liberatory model particularly strong on recognizing differences based on race, class, and gender; nevertheless, "they focus too much on structures, and do not account for the individual's capacity for agency, the capacity to have some control outside of these social structures" (1996a, p. 310). The gender or psychological model, on the other hand, because it tends to emphasize similarities among women, does not much account for differences among women or differences in power relations based on race, class, sexual orientation, and so on. The way to take into account all four themes, Tisdell proposes, is through a poststructural feminist pedagogy, which weds the psychological orientation of the gender model with the structural factors of the liberatory perspective. Tisdell (1996a) explains:

> A synthesis of these models in the form of poststructural feminist pedagogies would take into account both the intellectual *and* emotional components of learning, the individual's capacity for agency, as well

as the psychological and social and political factors that affect learning. It would emphasize the importance of relationship and connection to learning, but also account for the fact that power relations
based on a multitude of factors including gender, race, and class are
always present in the learning environment and affect both how
knowledge is constructed on the individual level as well as the social
and political factors that affect what counts as "official" knowledge and
how it is disseminated. [p. 311]

Tisdell's poststructural feminist pedagogy model has several implications for the teaching and learning transaction. First, it speaks to
differences among learners themselves: "Most women and some men
may have different learning needs from men who represent the dominant culture" (1995, p. 73). Second, there is attention given to the role
of power in the construction of knowledge itself—power's role in how
knowledge is shaped and disseminated in the classroom, and in society at large. Third, a poststructural pedagogy, or what Tisdell (1995)
also calls positional pedagogy, examines how "various positionalities—
the gender, race, class, sexual orientation—of both the participants
and the instructor matter and have an effect on the learning environment" (p. 75). Finally, this perspective problematizes the power and
authority of the teacher and considers the ramifications of redistrib-
uting this power.

Tisdell's poststructuralist feminist pedagogy model highlights *connections*: connections between "the individual and the intersecting
structural systems of privilege and oppression" and connections
between "one's individual (constantly shifting) identity and social
structures" (1998, p. 146). She suggests how these connections might
lead to change in an adult learning setting:

As learners examine how social systems of privilege and oppression
have affected their own identity, including their beliefs and values, the
"discourse" is disrupted, thus shifting their identity, as well as increasing their capacity for agency. For example, if one has embraced societal
prescriptions of particular gender roles (or race roles, or sexual roles
that are exclusively heterosexual), and one becomes conscious of and
examines the social construction of such roles, one's identity is likely
to shift, and one could develop new ways of acting in the world. One
also begins to see that there are different "truths" and perhaps not one
"Truth," and that social systems have allowed members of privileged

groups to control what has counted as "knowledge" in determining the official curriculum through the politics of the knowledge production process. [Tisdell, 1998, p. 146]

In making these observations, Tisdell echoes the sentiments about the nature of knowledge described by Cunningham and Curry (1997) and noted previously in this chapter.

Weiler (1996) identifies three issues from which a feminist pedagogy can be forged. The first is the role and authority of the teacher. The tension between the feminist teacher's need "to *claim* authority in a society that denies it to them" (p. 139) and sharing of authority in the community of the classroom needs to be addressed. Second, space needs to be made for personal experience as a source of knowledge and truth. How much space and what kind of space in regard to other sources of knowledge needs to be negotiated. Weiler cites the black lesbian feminist Audre Lorde for articulating the challenge of incorporating feelings, "those hidden sources of power from where true knowledge and, therefore, lasting action comes," into the discourse around types of knowledge (cited by Weiler, 1996, p. 142). The third issue for Weiler is the question of difference. There is no unitary, universal women's experience on which to base a pedagogy of practice. Women who have been marginalized and oppressed by the dominant society, by the dominant female norms, have had very different experiences from those of the mainstream. "The turning to experience thus reveals not a universal and common women's essence, but, rather, deep divisions in what different women have experienced, and in the kinds of knowledge they discover when they examine their own experience. The recognition of the differences among women raises serious challenges to feminist pedagogy" (p. 145). Johnson-Bailey and Cervero's (1996) study of the educational experiences of reentry black women underscores Weiler's point.

Tisdell's and Weiler's work is part of an expanding body of literature in adult education that addresses various aspects of adult teaching and learning contexts from a feminist pedagogy perspective. Hayes (1989), for example, drew from Belenky, Clinchy, Goldberger, and Tarule (1986) to suggest strategies for teaching women. A number of writers have researched and presented guidelines for establishing collaborative and connected learning environments (Caffarella, 1992, 1996; Daloz, 1986; Hayes and Colin, 1994a; Ross-Gordon, 1994; Taylor and Marienau, 1995). Stalker's (1993c) feminist analysis of women teachers' mentoring women learners centers on women academics' location in a patriarchal system. In another study, Stalker (1993a) examines sexual harassment in the adult learner–teacher relationship as a function of unequal power, authority, and control. Similarly, Jarvis and Zukas (1998) conducted a feminist analysis of teaching, research, and supervision in adult education, and Bierema (1998) analyzed human resource development research from a feminist perspective. Sheared (1994, p. 31) argues for a "polyrhythmic" pedagogy in which each learner's multiple positions, statuses, and connections can be given voice: "Polyrhythmic reality reflects the wholeness, the uniqueness, and—most important—the connectedness of individuals to others in society, their both/and realities."

With few exceptions (see Mezirow and Associates, 1990, for one), critical theory offers little guidance on how to manage the teaching and learning encounter to effect the theory's desired ends (emancipation through rational discourse). There is much more in the feminist pedagogy literature, as the references indicate. Tisdell in particular lays out concrete strategies (1993, 1995) and a comprehensive model (1995, 1998) for applying feminist pedagogy to the practical realm of adult education. She suggests attending to the specific curriculum materials used in the classroom, adopting particular teaching strategies that lead to emancipation, designing courses or workshops where the content specifically deals with power relations based on gender, race, and class, and encouraging adult educators to examine how their own views and behaviors challenge or reproduce "society's inequitable distribution of power" (1993, p. 102). Tisdell (1995, p. 90) has expanded these guidelines to include the literature on multicultural education in her suggestions for creating inclusive learning environments:

- Integrate affective and experiential knowledge with theoretical concepts.

- Pay attention to the power relations inherent in knowledge production.

- Be aware that participants are positioned differently in relationship to each other and to the knowledge being acquired.

- Acknowledge the power disparity between the teacher/facilitator and the students.

- Identify all stakeholders and their positionality in the educational program.

- Consider the levels of inclusivity and the levels of contexts involved in the educational activity.

- Consider how curricular choices implicitly or explicitly contribute to challenging structured power relations.

- Adopt emancipatory teaching strategies.

- Be conscious of the ways in which unconscious behavior contributes to challenging or reproducing unequal power relations.

- Build a community based on both openness and intellectual rigor to create a democratic classroom.

Because Tisdell's guidelines draw from many strands of feminist pedagogy, which in turn reflect a number of theoretical and philosophical positions, Tisdell's suggestions cover principles or tenets from a wide range of literature, the most influential being critical theory and postmodernism.

It is clear that approaching adult learning from a power relations perspective can be a rather eclectic activity incorporating any number of assumptions and concepts. Indeed, several adult educators have attempted a theoretical synthesis of several orientations. We have just reviewed Tisdell's (1998) model, which weds feminist pedagogy and poststructuralism. In a similar vein, Grace (1996a, p. 145) admits to "an eclectic theoretical scaffolding . . . using insights from discourses including critical theory, feminism, and postmodernism." He proposes a critical theory of the adult learning community grounded in five assumptions (1997). First, the theory emphasizes community between educators and learners. Second, the focus is on knowledge production, not consumption; experiential knowledge is valued as well as technical. Third, theory and practice are mutually informative. "Practice is theory lived out in the everyday" (p. 129), he writes, meaning that what goes on in the classroom mirrors theory and at the same time can inform theory. His fourth assumption is that there is value in being informed by the foundations of adult education, and in particular the tension between maintaining the status quo and changing it. Closely related to this assumption is that instrumental, social, and cultural forms of adult education should be valued. For those who eschew learners' instrumental and training needs in favor of emancipatory ones, he argues that "instrumental forms of adult education must be given space and place in an inclusionary, reflexive practice of adult education" (p. 130). These assumptions translate into actual classroom practices through honoring personal experience along with theoretical analyses; through being sensitive to intersections of power "where race, ethnicity, class, gender, sexual orientation, ableness, and age impact learning, life, and work" (1996a, p. 147); through conflict and dialogue; and through practices that are inclusionary of the diversity of peoples and their knowledge.

Finally, Youngman (1996, p. 8) points out that undertaking a critical analysis of adult education practice from any of the perspectives reviewed in this chapter "has practical consequences for the identification of appropriate forms of action for social change. Is there a 'main enemy' in a particular context? Should single issue struggles take priority?" However, "those frameworks which are multidimensional in their analysis are likely to provide the most fruitful basis for unified social action that will meet the diverse interests of the different dominated groups in society" (p. 8).

SUMMARY

In this chapter we have presented an overview of several perspectives on adult learning, all of which deal with power relations. The mound of writing and research, the plethora of viewpoints, and the complexity and density of language and concepts that make up this perspective have made this effort a daunting one. What we have done is to sketch the outlines, name some of the major concepts and players, and, drawing from the work of colleagues in adult education, show how this perspective is shaping our understanding of adult learning and adult education practice.

To this end, and drawing from Marxist theory, critical theory, multiculturalism, postmodernism, and feminist theory, we briefly discussed three themes that characterize this perspective. The first theme, race, class, and gender, leads to the second theme, of how the intersections of race, class, and gender affect the distribution of resources and power such that some groups in our society are privileged and some are oppressed. The third theme, of knowledge and truth, considers the nature and construction of knowledge as it relates to learning.

The second half of the chapter reviewed critical theory, postmodernism, and feminist pedagogy and their contributions to understanding adult learning. Drawing from Welton's (1993) framework, several aspects of critical theory were discussed: Habermas's three distinct types of knowledge and the conditions necessary for ideal discourse; how to make institutions sites for learning; and the relationship between systemic forces based on money and power, and the everyday lifeworld of adults.

Postmodernism challenges the certainty and rationality that characterize modernity. Uncertainty, diversity, and multiplicity can be fragmenting and disempowering for some, energizing and powerful for others. Postmodernity's major contribution to adult education has been to foreground previously oppressed and marginalized groups.

Finally, feminist pedagogy, the application of feminist theory to education, was reviewed with attention to adult education. What Maher (1987) categorizes as liberatory (focusing on social structures) and gender (emphasizing the psychological) models of feminist pedagogy were presented, followed by Tisdell's (1995, 1996a, 1998) synthesis of the two into a poststructural model of feminist pedagogy. The work of adult educators in applying feminist pedagogy to adult learning transactions and contexts was also reviewed. The chapter concludes with a review of Grace's (1997) effort to synthesize critical theory, postmodernism, and feminist theory into what he calls a general critical theory of adult learning.

PART FIVE

Reflections on Practice

In this final part of *Learning in Adulthood*, we step back and reflect on some important issues in both the theory and the practice of adult learning. Thus far in this book, we have reviewed the accumulation of knowledge about learning in adulthood: the context in which it takes place, the learner, the learning process, and theory building specific to the learning transaction with adults. This knowledge only partly informs the decisions that educators make in practice, however. Another kind of knowledge, that lodged in values and beliefs, also defines practice to a great extent. Thus, what we have chosen to address in this final part are some of the ethical issues inherent in the teaching-learning transaction and program planning, and our own beliefs about the theory and practice of learning in adulthood.

Chapter Sixteen explores the ethical questions inherent in instruction and program planning. To what extent, for example, should we be concerned with a person's growth and development versus what is "good" for society? To what extent do we do an injustice by raising expectations that learning to read will lead to a better job and a better life? Whose responsibility is it to determine the goals of a learning activity? How much responsibility for planning and implementing a learning activity should be the teacher's versus the learner's? What about the outcomes of a learning activity? As everyone knows who has seen the film *Educating Rita,* the growth that results from learning can be painful and disorienting, and have unintended consequences. We offer three frameworks for examining the many ethical dilemmas we face in our practice as educators. To illustrate how each of these frameworks can be used, we integrate examples of typical ethical dilemmas often encountered by planners and teachers.

In Chapter Seventeen we reflect on our own beliefs about the theory and practice of adult learning. We frame this discussion in terms of how learning in adulthood can be distinguished from learning in childhood. For us it is the unique configuration of the context, the learner, and the learning process that makes learning different in adulthood. The final section of the chapter examines the relationship between the accumulated knowledge base of adult learning represented in this book and practice. We use Cervero's (1991) model of four types of interaction between knowledge and practice to frame this discussion.

CHAPTER SIXTEEN

Ethics and Adult Learning

I n "The Story of Gladys Who Refused to Grow: A Morality Tale for Mentors," Daloz (1988b) recounts his experience in advising an adult learner who stubbornly resists thinking critically or imaginatively about her life experiences. It becomes clear to him that "not all students grow from their education." Such students "contradict our best hopes and some of our fonder theories." "People like me," Daloz admits, "prefer to look the other way" (p. 7). Daloz goes on to explain what students like Gladys can teach us about learning in adult life: how the price of change may be too expensive for some. Daloz's encounter with Gladys raises questions about the adult learning transaction, questions that are ethical in nature. What is the right way to act in the teaching-learning situation? What are the responsibilities of the instructor and the learner? Do we have the right to challenge learners to grow?

Program planners also face many ethical dilemmas as they go about their practice. Should they respond primarily to market demands, when they know in doing so certain segments of the population, such as the poor or those with little formal education, are almost always excluded? What about advertising that is misleading—that says, for example, that everyone will be employed as a result of our program? Is it right to continue to use promotional campaigns that work in terms of bringing in learners, but in fact are only partially true? And what if you know that instructors you have selected for programs are only marginal, or perhaps downright poor, but they are all you can afford or can find? Is it right to go with what you can get? After all, participants can opt out of programs if they do not like them (or at least in some situations they can).

In making decisions like these in everyday practice, one cannot rely solely on the kind of knowledge described in previous chapters on the learner and the learning process. That is, knowing something about how adults learn does not necessarily tell you how to respond to Gladys or the conflicting ethical situations both instructors and program planners find themselves facing.

This chapter explores some of the ethical issues related to learning— in particular, those present in the teaching-learning transaction and in program planning. We first describe the nature of ethical practice and adult education. Next, we explore three frameworks through which educators of adults can examine ethical dilemmas they face as instructors and program planners. To illustrate how each framework can be used, we integrate examples of typical ethical dilemmas planners and teachers often encounter. We conclude the chapter with a discussion of assessing the consequences of acting ethically in our practice as educators of adults.

ETHICAL PRACTICE AND ADULT EDUCATION

Adult education is a social activity. It involves people and their interactions with one another—people who have differing views on how things should be done, who feel obligated and responsible in different ways. Conflicting obligations and competing values underlie the ethical dilemmas of practice. Because ethics is socially defined, acting in an ethical manner is not free from political pressures, and rarely are judgments made in isolation about ethical dilemmas. Rather, the mix of differing individuals, groups, and contexts of practice influences how we respond to the many dilemmas we face as practitioners.

Furthermore, being involved in the provision of formal and nonformal learning is a moral activity. Regardless of our specific role or the organization that employs us, we are engaged in bringing about change, and the change process often involves us in situations where there is no one right way to respond. Education, like public policy, military intervention, community development, and psychotherapy, is a form of social intervention, which is defined as "any act, planned or unplanned, that alters the characteristics of another individual or the pattern of relationships between individuals" (Kelman and Warwick, 1978, p. 3). Although most of adult education is designed to educate the learner in specified ways, there are often unintended outcomes affecting the people involved or their pattern of relationships. Gladys is a case in point. Her academic experience affected her only marginally; rather, the interaction became an unplanned learning experience for her mentor. Daloz learned that there are good reasons for which adults resist change, reasons that have to do with maintaining rather than altering the pattern of relationships:

> Most adults are richly enmeshed in a fabric of relationships which hold them as they are, and many of their friends and relations do not wish to see them change. . . . Change demands a complex kind of re-negotiation of relationships among spouses, children, friends, parents, and teachers. Complex enough for young adults in college for the first time, the mix can be boggling for adults. Sometimes it is just plain simpler to stay right where they are, or at least appear that way. [Daloz, 1988b, p. 7]

Just because we as educators believe it is right for adults to grow and become personally empowered as a result of their educational experiences, it may not be what the learners themselves want or need in their lives, at least perhaps not at that time.

Adult learning thus becomes both a moral activity and a social intervention accompanied by dilemmas over good versus bad and right versus wrong. Ethical dilemmas are grounded in conflicting yet often equally legitimate views of what is good and right. For example, is there a universal ethic or set of ethics to which all humankind should adhere? Does the situation make a difference in how one addresses ethical issues? And what is the role of culture, if any, in ethical practice? There are some scholars like Jarvis (1997), who argue "that there is one universal moral good, which consists of being concerned for the Other" (p. 16). Although Jarvis observes there are also "other morally good values which find their origin in culture," he views the universal good as "the underlying principle of all morally good action" (p. 16).

Others contend that there are a number of basic principles that could undergird how ethical practice should be defined for different professions. More specifically, Connelly and Light (1991) have proposed "five basic principles which could serve as a common ground for all adult educators: social responsibility as the most important principle, an inclusive philosophy of education for a foundation, pluralism as a strength but greater unity a worthy goal, respect for learners, and [respect] for educators" (p. 233). Murk (1996) has posited a similar set of fundamental ethical principles based on the work of J. E. Sieber (1980, p. 54, as cited by Murk, 1996) "that could apply to adult educators[:] *beneficence* (avoidance of unnecessary harm and maximization of good outcomes), *respect* (acceptance of people as unique individuals), *justice* (treating all individuals or groups equally according to their own needs [or] merits), and *obligations to clients* (an open discussion of and adherence to the rights and responsibilities of the learners)" (p. 11). And still others believe that there is no one right or ethical way—that the specific context of a situation must be taken into consideration whenever decisions of an ethical nature are made (Strike and Soltis, 1985). The most common path that most professions have taken, such as medicine and law, is adopting a common set of principles, which often have been formalized into codes of ethics, on which to base their decision making. For example, "several adult education organizations in the United States have developed codes of ethics or guidelines for developing codes" (Sork, 1996), such as the Coalition of Adult Education Organizations (CAEO) and the Learning Resources Network (LERN).

Ethical dilemmas are dilemmas because of this complexity in thinking about what constitutes right and wrong. There are no simple answers. An ethical dilemma forces choice between competing courses of action, each with its own values. An ethical dilemma is in fact "a choice that has no totally acceptable resolution" (Sork, 1988, p. 37). This lack of totally acceptable solutions makes acting in an ethical manner very difficult at times, and often painful for those who must make those judgments.

Ethical frameworks can be useful in helping educators of adults think through the ethical dilemmas they face in their practice. These frameworks do not necessarily make the decision-making process any less intense, but they can provide useful analytical tools to guide the thinking of practitioners through what can be exceedingly trying times.

Presented next are three frameworks that we have found helpful in practice. The first framework, that of Robert Starratt (1991, 1994), provides a theoretical lens for viewing ethical dilemmas. The other two frameworks represent ways of looking at ethical issues through personal and organizational lenses.

A THEORETICAL LENS

Starratt (1991, 1994) provides a picture of how instructors and program planners can view ethical decision making from three important frames: justice, care, and critique (see Figure 16.1). Depending on which lens or frame you use, how you view ethical dilemmas and alternative ways of solving those dilemmas will be very different. Starratt argues that all three lenses are necessary to build ethical environments for learning. The ethic of justice implies "values such as equality, the common good, human and civil rights, democratic participation and the like" (Starratt, 1994, p. 49). In the practice of adult education, two understandings of justice, "justice understood as individual choice to act justly and justice understood as the community's choice to direct or govern its actions justly" (p. 51), are needed. What is important is a balance between the common good and individual rights and responsibilities—a balance maintained by treating each other uniformly through accepted standards of conduct and social contracts. In order to maintain communal groups and societies, we need to surrender some of our freedom in return for some protection from the self-seeking behaviors of individuals.

Kohlberg (1973) is an often-quoted spokesperson for the ethic of justice, with his emphasis on fostering higher levels of moral development. More recently Daloz, Keen, Keen, and Parks (1996) have also outlined what they have termed "habits of the mind," which lead people to act for the common good. Their work differs somewhat from the traditional ways of thinking about how we reach this common good in that they stress interdependence and holistic thought processes as key. One of the inherent limitations of our more traditional notions of the ethic of justice "is the inability of the theory to determine claims in conflict. What is just for one person might not be considered just by another person" (Starratt, p. 52, 1994). This can lead to a minimalist mentality where the task becomes to create only the most basic condition in order to fulfill the claim of justice. The

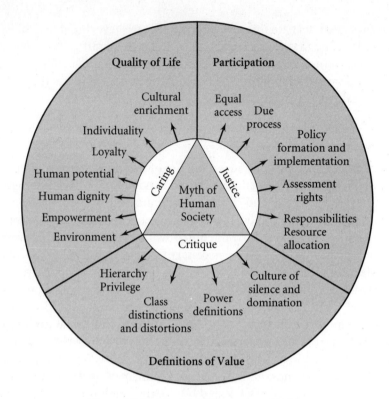

**Figure 16.1. The Multidimensional Ethic
at Work in an Educational Setting.**
Source: Starratt, 1994, p. 56.

ethic of justice is manifested in adult education through attention to such things as equal access, due process, and promotion of fair and equitable policies and procedures (see Figure 16.2).

The ethic of care "implies fidelity to persons, a willingness to acknowledge their right to be who they are, an openness of encountering them in their authentic individuality, a loyalty to the relationship. . . . It honors the dignity of each person and desires to see that person enjoy a fully human life" (Starratt, 1994 p. 52). One becomes whole only when functioning with others. Scholars such as Gilligan (1982), Noddings (1984, 1992), and Beck (1994) have promoted the importance of the ethic of care as a critical component, and perhaps the most important one, of educational practice. Noddings (1984) has worked in her research "deliberately toward a criterion that will preserve our deepest and more tender human feelings" (p. 87), those of

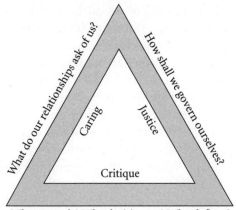

Figure 16.2. The Multidimensional Ethic.
Source: Starratt, 1994, p. 56.

nurturing and love. Beck (1994) sees fostering "communal relationships with other people [as] inextricably related to the welfare of others so that one caring for others in fact cares for herself or himself" (p. 20). In other words, a caring relationship fosters a real commitment to another, which leads to mutual benefits for both. Developing and maintaining caring relationships through an ethic of care as an instructor or program planner is a very time-consuming commitment, especially when working with others who are reluctant to adopt a culture that embraces care as foundational to practice. Also, sometimes we are just too weary or overwhelmed "to care," part of the human condition of modern life. The ethic of care is seen in adult learning programs in the mutual respect between learners and instructors, and in how we empower all in our work environments, learners and staff alike, to be all that they can be.

Starratt's final ethic, critique, asks, for example, who benefits from how programs are organized and taught? Which group dominates in determining which programs we offer and when? And "'Who defines what is valued and disvalued in this situation?' The point of this critical stance is to uncover which group has the advantage over the others, how things got to be the way they are, and to expose how situations are structured and language used so as to maintain the legitimacy of what is currently happening" (Starratt, 1994, p. 47). (See Chapter Four for a more through discussion of these and similar questions.) The critical lens is drawn primarily from the work of critical theorists, but we also see ideas of feminist theory woven into this frame (see Chapter Fifteen).

Representative spokespersons for an ethic of critique from the adult education community include Cervero and Wilson (1994), Collins (1991), Welton (1995b), and Tisdell (1995). By challenging the inherent injustices embedded within our many systems, such as racism, classism, and sexism, those practicing from an ethic of critique want to change the way we teach and plan programs by addressing how issues of unequal power and oppression affect our work as educators of adults. Cervero and Wilson (1994), for example, ask educational planners to think in ethical terms when considering who to invite to the "planning table." How we make decisions about who is allowed a voice in the program planning process, they say, "is the fundamental ethnical question that every planner [of programs for adults] has to negotiate" (Wilson and Cervero, 1996, p. 21). Two major criticisms of the ethic of critique are that the language used to describe this ethic is often obtuse and dense (even though they criticize the power of language used by others) and their blueprints for action are not always clear or practical. When questioning the privilege of class, race, and gender in how a program is formulated or altering the power mix related to who controls instructional practices, adult educators are using an ethic of critique.

These three lenses of justice, care, and critique are not mutually exclusive. People often operate out of more than one lens, though many have a preferred style. For example, Gilligan (1982) and Lyons (1983) have found that most women resonate to the ethic of care, most men look to the ethic of justice, and more women than men use both the ethic of care and justice. The consequences for practice of which ethical framework a person primarily uses are many. The most obvious consequence is that the parameters one uses to solve ethical dilemmas will be quite different, and therefore the outcome of that decision-making process may also be different. For example, when to dismiss learners from job training programs designed for welfare mothers often poses ethical dilemmas for staff. They know these mothers may be required by law to attend these programs or lose their benefits. For some of these women, this may be their last hope for possible employment. Those operating out of an ethic of justice would most likely look to the guidelines and rules that have been developed for continued participation in the program. They would carefully document any infringements based on those guidelines and keep those learners informed of their progress and what the consequences would be if their performance did not change to meet the required standards. In dismissing participants from the program because of poor performance, they would ensure these learners were given due process rights but would hold fast to the performance standards set for continued program participation. Individual situations and factors would most likely not be taken into account in their decision-making process about dismissing participants who performed below the standards.

Although those coming from an ethic of care would also pay attention to the basic guidelines for the job training program, they would approach the problem of poor performance by participants in a very different way. First, they would make it a point to establish an open and trusting relationship with as many participants as possible. In building these relationships, they would foster a sense of personal worth and dignity in each participant, looking to enhance the strengths she brings to the program, while encouraging her to embrace the program's goal of strengthening her work skills and habits. As the program progressed, instructors would then target their time, without slighting other program participants, in working with learners who were performing poorly in the program. They would more likely take a counseling stance with these participants and try to find ways to help each learner based on her individual needs and circumstances. They probably would allow more leeway in interpreting the program rules and guidelines depending on the situation of the participant. For example, they might excuse participants from missing classes, even if they went over the allotted amount, if they were caring for a sick child or relative. In dismissing participants from the program, they would assist as much as possible in helping these participants locate alternative programs or other type of interventions more appropriate to their individual needs (for example, a shelter for battered women or a drug treatment program).

Those operating from an ethic of critique would probably approach the problem of poor participation in a very different way. They would first want to know the racial, ethnic, and economic composition of the class and whether the poor performers fit any specific profile. If they did, they would then ask whether how the program was designed and implemented took into account the sociocultural background of these participants. For example, if most of the poor performers were of Hispanic or Latino background, they would seek to determine whether there was a language problem or whether the program was not recognizing the communal aspect of learning as important. Or, if there was no specific profile of learners who were not successful, they would then ask other questions, such as: Are instructors using their privileged positions to silence those who do not perform up to their standards? Are the instructional methods employed foreign to the participants who are doing poorly, thus making the learning process difficult for them? Are these participants usually silent whenever confronted by any type of authority figure (like an instructor), no matter what the beliefs and actions of those in authority? In essence, they would challenge the status quo of how the program was designed and being taught in the light of the backgrounds of the participants. They would also work hard at not having any participants dismissed because they would probably view components of the program (such as the way the program was being taught, the lack of ensuring that participants had a voice) as oppressive.

Practitioners need to be aware of the primary frame within which they operate when confronting ethical dilemmas and understand and honor the opinions of those who come from different perspectives. This recognition that we view ethical dilemmas through different lenses does not necessarily make the decision-making process any easier, but it does allow for more open and respectful dialogue when confronting problems and issues of an ethical nature. In addition, it helps to clarify the basis for the decision-making process. In understanding our own personal stance related to ethical dilemmas, a second modified version of a framework, proposed originally by Brockett (1988), is very useful.

THE PERSONAL LENS

As educators of adults, it is critical that we understand what influences our thinking and actions when faced with ethical dilemmas. Using a framework like Starratt's helps us to identify which conceptual lens we usually operate from, but confronting ethical issues goes much deeper than just thinking about issues in a conceptual way. Making ethical decisions and taking a stand based on those decisions is often painful and can have important consequences for both ourselves and others, depending on what course of action we choose. For example, if we believe our supervisors are acting in an unethical manner toward learners, to question their practices could cost us our jobs. On the other hand, if we do not raise the questions, we may cost learners their dignity, respect, and even access to our programs. Using a modified version of Brockett's (1988) framework of dimensions of ethical practice can assist us in gaining a deeper understanding of our basic beliefs and values related to our practice and how these values are related to and shaped by the wider world in which we work.

Four dimensions form the core of this framework: our personal value systems, the consideration of our multiple responsibilities, the expectations of our professional fields, and the values of the wider communities in which we work. Each of these dimensions is inter-related and affects one another. Our personal values are "at the heart of ethical practice" (Brockett, 1988, p. 10). These values become particularly important in situations where our fundamental values are challenged by dilemmas we face. For example, if we firmly believe that all learners should be treated with care and respect, and we see learners being abused by instructors through their use of racist and sexist language, we will be more likely to challenge the practice of those instructors, no matter what the consequences to ourselves. On the other hand, if we only espouse those values, but do not really believe they are fundamental to our practice, we are more likely to overlook the situation.

The second dimension of the framework acknowledges the multiple roles and responsibilities we often hold as educators of adults, and how these roles may come into conflict. Although we might firmly believe in the worth and dignity of each learner and that caring about learners is an important part of our practice, we may get so caught up in the multiple roles and daily demands of our jobs that we do not operationalize these beliefs, either in our own practice or in questioning the practice of others. Program administrators in adult education and training programs who also must serve as instructors are good examples of people who often get caught in this dimension of multiple roles. Administrative demands may get in the way of adequately preparing for classes and having time to spend assisting individual students. The tension may become especially unbearable for both learners and the administrator-instructor if the participants in the class believe how they are being evaluated is either unfair or they are given only cursory feedback on their work.

Professional expectations, the third dimension of the framework, also bear on how we respond to ethical dilemmas. These expectations may just be the norms of practice, which could be organizationally based as well as embedded within one's professional field, or they could be formalized in codes of ethics. Norms of practice, for example, might involve an unspoken, but clearly understood, norm that what the boss wants in the way of programs always takes priority in choosing which programs will be offered. This norm may be in conflict with people's personal values and how they think they should practice their roles as professional educators. But because they otherwise like their jobs, and the norm does not seem to harm program participants, they are willing to go along with it. In terms of formalized codes of ethics, depending on the background of the educator or trainer, they may have professional codes that act as guides for their practice, such as educators with formal degrees in health-related fields or law or those who work in settings that serve clientele in these arenas. Although codes of ethics are not yet common for the field of adult education, and debates still abound as to whether adult educators should develop such codes, there has been recent movement in developing guidelines or actual codes of ethics specifically for adult educators (Griffith, 1991; McDonald and Wood, 1993; Robertson, 1996; Sork, 1992, 1996; Wood, 1996). In addition, since many educators of adults come from varying professional backgrounds (for example, educators from medical fields or staff developers within public schools), they often have their own professional code of ethics within which their practice must be framed.

The final dimension, that of the values of the wider community in which we work, can cloud the issue of ethical decision making if we take those values seriously in our practice. This wider community may include cities, towns, and counties where we are physically located, specific types of groups with whom we work (for example, ethnic, racial, or religious communities), and even wider boundaries of national or even international scope. In launching family literacy programs, for example, we are often bound by both state and national legislative actions, as well as local community attitudes about literacy and the backgrounds of individual learners (such as language and cultural norms). In taking into consideration this fourth dimension of ethical practice, it first means we need to seek out and understand the values of the one or multiple communities that we serve. Second, often the values held by the wider communities in which we work are in conflict with each other, and sometimes in conflict with our professional standards and even our personal values, so understanding and sorting through all of these value stances can be time-consuming and, at times, frustrating. Yet it is important that educators of adults recognize this diversity in values and beliefs, although we know that even when we acknowledge this diversity, we will rarely, if ever, be able to respond to all of the parties involved. Again, the nature of addressing ethical dilemmas—that there is usually no one acceptable solution—makes acting ethically as educators of adults a demanding but critical part of our practice.

THE ORGANIZATIONAL LENS

The ethical practices analysis (EPA) is designed specifically for organizations to use as a tool for exploring the ethical aspects of their work (Sork, 1988, 1990). This analysis framework "provides a systematic way of structuring the identification and analysis of practices that have moral consequences and produces data useful for understanding the ethical dimension of adult education practice" (Sork, 1990, p. 2). Areas of ethical practice may include current or planned actions, policies and procedures, or behaviors of staff and other people associated with the organization, such as board members or financial sponsors. Sork (1990, p. 2) cautions that examining "the ethics of practice has the potential to be both exhilarating and destructive." When using the EPA, several prerequisites need to be met. More specifically, he recommends that "participation in the process should be voluntary . . . [and done] for professional or organizational development purposes rather than as a means of publicly exposing the perceived ethical shortcomings of individuals and organizations" (p. 2). In addition, the EPA "should not be used as a response to an accusation of unethical or improper behavior" (p. 2). Rather such accusations "should be adjudicated separately from and prior to the audit" (Sork, 1988, p. 394), although they may serve as one of the reasons for choosing to do an EPA.

Organizations that are using the EPA should review any "explicit mission statement or other document that provides evidence of an organizational philosophy, or [a] consensus on a set of principles that should guide practice within the organization" (Sork, 1990, p. 2) prior to initiating the process. These types of statements provide ways of comparing actual actions of staff versus the espoused principles of the organization.

The EPA in its current form consists of ten specific steps, which are outlined in Exhibit 16.1.

Step 1: Decide who to involve. An Ethical Practices Analysis could be proposed by anyone interested in exploring the ethics of practice, but the decision about who to involve in the process should be both deliberate and defensible. [This decision usually needs to] be reconsidered after Step 2 or Step 3 when it becomes clear what functions and practices will be included.

Step 2: Identify the functions to be included. The word "functions" . . . is meant to represent clusters of activities that are amenable to analysis and can logically be placed under one heading. Examples include instruction, admissions, marketing, administration, counseling, planning, and evaluation.

Step 3: Specify the practices to be analyzed for each function. Practices are current or planned actions, policies, or behaviors that affect others. While it is important to the success of the EPA to identify all practices that are judged relevant to the function, it is desirable to exclude practices that are judged morally benign—that is, practices with no conceivable moral consequences.

Step 4: Prepare moral arguments to justify and refute each practice. Here the task becomes one of developing arguments using what Talmor calls value language. Value language invokes explicit prescriptive statements [which] commends or condemns an action based on a value held by the analyst rather than on the basis of empirically-verifiable consequence of the action. The point of this step is to make explicit the moral reasoning which can be used to justify and refute each practice.

Step 5: Refine the arguments. The initial arguments from the previous step are now reviewed and refined so that they are as compelling and complete as possible.

Step 6: Discuss and debate the arguments. Although a great deal of discussion and debate may take place during the preparation and refinement of arguments, this step focuses attention on the task of deliberate and thorough consideration of all arguments presented to justify and refute each practice.

Step 7: Identify and discuss ethical consequences of continuing, modifying, terminating, or instituting each practice. These four outcomes represent the most likely outcomes of the ethical practices analysis. The task here is to consider what will happen from a moral/ethical perspective if these actions are taken. It is at this point that the ethical dilemmas may become apparent.

Step 8: Identify and discuss practical consequences of continuing, modifying, terminating, or instituting each practice. Now the discussion shifts from consideration of the abstract (moral consequences) to the concrete (practical consequences). Consideration of consequences is, to a large extent, speculative. That is, analysts will be making "best guesses" about what will happen given certain actions.

Step 9: Decide which practices will be continued, modified, terminated, or instituted. This step calls for the making of a decision about each practice included in the analysis. The decisions reached may be communicated in the form of recommendations to be considered by agency administrators or others who reserve the "final word" on changes likely to alter the nature of the organization.

Step 10: Prepare summary report and action plan. This step involves preparing a summary report and an action plan that stipulates how the decisions made in Step 9 will be implemented. The report should [summarize each step of the process] and how any changes to current practice will be evaluated—that is, what the expected outcomes will be of the proposed changes. In addition, the report should specify any moral/ethical principles proposed as guides for practice.

Exhibit 16.1. Steps in the Ethical Practices Analysis.

Source: Sork, 1990, pp. 3–6. Adapted with permission.

Using the EPA does require a large commitment of time and energy from those involved in the process. Completing the analysis, especially when decisions are made about which practices should be continued, modified, terminated, or instituted, may create high discord and disagreement among all parties involved. Although this process is called an ethical practices analysis, engaging in a process of this nature is not just an analytical exercise. Emotions often run high, and people become very invested in both the process and the proposed outcomes. An outside facilitator may be needed, especially for highly sensitive issues. This facilitator must be highly skilled in group process, conflict resolution, and meeting management.

ASSESSING THE ETHICAL CONSEQUENCES

In the movie *Educating Rita,* the protagonist enrolls in an open university course and is introduced to a world very different from the one she has inhabited all of her life. Midway through her transformation from a working-class London hairdresser to an articulate student of great literature, Rita is invited to a party at her professor's home. In a particularly poignant scene, she stands outside the house afraid to go in. Instead, she joins her husband and parents in a tavern where they are singing and drinking. She sits with them but remains separated from the activity. The next day she tells her professor that she can no longer relate to her family's world, but she is not comfortable in his world either. She is clearly in a great deal of pain. The changes that occur as the result of actively engaging in learning activities can be profound and disturbing to the learner. What is the educator's responsibility for the consequences of learning?

Most educators believe in the "goodness" of continued learning—that more is better than less, that through education both individuals and society can advance to higher levels of development. But what of the unintended outcomes of learning, such as those we discussed earlier related to Gladys? What responsibility do we have for the pain and discomfort of our learners as well as their growth and successes? Rita for a time finds herself between two worlds, a member of neither. Fingeret's research (1983) with adult illiterates underscores this concern. She found that adult illiterates are in tightly knit interpersonal networks where there is an exchange of goods and services. In exchange for reading, for example, the illiterate might baby-sit for the reader's child or employ a relative at work. Learning to read may disrupt the network, perhaps isolating the learner from important support. Research on reentry women reveals the pain and disruption to their personal lives that many of these women feel as they become exposed to new ways of thinking and being (Robertson, 1996; Taylor and Marienau, 1995).

For those who follow an empowerment model of education, the consequences of enabling adults to take control of their own lives are fraught with ethical questions. Empowerment involves the important notion of praxis-reflection and action (Freire, 1970b). Learners who become aware of their oppression become empowered to take action to change not only their situation but the social structure that led to oppression in the first place. An example provided by Ewert (1982, p. 33) describes his experiences working in an African village where "linkages between oppressive social structures and local economic problems were established beyond reasonable doubt." But rather than addressing the economic problems through community development projects, the community focused on the need for revolution. It was felt that "the program could generate more lasting changes by distributing guns than by talking about agriculture and health" (p. 33). This would have been a suicidal course of action. Ewert comments on the ethics involved: "Freire has been criticized by many for not coming to grips with the ethical implications of raising people's levels of consciousness through discussion of community problems. Few would now deny that defining problems in structural terms is a political process that might result in putting bullets in disadvantaged people's guns, at least within an oppressive social system. The responsibility for unleashing a process that can potentially exceed controllable limits rests with the adult educator" (p. 34).

The consequences of empowerment at the individual level are explored by Day (1988). For him, the goal of a learning activity is choice: the freedom and capacity "to choose for oneself from a set of possible alternatives" (p. 119). Developing a person's capacity to know, weigh, choose, and act, he says (p. 124), involves being aware of the following issues:

1. We are decision-making beings and are ultimately responsible for the decisions we make.

2. Our participation in a learning activity cannot be viewed in isolation from the wholeness of our lives, that is, what we learn affects what we feel and what we do.

3. The idea of increased choices and options may indeed serve as a powerful motivator for participation in learning activities.

4. The results of our learning experiences may as likely lead to discontent as to a state of well-being.

5. Generally speaking, learning produces consequences.

Learning, Day (1988, p. 123) concludes, sets in motion changes that "an educator with the best of intentions has little final control over." What the educator can and should do is to explore with learners the potential consequences of various courses of action. Frameworks like Starratt's (1994) and the modified version of Brockett's (1988) are helpful tools to use with learners in discussing the changes they are making or would like to make. The decision to proceed in a particular direction lies ultimately with the learner, not the educator. This is indeed what Daloz learned from Gladys, who "refused to grow."

SUMMARY

There are no simple answers to the ethical dilemmas raised in this chapter. The systematic knowledge that we do have about the context of adult learning, who the adult learners are, why and how they learn—information presented earlier in this book—is only partly helpful in making ethical decisions. Societal, community, professional, and individual values play a much larger role in shaping our practice. Competing courses of action and alternative choices, each with its own merits, means that educational planners, instructors, and learners themselves must examine the beliefs and values that form the basis for choosing among alternatives. It is this kind of awareness—awareness of why we do things the way we do—that leads to responsible, ethical practice in adult learning.

In creating an awareness of why we practice as we do and exploring the ethical dilemmas we face as educators of adults, frameworks for ethical practice are useful. Having conceptual, personal, and organizational lenses to examine who we are and the nature of the dilemmas we confront are helpful for both individuals and groups who want to gain a clearer understanding of the issues they face and the actions they take related to those dilemmas. We have found the frameworks of Starratt (1994), Brockett (1988), and Sork (1990) to be especially effective analytical tools for thinking through ethical dilemmas from a theoretical, personal, and organizational perspective. Yet we recognize that using these frameworks to examine ethical aspects of practice is much more than just an analytical exercise. Coping with ethical dilemmas is often heart wrenching and painful, especially when these dilemmas challenge our fundamental values and beliefs as educators. Therefore, we need to be mindful of the possible consequences of our actions in addressing practices that involve ethical dimensions for both ourselves and those with whom we work.

CHAPTER SEVENTEEN

Integrating Theory
and Practice

━◠◠◠━ T
his book is testimony to the fact that we know quite
a lot about learning in adulthood. Each chapter in the parts on context, the learner, the process, and the learning transaction with adults
is an interpretive summary of information about some aspect of
learning in adulthood. In the process of reviewing and reflecting on
all of this material, we arrived at our own understanding of learning
in adulthood. This last chapter is our opportunity to articulate what
we ourselves have learned about this phenomenon.

Most who have written on the topic of adult learning have tried to
delineate principles summarizing what has been learned from research
or observed in practice and axioms that can be applied to practice.
Knowles's (1980) assumptions underlying andragogy, discussed in
Chapter Twelve, are a good example of a set of principles about adult
learners that has implications for practice. Others have advanced similar lists, often with a distinctive orientation. Smith (1982) distinguishes
the learning process from the learners. He presents six observations
about learning, such as "learning is a personal and natural process" and
"learning has its intuitive side" (p. 35), and notes four critical characteristics of adult learners: a different orientation to education and

learning, an accumulation of experience, special developmental trends, and anxiety and ambivalence. In a popular version of this approach, Zemke and Zemke (1995) in an update of an earlier article (1981) that listed "thirty things we know for sure about adult learning" divide principles of adult learning into the three categories: adult motivation, curriculum design, and classroom practice. MacKeracher (1996), who makes sense of adult learning through looking at the complex interaction of cognitive, affective, physical, social, and spiritual aspects of learning, offers practical advice to both learners and facilitators for enhancing the learning activity. Learners, for example, should "trust the process," be willing to take risks, and be "open to new ideas and experiences" (p. 243). Instructors should be reflective, passionate, responsive, and "keep in mind that you are a model for learners whether you want to be or not" (p. 253).

Brookfield (1986) takes a somewhat different angle; he proposes six principles that underlie effective facilitation of learning and address participation, mutual respect, collaboration, praxis, critical reflection, and self-direction. More recently, Brookfield (1995) has focused on incorporating critical reflection into our roles as teachers. Developing a critically reflective instructional practice means identifying and examining our underlying assumptions. The best way to do that, he suggests, "is to look at what we do from as many unfamiliar angles as possible . . . to stand outside ourselves and see how some of our most deeply held values and beliefs lead us into distorted and constrained ways of being" (p. 28). Brookfield suggests four lenses for examining our teaching: our autobiographies as teachers and learners, how students see us, how colleagues perceive us, and the theoretical literature, which "can help us understand our experience by naming it in different ways" (p. 30). It is this fourth lens—the theoretical literature—where our book makes a contribution.

We considered doing a meta-analysis of the principles, concepts, and characteristics found in these sources as well as those delineated elsewhere in this book and in some of our own work (Caffarella, 1992, 1994, 1996; Merriam and Brockett, 1997). That undertaking, however, would probably have resulted in another set of principles that would not truly capture what we have come to understand about learning in adulthood. Furthermore, there is some question in our minds as to the usefulness of any one set of principles for guiding either research or practice. If, as we have tried to bring out in previous chapters, learning in adulthood is embedded in its context, a single set of principles is not likely to hold true for the wide-ranging diversity of learners and learning situations.

What we have done, therefore, is to step back and think about how learning in adulthood can be distinguished from learning in childhood. Our answer, in essence a summary of the book, is that learning in adulthood can be distinguished from childhood in terms of the learner, the context, and to some extent the learning process. Furthermore, it is not just that differences can be seen in these areas. Equally important, the configuration of learner, context, and process *together* makes learning in adulthood distinctly different from learning in childhood. In this chapter we first explore these differences and then discuss how well our understanding of the phenomenon is addressed by theory and practice. Finally, we speculate on the next steps to furthering our understanding of adult learning.

THE LEARNER

The focus on the individual learner, grounded primarily in the psychological paradigm, has driven research and practice in adult learning until this past decade. Representative lines of inquiry from this perspective include the ways we have traditionally framed the life experiences of individual learners, the linking of the psychological frame of development to learning, much of our research on motivation and participation, the information processing framework of cognition and memory, and the neurobiology of learning.

The comparatively richer life experiences of individual adults have been cited by nearly all writers as a key factor in differentiating adult learning from child learning. As Kidd (1973, p. 46) noted more than twenty-five years ago, "Adults have *more* experiences, adults have different *kinds* of experiences, and adult experiences are *organized differently.*" He goes on to observe that "these points seem self-evident. An adult's sexual or social experiences are of a kind that mark him [sic] off from the world of children. The same can be said of his experiences of a job, or politics, or war" (p. 46). If accumulated life experiences differentiate children from adults, they also differentiate one adult from another. A group of sixty year olds will have less in common than a group of twenty year olds.

Experience is a major assumption "that can arguably lay claim to be viewed as a 'given' in the literature of adult learning" (Brookfield, 1986, p. 98). Knowles (1980, p. 44) conceives of it in terms of a "growing reservoir of experience" that functions as "a rich resource for learning." It also establishes a person's self-identity: "Adults derive their self-identity from their experience. They define who they are in terms of the accumulation of their unique sets of experiences." And "because adults define themselves largely by their experience, they have a deep investment in its value" (p. 50).

Life experience, as discussed in Chapter Ten, functions in several ways that are idiosyncratic to adult learning. First, as Knowles observes, adult learners themselves become important resources for learning. Adults can call on their experiences in the formulation of learning activities, as well as serve as resources for others in a learning event. Second, the need to make sense out of one's life experiences is often an incentive for engaging in a learning activity in the first place. Third, the actual engagement of past experiences with learning is somewhat different for adults than children. An adult's major use of experience in learning is on "modifying, transferring, and reintegrating meanings, values, strategies, and skills" (Brundage, cited by Smith, 1982, p. 41), while children use their experiences in accumulating new knowledge and skills. Finally, it should be noted that an adult's past experiences can become obstacles to new learning. Some may have to unlearn negative attitudes toward learning, old ways of doing things, prejudicial views, and so on.

The arena of development from a psychological perspective is another way in which adults are differentiated from children. While it is true that both adults and children are involved in developmental processes, the *nature* of the process is qualitatively different. This difference can be clearly illustrated with Havighurst's (1972) developmental tasks for different life stages. For infancy through adolescence, the tasks reflect physical maturation (learning to walk, getting ready to read) or preparatory activities needed for future adult roles. Beginning with the tasks of young adulthood, there is a shift to functioning well as an adult—bringing up young children, managing a home, achieving adult civic and social responsibilities, and so on. Erikson's (1963) life stages also reflect a shift from childhood dependence to adult-oriented dilemmas. In the first five stages of infancy through adolescence, the child deals with establishing trust, autonomy, initiative, industry, and identity. Adults struggle with intimacy, generativity, and integrity, characteristics manifested in adult roles of spouse, parent, worker, and citizen. In at least one developmental theory, the notions of adult experience and development converge. Part of

Kohlberg's (1973) theory of moral development stipulates that one cannot attain the higher stages of development until one has experienced irrevocable moral decision making. Fowler (1981), whose stages of faith build on Kohlberg's idea, also maintains that later stages cannot be attained until adult life. Even some models of cognitive change and development, as discussed in Chapters Seven and Fourteen, assume an accumulation of experience with age (Baxter Magolda, 1992, 1995; Kegan, 1994; King and Kitchener, 1994; Mezirow, 1991). Mezirow (1991, p. 193), for example, asserts that "transformations likely to produce developmentally advanced meaning perspectives usually appear to occur after the age of thirty," while Kegan (1994) asserts that most people do not even enter the highest levels of consciousness until their forties.

In addition to a sequential stage-phase view of development, life events and transitions differentiate adult learning from child learning. Many of the life events and transitions that adults face are peculiar to adulthood and require adjustments—adjustments often made through systematic learning activity. It is these transitions and life events that are likely to result in significant, meaningful learning (Merriam and Clark, 1991). They are also what motivate many adults to seek out learning. Aslanian and Brickell (1980), for example, found that 83 percent of adult learners in their study were involved in learning to cope with a transition. The transitions were primarily career related (56 percent), followed by family life transitions (35 percent). "To know an adult's life schedule," they concluded, "is to know an adult's learning schedule" (pp. 60–61).

As noted in Chapter Three, there is a strong link between the motivation to participate in a learning activity and an adult's life experiences and developmental issues. Several theories of adult learning acknowledge this link. Knox's proficiency theory, for example, is based on the premise that adults experience a gap between their current level of proficiency and a desired level (1985). The proficiencies are related to major adult roles such as spouse or worker. Mezirow's (1991, p. 192) process of perspective transformation is precipitated by a "disorienting dilemma"—that is, one's familiar patterns of coping with life events prove ineffective. Daloz (1988a, p. 238) talks about two major "crossings" in the journey of human development: One is moving from childhood into adulthood; the second is attempted when the beliefs, behavior, or mores of one's "tribe" come into question. In both cases there is a "gap between old givens and new discoveries." Further, many of the models explaining the relationship between motivation and participation (see Chapter Three) focus on the individual adult engaging in learning as a function of particular life experiences.

How we have conceptualized human memory and how the brain functions, as described in Chapter Nine, has also been driven primarily by psychological or biological paradigms, with little, if any, credence given to how the world outside affects these functions. From these perspectives learning has been conceived as something that primarily goes on inside of the heads of individual learners. Through studying memory we continue to try to decipher how adults receive, store, transform, and retrieve information. We have even tried to see if we could improve these processes within individual learners as they age through both formal learning activities and more recently by using various forms of pharmaceutical interventions. One of the most intriguing knowledge bases on which to draw about learning in adulthood in the last few years is that of the neurobiological basis of learning. By discovering more about how the brain actually functions, we have a better chance of unlocking lifelong learning disabilities and such disastrous diseases of the mind as Alzheimer's and Parkinson's, which render adults incapable of learning even at a rudimentary level. There is a great deal of potential to enhance what we know about individual learners, especially when we merge the ideas from the cognitive and neurobiological sciences.

Just being an adult is thus a crucial factor in distinguishing between learning in adulthood and learning in childhood. The accumulation of experience, the nature of that experience, the developmental issues adults address, how the notions of development and experience relate to learning, and how aging affects our memory and the more general neurological basis for learning—all of these differentiate adult learners from children.

THE CONTEXT

The recognition of the importance of context in learning has gained more acceptance in the past decade. Although historically adult educators in social action and community-based learning programs have always incorporated the concept of context as integral to their work, this idea has not received as much attention from educators of adults in other settings until very recently. A contextual approach to learning encompasses two important dimensions: the interactive and the structural. The interactive dimension acknowledges that learning is a product of the individual interacting with the context. Recent theories of situated cognition, reflective practice, and cognitive development are representative of this interactive dimension. The structural dimension includes consideration of factors such as race, class, gender, cultural diversity, and power and oppression. Each of these two contextual dimensions are discussed in more depth in this and in a later section of the chapter.

The interactive dimension of the context acknowledges an adult's life situation is quite different than that of a child's. A child's life situation is usually characterized by dependency on others for his or her well-being. The majority of adults, on the other hand, are adults because they have assumed responsibility for managing their own lives. As Paterson (1979, p. 10) reminds us, "To say that someone is an adult is to say that he [sic] is entitled, for example, to a wide-ranging freedom of life-style and to a full participation in the making of social decisions; and it is also to say that he is obliged, among other things, to be mindful of his own deepest interests and to carry a full share of the burdens involved in conducting society and transmitting its benefits. His adulthood consists in his full employment of such rights and his full subjection to such responsibilities." The taking on of social roles characteristic of adulthood—roles such as worker, spouse or partner, voter, and parent—differentiates adults from children better than chronological age does.

This difference in the social position of adults and children is reflected in contextual differences in their lives and their learning. A child's life is bounded by home and school, whereas an adult's life situation is defined primarily by work, family, and community. Through home and school, children learn to be adults; going to school is a full-time job. Theoretically at least, both home and school are sites where young people learn how to function as adults. The curriculum in both settings is determined primarily by others, who decide what is important to know in order to become responsible members of society. Education, even undergraduate education for traditional-aged students, is basically preparatory—young people are "prepared" to be adults.

Adults, on the other hand, typically add the role of learner to other full-time roles and responsibilities. The learning that adults do arises from the context of their lives, which is intimately tied to the sociocultural setting in which they live. As Jarvis (1992, p. 11) has observed: "Learning . . . is about the continuing process of making sense of everyday experience." Jarvis also draws a connection between motivation and context: "The reason for participation does not always lie within the learner but in the dynamic tension that exists between the learner and [the] socio-cultural world" (1983, p. 67). For example, an assembly-line worker whose job is taken over by a robot will need to retrain for other employment, and a nurse will need to keep up with changes in the health care system and technology. Zoning and tax laws, waste disposal management, and so on that affect citizens' lives in communities also lead to new learning. Thus learning in adulthood is characterized by its usefulness for immediate application to the duties and responsibilities inherent in the adult roles of worker, spouse, partner, parent, citizen, and so on.

The differences in context between children's and adults' lives and how these differences influence learning are highlighted in an article by Resnick (1987) contrasting learning in school and outside school. She writes that "school is a special place and time for people—discontinuous in some important ways with daily life and work" (p. 13). There are four ways that school learning differs from other (mostly adult) learning. First, in school, individual cognition has, until recently, been primarily rewarded, whereas outside school shared cognition is the norm. Except in situations where models such as cooperative learning are used extensively, "a student succeeds or fails at a task independently of what other students do. . . . In contrast, much activity outside school is socially shared. Work, personal life, and recreation take place within social systems, and each person's ability to function successfully depends on what others do and how several individuals' mental and physical performances mesh" (p. 13). Second, with the exception of situations where computers are integrated into the curriculum, schools value pure mentation as opposed to the tool manipulation that is valued outside. That is, "school is an institution that values thought that proceeds independently, without aid of physical and cognitive tools," at least in testing situations (p. 13). In the real world, people use all sorts of tools on a regular basis, such as books, notes, calculators, and computers, to solve problems and function more effectively. Resnick points out that it is the use of tools that allows "people of limited education to participate in cognitively complex activity systems" and cites Brazilian black market bookies' use of prepared probability tables for functioning in a demanding mathematical system (p. 14). In our own society, personnel in fast food restaurants ring up orders on a computer where the food items are keyed by picture and word.

The third and fourth distinctions between learning inside school and outside are closely related. Resnick notes that symbol manipulation is valued in school, whereas outside, one's "actions are intimately connected with objects and events . . . without necessarily using symbols to represent them" (p. 14). Too often school learning is decontextualized, resulting in little transfer between school and real-world reasoning. Resnick's fourth observation is that generalized learning occurs in school, but situation-specific competencies are needed out of school: "Schools aim to teach general, widely usable skills and theoretical principles. . . . Yet to be truly skillful outside school, people must develop situation-specific forms of competence" (p. 15). What people in all settings (including, Resnick points out, adult technical training, management, and continuing professional education) need to learn is "to be good *adaptive learners,* so that they can perform effectively when situations are unpredictable and task demands change" (p. 18). Resnick's analysis underscores the contextual differences between learning in childhood and in adulthood and acknowledges the importance of the more recent work on situated cognition (Clancey, 1997; Hansman and Wilson, 1998; Wilson, 1993a, 1993c) and selected models of reflective practice (Boud and Walker, 1990, 1992; Usher, Bryant, and Johnston, 1997).

In delineating differences between children and adults regarding the context, we note that these differences have ramifications with regard to social and ethical issues. Since children's education is preparatory, for example, they are expected to learn certain social and moral values as well as specific bodies of knowledge. As discussed in Chapters Four and Sixteen, adult education struggles with issues of provision and access to learning opportunities, perhaps because adult education is primarily a voluntary activity, whereas schooling for children is compulsory. Similarly, the ethical issues involved in adult learning differ somewhat in that an adult's learning is often intimately tied to his or her life situation and status as an adult. Questions thus arise regarding agency and responsibility in the learning activity, as well as the outcomes of that interaction.

The context, then, in which adult learning takes place generally differs from the context of most childhood learning. Moreover, as we pointed out in Chapters Two, Six, and Twelve, every adult learning situation differs from every other situation, whether the learning is done in a formal or nonformal setting or on one's own. Certainly informal learning contexts, including social action and community-based learning, are where much of adult learning takes place. While these contexts vary from individual to individual, they all hold the potential for learning and in fact *organize* our learning. We need only see them as sites for learning. In a delightful and insightful book on the integration of learning and living, Bateson (1994, p. 9) writes, "When the necessary tasks of learning cannot be completed in a portion of the life cycle set aside for them, they have to join life's other tasks and be done concurrently. We can carry on the process of learning in everything we do, like a mother balancing her child on her hip as she goes about her work with the other hand or uses it to open the doors of the unknown. Living and learning, we become ambidextrous." At another point, she comments on the unfortunate tendency of our society to compartmentalize: "If only for tax purposes, we are forced to label activities as work, or play, or learning, or therapy, or exercise, or stress reduction, missing the seriousness of play, the delight of good work, the healing that happens in the classroom. For adults, learning is rarely the only activity going on. . . . By emphasizing a single thread of activity, we devalue the learning running throughout" (p. 108).

The second aspect of the context of adult learning, the structural dimension, acknowledges the fact that our society has become highly multicultural and diverse and that political and economic conditions often shape the learning experience. It is no longer a question of whether in adult learning situations we need to address issues of race, class, gender, culture, ethnicity, and sexual orientation, but rather a question of how should we deal with these issues, both in terms of who presently constitutes the majority of learners, at least in formal adult learning activities, and who should be involved. We need to know the backgrounds and experiences of our learners, as individual learners, but also as members of social and culturally constructed groups such as women and men; poor, middle-class, and rich; and black, white, and brown. These socially constructed notions of who our learners and we are as educators and subsequent power dynamics should be given the same attention in teaching and learning, planning, and administrative functions as the technology of our practice.

Further, exposure to other groups of people and cultures has been greatly expanded through travel, participation in the global marketplace, and technological wonders such as the World Wide Web. These changes afford all adults opportunities to learn from others and to expand their worldviews. Bateson (1994, p. 17) explains how this kind of exposure can lead to learning: "Each person is calibrated by experience, almost like a measuring instrument for difference, so discomfort [in encountering difference] is informative and offers a starting point for new understanding." She recognizes that "a certain amount of friction is inevitable whenever peoples with different customs and assumptions meet. . . . As migration and travel increase, we are going to have to become more self-conscious and articulate about differences, and to find acceptable ways of talking about the insights gained through such friction-producing situations, gathering up the harvest of learning along the way" (p. 23). "It is contrast," she writes, "that makes learning possible" (p. 27).

THE LEARNING PROCESS

Of the three areas of learner, context, and process, there are fewer dramatic differences between adults and children in the learning process than in the other two areas. Houle (1972), one of the field's most respected adult educators, maintains that the process of learning is fundamentally the same for adults as for children. Research in the past twenty years, however, has uncovered some differences—differences that when linked with context and learner help distinguish adult learning from child learning. This section draws from Chapters Five and Seven through Eleven to highlight some of the learning process differences between adults and children.

Two process factors in particular—speed and meaningfulness— have been shown to affect adult learning. Speed refers to the time a person has to examine a problem or respond to a situation. An adult's ability to respond slows with age, and time limits and pressures have a negative effect on learning performance. Perhaps because an adult's learning is so closely tied to his or her life situation, adults are not inclined to engage in learning unless it is meaningful. Adults are thus likely to do poorly on recall of nonsense syllables, for example, compared with younger learners, who are more conditioned by school experiences to learn material that may not be immediately relevant. Linked to the meaningfulness of material is the variable of motivation. MacKeracher (1996, p. 80) defines motives as "the needs that learners feel when starting a learning activity. They may relate to unmet needs or unwanted conditions in life and to the pursuit of positive growth toward desired goals. As learners proceed toward meeting unmet needs, resolving unwanted conditions, or reaching desired goals, motives for learning tend to change in relation to any feelings and experiences of success/failure and satisfaction/dissatisfaction." In summarizing the literature on motivation, MacKeracher observes that "the tendencies which are labeled 'motives' arise from *within the learner.* Despite encouragement from some writers to 'motivate learners,' facilitators cannot do this directly" (p. 79).

In addition, there are other age-related factors that may affect learning in adulthood. Adults are more likely than children to have health problems. Fatigue, medication, disuse of abilities, interference from previous learning, environmental conditions, and so on certainly affect new learning. Acquisition of information may become more difficult as the rate at which working memory processes information seems to be slower with age. These and other factors have been covered in depth in Chapters Five, Eight, and Nine. The point to be made here is that the nature of the learning process in adulthood is likely to be different from a child's because of the greater incidence of these occurrences and the greater impact of these factors on older learners.

By linking an adult's greater experiential base to learning, a case can be made that cognitive functioning in adulthood may also be qualitatively different from childhood. Ausubel (1968) and J. Anderson (1996), for example, maintain that the prior accumulation of knowledge is crucial to the integration of new learning. By extension, then, "adults who have accumulated more knowledge than children are in a better position to learn new things, and, barring physiological impairments, learning potential [at least in some areas] increases with age" (Darkenwald and Merriam, 1982, p. 104). For example, as discussed in Chapter Fourteen, others focus not so much on the accumulation of knowledge as on the *transformation* of experience as a characteristic of adult learning.

Finally, it should be noted that those who posit stages of cognitive development in adulthood different from those unfolding in childhood contribute to our understanding of how the learning process may be different for adults. Arlin (1975), Kegan (1994), Riegel (1973), and others "introduce the hypothesis that mature adult thought, or the type of thought which adults have the potential to develop, is qualitatively different from the thought of adolescents or very young adults" (Allman, 1983, p. 112). Arlin (1975), for example, proposes a fifth stage (after Piaget's four stages) of cognitive development occurring in adulthood called problem finding. Kegan (1994) proposes a level of consciousness model in which dialectical thinking becomes the hallmark, or highest level of mature adult thinking. Framed from the assumption that our postmodern world necessitates this form of thinking in order to respond effectively to the demands of adult life, Kegan asserts that adults rarely expand their thinking to this level until their forties or fifties. As Kegan observes, "I suggest that we are gradually seeing more adults working on a qualitatively different order of consciousness than did adults one hundred years ago because we live twenty or more years longer than we used to" (p. 352).

THE CONFIGURATION OF CONTEXT, LEARNER, AND PROCESS

We believe that learning in adulthood can be distinguished from childhood learning by the way in which learner, context, and some aspects of the learning process blend in adulthood. The configuration looks different than it does in childhood. In our discussion of each component, we noted how adults are different from children, how the context of adult learning is different from the context of child learning, and how certain features of the learning process are unique to adults. Although we have attempted to discuss these components separately, our discussion reflects their natural interaction. An adult's life experiences, for example, are a function of the sociocultural environment and the learner's personality. We can think about this interaction with regard to an adult's work experiences. As everyone is aware, the context of work has changed dramatically with the emergence of a global marketplace, advances in technology, and the shift from an industrial to a service and knowledge-based economy. Some adults are training for jobs that did not exist five years ago, many are changing jobs often, and a growing number are experimenting with alternative job structures, such as consulting, telecommuting, and job sharing. Previous experiences as well as one's personality will determine how these changes are accommodated, which in turn affects one's self-concept as a worker, as well as notions of career development.

How an adult processes information from the sociocultural context, and even what an adult attends to in the environment, is wrapped up with the developmental concerns of the moment. A parent of teenagers, for example, is much more likely to notice and perhaps attend a workshop on teenagers and drugs than someone not involved with that age group. And the state of the economy is likely to be of great interest to someone nearing retirement, who might then design a learning project on the topic. In both examples, the sociocultural context, the accumulated life experiences, developmental concerns, and presumably the nature of ensuing learning experiences converge to make learning in adulthood qualitatively different from learning in childhood.

In presenting this summary of learning in adulthood, we also asked ourselves to what extent theory and practice might reflect this integrated perspective of adult learning. The work on self-directed learning reviewed in Chapter Thirteen and the models of participation reviewed in Chapter Three by definition focus on a particular aspect of the phenomenon. The self-directed learning frameworks emphasize the process and, to a lesser extent, the context and the learner. Similarly, the participation models do not deal with the learning process per se—the context and the learner are the most important variables.

Chapters Twelve, Fourteen, and Fifteen present theory-building efforts that purport to explain learning in adulthood. Some theories focus on adult characteristics, some emphasize an adult's life situation, and others center on changes in consciousness. These three emphases can be loosely equated with the adult, the context, and the learning process. Knowles's (1970) original popular notion of andragogy is almost entirely focused on how the adult learner is different from a preadult learner. So too is Cross's model, although she does bring in contextual variables. McClusky, Knox, and Jarvis all attend to the adult's life situation and social context from which the need or motivation to learn arises. Of the three, Jarvis devotes the most attention to the learning process in addition to the context. He has not yet explained, however, how his model might be a uniquely *adult* model.

For Mezirow and Freire, learning in adulthood is a transformative rather than an additive process. It requires the ability to reflect critically on one's thoughts and assumptions—a particularly adult skill. Both theories also account for adult characteristics, in particular life experiences and developmental concerns unique to adulthood. And in both theories the sociocultural context is a critical component. It is in the sociocultural context that adults have experiences that must be processed. The two differ, however, in the notion of being emancipated through this learning process. Mezirow (1991), while not outlawing social change as an outcome of perspective transformation, emphasizes personal psychological change. And while Mezirow's theory of perspective transformation perhaps comes closest to taking into account our notions of context, learner, and process, there are still some questions as to just how comprehensive his theory is. Is the process he outlines unique to adulthood? What about adults who do not reflect critically? Can transformations occur through other mechanisms? His theory seems most appropriate for informal, self-directed learning situations, although several have sought application in more institutionally-based settings (Cranton 1994b, 1996, 1997; Mezirow and Associates, 1990).

For Freire, on the other hand, being emancipated from false consciousness requires political action aimed at changing society. Critical theory and feminist pedagogy draw from Freire in their emphases on emancipation and empowerment. Further, both of these orientations *begin* with the sociopolitical context of people's lives. Critical theory attends to socioeconomic class as the major variable creating inequities and oppression, while feminists look to gender as well as the intersection of race, class, and gender. Both perspectives call for adults to reflect critically on their oppression and engage with other like-minded adults in a radical restructuring of society.

How well does practice account for the uniqueness of adult learning? This question is difficult to answer without looking at a specific learning situation. Furthermore, it is basically a question about the relationship between theory and practice. To what extent is the knowledge that we have accumulated about adult learning, knowledge reviewed in this book, reflective of what actually happens in practice? Moreover, to what extent is the knowledge that we do have derived from practice, and to what extent does it inform our practice? Cervero (1991) has delineated four positions relative to the interaction between knowledge and practice, each of which can be applied to adult learning. A review of these positions allows us to see how the knowledge presented in this book and practice are related.

The first position posits that the practice of adult learning has been carried out without reference to what is known about how adults learn. This position in fact characterizes much of adult learning, since only a small percentage of teachers, administrators, program developers, and others have had any formal training in adult education. From this position, those working with adult learners rely on common sense and intuition—less formal but certainly no less valuable sources of guidance for practice.

The second position is that a systematically collected knowledge base illuminates practice. It is thought that if this knowledge is disseminated through professional preparation, in-service staff development, and so on, practice will be strengthened. Lists of principles and guidelines, for example, such as those reviewed at the beginning of the chapter, are often disseminated through workshops and in-house publications, ostensibly to improve one's practice in adult learning. There are also numerous publications that attempt to show how knowledge about context, learner, and process could be put into practice. *Andragogy in Action* (Knowles and Associates, 1984), for example, presents thirty-six case studies of how characteristics of adult learners can be incorporated into the planning of learning activities in settings ranging from business and government to universities and volunteer organizations. In another publication, *Improving Higher Education Environments for Adults* (1989), Schlossberg, Lynch, and Chickering show how adult life experiences and adult developmental theory can form the basis for programs and support services for learners in higher education. Finally, Cranton's *Transformative Learning in Action: Insights from Practice* (1997) and Mezirow and Associates' *Fostering Critical Reflection in Adulthood* (1990) review exemplary programs and suggest methods "for precipitating and fostering transformative learning in the context of the classroom, in special workshops, in informal group settings, in collective social action, in counseling sessions, and in the workplace" (Mezirow and Associates, 1990, p. xv).

The third position on the relationship between knowledge and practice is that educators operate intuitively with an understanding of adult learning whether or not that knowledge is articulated. This theory-in-practice position holds that "practitioners actually do operate on the basis of theories and knowledge" and that "theory can be derived from practice by systematically articulating the subjective meaning structures that influence the ways that real individuals act in concrete situations" (Cervero, 1991, pp. 26–27). This notion has been investigated with regard to professional practice (Schön, 1983, 1987, 1991, 1996) and is now being developed in adult education (Cervero and Wilson, 1994; Johnson-Bailey, Tisdell, and Cervero, 1994). With regard to the learning situation and other aspects of adult education, the central task of this approach is to "describe educational practice and help practitioners become more reflective about their own individual actions" (Cervero, 1991, p. 29). The orientation of our book—

in particular, our attending to context and exploring social and ethical issues—models the critical stance toward practice inherent in this position.

The fourth position on theory and practice is that they are indivisible. Here the focus is on "what counts as knowledge and how, where, and by whom this knowledge is produced" (Cervero, 1991, p. 31). Understanding the production of knowledge is emancipating. This perspective is best illustrated by critical theory, postmodernism, and feminist theoretical assumptions about knowledge and learning. More than the first three positions, this perspective—that theory and practice are indivisible—takes into account the political, economic, and sociocultural context in which learning occurs. Examples of adult education practice from this perspective are community-based literacy programs (Sissel, 1996), feminist pedagogy (Tisdell, 1993, 1995, 1998), critical pedagogy (Freire, 1970b; Shor and Freire, 1987), popular education programs and movements (Cunningham and Curry, 1997; Galbraith, 1990; Hamilton, 1992; Hamilton and Cunningham, 1989; Smith, 1994), and participatory research activities (Merriam, 1991). Participatory research "has faith in people's ability to produce their own knowledge through collective investigation of problems and issues, collective analysis of the problems, and collective action to change the conditions that gave rise to the problems in the first place" (Gaventa, 1988, p. 19). This method of producing knowledge "represents an effort to recover alternative knowledge systems that have been excluded from the 'official' body of knowledge in adult education" (Cervero, 1991, chap. 2). For the most part, the material presented in this book is representative of "official" knowledge. More certainly could be done through collaborative research efforts with learners themselves to illuminate learning in adulthood.

SOME CONCLUDING THOUGHTS

In this final chapter, we have articulated our understanding of learning in adulthood and assessed how well learner, context, and process as a unique configuration in adulthood are reflected in theory and in practice. We conclude with some observations and suggestions. First, we think the field has developed a significant knowledge base about learning in adulthood, much of it fairly recent. We are optimistic that learning in adulthood will continue to interest researchers and educators and that we will know quite a bit more within the next several years. Second, the nature of contributions in this area is changing. Adult educators are moving from description to theory building. We are considering the sociocultural context in which learning takes place, how race, class, gender, able-bodiedness, sexual orientation, and so on affect learning, thus shifting from a primarily psychological orientation to a broader contextual view. We are more cognizant of the social issues and ethical dilemmas involved in the provision and practice of adult learning. And we are examining notions about how knowledge about adult learning itself is produced and legitimized.

We are hopeful that learners themselves will be a major source of our understanding of learning in adulthood. We in fact suggest that future research in adult learning be collaboratively designed with adults who are learning on their own or in informal ways, as well as with participants in formal and nonformal learning activities. We also suggest that research that takes into account the sociocultural and political context of adult learning might well advance our understanding of the problems of access and opportunity that continue to trouble the field. Finally, much of what we know about learning itself is derived from nonadults or select adult populations such as college students and the elderly. We suggest that there is still much to be learned about learning that takes place in adulthood.

—˜— References

Adenuga, T. "Demographic and Personal Factors in Predicting Self-Directedness in Learning." In H. B. Long and others (eds.), *Self-Directed
Learning: Consensus and Conflict*. Norman: Oklahoma Research
Center for Continuing Professional and Higher Education, University of Oklahoma, 1991.

Adult Learning, 1996, *7*(6).

Advances in Motivation and Achievement. Vol. 4: *Motivation in Adulthood*.
Greenwich, Conn.: JAI Press, 1985.

Agrawal, R., and Kumar, A. "Everyday Memory in Adulthood." *Psychological Studies*, 1992, *37*(2/3), 161–172.

Ahteenmaki-Pelkonen, L. "From Self-Directedness to Interdependence? An
Analysis of Mezirow's Conceptualization of Self-Directed Learning."
In S. Tosse, B. Wahlgren, J. Manninen, and M. Klasson (eds.), *Social
Change and Adult Education Research: Adult Education Research in
Nordic Countries 1992/93*. Linkoping, Sweden: Linkoping Adult Edu-
cation Research Group, Linkoping University, 1994. (ED 374 213)

Allman, P. "The Nature and Process of Adult Development." In M. Tight
(ed.), *Adult Learning and Education*. London: Croom Helm, 1983.

Alpaugh, K. P., Parham, I. A., Cole, K. D., and Birren, J. E. "Creativity in
Adulthood and Old Age: An Exploratory Study." *Educational Gerontology*, 1982, *8*, 101–116.

Amstutz, D. D. "Staff Development: Addressing Issues of Race and Gender."
In E. Hayes and S. A. J. Colin III (eds.), *Confronting Racism and Sex-
ism*. New Directions for Adult and Continuing Education, no. 61.
San Francisco: Jossey-Bass, 1994.

Anderson, J. R. "Cognitive Styles and Multicultural Populations." *Journal of
Teacher Education*, 1988, *39*(1), 2–9.

Anderson, J. R. *Rules of the Mind*. Hillsdale, N.J.: Erlbaum, 1993.

Anderson, J. R. *Cognitive Psychology and Its Implications*. (4th ed.) New
York: Freeman, 1996.

Anderson, J. R., Reder, L. M., and Simon, H. A. "Situated Learning and Education." *Educational Researcher,* 1996, *25*(4), 5–11.

Anderson, J. R., Reder, L. M., and Simon, H. A. "Rejoinder: Situative Versus Cognitive Perspectives: Form Versus Substance." *Educational Researcher,* 1997, *26*(1), 18–21.

Anderson, N. H. *A Functional Theory of Cognition.* Hillsdale, N.J.: Erlbaum, 1996.

Apps, J. W. *Improving Practice in Continuing Education.* San Francisco: Jossey-Bass, 1985.

Apps, J. W. "Adult Education and the Learning Society." *Educational Considerations,* 1987, *14*(2–3), 14–18.

Apps, J. W. *Higher Education in a Learning Society.* San Francisco: Jossey-Bass, 1988.

Apps, J. W. "Providers of Adult and Continuing Education: A Framework." In S. B. Merriam and P. M. Cunningham (eds.), *Handbook of Adult and Continuing Education.* San Francisco: Jossey-Bass, 1989.

Apter, T. *Secret Paths: Women in the New Midlife.* New York: Norton, 1995.

Argyris, C., and Schön, D. A. *Theory in Practice: Increasing Professional Effectiveness.* San Francisco: Jossey-Bass, 1974.

Argyris, C., and Schön, D. A. *Organizational Learning: A Theory of Action Perspective.* San Francisco: Jossey-Bass, 1978.

Arlin, P. K. "Cognitive Development in Adulthood: A Fifth Stage?" *Developmental Psychology,* 1975, *11,* 602–606.

Arlin, P. K. "Adolescent and Adult Thought: A Structural Interpretation." In M. L. Commons, F. A. Richards, and C. Armon (eds.), *Beyond Formal Operations: Late Adolescent and Adult Cognitive Development.* New York: Praeger, 1984.

Ashar, H., and Skenes, R. "Can Tinto's Student Departure Model Be Applied to Nontraditional Students?" *Adult Education Quarterly,* 1993, *43*(2), 90–100.

Aslanian, C. B., and Brickell, H. M. *Americans in Transition: Life Changes as Reasons for Adult Learning.* New York: College Entrance Examination Board, 1980.

Attewell, P. A. "The Productivity Paradox." *Chronicle of Higher Education,* Mar. 15, 1996, p. A56.

Ausubel, D. P. "A Cognitive Structure Theory of School Learning." In L. Siegel (ed.), *Instruction: Some Contemporary Viewpoints.* San Francisco: Chandler, 1967.

Ausubel, D. P. *Educational Psychology: A Cognitive View.* New York: Holt, Rinehart & Winston, 1968.

Bagnall, R. G. "Researching Participation in Adult Education: A Case of Quantified Distortion." *International Journal of Lifelong Education,* 1989, *8*(3), 251–260.

Bagnall, R. G. "Education Beyond Macro-level Needs: A Critique of Boshier's Model for the Future." *International Journal of Lifelong Education,* 1990, *9*(4), 317–330.

Bagnall, R. G. "Discriminative Justice and Responsibility in Postmodernist Adult Education." *Adult Education Quarterly,* 1995, *45*(2), 79–94.

Bailey, J. J., Tisdell, E. J., and Cervero, R. M. "Race, Gender, and the Politics of Professionalism." In E. Hayes and S. A. J. Colin III (eds.), *Confronting Racism and Sexism* (pp. 63–76). New Directions for Adult and Continuing Education, no. 61. San Francisco: Jossey-Bass, 1994.

Bakari, S. "Epistemology from an Afrocentric Perspective." Unpublished paper. Greeley: University of Northern Colorado, Division of Educational Leadership and Policy Studies, 1997.

Baltes, P. B. "Life-Span Development Psychology: Some Conveying Observations on History and Theory." In K. W. Schaie and J. Geiwitz (eds.), *Readings in Adult Development and Aging.* Boston: Little, Brown, 1982.

Baltes, P. B. "Theoretical Propositions of Life-Span Developmental Psychology: On the Dynamics Between Growth and Decline." *Developmental Psychology,* 1987, *23*, 611–626, 1987.

Baltes, P. B. "The Aging Mind: Potential and Limits." *Gerontologist,* 1993, *33*(5), 580–594.

Baltes, P. B., Dittmann-Kohli, F., and Dixon, R. "New Perspectives on the Development on Intelligence in Adulthood: Toward a Dual Process Conception and a Model of Selective Optimization with Compensation." In P. B. Baltes and O. G. Brim (eds.), *Life-Span Development and Behavior.* Vol. 6. Orlando, Fla.: Academic Press, 1984.

Baltes, P. B., and Lindenberger, U. "Emergence of a Powerful Connection Between Sensory and Cognitive Functions Across the Adult Life Span: A New Window to the Study of Cognitive Aging?" *Psychology and Aging,* 1997, *12*(1), 12–21.

Baltes, P. B., and Reese, H. W. "The Life-Span Perspective in Developmental Psychology." In M. Bornstein and M. E. Lamb (eds.), *Developmental Psychology: An Advanced Textbook.* Hillsdale, N.J.: Erlbaum, 1984.

Baltes, P. B., and Smith, J. "Toward a Psychology of Wisdom and Its Ontogenesis." In R. J. Sternberg (ed.), *Wisdom: Its Nature, Origins, and Development.* Cambridge, Mass.: Harvard University Press, 1990.

Baltes, P. B., and Willis, S. L. "Plasticity and Enhancement of Intellectual

Functioning: Penn State's Adult Development and Enrichment Project (ADEPT)." In M. Craig and S. Trehub (eds.), *Aging and Cognitive Processes.* New York: Plenum, 1982.

Bandura, A. "Modeling Theory." In W. S. Sahakian (ed.), *Learning: Systems, Models, and Theories.* (2nd ed.) Chicago: Rand McNally, 1976.

Bandura, A. *Social Foundations of Thought and Action: A Social Cognitive Theory.* Englewood Cliffs, N.J.: Prentice Hall, 1986.

Baptiste, I. "Towards a Pedagogy of Disempowering Our Enemies." *Proceedings of the Adult Education Research Conference,* no. 39. San Antonio, Tex.: University of the Incarnate Word and Texas A&M University, 1998.

Baptiste, I., and Brookfield, S. "Your So-Called Democracy Is Hypocritical Because You Can Always Fail Us: Learning and Living Democratic Contradictions in Graduate Adult Education." In P. Armstrong, N. Miller, and M. Zukas (eds.), *Crossing Borders, Breaking Boundaries: Proceedings of the 27th Annual SCUTREA Conference.* London: Birkbeck College, University of London, July 1997.

Barnett, B. G. "Reflection: The Cornerstone of Learning from Experience." Paper presented at the University Council for Educational Administrators Annual Convention, Scottsdale, Ariz., October 1989.

Baruch, G. K., Barnett, R. C., and Rivers, C. *Lifeprints.* New York: McGraw-Hill, 1983.

Basseches, M. *Dialectical Thinking and Adult Development.* Norwood, N.J.: Ablex, 1984.

Bateson, M. C. *Composing a Life.* New York: Atlantic Monthly Press, 1989.

Bateson, M. C. *Peripheral Visions: Learning Along the Way.* New York: HarperCollins, 1994.

Baum, J. "Testing the Theory of Margin Using a Population of Widows." *Proceedings of the Adult Education Research Conference,* no. 21. Vancouver: University of British Columbia, 1980.

Baxter Magolda, M. *Knowing and Reasoning in College: Gender-Related Patterns in Students' Intellectual Development.* San Francisco: Jossey-Bass, 1992.

Baxter Magolda, M. "The Integration of Relational and Impersonal Knowing in Young Adults' Epistemological Development." *Journal of College Student Development,* 1995, *36*(3), 205–216.

Bayha, R. A. "Self-Directed Learning of Northwest Missouri Farmers as Related to Learning Resource Choice and Valuing." Unpublished doctoral dissertation, Kansas State University, 1983.

Beatty, P. T., and Wolf, M. A. *Connecting with Older Adults: Educational Responses and Approaches.* Malabar, Fla.: Krieger Publishing, 1996.

Beck, L. G. *Reclaiming Educational Administration as a Caring Profession.* New York: Teachers College Press, 1994.

Beder, H. "Dominant Paradigms, Adult Education, and Social Justice." *Adult Education Quarterly,* 1987, *37*(2), 105–113.

Beder, H. "Popular Education: An Appropriate Educational Strategy for Community-Based Organizations." In P. A. Sissel (ed.), *A Community-based Approach to Literacy Programs: Taking Learners' Lives into Account.* New Directions for Adult and Continuing Education, no. 70. San Francisco: Jossey-Bass, 1996.

Beder, H., and Carrea, N. "The Effects of Andragogical Teacher Training on Adult Students' Attendance and Evaluation of Their Teachers." *Adult Education Quarterly,* 1988, *40*(4), 207–218.

Beder, H., and Darkenwald, G. "Differences Between Teaching Adults and Pre-Adults: Some Propositions and Findings." *Adult Education,* 1982, *32*(3), 142–155.

Bee, H. L. *Journey of Adulthood.* (3rd ed.) Englewood Cliffs, N.J.: Prentice Hall, 1996.

Bejot, D. D. "The Degree of Self-Directedness and the Choices of Learning Methods as Related to a Cooperative Extension Program." Unpublished doctoral dissertation, Iowa State University, 1981.

Belanger, P. "Trends in Adult Education Policy." *Adult Education and Development,* 1996, *47,* 19–29.

Belenky, M. F., Bond, L. A., and Weinstock, J. S. *A Tradition That Has No Name: Nurturing the Development of People, Families, and Communities.* New York: Basic Books, 1997.

Belenky, M. F., Clinchy, B. M., Goldberger, N. R., and Tarule, J. M. *Women's Ways of Knowing: The Development of Self, Voice, and Mind.* New York: Basic Books, 1986.

Bell, Y. R. "A Culturally Sensitive Analysis of Black Learning Style." *Journal of Black Psychology,* 1994, *20*(1), 47–61.

Bell-Scott, P. "Telling Flat-Footed Truths: An Introduction." In P. Bell-Scott with J.Johnson-Bailey, *Flat-Footed Truths: Telling Black Women's Lives.* New York: Henry Holt, 1998.

Bell-Scott, P., with Johnson-Bailey, J. *Flat-Footed Truths: Telling Black Women's Lives.* New York: Henry Holt, 1998.

Bem, S. L. *The Lenses of Gender: Transforming the Debate on Sexual Inequality.* New Haven, Conn.: Yale University Press, 1993.

Benack, S., and Basseches, M. A. "Dialectical Thinking and Relativistic Epistemology: Their Relation in Adult Development." In M. L. Commons, J. D. Sinnott, F. A. Richards, and C. Armon (eds.), *Adult Development*. New York: Praeger, 1989.

Bengtson, V. L. (ed.) *Adulthood and Aging: Research on Continuities and Discontinuities*. New York: Springer, 1996.

Benn, R. "Participation in Adult Education: Breaking Boundaries or Developing Inequalities?" In P. Armstrong, N. Miller, and M. Zukas (eds.), *Crossing Borders, Breaking Boundaries: Proceedings of the 27th Annual SCUTREA Conference*. London: Birbeck College, University of London, July 1997.

Bennett-Woods, D. "Reflections on Wisdom." Unpublished paper, University of Northern Colorado, 1997.

Berg, C. A. "Perspectives for Viewing Intellectual Development Throughout the Life Course." In R. J. Sternberg and C. A. Berg (eds.), *Intellectual Development*. New York: Cambridge University Press, 1992.

Berg, C. A., and Sternberg, R. J. "Adults' Conceptions of Intelligence Across the Adult Life Span." *Psychology and Aging*, 1992, *7*(2), 221–231.

Berger, K. S. *The Developing Person Through the Life Span*. (4th ed.) New York: Worth Publishers, 1998.

Berger, N. "A Qualitative Study of the Process of Self-Directed Learning." Unpublished doctoral dissertation, Virginia Commonwealth University, 1990.

Berry, J. W. "A Cultural Ecology of Cognition." In I. Dennis and P. Tapsfield (eds.), *Human Abilities*. Hillsdale, N.J.: Erlbaum, 1996.

Bierema, L. "A Feminist Critique of Human Resource Development Research." *Proceedings of the Adult Education Research Conference*, no. 39. San Antonio, Tex.: University of the Incarnate Word and Texas A&M University, 1998.

Binet, A. *The Development of Intelligence in Children (the Binet-Simon Scale)*. Baltimore: Williams & Williams, 1916.

Bischof, L. J. *Adult Psychology*. New York: HarperCollins, 1969.

Bissette, G. "Chemical Messengers." In E. W. Busse and D. G. Blazer (eds.), *Textbook of Geriatric Psychiatry*. (2nd ed.) Washington, D.C.: American Psychiatric Press, 1996.

Blackburn, J. A., and Papalia, D. E. "The Study of Adult Cognition from a Piagetian Perspective." In R. J. Sternberg and C. A. Berg (eds.), *Intellectual Development*. New York: Cambridge University Press, 1992.

Blaxter, L., and Tight, M. "Life Transitions and Educational Participation by Adults." *International Journal of Lifelong Education,* 1995, *14*(3), 231– 246.

Bloom, M. "Multiple Roles of the Mentor Supporting Women's Adult Development." In K. Taylor and C. Marienau (eds.), *Learning Environments for Women's Adult Development: Bridges Toward Change.* New Directions for Adult and Continuing Education, no. 65. San Francisco: Jossey-Bass, 1995.

Bock, J. C., and Bock, C. M. "Nonformal Education Policy: Developing Countries." In C. J. Titmus (ed.), *Lifelong Education for Adults: An International Handbook.* Oxford: Pergamon Press, 1989.

Bode, H. B. *Conflicting Psychologies of Learning.* New York: Heath, 1929.

Bonham, L. A. "Theoretical and Practical Differences and Similarities Among Selected Cognitive and Learning Styles of Adults: An Analysis of the Literature, Vol. I and II." Unpublished doctoral dissertation, University of Georgia, 1987.

Bonham, L. A. "Learning Style Use: In Need of Perspective." *Lifelong Learning,* 1988, *11*(5), 14–17.

Bors, D. A., and Forrin, B. "Age, Speed of Information Processing, Recall, and Fluid Intelligence." *Intelligence,* 1995, *20*(3), 229–248.

Boshier, R. "Motivational Orientations of Adult Education Participants: A Factor Analytic Exploration of Houle's Typology." *Adult Education,* 1971, *21*(2), 3–26.

Boshier, R. "Educational Participation and Dropout: A Theoretical Model." *Adult Education,* 1973, *23,* 255–282.

Boshier, R. "Motivational Orientation Re-visited: Life-Space Motives and the Education Participation Scale." *Adult Education,* 1977, *27*(2), 89–115.

Boshier, R. "Proaction for Change: Some Guidelines for the Future." *International Journal of Lifelong Education,* 1986, *5*(1), 15–31.

Boshier, R., and Collins, J. B. "The Houle Typology After Twenty-Two Years: A Large-Scale Empircal Test." *Adult Education Quarterly,* 1985, *35*(3), 113– 130.

Botwinick, J. "Intellectual Abilities." In J. E. Birren and K. W. Schaie (eds.), *Handbook of the Psychology of Aging.* New York: Van Nostrand Reinhold, 1977.

Bouchard, P. "Self-Directed Professionals and Autodidactic Choice: A Framework for Analysis." Unpublished paper, Concordia University, 1994. (ED 377 298)

Boucouvalas, M. "Learning Throughout Life: The Information-Knowledge-Wisdom Framework." *Educational Considerations,* 1987, *14*(2–3), 32–38.

Boucouvalas, M. "An Analysis and Critique of the Concept of Self in Self-Directed Learning: Toward a More Robust Construct for Research and Practice." In M. Zukas (ed.), *Papers from the Transatlantic Dialogue: SCUTREA 1988.* Leeds, England: School of Continuing Education, University of Leeds, July 1988a, 56–61.

Boucouvalas, M. "Research and Development in the Neurosciences: Relevance for Adult Education." *Proceedings of the Adult Education Research Conference,* no. 29. Calgary, Alberta, Canada: University of Calgary, 1988b.

Boucouvalas, M. "Consciousness and Learning: New and Renewed Approaches." In S. B. Merriam (ed.), *An Update on Adult Learning Theory.* New Directions for Adult and Continuing Education, no. 57. San Francisco: Jossey-Bass, 1993.

Boucouvalas, M. "An Analysis and Critique of Transformation Theory and Adult Learning: Contributions from Consciousness Studies." In P. Armstrong, N. Miller, and M. Zukas (eds.), *Crossing Borders, Breaking Boundaries: Proceedings of the 27th Annual SCUTREA Conference.* London: Birbeck College, University of London, July 1997.

Boud, D., Keogh, R., and Walker, D. (eds.) *Reflection: Turning Experience into Learning.* New York: Kogan Page, 1985.

Boud, D., Keogh, R., and Walker, D. "Promoting Reflection in Learning: A Model." In R. Edwards, A. Hanson, and P. Raggatt (eds.), *Boundaries of Adult Learning.* New York: Routledge, 1996.

Boud, D., and Miller, N. "Synthesizing Traditions and Identifying Themes in Learning from Experience." In D. Boud and N. Miller (eds.), *Working with Experience: Animating Learning.* New York: Routledge, 1996a.

Boud, D., and Miller, N. (eds.). *Working with Experience: Animating Learning.* New York: Routledge, 1996b.

Boud, D., and Miller, N. "Animating Learning: New Conceptions of the Role of the Person Who Works with Learners." *Proceedings of the Adult Education Research Conference,* no. 39. San Antonio, Tex.: University of the Incarnate Word and Texas A&M University, 1998.

Boud, D., and Walker, D. "Making the Most of Experience." *Studies in Continuing Education,* 1990, *12*(2), 61–80.

Boud, D., and Walker, D. "In the Midst of Experience: Developing a Model to Aid Learners and Facilitators." In J. Mulligan and C. Griffin (eds.), *Empowerment Through Experiential Learning.* London: Kogan Page, 1992.

Bowman, C. "BLS Projections to 2006—A Summary." *Monthly Labor Review,* 1977, *120*(11), 3–5.

Brandt, B. L., Farmer, J. A., Jr., and Buckmaster, A. "Cognitive Apprenticeship Approach to Helping Adults Learn." In D. D. Flannery (ed.), *Applying Cognitive Learning Theory to Adult Learning.* New Directions for Adult and Continuing Education, no. 59. San Francisco: Jossey-Bass, 1993.

Brennan, B. "Indigenous Learning Re-Visited." *Adult Education and Development,* 1990, *35,* 73–83.

Brennan, B. "Reconceptualizing Non-Formal Education." *International Journal of Lifelong Education,* 1997, *16*(3), 185–200.

Bridges, W. *Transitions.* Reading, Mass.: Addison-Wesley, 1980.

Bridges, W. *Managing Transitions: Making the Most of Change.* Reading, Mass.: Addison-Wesley, 1991.

Brim, O. G., and Ryff, C. D. "On the Properties of Life Events." In R. Baltes and O. Brim (eds.), *Life-Span Development and Behavior.* Vol. 3. Orlando, Fla.: Academic Press, 1980.

Briscoe, D. B., and Ross, J. M. "Racial and Ethnic Minorities and Adult Education." In S. B. Merriam and P. M. Cunningham (eds.), *Handbook of Adult and Continuing Education.* San Francisco: Jossey-Bass, 1989.

Brockett, R. G. "Methodological and Substantive Issues in the Measurement of Self-Directed Learning Readiness." *Adult Education Quarterly,* 1985a, *36* (1), 15–24.

Brockett, R. G. "The Relationship Between Self-Directed Learning Readiness and Life Satisfaction Among Older Adults." *Adult Education Quarterly,* 1985b, *35*(4), 210–219.

Brockett, R. G. (ed.). *Ethical Issues in Adult Education.* New York: Teachers College Press, 1988.

Brockett, R. G. "Resistance to Self-Direction in Adult Learning: Myths and Misunderstandings." In R. Hiemstra and R. G. Brockett (eds.), *Overcoming Resistance to Self-Directed Adult Learning.* New Directions for Adult and Continuing Education, no. 64. San Francisco: Jossey-Bass, 1994.

Brockett, R. G., and Hiemstra, R. *Self-Direction in Adult Learning: Perspectives on Theory, Research, and Practice.* New York: Routledge, 1991.

Bronfenbrenner, U. "Developmental Ecology Through Space and Time: A Future Perspective." In P. Moen, G. H. Elder, and K. Lüscher (eds.), *Examining Lives in Context: Perspectives on the Ecology of Human Development.* Washington, D.C.: American Psychological Association, 1995.

Brookfield, S. "Self-Directed Adult Learning: A Critical Paradigm." *Adult Education Quarterly,* 1984, *35*(2), 59–71.

Brookfield, S. "Self-Directed Learning: A Critical Review of Research." In S. Brookfield (ed.), *Self-Directed Learning: From Theory to Practice.* New Directions for Continuing Education, no. 25. San Francisco: Jossey-Bass, 1985.

Brookfield, S. *Understanding and Facilitating Adult Learning.* San Francisco: Jossey-Bass, 1986.

Brookfield, S. *Developing Critical Thinkers.* San Franciso: Jossey-Bass, 1987.

Brookfield, S. *The Skillful Teacher.* San Francisco: Jossey-Bass, 1990.

Brookfield, S. "Breaking the Code." *Studies in the Education of Adults,* 1993a, *25*(1), 64–91.

Brookfield, S. "Self-Directed Learning, Political Clarity, and the Critical Practice of Adult Education." *Adult Education Quarterly,* 1993b, *43*(4), 227–242.

Brookfield, S. "Tales from the Dark Side: A Phenomenography of Adult Critical Reflection." *Proceedings of the Adult Education Research Conference,* no. 35. Knoxville: University of Tennessee, May 1994.

Brookfield, S. *Becoming a Critically Reflective Teacher.* San Francisco: Jossey-Bass, 1995.

Brookfield, S. "Breaking the Code: Engaging Practitioners in Critical Analysis of Adult Educational Literature." In R. Edwards, A. Hanson, and P. Raggatt (eds.), *Boundaries of Adult Learning.* New York: Routledge, 1996a.

Brookfield, S. "Helping People Learn What They Do: Breaking Dependence on Experts." In D. Boud and N. Miller (eds.), *Working with Experience: Animating Learning.* New York: Routledge, 1996b.

Brookfield, S. "The Postmodern Challenge to Clarity: The Meaning of George Orwell's *Politics and the English Language* for Adult Education Theory." *Proceedings of the Adult Education Research Conference,* no. 37. Tampa, Fla.: University of South Florida, 1996c.

Brooks, A. K., and Edwards, K. "Rewriting the Boundaries of Social Discourse: Collaborative Inquiry into Women's Sexual Identity Development." *Proceedings of the SCUTREA Conference,* no. 27. London: University of London, 1997.

Brougher, J. Z. "Creating a Nourishing Learning Environment for Adults Using Multiple Intelligence Theory." *Adult Learning,* 1997, 8(4), 28–29.

Brown, J. S., Collins, A., and Duguid, P. "Situated Cognition and the Culture of Learning." *Educational Researcher,* 1989, *18*(1), 32–42.

Brown, L. M., and Gilligan, C. *Meeting at the Crossroads: Women's Psychol-

ogy and Girls' Development. Cambridge, Mass.: Harvard University Press, 1992.

Bruer, J. T. *Schools for Thought: A Science of Learning in the Classroom.* Cambridge, Mass.: MIT Press, 1993.

Bruer, J. T. "Education and the Brain: A Bridge Too Far." *Educational Researcher,* 1997, *26*(8), 4–16.

Bruner, J. "In Defense of Verbal Learning." In R. C. Anderson and D. P. Ausubel (eds.), *Readings in the Psychology of Cognition.* New York: Holt, Rinehart & Winston, 1965.

Bryant, J. "Normal Adult Development: But What About the Rest of Us?" Unpublished paper, Virginia Commonwealth University, 1989.

Burgess, P. "Reasons for Adult Participation in Group Educational Activities." *Adult Education,* 1971, *22,* 3–29.

Caffarella, R. S. *Psychosocial Development of Women: Linkages to Teaching and Leadership in Adult Education.* Information Series No. 350. Columbus, Ohio: ERIC Clearinghouse of Adult, Career, and Vocational Education, 1992.

Caffarella, R. S. "Facilitating Self-Directed Learning as a Staff Development Option." *Journal of Staff Development,* 1993a, *14*(2), 30–34.

Caffarella, R. S. "Self-Directed Learning." In S. B. Merriam (ed.), *An Update on Adult Learning Theory.* New Directions for Adult and Continuing Education, no. 57. San Francisco: Jossey-Bass, 1993b.

Caffarella, R. S. *Planning Programs for Adult Learners: A Practical Guide for Educators, Trainers, and Staff Developers.* San Francisco: Jossey-Bass, 1994.

Caffarella, R. S. "What Women Have Taught Us About Teaching Adults." *Journal of Staff Development,* 1996, *17*(4), 40–45.

Caffarella, R. S., and Caffarella, E. P. "Self-Directedness and Learning Contracts in Adult Education." *Adult Education Quarterly,* 1986, *36,* 226–234.

Caffarella, R. S., and O'Donnell, J. M. "Self-Directed Adult Learning: A Critical Paradigm Revisited." *Adult Education Quarterly,* 1987, *37,* 199–211.

Caffarella, R. S., and O'Donnell, J. M. "Self-Directed Learning: The Quality Dimension." *Proceedings of the Adult Education Research Conference,* no. 29. Calgary: University of Calgary, 1988.

Caffarella, R. S., and O'Donnell, J. M. *Self-Directed Learning.* Nottingham, England: Department of Adult Education, University of Nottingham, 1989.

Caffarella, R. S., and Olson, S. K. "Psychosocial Development of Women: A Critical Review of the Literature." *Adult Education Quarterly,* 1993, *43*(3), 125–151.

Cain, M. L. "A Critical Ethnography of Adult Learning in the Context of a Social Movement Group." *Proceedings of the Adult Education Research Conference,* no. 39. San Antonio, Tex.: University of the Incarnate Word and Texas A&M University, 1998.

Caine, R. N., and Caine, G. *Making Connections: Teaching and the Human Brain.* Menlo Park, Calif.: Addison-Wesley, 1994.

Cajete, G. *Look to the Mountain: An Ecology of Indigenous Education.* Skyland, N.C.: Kivaki Press, 1994.

Cameron, S. W. "The Perry Scheme: A New Perspective on Adult Learners." *Proceedings of the Adult Education Research Conference,* no. 24. Montreal: Université de Montreal, 1983.

Candy, P. C. "Evolution, Revolution or Devolution: Increasing Learner Control in the Instructional Setting." In D. Boud and V. Griffin (eds.), *Appreciating Adults Learning: From the Learner's Perspective.* London: Kogan Page, 1987.

Candy, P. C. *Self-Direction for Lifelong Learning.* San Francisco: Jossey-Bass, 1991.

Carre, P. "Self (-Directed) Learning in France." In G. A. Straka (ed.), *European Views of Self-Directed Learning: Historical, Conceptional, Empirical, Practical, Vocational.* Munster, Germany: Waxmann, 1997.

Cass, V. C. "Homosexual Identity: A Concept in Need of Definition." *Journal of Homosexuality,* 1979, *9,* 214–235.

Cattell, R. B. "Theory of Fluid and Crystallized Intelligence: A Critical Approach." *Journal of Educational Psychology,* 1963, *54*(1), 1–22.

Cattell, R. B. *Intelligence: Its Structure, Growth and Action.* Amsterdam: North-Holland 1987.

Cavaliere, L. A. "The Wright Brothers' Odyssey: Their Flight of Learning." In L. A. Cavaliere and A. Sgroi (eds.), *Learning for Personal Development.* New Directions for Adult and Continuing Education, no. 53. San Francisco: Jossey-Bass, 1992.

Cervero, R. M. *Effective Continuing Education for Professionals.* San Francisco: Jossey-Bass, 1988.

Cervero, R. M. "Relationships Between Theory and Practice." In J. Peters and P. Jarvis (eds.), *Adult Education: Evolution and Achievements in a Developing Field of Study.* San Francisco: Jossey-Bass, 1991.

Cervero, R. M., and Kirkpatrick, T. E. "The Enduring Effects of Pre-Adult

Factors on Participation in Adult Education." *American Journal of Education,* 1990, *99,* 77–94.

Cervero, R. M., and Wilson, A. L. *Planning Responsibly for Adult Education: A Guide to Negotiating Power and Interests.* San Francisco: Jossey-Bass, 1994.

Chapman, V. L. "Adult Education and the Body: Changing Performances of Teaching and Learning." *Proceedings of the Adult Education Research Conference,* no. 39. San Antonio, Tex.: University of the Incarnate Word and Texas A&M University, 1998.

Charner, I., and Rolzinski, C. A. "New Directions for Responding to a Changing Economy: Integrating Education and Work." In I. Charner and C. A. Rolzinski (eds.), *Responding to the Educational Needs of Today's Workplace.* New Directions for Continuing Education, no. 33. San Francisco: Jossey-Bass, 1987.

Chávez, A. F., Guido-DiBrito, F., and Mallory, S. "Learning to Value the 'Other': A Model of Diversity Development." Unpublished paper, 1996.

Chene, A. "The Concept of Autonomy: A Philosophical Discussion." *Adult Education Quarterly,* 1983, *34,* 38–47.

Chi, M. T. H., Glaser, R., and Farr, M. J. (eds.). *The Nature of Expertise.* Hillsdale, N.J.: Erlbaum, 1988.

Chickering, A. W., and Reisser, L. *Education and Identity.* (2nd ed.) San Francisco: Jossey-Bass, 1993.

Choi, J., and Hannafin, M. "Situated Cognition and Learning Environments: Roles, Structures, and Implications for Design." *Educational Technology Research and Design,* 1995, *43*(2), 53–69.

Christensen, H. "Age Differences in Tests of Intelligence and Memory in High and Low Ability Subjects: A Second Sample of Eminent Academics and Scientists." *Personality and Individual Differences,* 1994, *16*(6), 919–929.

Clancey, W. J. *Situated Cognition: On Human Knowledge and Computer Representations.* New York: Cambridge University Press, 1997.

Clark, M. C. "Structuring and Restructuring of Meaning: An Analysis of the Impact of Context on Transformational Learning." Doctoral dissertation prospectus, University of Georgia, 1990.

Clark, M. C. "Changing Course: Initiating the Transformational Learning Process." *Proceedings of the Adult Education Research Conference,* no. 33. Saskatoon: University of Saskatchewan, May 1993a.

Clark, M. C. "Transformational Learning." In S. B. Merriam (ed.), *An*

Update on Adult Learning Theory. New Directions for Adult and Continuing Education, no. 57. San Francisco: Jossey-Bass, 1993b.

Clark, M. C. "Learning as a Non-Unitary Self: Implications of Postmodernism for Adult Learning Theory." In P. Armstrong, N. Miller, and M. Zukas (eds.), *Crossing Borders, Breaking Boundaries: Proceedings of the 27th Annual SCUTREA Conference.* London: Birkbeck College, University of London, July 1997.

Clark, M. C., and Wilson, A. L. "Context and Rationality in Mezirow's Theory of Transformational Learning." *Adult Education Quarterly,* 1991, *41*(2), 75–91.

Clausen, J. A. *American Lives: Looking Back at the Children of the Great Depression.* New York: Free Press, 1993.

Clausen, J. A. "Gender, Contexts, and Turning Points in Adults' Lives." In P. Moen, G. H. Elder, and K. Lüscher (eds.), *Examining Lives in Context: Perspectives on the Ecology of Human Development.* Washington, D.C.: American Psychological Association, 1995.

Claxton, C. S., and Murrell, P. H. *Learning Styles: Implications for Improving Educational Practices.* ASHE-ERIC Higher Education Reports, no. 4. Washington, D.C.: Association for the Study of Higher Education, 1987.

Cobb, P. "Where Is the Mind? Constructivist and Sociocultural Perspectives on Mathematical Development." *Educational Researcher,* 1994, *23*(7), 13–20.

Cognition and Technology Group at Vanderbilt. "Anchored Instruction and Its Relationship to Situated Cognition." *Educational Researcher,* 1990, *19*(6), 2–10.

Cognition and Technology Group at Vanderbilt. "The Jasper Experiment: An Exploration of Issues in Learning and Instructional Design." *Educational Technology,* 1992, *40*(1), 65–80.

Cognition and Technology Group at Vanderbilt. "Anchored Instruction and Situated Cognition Revisited." *Educational Technology,* 1993, *33*(3), 52–70.

Cohen, N. H. *Mentoring Adult Learners: A Guide for Educators and Trainers.* Melbourne, Fla.: Krieger Publishing Company, 1995.

Coles, R., and Coles, J. H. *Women of Crisis.* New York: Dell, 1978.

Coles, R., and Coles, J. H. *Women of Crisis II.* New York: Dell, 1980.

Colin, S. A. J., III, and Preciphs, T. K. "Perceptual Patterns and the Learning Environment: Confronting White Racism." In R. Hiemstra (ed.), *Creating Environments for Effective Adult Learning.* New Directions for Adult and Continuing Education, no. 50. San Francisco: Jossey-Bass, 1991.

Collard, S. "Remapping Adult Education: Beyond Social Movement and Professionalization." *Proceedings of the Adult Education Research Conference*, no. 36. Edmonton, Alberta: University of Alberta, May 1995.

Collard, S., and Law, M. "The Limits of Perspective Transformation: A Critique of Mezirow's Theory." *Adult Education Quarterly*, 1989, *39(2)*, 99–107.

The College Board. *Adult Learning in America: Why and How Adults Go Back to School*. New York: The College Board, in press.

Collins, M. "Self-Directed Learning or an Emancipatory Practice of Adult Education: Re-Thinking the Role of the Adult Educator." *Proceedings of the Adult Education Research Conference*, no. 29. Calgary: University of Calgary, 1988.

Collins, M. *Adult Education as Vocation*. New York: Routledge, 1991.

Collins, M. "Current Trends in Adult Education: From Self-Directed Learning to Critical Theory." Paper presented at the sixth annual meeting of the Association of Process Philosophy of Education, American Philosophical Association (Central Division) Annual Meetings, Louisville, Ky., April 1992.

Collins, M. "From Self-Directed Learning to Post-Modernist Thought in Adult Education: Relocating our Object of Theory and Practice." *Proceedings of the Adult Education Research Conference*, no. 35. Knoxville: University of Tennessee, 1994.

Collins, M. "Critical Commentaries on the Role of the Adult Educator: From Self-Directed Learning to Postmodernist Sensibilities." In M. R. Welton (ed.), *In Defense of the Lifeworld* (pp. 71–98). Albany, N.Y.: State University of New York Press, 1995a.

Collins, M. "In the Wake of Postmodernist Sensibilities and Opting for a Critical Return." In M. R. Welton (ed.), *In Defense of the Lifeworld* (pp. 195–201). Albany, N.Y.: State University of New York Press, 1995b.

Collins, M. "On Contemporary Practice and Research: Self-Directed Learning to Critical Theory." In R. Edwards, A. Hanson, and P. Raggatt (eds.), *Boundaries of Adult Learning: Adult Learners, Education and Training*. New York: Routledge, 1996.

Collins, M., and Collard, S. "Examining the Case for Class Analysis in Adult Education Research." *Proceedings of the Adult Education Research Conference*, no. 36. Edmonton, Alberta: University of Alberta, May 1995.

Collins, M. A., Brick, J. M., and Kim, K. "The Measurement of Participation in Adult Education." *Proceedings of the Adult Education Research Conference*, no. 38. Stillwater: Oklahoma State University, May 1997.

Collins, P. H. *Black Feminist Thought: Knowledge, Consciousness and the Politics of Empowerment*. New York: Routledge, 1990.

Confessore, G. J., and Confessore, S. J. *Guideposts to Self-Directed Learning: Expert Commentary on Essential Concepts*. King of Prussia, Pa.: Organizational Design and Development, 1992.

Confessore, S. J., and Confessore, G. J. "Learner Profiles: A Cross-Sectional Study of Selected Factors Associated with Self-Directed Learning." In H. B. Long and others (eds.), *New Ideas about Self-Directed Learning*. Norman: Oklahoma Research Center for Continuing Professional and Higher Education, University of Oklahoma, 1994.

Connelly, R. J., and Light, K. M. "An Interdisciplinary Code of Ethics for Adult Education." *Adult Education Quarterly*, 1991, *41*(4), 233–240.

Cookson, P. S. "A Framework for Theory and Research on Adult Education Participation." *Adult Education Quarterly*, 1986, *36* (3), 130–141.

Cookson, P. S. "The Interdisciplinary, Sequential Specificity, Time Allocation, Lifespan Model of Social Participation: A Report of Two Applications in Adult Education." *Proceedings of the 1987 Lifelong Learning Research Conference*. College Park: University of Maryland, 1987.

Coombs, P. H. *The World Crisis in Education: A View from the Eighties*. New York: Oxford University Press, 1985.

Coombs, P. H., Prosser, R. C., and Ahmed, M. *New Paths to Learning: For Rural Children and Youth*. New York: International Council for Educational Development, 1973.

Costa, P. T., Jr., and McCrae, R. R. "Still Stable After All These Years: Personality as a Key to Some Issues in Adulthood and Old Age." In P. Baltes and O. G. Brim (eds.), *Life-Span Development and Behavior*. Vol. 3. Orlando, Fla.: Academic Press, 1980.

Costa, P. T., Jr., and McCrae, R. R. "Set Like Plaster? Evidence for the Stability of Adult Personality." In T. F. Hetherton and J. L Weinberger (eds.), *Can Personality Change?* Washington, D.C.: American Psychological Association, 1994.

Courtenay, B. C., Arnold, G. W., and Kim, K. "An Examination of the Empirical Basis for Involving Adult Learners in Planning Their Learning Experiences." *International Journal of Lifelong Education*, 1994, *13*(4), 291–300.

Courtenay, B. C., Merriam, S. B., and Reeves, P. "The Centrality of Meaning-Making in Transformational Learning: How HIV-Positive Adults Make Sense of Their Lives." *Adult Education Quarterly*, 1998, *48*(2), 63–82.

Courtney, S. *Why Adults Learn: Toward a Theory of Participation in Adult Education*. New York: Routledge, 1992.

Cranton, P. "Self-Directed and Transformative Instructional Development." *Journal of Higher Education,* 1994a, *65*(6), 726–744.

Cranton, P. *Understanding and Promoting Transformative Learning.* San Francisco: Jossey-Bass, 1994b.

Cranton, P. *Professional Development as Transformative Learning.* San Francisco: Jossey-Bass, 1996.

Cranton, P. (ed.). *Transformative Learning in Action: Insights from Practice.* New Directions for Adult and Continuing Education, no. 74. San Francisco: Jossey-Bass, 1997.

Creel, D. W. "Transitions in Adult Development: Implications for Adult Education." *Research and Teaching in Developmental Education,* 1996, *12*(2), 61–69.

Crick, F., and Koch, C. "The Problem of Consciousness." *Scientific American,* 1992, *267*(3), 153–159.

Criticos, C. "Experiential Learning and Social Transformation for a Post-Apartheid Learning Future." In D. Boud, R. Cohen, and D. Walker (eds.), *Using Experience for Learning.* Buckingham, England, and Bristol, Pa.: Society for Research into Higher Education and Open University Press, 1993.

Cropley, A. J. "Factors in Participation." In C. J. Titus (ed.), *Lifelong Education for Adults: An International Handbook* (pp. 145–147). New York: Pergamon Press, 1989.

Crose, R. *Why Women Live Longer Than Men.* San Francisco: Jossey-Bass, 1997.

Cross, K. P. *Adults as Learners: Increasing Participation and Facilitating Learning.* San Francisco: Jossey-Bass, 1981.

Cross, K. P., and McCartan, A. *Adult Learning: State Policies and Institutional Practices.* ASHE-ERIC Higher Education Research Reports, no. 1. Washington, D.C.: Association for the Study of Higher Education, 1984.

Cross, W. E. *Shades of Black: Diversity in African-American Identity.* Philadelphia: Temple University Press, 1991.

Cross, W. W., Jr. "The Psychology of Nigrescence: Revising the Cross Model." In J. G. Ponterrotto, J. M. Casas, L. A. Suzuki, and C. M. Alexander (eds.), *Handbook of Multicultural Counseling.* Thousand Oaks, Calif.: Sage, 1995.

Cunningham, J., and Fitzgerald, J. "Epistemology and Reading." *Reading Research Quarterly,* 1996, *31*(1), 36–60.

Cunningham, P. M. "The Adult Educator and Social Responsibility." In R. G. Brockett (ed.), *Ethical Issues in Adult Education.* New York: Teachers College Press, 1988.

Cunningham, P. M. "From Freire to Feminism: The North American Experience with Critical Pedagogy." *Adult Education Quarterly,* 1992, *42,* 180–191.

Cunningham, P. M., and Curry, R. "Learning Within a Social Movement: The Chicago-African-American Experience." *Proceedings of the Adult Education Research Conference,* no. 38. Stillwater: Oklahoma State University, May 1997.

Daley, B. J. "Novice to Expert: How Do Professionals Learn?" *Proceedings of the Adult Education Research Conference,* no. 39. San Antonio, Tex.: University of the Incarnate Word and Texas A&M University, 1998.

Daloz, L. A. *Effective Teaching and Mentoring: Realizing the Transformational Power of Adult Learning Experiences.* San Francisco: Jossey-Bass, 1986.

Daloz, L. A. "Beyond Tribalism: Renaming the Good, the True, and the Beautiful." *Adult Education Quarterly,* 1988a, *38*(4), 234–241.

Daloz, L. A. "The Story of Gladys Who Refused to Grow: A Morality Tale for Mentors." *Lifelong Learning: An Omnibus of Practice and Research,* 1988b, *11*(4), 4–7.

Daloz, L. A., Keen, C. H., Keen, J. P., and Parks, S. D. *Common Fire: Lives of Commitment in a Complex World.* Boston: Beacon Press, 1996.

Danis, C. "A Unifying Framework for Date-Based Research into Adult Self-Directed Learning." In H. B. Long and others (eds.), *Self-Directed Learning: Application and Research.* Norman: Oklahoma Research Center for Continuing Professional and Higher Education, University of Oklahoma, 1992.

Danis, C., and Tremblay, N. A. "Propositions Regarding Autodidactic Learning and Their Implications for Teaching." *Lifelong Learning: An Omnibus of Practice and Research,* 1987, *10*(7), 4–7.

Danis, C., and Tremblay, N. A. "Autodidactic Learning Experiences: Questioning Established Adult Learning Principles." In H. B. Long and others (eds.), *Self-Directed Learning: Application and Theory.* Athens: Adult Education Department, University of Georgia, 1988.

Dannefer, D. "Adult Development and Social Theory: A Paradigmatic Reappraisal." *American Sociological Review,* 1984, *49,* 100–116.

Dannefer, D. "Human Action and Its Place in Theories of Aging." *Journal of Aging Studies,* 1989, *3,* 1–20.

Dannefer, D. "Commentary." *Human Development,* 1996, *39,* 150–152.

Darkenwald, G. G., and Merriam, S. B. *Adult Education: Foundations of Practice.* New York: HarperCollins, 1982.

Darkenwald, G. G., and Valentine, T. "Factor Structure of Deterrents to

Public Participation in Adult Education." *Adult Education Quarterly,* 1985, *35*(4), 177–193.

D'Augelli, A. R. "Identity Development and Sexual Orientation: Toward a Model of Lesbian, Gay, and Bisexual Development." In E. J. Trickett, R. J. Watts, and D. Birman (eds.), *Human Diversity: Perspectives on People in Context.* San Francisco: Jossey-Bass, 1994.

D'Augelli, A. R., and Patterson, C. J. *Lesbian, Gay, and Bisexual Identities over the Lifespan: Psychological Perspectives.* New York: Oxford University Press, 1995.

Davenport, J., and Davenport, J. "A Chronology and Analysis of the Andragogy Debate." *Adult Education Quarterly,* 1985, *35*(3), 152–159.

Davis, S. M., and Botkin, J. W. *The Monster Under the Bed.* New York: Simon & Schuster, 1994.

Davis-Harrison, D. "Nonparticipation in Adult Education Programs: Views of Blue-Collar Male Workers with Low-Literacy Skills." *Proceedings of the Adult Education Research Conference,* no. 37. Tampa: University of South Florida, May 1996.

Day, M. "Educational Advising and Brokering: The Ethics of Choice." In R. G. Brockett (ed.), *Ethical Issues in Adult Education.* New York: Teachers College Press, 1988.

De Beauport, E. *The Three Faces of Mind: Developing Your Mental, Emotional, and Behavioral Intelligences.* Wheaton, Ill.: Quest Books, 1996.

Delahaye, B. L., Limerick, D. C., and Hearn, G. "The Relationship Between Andragogical and Pedagogical Orientations and the Implications for Adult Learning." *Adult Education Quarterly,* 1994, *44*(4), 187–200.

Delahaye, B. L., and Smith, H. E. "The Validity of the Learning Preference Assessment." *Adult Education Quarterly,* 1995, *45*(3), 159–173.

deMarrais, K. "John's Story: An Exploration into Critical Theory in Education." *Adult Learning,* 2(8), 1991, 9–10.

Demick, J. "Life Transitions as a Paradigm for the Study of Adult Development." In M. L. Commons, J. Demick, and C. Goldberg (eds.), *Clinical Approaches to Adult Development.* Norwood, N.J.: Ablex, 1996.

Demko, D. J. "Human Resources Correlates of Older Adult Participation in Self-Selected Community College Settings." Abstract from Dissertation Abstracts International: DAI43–06A: 1792, 1982.

Denney, N. W. "Aging and Cognitive Changes." In B. B. Wolman (ed.), *Handbook of Developmental Psychology.* Englewood Cliffs, N.J.: Prentice Hall, 1982.

Derber, C. "Worker Education for a Changing Economy: New Labor-Academic Partnerships." In I. Charner and C. A. Rolzinski (eds.),

Responding to the Educational Needs of Today's Workplace. New Directions for Continuing Education, no. 33. San Francisco: Jossey Bass, 1987.

Deroos, K. K. B. "Persistence of Adults in Independent Study." Unpublished doctoral dissertation, University of Minnesota, 1982.

Deshler, D. "Metaphor Analysis: Exorcising Social Ghosts." In J. Mezirow and Associates, *Fostering Critical Reflection in Adulthood: A Guide to Transformative and Emancipatory Learning* (pp. 296–313). San Francisco: Jossey-Bass, 1990.

Devine, P. "Stereotypes and Prejudice: Their Automatic and Controlled Components." *Journal of Personality and Social Psychology,* 1989, *56*(1), 5–18.

Dewey, J. *How We Think: A Restatement of the Relation of Reflective Thinking on the Educative Practice.* Lexington, Mass.: Heath, 1933.

Dewey, J. *Experience and Education.* New York: Collier Books, 1938.

Di Bella, A. J., and Nevis, E. C. *How Organizations Learn: An Integrated Strategy for Building Learning Capability.* San Francisco: Jossey-Bass, 1998.

Di Bella, A. J., Nevis, E. C., and Gould, J. M. "Organizational Learning Style as a Core Capability." In B. Moingeon and A. Edmondson (eds.), *Organizational Learning and Competitive Advantage.* London: SAGE Publications, 1996.

Di Vesta, F. J. "The Cognitive Movement and Education." In J. Glover and R. Ronning (eds.), *Historical Foundations of Education.* New York: Plenum, 1987.

Dirkx, J. M. "Nurturing Soul in Adult Learning." In P. Cranton (ed.), *Transformative Learning in Action: Insights from Practice.* New Directions for Adult and Continuing Education, no. 74. San Francisco: Jossey-Bass, 1997.

Dirkx, J. M. "Transformative Learning Theory in the Practice of Adult Education: An Overview." *PAACE Journal of Lifelong Learning,* 1998, *7,* 1–14.

Dirkx, J. M., and Jha, L. R. "Completion and Attrition in Adult Basic Education: A Test of Two Pragmatic Prediction Models." *Adult Education Quarterly,* 1994, *45*(1), 269–285.

Dittmann-Kohli, F., and Baltes, P. B. "Toward a Neofunctionalist Conception of Adult Intellectual Development: Wisdom as a Prototypical Case of Intellectual Growth." In C. N. Alexander and E. J. Langer (eds.), *Higher Stages of Human Development: Perspective on Adult Growth.* Oxford: Oxford University Press, 1990.

Dixon, N. M. "The Hallways of Learning." *Organizational Dynamics,* 1997, *25*(4), 23–34.

Dixon, R. A. "Contextual Approaches to Adult Intellectual Development." In R. J. Sternberg and C. A. Berg (eds.), *Intellectual Development.* New York: Cambridge University Press, 1992.

Driver, R., Asoko, H., Leach, J., Mortimer, E., and Scott, P. "Constructing Scientific Knowledge in the Classroom." *Educational Reseacher,* 1994, *23*(7), 5–12.

Durr, R., Guglielmino, L. M., and Guglielmino, P. J. "Self-Directed Learning Readiness and Occupational Categories." In G. N. McLean (ed.), *Human Resource Development Quarterly,* 1996, *7(4),* 349–358.

Dychtwald, K., and Flower, J. "The Third Age." *New Age Journal,* 1989, *6*(1), 50–59.

Eichorn, D. H., Clausen, J. A., Hann, N., Honzik, M. P., and Mussen, P. H. (eds.). *Present and Past in Middle Life.* Orlando, Fla.: Academic Press, 1981.

Elder, G. H. "The Life Course Paradigm: Social Change and Individual Development." In P. Moen, G. H. Elder, and K. Luscher (eds.), *Examining Lives in Context.* Washington, D.C.: American Psychological Association, 1995.

Elias, D. "It's Time to Change Our Minds: An Introduction to Transformative Learning." *ReVision,* 1997, *20*(1), 2–6.

Elias, J. L. "Critique: Andragogy Revisited." *Adult Education,* 1979, *29,* 252–255.

Elias, J. L., and Merriam, S. B. *Philosophical Foundations of Adult Education.* (2nd ed.) Malabar, Fla.: Krieger Publishing Company, 1995.

Elias, J. W., Elias, M. R., and Elias, P. K. "Normal Aging and Disease as Contributors to the Study of Cognitive Processing in Aging." In J. D. Sinnott and J. C. Cavanaugh (eds.), *Bridging Paradigms: Positive Development in Adulthood and Cognitive Aging.* New York: Praeger, 1991.

Ellsworth, E. "Why Doesn't This Feel Empowering? Working Through the Repressive Myths of Critical Pedagogy." *Harvard Educational Review,* 1989, 59(3), 297–324.

Erikson, E. H. *Childhood and Society.* (2nd ed., rev.) New York: Norton, 1963.

Erikson, E. H. *Adulthood.* New York: Norton, 1978.

Erikson, E. H. *The Lifecycle Completed: A Review.* New York: Norton, 1982.

Erikson, E. H., Erikson, J. M., and Kivnick, H. O. *Vital Involvement in Old Age.* New York: Norton, 1986.

Erikson, J. M. *Wisdom and the Senses: The Way of Creativity.* New York: Norton, 1988.

Estes, C. P. *Women Who Run with the Wolves: Myths and Stories of the Wild Woman Archetype.* New York: Ballantine Books, 1992.

Etter-Lewis, G. Introduction to G. Etter-Lewis and M. Foster (eds.), *Unrelated Kin: Race and Gender in Women's Personal Narratives.* New York: Routledge, 1996.

Etter-Lewis, G., and Foster, M. (eds.) *Unrelated Kin: Race and Gender in Women's Personal Narratives.* New York: Routledge, 1996.

Eurich, N. *Corporate Classrooms: The Learning Business.* Princeton, N.J.: Carnegie Foundation for the Advancement of Teaching, 1985.

Eurich, N. *The Learning Industry.* Princeton, N.J.: Carnegie Foundation for the Advancement of Teaching, 1990.

Evans, N. J., Forney, D. S., and Guido-DiBrito, F. *Student Development in College: Theory, Research, and Practice.* San Francisco: Jossey-Bass, 1998.

Ewert, D. M. "Involving Adult Learners in Program Planning." In S. B. Merriam (ed.), *Linking Philosophy and Practice.* New Directions for Continuing Education, no. 15. San Francisco: Jossey-Bass, 1982.

Farley, F. "Biology and Adult Cognition." In R. A. Fellenz (ed.), *Cognition and the Adult Learner.* Bozeman: Center for Adult Learning Research, Montana State University, 1988.

Farmer, J. A., Buckmaster, A., and LeGrand, B. "Cognitive Apprenticeship: Implications for Continuing Professional Education." In H. K. Morris Baskett and V. J. Marsick (eds.), *Professionals' Ways of Knowing: New Findings on How to Improve Professional Education.* New Directions in Adult and Continuing Education, no. 55. San Francisco: Jossey-Bass, 1992.

Fay, C. H., McCune, J. T., and Begin, J. P. "The Setting for Continuing Education in the Year 2000." In R. G. Brockett (ed.), *Continuing Education in the Year 2000.* New Directions for Continuing Education, no. 36. San Francisco: Jossey-Bass, 1987.

Fenimore, M. A. "'My Brain Is Still Working!': Conversations with Centenarians About Learning in Adulthood." *Canadian Journal for the Study of Adult Education,* 1997, *11*(1), 57–70.

Ferry, N., and Ross-Gordon, J. "An Inquiry into Schön's Epistemology of Practice: Exploring Links Between Experience and Reflective Practice." *Adult Education Quarterly,* 1998, *48*(2), 98–112.

Fiddler, M., and Marienau, C. "Linking Learning, Teaching, and Development." In K. Taylor and C. Marienau (eds.), *Learning Environments* for Women's Adult Development: Bridges Toward Change. New Directions for Adult and Continuing Education, no. 65. San Francisco: Jossey-Bass, 1995.

Field, D., Schaie, K. W., and Leino, V. E. "Continuity in Intellectual Functioning: The Role of Self-Reported Health." *Psychology and Aging*, 1988, *3*(4), 385–392.

Field, L. "An Investigation into the Structure, Validity, and Reliability of Guglielmino's Self-Directed Learning Readiness Scale." *Adult Education Quarterly*, 1989, *39*(4), 235–245.

Field, L. "Guglielmino's Self-Directed Learning Readiness Scale: Should It Continue to Be Used?" *Adult Education Quarterly*, 1991, *41*(2), 100–103.

Finger, M. "Adult Education and Society Today." *International Journal of Lifelong Education*, 1995, *14*(2), 110–119.

Fingeret, A. "Social Network: A New Perspective on Independence and Illiterate Adults." *Adult Education* Quarterly, 1983, *33*(3), 133–146.

Fischback, G. D. "Mind and Brain." *Scientific American*, 1992, *267*(3), 48–57.

Flannery, D. D. *Applying Cognitive Learning Theory to Adult Learning.* New Directions for Adult and Continuing Education, no. 59. San Francisco: Jossey-Bass, 1993a.

Flannery, D. D. "Book Review." *Adult Education Quarterly*, 1993b, *43*(2), 110–112.

Flannery, D. D. "Global and Analytical Ways of Processing Information." In D. D. Flannery (ed.), *Applying Cognitive Learning Theory to Adult Learning.* New Directions for Adult and Continuing Education, no. 59. San Francisco: Jossey-Bass, 1993c.

Forest, L. B. "The Cooperative Extension Service." In S. B. Merriam and P. M. Cunningham (eds.), *Handbook of Adult and Continuing Education.* San Francisco: Jossey-Bass, 1989.

Fowler, J. *Stages of Faith: The Psychology of Human Development and the Quest for Meaning.* New York: HarperCollins, 1981.

Fox, R. D., and West, R. F. "Personality Traits and Perceived Benefits Associated with Different Approaches of Medical Students to Self-Directed Learning Projects." *Proceedings of the Adult Education Research Conference*, no. 24. Montreal: Université de Montreal, 1983.

Fraser, S. *The Bell Curve Wars: Race, Intelligence, and the Future of America.* New York: Basic Books, 1995.

Freire, P. *Cultural Action for Freedom.* Harvard Educational Review Monograph Series No. 1. Cambridge, Mass.: Center for the Study of Development and Social Change, 1970a.

Freire, P. *Pedagogy of the Oppressed.* New York: Seabury Press, 1970b.

Freire, P. *Education for Critical Consciousness.* New York: Seabury Press, 1973.

Fujita-Starck, P. J. "Motivations and Characteristics of Adult Students: Factor Stability and Construct Validity of the Educational Participation Scale." *Adult Education Quarterly,* 1996, *47*(1), 29–40.

Gagne, R. M., Briggs, L. J., and Wager, W. W. *Principles of Instructional Design.* (4th ed.) Orlando, Fla.: Harcourt Brace, 1992.

Galbraith, M. W. (ed.) *Education Through Community Organizations.* New Directions for Adult and Continuing Education, no. 47. San Francisco: Jossey-Bass, 1990.

Galbraith, M. W., and Cohen, N. H. (eds.). *Mentoring: New Strategies and Challenges.* New Directions for Adult and Continuing Education, no. 66. San Francisco: Jossey-Bass, 1995.

Gardner, H. *Frames of Mind.* New York: Basic Books, 1983.

Gardner, H. *Multiple Intelligences: The Theory in Practice.* New York: Basic Books, 1993.

Gardner, H. "Reflections on Multiple Intelligences: Myths and Messages." *Phi Delta Kappan,* 1995, *77*(3), 200–209.

Gardner, H., and Hatch, T. "Multiple Intelligences Go to School." *Educational Researcher,* 1989, *18*(8), 4–10.

Gardner, P. "Demographic and Attitudinal Trends: The Increasing Diversity of Today's and Tomorrow's Learner." *Journal of Cooperative Education,* 1996a, *31*(2–3), 58–82.

Gardner, P. "Transitions: Understanding Economic and Workplace Changes at the End of the Century." *Journal of Cooperative Education,* 1996b, *31*(2–3), 41–57.

Garrison, D. R. "An Analysis and Reformulation of McClusky's Concept of Margin for Predicting Adult Dropout." *Proceedings of the Adult Education Research Conference,* no. 27. Syracuse, N.Y.: Syracuse University, May 1986.

Garrison, D. R. "Dropout Prediction Within a Broad Psychological Context: An Analysis of Boshier's Congruence Model." *Adult Education Quarterly,* 1987, *37*(4), 212–222.

Garrison, D. R. "Critical Thinking and Adult Education: A Conceptual Model for Developing Critical Thinking in Adult Learners." *International Journal of Lifelong Learning,* 1991, *10*(4), 287–303.

Garrison, D. R. "Critical Thinking and Self-Directed Learning in Adult Education: An Analysis of Responsibility and Control Issues." *Adult Education Quarterly,* 1992, *42,* 136–148.

Garrison, D. R. "Self-Directed Learning: Toward a Comprehensive Model." *Adult Education Quarterly,* 1997, *48*(1), 18–33.

Gaventa, J. "Participatory Research in North America." *Convergence,* 1988, *21*(2–3), 19–28.

Geisler, K. K. "Learning Efforts of Adults Undertaken for Matriculating into a Community College." Unpublished doctoral dissertation, Texas A&M University, 1984.

Geissler, K. A. "Adult Education in Modern Times—Development and Quality." *Adult Education and Development,* 1996, *47,* 31–54.

Gergen, K. J. *The Saturated Self.* New York: Basic Books, 1991.

Gerstner, L. S. "On the Theme and Variations of Self-Directed Learning: An Exploration of the Literature." Unpublished doctoral dissertation, Teachers College, Columbia University, 1987.

Gerstner, L. S. "What's in a Name? The Language of Self-Directed Learning." In H. B. Long and others (eds.), *Self-Directed Learning: Application and Research.* Norman: Oklahoma Research Center for Continuing Professional and Higher Education, University of Oklahoma, 1992.

Gilligan, C. "Women's Places in Man's Life Cycle." *Harvard Educational Review,* 1979, *49*(4), 431–446.

Gilligan, C. *In a Different Voice.* Cambridge, Mass.: Harvard University Press, 1982.

Gilligan, C. "Remapping Development: The Power of Divergent Data." In L. Cirillo and S. Wapner (eds.), *Value Presuppositions in Theories of Human Development.* Hillsdale, N.J.: Erlbaum, 1986.

Giroux, H. A. "Literacy and the Pedagogy of Voice and Political Empowerment." *Educational Theory,* 1988, *38,* 61–75.

Giroux, H. *Border Crossings: Cultural Workers and the Politics of Education.* New York: Routledge, 1992.

Glaser, R. "Education and Thinking: The Role of Knowledge." *American Psychologist,* 1984, *39*(2), 93–104.

Glaser, R. "Thoughts on Expertise." In C. Schooler and K. Schaie (eds.), *Cognitive Functioning and Social Structure over the Life Course.* Norwood, N.J.: Ablex, 1987.

Glaser, R., and Chi, M. T. H. "Overview." In M. T. H. Chi, R. Glaser, and M. J. Farr (eds.), *The Nature of Expertise.* Hillsdale, N.J.: Erlbaum, 1988.

Goldberger, N. R. "Cultural Imperatives and Diversity in Ways of Knowing." In N. R. Goldberger, J. M. Tarule, B. M. Clinchy, and M. F. Belenky (eds.), *Knowledge, Difference, and Power: Essays Inspired by Women's Ways of Knowing.* New York: Basic Books, 1996a.

Goldberger, N. R. "Looking Backward, Looking Forward." In N. R. Goldberger, J. M. Tarule, B. M. Clinchy, and M. F. Belenky (eds.), *Knowledge, Difference, and Power: Essays Inspired by Women's Ways of Knowing.* New York: Basic Books, 1996b.

Goldberger, N. R., Tarule, J. M., Clinchy, B. M., and Belenky, M. F. (eds.). *Knowledge, Difference, and Power: Essays Inspired by Women's Ways of Knowing.* New York: Basic Books, 1996.

Goleman, D. *Emotional Intelligence: Why It Can Matter More Than IQ.* New York: Bantam Books, 1995.

Gooderham, P. N. "A Conceptual Framework of Sociological Perspectives on the Pursuit by Adults of Access to Higher Education." *International Journal of Lifelong Education,* 1993, *12*(1), 27–39.

Goodnow, J. J. "Using Sociology to Extend Psychological Accounts of Cognitive Development." *Human Development,* 1990, *33,* 81–107.

Gorham, J. "Differences Between Teaching Adults and Pre-Adults: A Closer Look." *Adult Education Quarterly,* 1985, *35*(4), 194–209.

Gould, R. *Transformations: Growth and Change in Adult Life.* New York: Simon & Schuster, 1978.

Grabove, V. "The Many Facets of Transformative Learning Theory." In P. Cranton (ed.), *Transformative Learning in Action: Insights from Practice.* New Directions for Adult and Continuing Education, no. 74. San Francisco: Jossey-Bass, 1997.

Grace, A. P. "Adult Educators as Border Crossers: Using Transformative Pedagogy to Inform Classroom Practice." *Proceedings of the Adult Education Research Conference,* no. 37. Tampa, Fla.: University of South Florida, 1996a.

Grace, A. P. "Taking a Critical Pose: Andragogy—Missing Links, Missing Values." *International Journal of Lifelong Education,* 1996b, *15*(5), 382–392.

Grace, A. P. "Taking It to Practice: Building a Critical Postmodern Theory of Adult Learning Community." *Proceedings of the Adult Education Research Conference,* no. 38. Stillwater: Oklahoma State University, May 1997.

Greeno, J. G. "Response: On Claims That Answer the Wrong Question." *Educational Researcher,* 1997, *26*(1), 5–17.

Griffin, C. *Adult Education and Social Policy.* London: Croom Helm, 1987.

Griffith, W. S. "Do Adult Educators Need a Code of Ethics?" *Adult Learning,* 1991, *2*(8), 4.

Griffith, W. S., and Fujita-Starck, P. J. "Public Policy and Financing of Adult and Continuing Education." In S. B. Merriam and P. M. Cunningham (eds.), *Handbook of Adult and Continuing Education.* San Francisco: Jossey-Bass, 1989.

Grippin, P., and Peters, S. *Learning Theory and Learning Outcomes.* Lanham, Md.: University Press of America, 1984.

Grow, G. "Teaching Learners to Be Self-Directed: A Stage Approach." *Adult Education Quarterly,* 1991, *41*(3), 125–149.

Grow, G. "In Defense of the Staged Self-Directed Learning Model." *Adult Education Quarterly,* 1994, *44*(2), 109–114.

Gruber, H. E. "Courage and Cognitive Growth in Children and Scientists." In M. Schwebel and J. Raph (eds.), *Piaget in the Classroom.* New York: Basic Books, 1973.

Guglielmino, L. M. "Development of the Self-Directed Learning Readiness Scale." Unpublished doctoral dissertation, University of Georgia, 1977.

Guglielmino, L. M. "An Examination of Self-Directed Learning Readiness and Selected Demographic Variables of Top Female Executives." In H. B. Long and Associates (eds.), *Current Developments in Self-Directed Learning.* Norman: Public Managers Center, University of Oklahoma, 1996.

Guglielmino, L. M. "Contributions of the Self-Directed Learning Readiness Scale (SDLRS) and the Learning Preference Assessment (LPA) to the Definition and Measurement of Self-Direction in Learning." Paper presented at the First World Conference on Self-Directed Learning, Montreal, Canada, September 1997a.

Guglielmino, L. M. "Reliability and Validity of the Self-Directed Learning Readiness Scale and the Learning Preference Assessment." In H. B. Long and others (eds.), *Expanding Horizons in Self-Directed Learning.* Norman: Public Managers Center, University of Oklahoma, 1997b.

Guglielmino, L. M., and Guglielmino, P. "Self-Directed Learning in Business and Industry: An Information Age Imperative." In H. B. Long and others (eds.), *Self-Directed Learning: Applications and Theory.* Athens: Adult Education Department, University of Georgia, 1988.

Guglielmino, L. M., Long, H. B., and McCune, S. K. "Reactions to Field's Investigation into the SDLRS." *Adult Education Quarterly,* 1989, *39*(4), 235–245.

Guglielmino, L. M., and Nowocien, D. "Self-Directed Learning and Teachers' Professional Development." Paper presented at an International Symposium on Self-Directed Learning, Kissimmee, Fla., February 1997.

Guglielmino, P. J., and Roberts, D. G. "A Comparison of Self-Directed Learning Readiness in U.S. and Hong Kong Samples and the Implications for Job Performance." *Human Resource Development Quarterly,* 1992, *3*(3), 261–271.

Guilford, J. P. *The Nature of Human Intelligence.* New York: McGraw-Hill, 1967.

Guilford, J. P. "The Structure-of-Intellect Model." In B. B. Wolman (ed.), *Handbook of Intelligence: Theories, Measurements, and Applications.* New York: Wiley, 1985.

Habermas, J. *Knowledge and Human Interests.* Boston: Beacon Press, 1970.

Hacker, A. *Two Nations.* New York: Scribner, 1992.

Hall, A. G., and Donaldson, J. F. "An Exploratory Study of the Social and Personal Dynamics That Deter Underserved Women from Participating in Adult Education Activities." *Proceedings of the Adult Education Research Conference,* no. 38. Stillwater: Oklahoma State University, May 1997.

Hamilton, E. *Adult Education for Community Development.* Westport, Conn.: Greenwood Press, 1992.

Hamilton, E., and Cunningham, P. M. "Community-Based Adult Education." In S. B. Merriam and P. M. Cunningham (eds.), *Handbook of Adult and Continuing Education.* San Francisco: Jossey-Bass, 1989.

Hammond, M., and Collins, R. *Self-Directed Learning: Critical Practice.* London: Nichols/GP Publishing, 1991.

Hancock, E. "Age or Experience." *Human Development,* 1985, *28*(5), 274–280.

Hansen, A. H. "Model of Deficit/Growth Motives and Learning Needs of Older Participants." Abstract from Dissertation Abstracts International: DAI49–12A: 3588, 1988.

Hansen, T. L. "What Is Critical Theory? An Essay for the Uninitiated Organizational Communication Scholar." Paper presented at the Speech Communication Association of America Convention, Miami, 1993. (ED 368 008)

Hansman, C. A., and Wilson, A. L. "Teaching Writing in Community Colleges: A Situated View of How Adults Learn to Write in Computer-Based Writing Classrooms." *Community College Review,* 1998, *26*(1), 21–42.

Hanson, A. "The Search for a Separate Theory of Adult Learning: Does Anyone Really Need Andragogy?" In R. Edwards, A. Hanson, and P. Raggatt (eds.), *Boundaries of Adult Learning.* New York: Routledge, 1996.

Harris, E. M. "Not Essential to Teaching and Research: The Buchans Community Learning Process." *Canadian Journal for the Study of Adult Education,* 1997, *11*(1), 1–26.

Hart, G. "Investing in People for the Information Age." *Futurist,* 1983, *17*(1), 10–14.

Hart, M. "Liberation Through Consciousness-Raising." In J. Mezirow and Associates, *Fostering Critical Reflection in Adulthood: A Guide to Transformative and Emancipatory Learning* (pp. 47–73). San Francisco: Jossey-Bass, 1990.

Hart, M. *Working and Educating for Life: Feminist and International Perspectives on Adult Education.* New York: Routledge, 1992.

Hart, M. "Motherwork: A Radical Proposal to Rethink Work and Education." In M. R. Welton (ed.), *In Defense of the Lifeworld* (pp. 99–126). Albany, N.Y.: State University of New York Press, 1995.

Hartree, A. "Malcolm Knowles' Theory of Andragogy: A Critique." *International Journal of Lifelong Education,* 1984, *3*(3), 203–210.

Hassan, A. M. "An Investigation of the Learning Projects Among Adults of High and Low Readiness for Self-Direction in Learning." Unpublished doctoral dissertation, Iowa State University, 1981.

Havighurst, R. J. *Developmental Tasks and Education.* (3rd ed.) New York: McKay, 1972. (Originally published 1952.)

Hawkesworth, M. "Confounding Gender." *Signs: Journal of Women in Culture and Society,* 1997, *22*(2), 649–713.

Hayes, E. "Insights from Women's Experience for Teaching and Learning." In E. Hayes (ed.), *Effective Teaching Styles* (pp. 55–65). New Directions for Continuing Education, no. 43. San Francisco: Jossey-Bass, 1989.

Hayes, E., and Colin, S.A.J., III (eds.). *Confronting Racism and Sexism.* New Directions for Adult and Continuing Education, no. 61. San Francisco: Jossey-Bass, 1994a.

Hayes, E., and Colin, S.A.J., III. "Racism and Sexism in the United States: Fundamental Issues." In E. Hayes and S.A.J. Colin III, *Confronting Racism and Sexism.* New Directions for Adult and Continuing Education, no. 61. San Francisco: Jossey-Bass, 1994b.

Hayes, E., and Snow, B. R. "The Ends and Means of Adult Literacy Education." *Lifelong Learning: An Omnibus of Practice and Research,* 1989, *12*(8), 12–15.

Hayslip, B., and Panek, P. *Adult Development and Aging.* New York: HarperCollins, 1989.

Healy, P. "A 2-Year College in Arizona Bills Itself as a New Model for Public

Higher Education." *Chronicle of Higher Education,* Feb. 27, 1998, pp. A32–A33.

Heaney, T. *Adult Education for Social Change: From Center Stage to the Wings and Back Again.* Series No. 365. Columbus, Ohio: ERIC Clearinghouse on Adult, Career, and Vocational Education, 1996.

Heclo, H. "Move to Cut High-Tech Is Growing." *Atlanta Journal/Atlanta Constitution,* Sept. 11, 1994, pp. B1–B2.

Helms, J. D. (ed.). *Black and White Identity: Theory, Research, and Practice.* New York: Praeger, 1993.

Helms, J. D. "An Update of Helm's White and People of Color Racial Identity Models." In J. G. Ponterotto, J. M. Casas, L. A. Suzuki, and C. M. Alexander (eds.), *Handbook of Multicultural Counseling.* Thousand Oaks, Calif.: Sage, 1995.

Hemphill, D. F. "Critical Rationality from a Cross-Cultural Perspective." *Proceedings of the Adult Education Research Conference,* no. 35. Knoxville: University of Tennessee, May 1994.

Hemphill, D. F. "Flexibility, Innovation, and Collaboration: A Regional View of Community-Based Organizations in Adult Education." *Adult Learning,* 1996, *7*(6), 21–22.

Henry, G. T., and Basile, K. C. "Understanding the Decision to Participate in Formal Adult Education." *Adult Education Quarterly,* 1994, *44*(2), 64–82.

Henry, W. A. "Beyond the Melting Pot." *Time,* Apr. 9, 1990, pp. 28–31.

Herasymowych, M. A. "Increasing Learnable Intelligence Through Action Learning: A Practical Approach." Unpublished master's thesis, University of Calgary, 1997.

Hergenhahn, B. R. *An Introduction to Theories of Learning.* (3rd ed.) Englewood Cliffs, N.J.: Prentice Hall, 1988.

Herrnstein, R. J., and Murray, C. *The Bell Curve: Intelligence and Class Structure in American Life.* New York: Free Press, 1994.

Hersey, P., and Blanchard, K. *Management of Organizational Behavior: Utilizing Human Resources.* (5th ed.) Englewood Cliffs, N.J.: Prentice Hall, 1988.

Hiemstra, R. "The Older Adult's Learning Projects." *Educational Gerontology: An International Quarterly,* 1976, *1,* 331–341.

Hiemstra, R. "Creating the Future." In R. G. Brockett (ed.), *Continuing Education in the Year 2000.* New Directions for Continuing Education, no. 36. San Francisco: Jossey-Bass, 1987.

Hiemstra, R. "Individualizing the Instructional Process: What We Have Learned from Two Decades of Research on Self-Direction in Learning." In H. B. Long and others (eds.), *Self-Directed Learning: Application and Research*. Norman: Oklahoma Research Center for Continuing Professional and Higher Education, University of Oklahoma, 1992.

Hiemstra, R. "Three Underdeveloped Models for Adult Learning." In S. B. Merriam (ed.), *An Update on Adult Learning Theory*. New Directions for Adult and Continuing Education, no. 57. San Francisco: Jossey-Bass, 1993.

Hiemstra, R. "Helping Learners Take Responsibility for Self-Directed Activities." In R. Hiemstra and R. G. Brockett (eds.), *Overcoming Resistance to Self-Directed Adult Learning*. New Directions for Adult and Continuing Education, no. 64. San Francisco: Jossey-Bass, 1994.

Hiemstra, R. "What's in a Word? Changes in Self Directed Learning Language Over a Decade." Paper presented at the Tenth International Self-Directed Learning Symposium, West Palm Beach, Fla., 1996.

Hiemstra, R., and Brockett, R. G. *Overcoming Resistance to Self-Direction in Adult Learning*. New Directions for Adult and Continuing Education, no. 64. San Francisco: Jossey-Bass, 1994.

Hiemstra, R., and Sisco, B. *Individualizing Instruction: Making Learning Personal, Empowering, and Successful*. San Francisco: Jossey-Bass, 1990.

Hilgard, E. R., and Bower, G. H. *Theories of Learning*. New York: Appleton-Century-Crofts, 1966.

Hill, E. J., Hawkins, A. J., and Miller, B. C. "Work and Family in the Virtual Office: Perceived Influences of Mobile Telework." *Family Relations,* 1996, *45*(3), 293–301.

Hill, R. J. "Fugitive and Codified Knowledge: The Struggle to Control the Meaning of Environmental Hazards." *Proceedings of the Adult Education Research Conference*, no. 36. Edmonton, Alberta: University of Alberta, May 1995.

Hill, R. J. "From Motherhood to Sister-Solidarity: Homemaking as a Counterdiscourse to Corporate Environment Polluting." *Proceedings of the Adult Education Research Conference*, no. 39. San Antonio, Tex.: University of the Incarnate Word and Texas A&M University, 1998.

Hill, W. F. *Learning: A Survey of Psychological Interpretations*. (3rd ed.) New York: Crowell, 1977.

Hinton, G. E. "How Neural Networks Learn from Experience." *Scientific American,* 1992, *267*(3), 144–151.

Hofer, B. K., and Pintrich, P. R. "The Development of Epistemological Theories: Beliefs About Knowledge and Knowing and Their Relation to Learning." *Review of Educational Research,* 1997, *67*(1), 88–140.

Holford, J. "Why Social Movements Matter: Adult Education Theory, Cognitive Praxis, and the Creation of Knowledge." *Adult Education Quarterly,* 1995, *45*(2), 95–111.

Holliday, S. G., and Chandler, M. J. *Wisdom: Explorations in Adult Competence: Contributions to Human Development.* Vol. 17. Basel: Karger, 1986.

hooks, b. *Talking Back: Thinking Feminist—Thinking Black.* Boston: South End Press, 1989.

hooks, b. *Teaching to Transgress: Education as the Practice of Freedom.* New York: Routledge, 1994.

Horn, J. L. "Human Abilities: A Review of Research Theory in the Early 1970s." In M. R. Rosenzweig and L. W. Porter (eds.), *Annual Review of Psychology,* 1976, *27,* 437–485.

Horn, J. L. "The Theory of Fluid and Crystallized Intelligence in Relation to Concepts of Cognitive Psychology and Aging in Adulthood." In F.I.M. Craik and S. Trenub (eds.), *Advances in the Study of Communication Affect.* New York: Plenum Press, 1982.

Horn, J. L. "Remodeling Old Models of Intelligence." In B. B. Wolman (ed.), *Handbook of Intelligence: Theories, Measurements, and Applications.* New York: Wiley, 1985.

Horn, J. L., and Donaldson, G. "On the Myth of Intellectual Decline in Adulthood." *American Psychologist,* 1976, *31,* 701–719.

Horn, J. L., and Donaldson, G. "Cognitive Development in Adulthood." In O. G. Brim and J. Kagan (eds.), *Constancy and Change in Human Development.* Cambridge, Mass.: Harvard University Press, 1980.

Houle, C. O. *The Inquiring Mind.* Madison: University of Wisconsin Press, 1961.

Houle, C. O. *The Design of Education.* San Francisco: Jossey-Bass, 1972.

Houle, C. O. *Patterns of Learning: New Perspectives on Life-Span Education.* San Francisco: Jossey-Bass, 1984.

Houle, C. O. *The Inquiring Mind.* (2nd ed.) Madison: University of Wisconsin Press; Norman: Oklahoma Research Center for Continuing Professional and Higher Education, 1988.

Houle, C. O. *The Design of Education.* (2nd ed.) San Francisco: Jossey-Bass, 1996.

Hruska, S., Riechmann, S., and Grasha, A. F. "The Grasha-Riechmann's Student Learning Style Scales." In J. W. Keefe (ed.), *Student Learning Styles and Brain Behavior.* Reston, Va.: National Association of Secondary School Principals, 1982.

Huber, K. L. "Memory Is Not Only About Storage." In D. D. Flannery (ed.),

Applying Cognitive Theory to Adult Learning. New Directions for Adult and Continuing Education, no. 59. San Francisco: Jossey-Bass, 1993.

Hughes, D. C., Blazer, D. C., and George, L. K. "Age Differences in Life Events: A Multivariate Controlled Analysis." *International Journal of Aging and Human Development,* 1988, *27*(3), 207–219.

Hughes, J. A., and Graham, S. W. "Adult Life Roles: A New Approach to Adult Development." *Journal of Continuing Higher Education,* 1990, *38 (2),* 2–8.

Hull, C. L. *Essentials of Behavior.* New Haven, Conn.: Yale University Press, 1951.

Hultsch, D. F., and Plemons, J. K. "Life Events and Life Span Development." In P. B. Baltes and O. G. Brim (eds.), *Life-Span Development and Behavior.* Vol. 2. New York: Academic Press, 1979.

Hurtado, A. "Strategic Suspensions: Feminists of Color Theorize the Production of Knowledge." In N. R. Goldberger, J. M. Tarule, B. M. Clinchy, and M. F. Belenky (eds.), *Knowledge, Difference, and Power: Essays Inspired by Women's Ways of Knowing.* New York: Basic Books, 1996.

Huyck, M. H., and Hoyer, W. J. *Adult Development and Aging.* Belmont, Calif.: Wadsworth, 1982.

Inglis, T. "Empowerment and Emancipation." *Adult Education Quarterly,* 1997, *48*(1), 3–17.

Ireland, T. "Building on Experience: Working with Construction Workers in Brazil." In D. Boud and N. Miller (eds.), *Working with Experience: Animating Learning.* New York: Routledge, 1996.

Ivnik, R. J., Smith, G. E., Malec, J. F., Petersen, R. C., and Tangalos, E. G. "Long-Term Stability and Intercorrelations of Cognitive Abilities in Older Persons." *Psychological Assessment,* 1995, *7*(2), 155–161.

Jackson, L., and Caffarella, R. S. (eds.) *Experiential Learning: A New Approach.* New Directions for Adult and Continuing Education, no. 62. San Francisco: Jossey-Bass, 1994.

Jacobs, R. *Human Performance Technology: A Systems-Based Field for the Training and Development Profession.* Information Series No. 326. Columbus, Ohio: ERIC Clearinghouse on Adult, Carer, and Vocational Education, 1987.

Jacoby, R., and Glauberman, N. *The Bell Curve Debate: History, Documents, Opinions.* New York: Times Books, 1995.

James, J. M. "Instructor-Generated Load: An Inquiry Based on McClusky's Concepts of Margin." Unpublished doctoral dissertation, University of Wyoming, 1986.

James, W. B., and Blank, W. E. "Review and Critique of Available Learning-

Style Instruments for Adults." In D. D. Flannery (ed.), *Applying Cognitive Learning Theory to Adult Learning.* New Directions for Adult and Continuing Education, no. 59. San Francisco: Jossey-Bass, 1993.

James, W. B., Blank, W. E., Morrison, D., Koch, K., Shapiro, A., Schiaper, L., and Tindell, M. "Learning Styles: Are They Fact or Fiction?" *Proceedings of the Adult Education Research Conference,* no. 37. Tampa, Fla.: University of South Florida, 1996.

Jarvis, C., and Zukas, M. "Feminist Teaching, Feminist Research, Feminist Supervision: Feminist Praxis in Adult Education." *Proceedings of the Adult Education Research Conference,* no. 39. San Antonio, Tex.: University of the Incarnate Word and Texas A&M University, 1998.

Jarvis, P. *Adult and Continuing Education: Theory and Practice.* London: Croom Helm, 1983.

Jarvis, P. *The Sociology of Adult and Continuing Education.* London: Croom Helm, 1985.

Jarvis, P. *Sociological Perspectives on Lifelong Education and Lifelong Learning.* Athens, Ga.: Adult Education Department, University of Georgia, 1986.

Jarvis, P. *Adult Learning in the Social Context.* London: Croom Helm, 1987a.

Jarvis, P. "Meaningful and Meaningless Experience: Toward an Analysis of Learning from Life." *Adult Education Quarterly,* 1987b, *37*(3), 164–172.

Jarvis, P. *Paradoxes of Learning: On Becoming an Individual in Society.* San Francisco: Jossey-Bass, 1992.

Jarvis, P. *Ethics and Education for Adults in a Late Modern Society.* Leicester, England: National Institute of Adult Continuing Education, 1997.

Johns, J. W. E. "Selected Characteristics of the Learning Projects Pursued by Practicing Pharmacists." Unpublished doctoral dissertation, University of Georgia, 1973.

Johnson-Bailey, J., and Cervero, R. M. "An Analysis of the Educational Narratives of Reentry Black Women." *Adult Education Quarterly,* 1996, *46*(3), 142–157.

Johnson-Bailey, J. Tisdell, E. J., and Cervero, R. M. "Race, Gender, and the Politics of Professionalization." In E. Hayes and S.A.J. Colin III, *Confronting Racism and Sexism.* New Directions for Adult and Continuing Education, no. 61. San Francisco: Jossey-Bass, 1994.

Johnstone, J. W. C., and Rivera, R. J. *Volunteers for Learning: A Study of the Educational Pursuits of Adults.* Hawthorne, N.Y.: Aldine, 1965.

Jones, H. E., and Conrad, H. S. "The Growth and Decline of Intelligence." *Genetic Psychology Monographs,* 1933, *13*, 223–298.

Jones, J. W. *In the Middle of the Road We Call Our Life: The Courage to Search for Something More*. New York: HarperCollins, 1995.

Jordan, J. V. "Empathy and Self Boundaries." In J. V. Jordan, A. G. Kaplan, J. B. Miller, I. P. Striver, and J. L. Surrey (eds.), *Women's Growth in Connection: Writing from the Stone Center*. New York: Guilford Press, 1991a.

Jordan, J. V. "The Meaning of Mutuality." In J. V. Jordan, A. G. Kaplan, J. B. Miller, I. P. Striver, and J. L. Surrey (eds.), *Women's Growth in Connection: Writing from the Stone Center*. New York: Guilford Press, 1991b.

Jordan, J. V. "A Relational Perspective for Understanding Women's Development." In J. V. Jordan (ed.), *Women's Growth in Diversity*. New York: Guilford Press, 1997a.

Jordan, J. V. Introduction to J. V. Jordan (ed.), *Women's Growth in Diversity*. New York: Guilford Press, 1997b.

Jordan, J. V. (ed.), *Women's Growth in Diversity*. New York: Guilford Press, 1997c.

Jordan, J. V., Kaplan, A. G., Miller, J. B., Striver, I. P., and Surrey, J. L. (eds.), *Women's Growth in Connection: Writing from the Stone Center*. New York: Guilford Press, 1991.

Josselson, R. *Finding Herself*. San Francisco: Jossey-Bass, 1987.

Josselson, R. *Revising Herself: The Story of Women's Identity from College to Midlife*. New York: Oxford University Press, 1996.

Joughin, G. "Cognitive Style and Adult Learning Principles." *International Journal of Lifelong Education*, 1992, *11*(1), 3–14.

Kahana, E., and Kahana, B. "Conceptual and Empirical Advances in Understanding Aging Well Through Proactive Adaptation. In L. Bengtson (ed.), *Adulthood and Aging: Research on Continuities and Discontinuities*. New York: Springer, 1996.

Kandel, E. R., and Hawkins, R. D. "The Biological Basis of Learning and Individuality." *Scientific American*, 1992, *267*(3), 78–86.

Kasworm, C. E. "Toward a Paradigm of Developmental Levels of Self-Directed Learning." Paper presented at the American Educational Research Association, Montreal, 1983. (ED 230 705)

Kasworm, C. E. "The Adult's Learning Projects: A Fresh Approach to Theory and Practice in Adult Learning, 2nd Edition." In G. J. Confessore and S. J. Confessore (eds.), *Guideposts to Self-Directed Learning: Expert Commentary on Essential Concepts*. King of Prussia, Pa.: Organizational Design and Development, 1992.

Kathrein, M. A. "A Study of Self-Directed Continuing Professional Learning of Members of the Illinois Nurses' Association: Content and Process." Unpublished doctoral dissertation, Northern Illinois University, 1981.

Kaufman, A. S., Kaufman, J. C., Chen, T., and Kaufman, N. L. "Differences on Six Horn Abilities for 14 Age Groups Between 15–16 and 75–94 Years." *Psychological Assessment,* 1996, *8*(2), 161–171.

Kausler, D. H. *Learning and Memory in Normal Aging.* Orlando, Fla.: Academic Press, 1994.

Keats, D. M. "Cultural and Environmental Influences in the Acquisition of Concepts of Intellectual Development." In J. Valisner (ed.), *Child Development Within Culturally Structured Environments: Comparative-Cultural and Constructivist Perspectives.* Norwood, N.J.: Ablex, 1995.

Keddie, N. "Adult Education: An Ideology of Individualism." In J. L. Thompson (ed.), *Adult Education for a Change.* London: Hutchinson, 1980.

Kegan, R. *The Evolving Self: Problem and Processes in Human Development.* Cambridge, Mass.: Harvard University Press, 1982.

Kegan, R. *In over Our Heads: The Mental Demands of Modern Life.* Cambridge, Mass.: Harvard University Press, 1994.

Kelman, H. C., and Warwick, D. P. "The Ethics of Social Intervention: Goals, Means, and Consequences." In G. Bermant, H. C. Kelman, and D. P. Warwick (eds.), *The Ethics of Social Intervention.* Washington, D.C.: Hemisphere, 1978.

Kenney, W. R. "A Great Conspiracy: Self-Directed Learning Among Protestant Clergy in Russia." Paper presented at 37th Annual Adult Education Research Conference, University of South Florida, May 1996.

Kidd, J. R. *How Adults Learn.* (Rev. ed.) New York: Association Press, 1973.

Kidd, R. *The Popular Performing Arts, Non-Formal Education and Social Change in the Third World: A Bibliography and Review Essay.* The Hague, Netherlands: Centre for the Study of Education in Developing Countries, 1982.

Kidd, R., and Colletta, N. *Tradition for Development: Indigenous Structures and Folk Media in Non-Formal Education.* Berlin: International Council for Adult Education, 1980.

Kim, K., Collins, M., Stowe, P., and Chandler, K. *Forty Percent of Adults Participate in Adult Education Activities: 1994–95.* Washington, D.C.: National Center for Educational Statistics, Office of Educational Research and Improvement, U.S. Department of Education, 1995.

Kincheloe, J. L., and Steinberg, S. R. "A Tentative Description of Post-

Formal Thinking: The Critical Confrontation with Cognitive Theory." *Harvard Educational Review,* 1993, *63*(3), 296–319.

Kincheloe, J. L., Steinberg, S. R., and Gresson, A. D. *Measured Lies: The Bell Curve Examined.* New York: St. Martin's Press, 1996.

King, P. M., and Kitchener, K. S. *Developing Reflective Judgment.* San Francisco: Jossey-Bass, 1994.

King, P. M., and others. "The Justification of Beliefs in Young Adults: A Longitudinal Study." *Human Development,* 1983, *26,* 106–116.

Kirby, P. *Cognitive Style, Learning Style and Transfer Skill Acquisition.* Columbus: Ohio State University, National Center for Research in Vocational Education, 1979.

Kirshner, D., and Whitson, J. A. (eds.). *Situated Cognition: Social, Semiotic, and Psychological Perspectives.* Hillsdale, N.J.: Erlbaum, 1997.

Kitchener, K. S., and King, P. M. "Reflective Judgment: Concepts of Justification and Their Relationship to Age and Education." *Journal of Applied Developmental Psychology,* 1981, *2,* 89–116.

Kitchener, K. S., and King, P. M. "The Reflective Judgment Model: Transforming Assumptions About Knowing." In J. Mezirow and Associates, *Fostering Critical Reflection in Adulthood.* San Francisco: Jossey-Bass, 1990.

Kline, D. W., and Scialfa, C. T. "Visual and Auditory Aging." In J. E. Birren and K. W. Schaie (eds.), *Handbook of the Psychology of Aging.* (4th ed.) Orlando, Fla.: Academic Press, 1996.

Knopf, M. "Memory for Action Events: Structure and Development in Adulthood." In F. E. Weinert and W. Schneider (eds.), *Memory Performance and Competencies: Issues in Growth and Development.* Hillsdale, N.J.: Erlbaum, 1995.

Knowles, M. S. "The Field of Operations in Adult Education." In G. Jensen, A. A. Liveright, and W. Hallenbeck (eds.), *Adult Education: Outlines of an Emerging Field of University Study.* Washington, D.C.: Adult Education Association of the USA, 1964.

Knowles, M. S. "Andragogy, Not Pedagogy." *Adult Leadership,* 1968, *16*(10), 350–352, 386.

Knowles, M. S. *The Modern Practice of Adult Education: Andragogy Versus Pedagogy.* New York: Cambridge Books, 1970.

Knowles, M. S. *The Adult Learner: A Neglected Species.* Houston: Gulf 1973.

Knowles, M. S. *Self-Directed Learning.* New York: Association Press, 1975.

Knowles, M. S. *The Modern Practice of Adult Education: From Pedagogy to Andragogy.* (2nd ed.) New York: Cambridge Books, 1980.

Knowles, M. S. *The Adult Learner: A Neglected Species.* (3rd ed.) Houston: Gulf, 1984.

Knowles, M. S. "Adult Learning." In R. L. Craig (ed.), *Training and Development Handbook.* (3rd ed.) New York: McGraw-Hill, 1987.

Knowles, M. S. *The Making of an Adult Educator.* San Francisco: Jossey-Bass, 1989.

Knowles, M. S., and Associates. *Andragogy in Action: Applying Modern Principles of Adult Learning.* San Francisco: Jossey-Bass, 1984.

Knox, A. B. *Adult Development and Learning.* San Francisco: Jossey-Bass, 1977.

Knox, A. B. "Proficiency Theory of Adult Learning." *Contemporary Educational Psychology,* 1980, *5,* 378–404.

Knox, A. B. "Adult Learning and Proficiency." In D. Kleiber and M. Maehr (eds.), *Advances in Motivation and Achievement.* Vol. 4: *Motivation in Adulthood.* Greenwich, Conn.: JAI Press, 1985.

Knox, A. B. *Helping Adults Learn: A Guide to Planning, Implementing, and Conducting Programs.* San Francisco: Jossey-Bass, 1986.

Kohl de Oliveira, M. "The Meaning of Intellectual Competence: Views from a Favela." In J. Valsiner (ed.), *Child Development Within Culturally Structured Environments: Comparative-Cultural and Constructivist Perspectives.* Norwood, N.J.: Ablex, 1995.

Kohlberg, L. "Continuities in Childhood and Adult Moral Development." In P. Baltes and K. Schaie (eds.), *Life-Span Developmental Psychology: Personality and Socialization.* Orlando, Fla.: Academic Press, 1973.

Kohlberg, L., and Ryncarz, R. A. "Beyond Justice Reasoning: Moral Development and Consideration of a Seventh Stage." In C. N. Alexander and E. J. Langer (eds.), *Higher Stages of Human Development: Perspectives on Adult Growth.* New York: Oxford University Press, 1990.

Kolb, D. A. *Experiential Learning: Experience as the Source of Learning and Development.* Englewood Cliffs, N.J.: Prentice Hall, 1984.

Kopka, T.L.C., and Peng, S. S. *Adult Education: Main Reasons for Participating.* NCES 93–451. Washington, D.C.: National Center for Educational Statistics, Office of Educational Research and Improvement, U.S. Department of Education, 1993.

Kramer, D. A. "Post-Formal Operations? A Need for Further Conceptualization." *Human Development,* 1983, *26,* 91–105.

Kramer, D. A. "Development of an Awareness of Contradiction Across the Life Span and the Question of Postformal Operations." In M. L. Commons, J. D. Sinnott, F. A. Richards, and C. Armon (eds.), *Adult*

Development: Comparisons and Applications of Developmental Models. New York: Praeger, 1989.

Kramer, D. A., and Bacelar, W. T. "The Educated Adult in Today's World: Wisdom and the Mature Learner." In J. D. Sinnott (ed.), *Interdisciplinary Handbook of Adult Lifespan Learning.* Westport, Conn.: Greenwood Press, 1994.

Kramer, D. A., and Melchior, J. "Gender, Role Conflict, and the Development of Relativistic and Dialectical Thinking." *Sex Roles,* 1990, *23*(9), 553–575.

Kratz, R. J. "The Effects of Programs Which Foster Self-Directed Learning on the Dropout Rate, the Length of Stay, and the Preferences for Self-Directed Learning of Adult Basic Education Students." Unpublished doctoral dissertation, State University of New York, 1978.

Krupp, J. A. "Understanding and Motivating Personnel in the Second Half of Life." *Journal of Education,* 1987, *169*(1), 20–46.

Krupp, J. A. "Adults from the Inside Out." In A. Costa, J. Bellanca, and R. Fogarty (eds.), *If Minds Matter.* Palatine, Ill.: Skylight Publishing, 1992.

Labouvie-Vief, G. "Beyond Formal Operations: Uses and Limits of Pure Logic in Life-Span Development." *Human Development,* 1980, *23,* 141–161.

Labouvie-Vief, G. "Logic and Self-Regulation from Youth to Maturity: A Model." In M. L. Commons, F. A. Richards, and C. Armon (eds.), *Beyond Formal Operations: Late Adolescent and Adult Cognitive Development.* New York: Praeger, 1984.

Labouvie-Vief, G. "Models of Cognitive Functioning in the Older Adult: Research Needs in Educational Gerontology." In R. H. Sherron and D. B. Lumsden (eds.), *Introduction to Gerontology.* (3rd ed.) New York: Hemisphere, 1990.

Labouvie-Vief, G. "A New-Piagetian Perspective on Adult Cognitive Development." In R. J. Sternberg and C. A. Berg (eds.), *Intellectual Development.* New York: Cambridge University Press, 1992.

Labouvie-Vief, G. *Psyche and Eros: Mind and Gender in the Life Course.* New York: Cambridge University Press, 1994.

Lachman, M. E., and James, J. B. *Multiple Paths of Midlife Development.* Chicago: University of Chicago Press, 1997.

Langer, E. J. *The Power of Mindful Learning.* Reading, Mass.: Addison-Wesley, 1997.

Lavallee, M., Gourde, A., and Rodier, C. "The Impact of Lived Experience on Cognitivoethical Development of Today's Women." *International Journal of Behavioral Development,* 1990, *13*(4), 407–430.

Lave, J. *Cognition in Practice: Mind, Mathematics and Culture in Everyday Life.* Cambridge: Cambrige University Press, 1988.

Leeb, J. G. "Self-Directed Learning and Growth Toward Personal Responsibility: Implications for a Framework for Health Promotion." Unpublished doctoral dissertation, Syracuse University, 1983.

Lees, K. A. "Understanding How Female Doctoral Students' Interactions with Their Chairpersons During the Dissertation Process Affect Doctoral Persistence." Unpublished doctoral dissertation, University of Northern Colorado, 1996.

Lefrancois, G. R. *The Lifespan.* (5th ed.) Belmont, Calif.: Wadsworth, 1996.

Leithwood, K., Leonard, L., and Sharratt, L. "Conditions Fostering Organizational Learning in Schools." *Educational Administration Quarterly,* 1998, *34*(2), 243–276.

Lemonick, M. D. "Glimpses of the Mind." *Time,* Jul. 25, 1995, pp. 44–52.

Levenson, M. R., and Crumpler, C. A. "Three Models of Adult Development." *Human Development,* 1996, *39*(3), 135–149.

Levine, A. "Getting Smarter About IQ." *U.S. News and World Report,* Nov. 23, 1987, pp. 53–55.

Levine, S. L. *Promoting Adult Growth in Schools: The Promise of Professional Development.* Needham Heights, Mass.: Allyn & Bacon, 1989.

Levinson, D. J. "A Conception of Adult Development." *American Psychologist,* 1986, *41*(1), 3–13.

Levinson, D. J., Darrow, C. N., Klein, E. B., Levinson, M. H., and McKee, B. *The Seasons of a Man's Life.* New York: Ballantine, 1978.

Levinson, D. J., and Levinson, J.D. *The Seasons of a Woman's Life.* New York: Ballantine, 1996.

Levison, A. "Computers May Widen Social-Class Gap." *Atlanta Journal/ Atlanta Constitution,* Jul. 2, 1995, p. B5.

Lewin, K. "Frontiers in Group Dynamics: Concept, Method, and Reality in Social Science." *Human Relations,* 1947, *1*, 5–41.

Lindeman, E. *The Meaning of Adult Education.* New York: Harvest House, 1961.

Lindeman, E. C. *The Meaning of Adult Education in the United States.* Norman: Oklahoma Research Center for Continuing Professional and Higher Education, University of Oklahoma, 1989. (Originally published in 1926.)

Little, D. "Toward Recovering and Reconstructing Andragogy." In *Proceed-*

ings of the Adult Education Research Conference, no. 3. Knoxville: University of Tennessee, May 1994.

Loevinger, J. *Ego Development: Conceptions and Theories.* San Francisco: Jossey-Bass, 1976.

Lohman, D. F. "Human Intelligence: An Introduction to Advances in Theory and Research." *Review of Educational Research,* 1989, *59*(4), 333–373.

Lohman, D. F., and Scheurman, G. "Fluid Abilities and Epistemic Thinking: Some Prescriptions for Adult Education." In A. Tuijnman and M. van der Kamp (eds.), *Learning Across the Lifespan: Theories, Research, Policies.* Oxford: Pergamon Press, 1992.

Long, H. B. *Adult Learning: Research and Practice.* New York: Cambridge University Press, 1983.

Long, H. B. "Self-Directed Learning: Emerging Theory and Practice." In H. B. Long and others (eds.), *Self-Directed Learning: Emerging Theory and Practice.* Norman: Oklahoma Research Center for Continuing Professional and Higher Education, University of Oklahoma, 1989.

Long, H. B. "Evolution of a Formal Knowledge Base." In J. M. Peters, P. Jarvis, and Associates, *Adult Education: Evolution and Achievements in a Developing Field of Study.* San Francisco: Jossey-Bass, 1991a.

Long, H. B. "Self-Directed Learning: Consensus and Conflict." In H. B. Long and others (eds.), *Self-Directed Learning: Consensus and Conflict.* Norman: Oklahoma Research Center for Continuing Professional and Higher Education, University of Oklahoma, 1991b.

Long, H. B., and others. *Self-Directed Learning: Application and Theory.* Athens: Department of Adult Education, University of Georgia, 1988.

Long, H. B., and others. *Self-Directed Learning: Emerging Theory and Practice.* Norman: Oklahoma Research Center for Continuing Professional and Higher Education, University of Oklahoma, 1989.

Long, H. B., and others. *Advances in Research and Practice in Self-Directed Learning.* Norman: Oklahoma Research Center for Continuing Professional and Higher Education, University of Oklahoma, 1990.

Long, H. B., and others. *Self-Directed Learning: Application and Research.* Norman: Oklahoma Research Center for Continuing Professional and Higher Education, University of Oklahoma, 1992.

Long, H. B., and others. *Current Developments in Self-Directed Learning.* Norman: Public Managers Center, University of Oklahoma, 1996.

Long, H. B., and others. *Expanding Horizons in Self-Directed Learning.* Norman: Public Managers Center, University of Oklahoma, 1997.

Long, H. B., McCrary, K., and Ackerman, S. "Adult Cognition: Piagetian Based Research Findings." *Adult Education,* 1979, *30*(1), 3–18.

Long, H. B., and Morris, S. S. "The Relationship Between Self-Directed Learning Readiness and Academic Performance in a Nontraditional Higher Education Program." In H. B. Long and others (eds.), *Current Developments in Self-Directed Learning.* Norman: Public Managers Center, University of Oklahoma, 1996.

Long, H. B., and Walsh, S. M. "An Analysis of a Modified Form of Guglielmino's Self-Directed Learning Readiness Scale." In H. B. Long and others (eds.), *Self-Directed Learning: Application and Research.* Norman: Oklahoma Research Center for Continuing Professional and Higher Education, University of Oklahoma, 1992.

Luszcz, M. A. "Predictors of Memory in Young-Old and Old-Old Adults." *International Journal of Behavioral Development,* 1992, *15*(1), 147–166.

Luttrell, W. "Working-Class Women's Ways of Knowing: Effects of Gender, Race and Class." *Sociology of Education,* 1989, *62*(1), 33–46.

Lyons, N. P. "Two Perspectives: On Self, Relationships, and Morality." *Harvard Educational Review,* 1983, *53*(1), 125–145.

Macdonald, C. *Toward Wisdom: Finding Our Way to Inner Peace, Love, and Happiness.* Charlottesville, Va.: Hampton Roads, 1996.

Macias, C. J. "American Indian Academic Success: The Role of Indigenous Learning Strategies." *Journal of American Indian Education,* 1989, Special Issue, 43–52.

MacKeracher, D. *Making Sense of Adult Learning.* Toronto, Canada: Culture Concepts, 1996.

Magnusson, D. "Individual Development: A Holistic, Integrated Model." In P. Moen, G. H. Elder, and K. Lüscher (eds.), *Examining Lives in Context: Perspectives on the Ecology of Human Development.* Washington, D.C.: American Psychological Association, 1995.

Maher, F. A. "Toward a Richer Theory of Feminist Pedagogy: A Comparison of 'Liberation' and 'Gender' Models for Teaching and Learning." *Journal of Education,* 1987, *169*(3), 91–100.

Maher, F. A., and Tetreault, M. K. *The Feminist Classroom.* New York: Basic Books, 1994.

Maples, M. F., and Webster, J. M. "Thorndike's Connectionism." In G. M. Gazda and R. J. Corsini (eds.), *Theories of Learning.* Itasca, Ill.: Peacock, 1980.

Marsh, G. R. "Perceptual Changes with Aging." In E. W. Busse and D. G. Blazer (eds.), *Textbook of Geriatric Psychiatry.* Washington, D.C.: American Psychiatric Press, 1996.

Marsick, V. J., and Neaman, P. G. "Individuals Who Learn Create Organizations That Learn." In R. W. Rowden (ed.), *Workplace Learning: Debating Five Critical Questions of Theory and Practice.* New Directions for Adult and Continuing Education, no. 72. San Francisco: Jossey-Bass, 1996.

Marsick, V. J., and Watkins, K. E. "The Learning Organization: An Integrative Vision for HRD." *Human Resource Development Quarterly,* 1994, 5, 353–360.

Mashengele, D. "Africentricity: New Context, New Challenges, New Futures." In P. Armstrong, N. Miller, and M. Zukas (eds.), *Crossing Borders, Breaking Boundaries: Proceedings of the 27th Annual SCUTREA Conference.* London: Birkbeck College, University of London, July 1997.

Maslow, A. H. *Motivation and Personality.* New York: HarperCollins, 1954.

Maslow, A. H. *Toward a Psychology of Being.* (2nd ed.) New York: Van Nostrand Reinhold, 1968.

Maslow, A. H. *Motivation and Personality.* (2nd ed.) New York: HarperCollins, 1970.

McAdams, D. P. "Can Personality Change? Levels of Stability and Growth in Personality Across the Life Span." In T. F. Heatherton and J. L. Weinberger (eds.), *Can Personality Change?* Washington, D.C.: American Psychological Association, 1994.

McClusky, H. Y. "The Course of the Adult Life Span." In W. C. Hallenbeck (ed.), *Psychology of Adults.* Washington, D.C.: Adult Education Association, 1963.

McClusky, H. Y. "An Approach to a Differential Psychology of the Adult Potential." In S. M. Grabowski (ed.), *Adult Learning and Instruction.* Syracuse, N.Y.: ERIC Clearinghouse on Adult Education, 1970a. (ED 045 867)

McClusky, H. Y. "A Dynamic Approach to Participation in Community Development." *Journal of Community Development Society,* 1970b, 1(1), 25–32.

McClusky, H. Y. *Education: Background.* Report prepared for the 1971 White House Conference on Aging. Washington, D.C.: White House Conference on Aging, 1971.

McCune, S. L., and Guglielmino, L. M. "The Validity Generalization of Guglielmino's Self-Directed Learning Readiness Scale." In H. B. Long and others (eds.), *Self-Directed Learning: Consensus and Conflict.* Norman: Oklahoma Research Center for Continuing Professional and Higher Education, University of Oklahoma, 1991.

McDonald, B. L. "A Comparison of Mezirow's Transformation Theory with the Process of Learning to Become an Ethical Vegan." Unpublished doctoral dissertation, University of Georgia, 1997.

McDonald, K. S., and Wood, G. S. "Surveying Adult Education Practitioners About Ethical Issues." *Adult Education Quarterly,* 1993, *43*(4), 243–257.

McLaren, P. "Revolutionary Praxis: Toward a Pedagogy of Resistance and Transformation." *Educational Researcher,* 1997, *26*(6), 23–26.

Mercer, S. O., and Garner, J. D. "An International Overview of Aged Women." In J. D. Garner and O. Mercer (eds.), *Women as They Age: Challenge, Opportunity, and Triumph.* New York: Haworth Press, 1989.

Merriam, S. B. *Adult Development: Implications for Adult Education.* Columbus, Ohio: ERIC Clearinghouse on Adult, Career, and Vocational Education, 1984.

Merriam, S. B. "How Research Produces Knowledge." In J. M. Peters and P. Jarvis (eds.), *Adult Education: Evolution and Achievements in a Developing Field of Study* (pp. 42–65). San Francisco: Jossey-Bass, 1991.

Merriam, S. B. "Learning and Life Experience: The Connection in Adulthood." In J. D. Sinnott (ed.), *Interdisciplinary Handbook of Adult Lifespan Learning.* Westport, Conn.: Greenwood Press, 1994.

Merriam, S. B., and Brockett, R. G. *The Profession and Practice of Adult Education: An Introduction.* San Francisco: Jossey-Bass, 1997.

Merriam, S. B., and Clark, M. C. *Lifelines: Patterns of Work, Love, and Learning in Adulthood.* San Francisco: Jossey-Bass, 1991.

Merriam, S. B., and Clark, M. C. "Adult Learning in Good Times and Bad." *Studies in Continuing Education,* 1992, *14*(1), 1–13.

Merriam, S. B., and Heuer, B. "Meaning-Making, Adult Learning and Development: A Model with Implications for Practice." *International Journal of Lifelong Education,* 1996, *15*(4), 243–255.

Merriam, S. B., Mott, V. W., and Lee, M. "Learning That Comes from the Negative Interpretation of Life Experience." *Studies in Continuing Education,* 1996, *18*(1), 1–23.

Merriam, S. B., and Yang, B. "A Longitudinal Study of Adult Life Experiences and Developmental Outcomes." *Adult Education Quarterly,* 1996, *46*(2), 62–81.

Messick, S. "Personality Consistencies in Cognition and Creativity." In S. Messick and Associates, *Individuality in Learning: Implications of Cognitive Styles and Creativity in Human Development.* San Francisco: Jossey-Bass, 1976.

Messick, S. "The Nature of Cognitive Styles: Problems and Promise in Educational Practice." *Educational Psychologist,* 1984, *19*(2), 59–74.

Messick, S. "Human Abilities and Modes of Attention: The Issue of Stylistic Consistencies in Cognition." In I. Dennis and P. Tapsfield (eds.), *Human Abilities: Their Nature and Measurement.* Hillsdale, N.J.: Erlbaum, 1996.

Metzger, C. "Self-Directed Learning in Continuing Education—A Report from Switzerland." In G. A. Straka (ed.), *European Views of Self-Directed Learning: Historical, Conceptional, Empirical, Practical, Vocational.* Munster, Germany: Waxmann, 1997.

Mezirow, J. *Education for Perspective Transformation: Women's Re-entry Programs in Community Colleges.* New York: Teachers College, Columbia University, 1978.

Mezirow, J. "A Critical Theory of Adult Learning and Education." *Adult Education,* 1981, *32*(1), 3–27.

Mezirow, J. "Concept and Action in Adult Education." *Adult Education Quarterly,* 1985a, *35*(3), 142–151.

Mezirow, J. "A Critical Theory of Self-Directed Learning." In S. Brookfield (ed.), *Self-Directed Learning: From Theory to Practice.* New Directions for Continuing Education, no. 25. San Francisco: Jossey-Bass, 1985b.

Mezirow, J. "Conclusion: Toward Transformative Learning and Emancipatory Education." In J. Mezirow and Associates, *Fostering Critical Reflection in Adulthood: A Guide to Transformative and Emancipatory Learning.* San Francisco: Jossey-Bass, 1990a.

Mezirow, J. "How Critical Reflection Triggers Transformative Learning." In J. Mezirow and Associates, *Fostering Critical Reflection in Adulthood: A Guide to Transformative and Emancipatory Learning* (pp. 1–20). San Francisco: Jossey-Bass, 1990b.

Mezirow, J. *Transformative Dimensions of Adult Learning.* San Francisco: Jossey-Bass, 1991.

Mezirow, J. "Transformation Theory: Critique and Confusion." *Adult Education Quarterly,* 1992, *42*(2), 250–252.

Mezirow, J. "How Adults Learn: The Meaning of Adult Education." *Proceedings of the Adult Education Research Conference,* no. 34. University Park: Pennsylvania State University, 1993.

Mezirow, J. "Transformation Theory of Adult Learning." In M. R. Welton (ed.), *In Defense of the Lifeworld* (pp. 39–70). New York: State University of New York Press, 1995.

Mezirow, J. "Contemporary Paradigms of Learning." *Adult Education Quarterly,* 1996, *46*(3), 158–172.

Mezirow, J. "Transformative Learning: Theory to Practice." In P. Cranton (ed.), *Transformative Learning in Action: Insights from Practice.* New Directions for Adult and Continuing Education, no. 74. San Francisco: Jossey-Bass, 1997a.

Mezirow, J. "Transformative Theory Out of Context." *Adult Education Quarterly,* 1997b, *48*(1), 60–62.

Mezirow, J. "On Critical Reflection." *Adult Education Quarterly,* 1998, *48*(3), 185–198.

Mezirow, J., and Associates. *Fostering Critical Reflection in Adulthood: A Guide to Transformative and Emancipatory Learning.* San Francisco: Jossey-Bass, 1990.

Michelson, E. "Usual Suspects: Experience, Reflection and the (En)gendering of Knowledge." *International Journal of Lifelong Education,* 1996, *15*(6), 438–454.

Mikolaj, E. D. "The Intrapersonal Role Conflicts of Adult Women Undergraduate Students." Abstract from: Dissertation Abstracts International: DAI44–11A:3247, 1983.

Miles, C. B., and Miles, W. R. "The Correlation of Intelligence Scores and Chronological Age from Early to Late Maturity." *American Journal of Psychology,* 1932, *44,* 44–78.

Miller, H. L. *Participation of Adults in Education: A Force-Field Analysis.* Boston: Center for the Study of Liberal Education for Adults, Boston University, 1967.

Miller, J. B. *Toward a New Psychology of Women.* (2nd ed.) Boston: Beacon Press, 1986.

Miller, M. E., and Cook-Greuter, S. R. (eds.). *Transcendence and Mature Adult Thought in Adulthood: The Further Reaches of Adult Development.* London: Rowman & Littlefield, 1994.

Miller, N., and Boud, D. "Animating Learning from Experience." In D. Boud and N. Miller (eds.), *Working with Experience: Animating Learning.* New York: Routledge, 1996.

Miller, N., and others. "From Teaching to Facilitation to Animation: Crossing the Boundaries Between Traditions and Perspectives in the Promotion of Learning from Experience." In P. Armstrong, N. Miller, and M. Zukas (eds.), *Crossing Borders, Breaking Boundaries: Proceed-*

ings of the 27th Annual SCUTREA Conference. London: Birkbeck College, University of London, July 1997.

Miller, N. E., and Dollard, J. C. *Social Learning and Imitation.* New Haven, Conn.: Yale University Press, 1941.

Moen, P., Elder, G. H., and Lüscher, K. (eds.). *Examining Lives in Context: Perspectives on the Ecology of Human Development.* Washington, D.C.: American Psychological Association, 1995.

Moingeon, B., and Edmondson, A. (eds.). *Organizational Learning and Competitive Advantage.* London: SAGE Publications, 1996.

Morgan, M. *Mutant Message Down Under.* New York: HarperCollins, 1994.

Morris, J. F. "The Planning Behavior and Conceptual Complexity of Selected Clergymen in Self-Directed Learning Projects Related to Their Continued Professional Education." Unpublished doctoral dissertation, University of Toronto, 1977.

Morris, S. S. "Item Analysis of Guglielmino's Self-Directed Learning Readiness Scale: Revisiting the Issue of Internal Consistency." In H. B. Long and others (eds.), *Expanding Horizons in Self-Directed Learning.* Norman: Public Managers Center, University of Oklahoma, 1997.

Morstain, B. R., and Smart, J. C. "Reasons for Participation in Adult Education Courses: A Multivariate Analysis of Group Differences." *Adult Education,* 1974, *24*(2), 83–98.

Murk, P. "Up Front—Ethics in the Profession: Five Important Views." *Adult Learning,* 1996, *8*(2), 11–12.

Naisbitt, J., and Aburdene, P. *Megatrends 2000: Ten New Directions for the 1990s.* New York: Morrow, 1990.

Nelson, A. "Imaging and Critical Reflection in Autobiography: An Odd Couple in Adult Transformative Learning." *Proceedings of the Adult Education Research Conference,* no. 38. Stillwater: Oklahoma State University, 1997.

Nesbit, T. "The Social Reform Perspective: Seeking a Better Society." In D. Pratt and others (eds.), *Five Perspectives on Teaching in Adult and Higher Education.* Malabar, Fla.: Krieger, 1998.

Neugarten, B. "Adaptation and the Life Cycle." *Counseling Psychologist,* 1976, *6,* 16–20.

Neugarten, B. "Time, Age, and the Life Cycle." *American Journal of Psychiatry,* 1979, *136,* 887–893.

Neugarten, B., and Datan, N. "Sociological Perspectives on the Life Cycle." In P. Baltes and K. W. Schaie (eds.), *Life-Span Developmental Psychology: Personality and Socialization.* Orlando, Fla.: Academic Press, 1973.

Neugarten, B., and others. *Personality in Middle and Late Life: Empirical Studies.* New York: Atherton Press, 1964.

Neumann, A., and Peterson, P. L. *Learning from Our Lives: Women, Research, and Autobiography in Education.* New York: Teachers College Press, 1997.

Newman, M. *Defining the Enemy: Adult Education in Social Action.* Sydney: Stewart Victor, 1994a.

Newman, M. "Response to *Understanding Transformation Theory.*" *Adult Education Quarterly,* 1994b, 44(4), 236–242.

Noddings, N. *Caring: A Feminine Approach to Ethics and Moral Education.* Berkeley: University of California Press, 1984.

Noddings, N. *The Challenge to Care in Schools: An Alternative Approach to Education.* New York: Teachers College Press, 1992.

Nordhaug, O. "Structured Determinants of Publicly Subsidized Adult Education." *Adult Education Quarterly,* 1990, 40(4), 197–206.

Nuernberger, P. "The Structure of Mind and Its Resources." In M. E. Miller and S. R. Cook-Greuter (eds.), *Transcendence and Mature Adult Thought in Adulthood: The Further Reaches of Adult Development.* London: Rowman & Littlefield, 1994.

Ocitti, J. P. "Indigenous Education for Today: The Necessity of the Useless." *Adult Education for Today,* 1990, 35, 53–64.

Oddi, L. F. "Development of an Instrument to Measure Self-Directed Continuing Learning." Unpublished doctoral dissertation, Northern Illinois University, 1984.

Oddi, L. F. "Development and Validation of an Instrument to Identify Self-Directed Continuing Learners." *Adult Education Quarterly,* 1986, 36(2), 97–107.

Oliver, L. P. *Study Circles.* Washington, D.C.: Seven Locks Press, 1987.

Ormrod, J. E. *Human Learning.* (2nd ed.) Englewood Cliffs, N.J.: Merrill, 1995.

Osterman, K. F., and Kottkamp, R. B. *Reflective Practice for Educators: Improving Schooling Through Professional Development.* Newbury Park, Calif.: Corwin Press, 1993.

Owen, T. R. "The Relationship Between Wellness and Self-Directed Learning Among Graduate Students." Unpublished doctoral dissertation, University of Knoxville, 1996.

Padberg, L. F. "The Organizing Circumstance Revisited: Environmentally Structured Learning Projects Among Adults with Low Formal Education." In H. B. Long and others (eds.), *New Ideas About Self-Directed Learning.* Norman: Oklahoma Research Center for Continuing Professional and Higher Education, University of Oklahoma, 1994.

Papalia, D. E., and Bielby, D.D.V. "Cognitive Functioning in Middle and Old Age Adults." *Human Development*, 1974, *17*, 424–443.

Pascual-Leone, J. "Growing into Maturity: Towards a Metasubjective Theory of Adulthood Stages." In P. B. Baltes and O. G. Brim, Jr. (eds.), *Life Span Development and Behavior*. Vol. 5. Orlando, Fla.: Academic Press, 1983.

Paterson, K. W. *Values, Education, and the Adult*. New York: Routledge, 1979.

Pearson, E., and Podeschi, R. "Humanism and Individualism: Maslow and His Critics." *Proceedings of the Adult Education Research Conference*, no. 38. Stillwater: Oklahoma State University, May 1997.

Peck, T. A. "Women's Self-Definition in Adulthood: From a Different Model." *Psychology of Women Quarterly*, 1986, *10*, 274–284.

Pedler, M., Burgoyne, J., and Boydell, T. *The Learning Company: A Strategy for Sustainable Development*. London: McGraw-Hill, 1991.

Penland, P. R. *Self-Planned Learning in America*. Pittsburgh: University of Pittsburgh, 1977. (ED 184 589)

Penland, P. R. "Self-Initiated Learning." *Adult Education*, 1979, *29*, 170–179.

Percy, K., Burton, D., and Withnall, A. *Self-Directed Learning Among Adults: The Challenge for Continuing Educators*. Lancaster, England: Association for Lifelong Learning, 1994. (ED 382 882)

Perkins, D. *Outsmarting IQ: The Emerging Science of Learnable Intelligence*. New York: Free Press, 1995.

Perlmutter, M., and Hall, E. *Adult Development and Aging*. New York: Wiley, 1985.

Perry, W. G. *Forms of Intellectual and Ethical Development in the College Years*. Austin, Tex.: Holt, Rinehart & Winston, 1970.

Perry, W. G. "Cognitive and Ethical Growth: The Making of Meaning." In A. W. Chickering (ed.), *The Modern American College*. San Francisco: Jossey-Bass, 1981.

Pert, C. B. *Molecules of Emotion: Why You Feel the Way You Feel*. New York: Scribner, 1997.

Perun, P. J., and Bielby, D. D. "Structure and Dynamics of the Individual Life Course." In K. W. Back (ed.), *Life Course: Integrative Theories and Exemplary Populations*. Boulder, Colo.: Westview Press, 1980.

Peters, J. M. "Programming Through the Client's Lifespan." In D. J. Blackburn (ed.), *Foundations and Changing Practices in Extension*. Guelph, Ontario: University of Guelph, 1989.

Peters, J. M. "Strategies for Reflective Practice." In R. G. Brockett (ed.), *Professional Development for Educators of Adults*. New Directions for

Adult and Continuing Education, no. 51. San Francisco: Jossey-Bass, 1991.

Peters, J. M., and Gordon, R. S. *Adult Learning Projects: A Study of Adult Learning in Urban and Rural Tennessee.* Knoxville: University of Tennessee, 1974. (ED 102 431)

Peterson, C. C. "The Ticking of the Social Clock: Adults' Beliefs About the Timing of Transition Events." *International Journal of Aging and Human Development,* 1996, *42*(3), 189–203.

Peterson, D. A., and Masunaga, H. "Policy for Older Adult Education." In J. C. Fisher and M. A. Wolf (eds.), *Using Learning to Meet the Challenges of Older Adulthood.* New Directions for Adult and Continuing Education, no. 77. San Francisco: Jossey-Bass, 1998.

Peterson, E. A. "Our Students, Ourselves: Lessons of Challenge and Hope from the African American Community." In P. A. Sissel (ed.), *A Community-Based Approach to Literacy Programs: Taking Learners' Lives into Account.* New Directions for Adult and Continuing Education, no. 70. San Francisco: Jossey-Bass, 1996.

Petrella, R. "The Snares of the Market Economy for Future Training Policy: Beyond the Heralding There Is a Need for Denunciation." *Adult Education and Development,* 1997, *48,* 19–26.

Phares, E. J. "Rotter's Social Learning Theory." In G. M. Gazda and R. J. Corsini (eds.), *Theories of Learning.* Itasca, Ill.: Peacock, 1980.

Phelan, A. M., and Garrison, J. W. "Toward a Gender-Sensitive Ideal of Critical Thinking: A Feminist Poetic." *Curriculum Inquiry,* 1994, *24*(3), 255–268.

Phillips, D. C. "The Good, the Bad, and the Ugly: The Many Faces of Constructivism." *Educational Researcher,* 1995, *24*(7), 5–12.

Phinney, J. S. "Ethnic Identity in Adolescents and Adults: Review of Research." *Psychological Bulletin,* 1990, *108*(3), 499–514.

Piaget, J. *The Origins of Intelligence in Children.* New York: International Universities Press, 1952.

Piaget, J. *Psychology of Intelligence.* Totowa, N.J.: Littlefield, Adams, 1966.

Piaget, J. "Intellectual Evolution from Adolescent to Adulthood." *Human Development,* 1972, *16,* 346–370.

Picciano, A. G. *Educational Leadership and Planning for Technology.* (2nd ed.) Englewood Cliffs, N.J.: Prentice Hall, 1998.

Pietrykowski, B. "Knowledge and Power in Adult Education: Beyond Freire and Habermas." *Adult Education Quarterly,* 1996, *46*(2), 82–97.

Pilling-Cormick, J. "A Framework for Using Instruments in Self-Directed Learning Research." In H. B. Long and others (eds.), *Current Devel-*

opments in Self-Directed Learning. Norman: Public Managers Center, University of Oklahoma, 1996.

Piskurich, G. M. *Self-Directed Learning: A Practical Guide to Design, Development, and Implementation.* San Francisco: Jossey-Bass, 1993.

Piskurich, G. M. "Making Telecommuting Work." *Training and Development,* 1996, *50*(2), 20–27.

Plumb, D. "Critical Adult Education and Identity in Postmodernity." *Proceedings of the Adult Education Research Conference,* no. 36. Edmonton, Alberta: University of Alberta, May 1995a.

Plumb, D. "Declining Opportunities: Adult Education, Culture, and Postmodernity." In M. R. Welton (ed.), *In Defense of the Lifeworld* (pp. 157–194). Albany, N.Y.: State University of New York Press, 1995b.

Ponterotto, J. G., Casas, J. M., Suzuki, L. A., and Alexander, C. M. (eds.). *Handbook of Multicultural Counseling.* Thousand Oaks, Calif.: Sage, 1995.

Pratt, D. D. "Andragogical Assumptions: Some Counter-Intuitive Logic." *Proceedings of the Adult Education Research Conference,* no. 25. Raleigh: North Carolina State University, 1984.

Pratt, D. D. "Andragogy as a Relational Construct." *Adult Education Quarterly,* 1988, *38*(3), 160–181.

Pratt, D. D. "Conceptions of Self Within China and the United States: Contrasting Foundations for Adult Development." *International Journal of Intercultural Relations,* 1991, *15*(3), 285–310.

Pratt, D. D. "Andragogy After Twenty-Five Years." In S. B. Merriam (ed.), *An Update on Adult Learning Theory.* New Directions for Adult and Continuing Education, no. 57. San Francisco: Jossey-Bass, 1993.

Pratt, D. D., Kelly, M., and Wong, W. "The Social Constructs of Chinese Models of Teaching." *Proceedings of the Adult Education Research Conference,* no. 39. San Antonio, Tex.: University of the Incarnate Word and Texas A&M University, 1998.

Pratt, D. D., and others. *Five Perspectives on Teaching in Adult and Higher Education.* Malabar, Fla.: Krieger, 1998.

Prestine, N. A., and LeGrand, B. F. "Cognitive Learning Theory and the Preparation of Educational Administrators: Implications for Practice and Policy." *Educational Administration Quarterly,* 1991, *27*(1), 61–89.

Quigley, B. A. "Hidden Logic: Reproduction and Resistance in Adult Literacy and Adult Basic Education." *Adult Education Quarterly,* 1990, *40* (2), 103–115.

Rabbitt, P., and others. "The University of Manchester Age and Cognitive Performance Research Centre and North East Age Research Longitudinal Programmes, 1982 to 1997." *Zeitschrift fur Gerontologie,* 1993, *26,* 176–183.

Rachal, J. R. "The Social Setting of Adult and Continuing Education." In S. B. Merriam and P. M. Cunningham (eds.), *Handbook of Adult and Continuing Education.* San Francisco: Jossey-Bass, 1989.

Ratinoff, L. "Global Insecurity and Education: The Culture of Globalization." *Prospects,* 1995, *25*(2), 147–174.

Raykov, T. "Multivariate Structural Modeling of Plasticity in Fluid Intelligence of Aged Adults." *Multivariate Behavioral Research,* 1995, *30*(2), 255–287.

Reese, H. W., and Overton, W. F. "Models of Development and Theories of Development." In L. R. Goulet and P. B. Baltes (eds.), *Life-Span Developmental Psychology: Interventions.* Orlando, Fla.: Academic Press, 1970.

Reese, H. W., and Smyer, M. A. "The Dimensionalization of Life Events." In E. J. Callahan and K. A. McCluskey (eds.), *Life-Span Development Psychology: Nonnormative Events.* Orlando, Fla.: Academic Press, 1983.

Resides, D. "Learning and New Voices: Lesbian Development and the Implications for Adult Education." *Proceedings of the Adult Education Research Conference,* no. 37. Tampa: University of South Florida, 1996.

Resnick, L. "Learning In School and Out." *Educational Researcher,* 1987, *16*(9), 13–20.

Restak, R. M. *Brainscapes.* New York: Hyperion, 1995.

Reybold, L. E. "A Sociocultural Perspective on Knowing: A Grounded Theory of Epistemological Development of Malaysian Women." *Proceedings of the Adult Education Research Conference,* no. 38. Stillwater: Oklahoma State University, 1997.

Richards, F. A., and Commons, M. L. "Postformal Cognitive-Developmental Theory and Research: A Review of its Current Status." In C. N. Alexander and E. J. Langer (eds.), *Higher Stages of Human Development: Perspective on Adult Growth.* New York: Oxford University Press, 1990.

Richards, R. K. "Physicians' Self-Directed Learning." *Mobius,* 1986, *6*(4), 1–13.

Richardson, P. L. "The Lifelong Learning Project Revisited: Institutionalizing the Vision." *Educational Considerations,* 1987, *14*(2–3), 2–4.

Riegel, K. F. "Dialectic Operations: The Final Period of Cognitive Development." *Human Development,* 1973, *16,* 346–370.

Riegel, K. F. "Adult Life Crises: A Dialectical Interpretation of Development." In N. Datan and L. H. Ginsberg (eds.), *Life-Span Developmental Psychology: Normative Life Crises.* Orlando, Fla.: Academic Press, 1975.

Riegel, K. F. "The Dialectics of Human Development." *American Psychologist,* 1976, *31,* 689–700.

Robertson, D. L. "Facilitating Transformative Learning: Attending to the Dynamics of the Educational Helping Relationship." *Adult Education Quarterly,* 1996, *47*(1), 41–53.

Robinson, D. N. "Wisdom Through the Ages." In R. J. Sternberg (ed.), *Wisdom: Its Nature, Origins, and Development.* Cambridge: Cambridge University Press, 1990.

Rocco, T. S., and West, W. "Deconstructing Privilege: An Examination of Privilege in Adult Education." *Adult Education Quarterly,* 1998, *48*(3), 171–184.

Rodin, J., Schooler, C., and Schaie, K. W. *Self-Directedness: Cause and Effects Throughout the Life Course.* Hillsdale, N.J.: Erlbaum, 1990.

Rogers, C. R. *On Becoming a Person: A Therapist's View of Psychotherapy.* Boston: Houghton Mifflin, 1961.

Rogers, C. R. *Freedom to Learn.* Columbus, Ohio: Charles E. Merrill, 1969.

Rogers, C. R. *Freedom to Learn for the 80s.* Columbus, Ohio: Merrill, 1983.

Rogoff, B. *Apprenticeship in Thinking: Cognitive Development in Social Context.* Oxford: Oxford University Press, 1990.

Rohrlich, J. B. *Work and Love: The Crucial Balance.* Orlando, Fla.: Academic Press, 1980.

Rosenau, P. M. *Post-Modernism and the Social Sciences.* Princeton, N.J.: Princeton University Press, 1992.

Rosenblum, S., and Darkenwald, G. "Effects of Adult Learner Participation in Course Planning on Achievement." *Adult Education Quarterly,* 1983, *33*(3), 147–160.

Rosnow, R. L., Skleder, A. A., Jaeger, M. E., and Rind, B. "Intelligence and the Epistemics of Interpersonal Acumen: Testing Some Implications of Gardner's Theory." *Intelligence,* 1994, *19*(1), 93–116.

Ross-Gordon, J. "Toward a Critical Multicultural Pedagogy for Adult Education." *Proceedings of the Adult Education Research Conference,* no. 35. Knoxville: University of Tennessee, May 1994.

Ross-Gordon, J., Martin, L. G., and Briscoe, D. B. "Conclusion." In J. Ross-Gordon, L. G. Martin, and D. B. Briscoe (eds.), *Serving Culturally Diverse Populations.* New Directions in Adult and Continuing Education, no. 48. San Francisco: Jossey-Bass, 1990a.

Ross-Gordon, J., Martin, L. G., and Briscoe, D. B. *Serving Culturally Diverse Populations.* New Directions for Adult and Continuing Education, no. 48. San Francisco: Jossey-Bass, 1990b.

Rotter, J. B. *Social Learning and Clinical Psychology.* Englewood Cliffs, N.J.: Prentice Hall, 1954.

Rowden, R. W. "Conclusions." In R. W. Rowden (ed.), *Workplace Learning: Debating Five Critical Questions of Theory and Practice.* New Directions for Adult and Continuing Education, no. 72. San Francisco: Jossey-Bass, 1996a.

Rowden, R. W. "Current Realities and Future Challenges." In R. W. Rowden (ed.), *Workplace Learning: Debating Five Critical Questions of Theory and Practice.* New Directions for Adult and Continuing Education, no. 72. San Francisco: Jossey-Bass, 1996b.

Rowland, F., and Volet, S. "Self-Direction in Community Learning: A Case Study." *Australian Journal of Adult and Community Education,* 1996, *36*(2), 89–102.

Rubenson, K. "Participation in Recurrent Education: A Research Review." Paper presented at a meeting of national delegates on Developments in Recurrent Education, Organization for Economic Cooperation and Development, Paris, 1977.

Rubenson, K. "Background and Theoretical Context." In R. Hoghiel and K. Rubenson (eds.), *Adult Education for Social Change.* Lund, Sweden: Liber, 1980.

Rubenson, K. "Sociology of Adult Education." In S. B. Merriam and P. M. Cunningham (eds.), *Handbook of Adult and Continuing Education.* San Francisco: Jossey-Bass, 1989.

Rubenson, K. "Adults' Readiness to Learn: Questioning Lifelong Learning for All. *Proceedings of the Adult Education Research Conference,* no. 39. San Antonio, Tex: University of the Incarnate Word and Texas A&M University, 1998.

Rumelhart, D. E., and Norman, D. A. "Accretion, Tuning, and Restructuring: Three Models of Learning." In J. W. Cotton and R. L. Klatzky (eds.), *Semantic Factors in Cognition.* Hillsdale, N.J.: Erlbaum, 1978.

Rybash, J. M., Hoyer, W. J., and Roodin, P. A. *Adult Cognition and Aging: Developmental Changes in Processing, Knowing and Thinking.* New York: Pergamon Press, 1986.

Sabbaghian, Z. S. "Adult Self-Directedness and Self-Concept: An Exploration of Relationships." Unpublished doctoral dissertation, Iowa State University, 1979.

Sahakian, W. S. *Introduction to the Psychology of Learning.* (2nd ed.) Itasca, Ill.: Peacock, 1984.

Salovey, P., and Mayer, J. D. "Emotional Intelligence." *Imagination, Cognition and Personality,* 1990, *9*(3), 185–211.

Salthouse, T. A. *A Theory of Cognitive Aging.* Amsterdam: North-Holland, 1985.

Salthouse, T. A. *Mechanisms of Age-Cognition Relations in Adulthood.* Hillsdale, N.J.: Erlbaum, 1992a.

Salthouse, T. A. "Why Do Adult Age Differences Increase with Task Complexity?" *Developmental Psychology,* 1992b, *28*(5), 905–918.

Salthouse, T. A. "Processing Capacity and Its Role on the Relations Between Age and Memory." In F. E. Weinert and W. Schneider (eds.), *Memory Performance and Competencies: Issues in Growth and Development.* Hillsdale, N.J.: Erlbaum, 1995.

Savicevic, D. M. "Self-Directed Education for Lifelong Learning." *International Journal of Lifelong Education,* 1985, *4*(4), 285–294.

Schacter, D. L. *Searching for Memory: The Brain, the Mind, and the Past.* New York: Basic Books, 1996.

Schaie, K. W. "The Primary Mental Abilities in Adulthood: An Exploration in the Development of Psychometric Intelligence." In P. B. Baltes and O. G. Brim (eds.), *Life-Span Development and Behavior.* Vol. 2. Orlando, Fla.: Academic Press, 1979.

Schaie, K. W. *Manual for the Schaie-Thurston Adult Mental Abilities Test (STAMAT).* Palo Alto, Calif.: Consulting Psychologists Press, 1985.

Schaie, K. W. "Applications of Psychometric Intelligence to the Prediction of Everyday Competence in the Elderly." In C. Schooler and K. Schaie (eds.), *Cognitive Functioning and Social Culture over the Life Course.* Norwood, N.J.: Ablex, 1987.

Schaie, K. W. "The Course of Adult Intellectual Development." *American Psychologist,* 1994, *49*(4), 304–313.

Schaie, K. W. "Intellectual Development in Adulthood." In J. E. Birren and K. W. Schaie (eds.), *Handbook of the Psychology of Aging.* (4th ed.) Orlando, Fla.: Academic Press, 1996.

Schaie, K. W., and Hertzog, C. "Fourteen-Year Cohort-Sequential Analyses of Adult Intellectual Development." *Developmental Psychology,* 1983, *19*(4), 531–543.

Schaie, K. W., and Labouvie-Vief, G. "Generational Versus Ontogeneic Components of Change in Adult Cognitive Behavior: A Fourteen Year Cross Sectional Study." *Developmental Psychologist,* 1974, *10*(3), 305–320.

Schaie, K. W., and Parham, I. A. "Cohort-Sequential Analysis of Adult Intellectual Development." *Developmental Psychology,* 1977, *13*(6), 649–653.

Schaie, K. W., and Willis, S. L. *Adult Development and Aging.* (2nd ed.) Boston: Little, Brown, 1986.

Schaie, K. W., Willis, S. L., and O'Hanlon, A. M. "Perceived Intellectual Performance Change Over Seven Years." *Journal of Gerontology: Psychological Sciences*, 1994, *49*(3), 103–118.

Scheibel, A. B. "Structural and Functional Changes in the Aging Brain." In J. E. Birren and K. W. Schaie (eds.), *Handbook of the Psychology of Aging*. (4th ed.) Orlando, Fla.: Academic Press, 1996.

Schied, F. *Learning in Social Context: Workers and Adult Education in Nineteenth Century Chicago*. DeKalb, Ill.: LEPS Press, 1993.

Schied, F. "From Workers to Trade Unionists: Transformation and Instrumentalism in Workers and Adult Education After the First World War." *Proceedings of the Adult Education Research Conference*, no. 35. Knoxville: University of Tennessee, 1994.

Schied, F., Carter, V. K., Preston, J. A., and Howell, S. L. "The HRD Factory: An Historical Inquiry into the Production of Control in the Workplace." In P. Armstrong, N. Miller, and M. Zukas (eds.), *Crossing Borders, Breaking Boundaries: Proceedings of the 27th Annual SCUTREA Conference*. London: Birbeck College, University of London, July 1997.

Schlattner, C. J. "The Body in Transformative Learning." *Proceedings of the Adult Education Research Conference*, no. 35. Knoxville: University of Tennessee, 1994.

Schlossberg, N. K. *Counseling Adults in Transition*. New York: Springer, 1984.

Schlossberg, N. K. "Taking the Mystery Out of Change." *Psychology Today*, 1987, *21*(5), 74–75.

Schlossberg, N. K. *Overwhelmed: Coping with Life's Ups and Downs*. San Francisco: Lexington Books, 1989.

Schlossberg, N. K., Lynch, A. Q., and Chickering, A. W. *Improving Higher Education Environments for Adults*. San Francisco: Jossey-Bass, 1989.

Schlossberg, N. K., Waters, E. B., and Goodman, J. *Counseling Adults in Transition*. (2nd ed.). New York: Springer, 1995.

Schön, D. A. *The Reflective Practitioner: How Professionals Think in Action*. New York: Basic Books, 1983.

Schön, D. A. *Educating the Reflective Practitioner*. San Francisco: Jossey-Bass, 1987.

Schön, D. A. (ed.). *The Reflective Turn: Case Studies in and on Educational Practice*. New York: Teachers College Press, 1991.

Schön, D. A. "From Technical Rationality to Reflection-in-Action." In R. Edwards, A. Hanson, and P. Raggatt (eds.), *Boundaries of Adult Learning*. London: Routledge, 1996.

Schugurensky, D. "Paulo Freire: From Pedagogy of the Oppressed to Pedagogy of Hope." *Proceedings of the Adult Education Research Conference*, no. 37. Tampa: University of South Florida, 1996.

Schulz, R., and Ewen, R. B. *Adult Development and Aging*. New York: Macmillan, 1988.

Scientific American, 1992, *267*(entire issue 3).

Scott, S. M. "Conscientization as the Object of Practice." *Proceedings of the Adult Education Research Conference*, no. 37. Tampa: University of South Florida, 1996.

Scott, S. M. "The Grieving Soul in the Transformation Process." In P. Cranton (ed.), *Transformative Learning in Action*. New Directions for Adult and Continuing Education, no. 74, 1997.

Scribner, S. "Studying Working Intelligence." In B. Rogoff and J. Lave (eds.), *Everyday Cognition: Its Development in Social Context*. Cambridge, Mass.: Harvard University Press, 1984.

Senge, P. M. *The Fifth Discipline: The Art and Practice of the Learning Organization*. New York: Doubleday, 1990.

Settersten, R. A., and Hägestad, G. O. "What's the Latest? Cultural Age Declines for Family Transitions." *Gerontologist*, 1996, *36 (2)*, 178–188.

Sheared, V. "Giving Voice: An Inclusive Model of Instruction—A Womanist Perspective." In E. Hayes and S.A.J. Colin III (eds.), *Confronting Racism and Sexism*. New Directions for Adult and Continuing Education, no. 61. San Francisco: Jossey-Bass, 1994.

Shearer, C. B., and Jones, J. A. *The Validation of the Hillside Assessment of Perceived Intelligences (HAPI): A Measure of Howard Gardner's Theory of Multiple Intelligences*. Washington, D.C.: National Institute on Disability and Rehabilitation Research, 1994. (ED 372 077)

Sheehy, G. *Passages: Predictable Crises of Adult Life*. New York: Dutton, 1976.

Sheehy, G. *New Passages: Mapping Your Life Across Time*. New York: Random House, 1995.

Sheffield, S. B. "The Orientations of Adult Continuing Learners." In D. Solomon (ed.), *The Continuing Learner*. Chicago: Center for the Study of Liberal Education for Adults, 1964.

Shor, I., and Freire, P. A. *Pedagogy for Liberation*. Westport, Conn.: Bergin & Garvey, 1987.

Shores, E. F. "Howard Gardner on the Eighth Intelligence. Seeing the Natural World." *Dimensions of Early Childhood*, 1995, *23*(4), 5–9.

Shuell, T. J. "Cognitive Conceptions of Learning." *Review of Educational Research*, 1986, *56*, 411–436.

Siegler, I. C., Poon, L. W., Madden, D. J., and Welsh, K. A. "Psychological Aspects of Normal Aging." In E. W. Busse and D. G. Blazer (eds.), *Textbook of Geriatric Psychiatry.* Washington, D.C.: American Psychiatric Press, 1996.

Simmons, S., and Simmons, J. C. *Measuring Emotional Intelligence.* Arlington, Tex.: Summit Publishing Company, 1997.

Sinnott, J. D. "Postformal Reasoning: The Relativistic Stage." In M. L. Commons, F. A. Richards, and C. Armon (eds.), *Beyond Formal Operations: Late Adolescent and Adult Cognitive Development.* New York: Praeger, 1984.

Sinnott, J. D. "The Relationship of Postformal Thought, Adult Learning, and Lifespan Development." In J. D. Sinnott (ed.), *Interdisciplinary Handbook of Adult Lifespan Learning.* Westport, Conn.: Greenwood Press, 1994.

Sisco, B. R. "The Relevance of Robert Sternberg's Triarchic Theory of Human Intelligence to Adult Education." *Proceedings of the Adult Education Research Conference,* no. 30. Madison: University of Wisconsin, 1989.

Sissel, P. A. "Reflection as Vision: Prospects for Future Literacy Programming." In P. A. Sissel (ed.), *A Community-Based Approach to Literacy Programs: Taking Learners' Lives into Account.* New Directions for Adult and Continuing Education, no. 70. San Francisco: Jossey-Bass, 1996.

Sissel, P. A. "Participation and Learning in Head Start: A Sociopolitical Analysis." *Adult Education Quarterly,* 1997, *47*(3/4), 123–137.

Skinner, B. F. *Beyond Freedom and Dignity.* New York: Knopf, 1971.

Skinner, B. F. *About Behaviorism.* New York: Knopf, 1974.

Smith, A. D. "Memory." In J. E. Birren and K. W. Schaie (eds.), *Handbook of the Psychology of Aging.* Orlando, Fla.: Academic Press, 1996.

Smith, D. H. "Determinants of Individuals' Discretionary Use of Time." In D. H. Smith, J. Macaulay, and Associates, *Participation in Social and Political Activities.* San Francisco: Jossey-Bass, 1980.

Smith, J., Dixon, R. A., and Baltes, P. B. "Expertise in Life Planning: A New Research Approach to Investigating Aspects of Wisdom." In M. L. Commons, J. D. Sinnott, F. A. Richards, and C. Armon (eds.), *Adult Developmental Models: Comparisons and Applications of Development.* New York: Praeger, 1989.

Smith, M. K. *Local Education: Community, Conversation, Praxis.* Philadelphia: Open University Press, 1994.

Smith, R. M. *Learning How to Learn: Applied Learning Theory for Adults.* Chicago: Follett, 1982.

Smith, R. M. (ed.). *Theory Building for Learning How to Learn.* Chicago: Educational Studies Press, 1987.

Smith, R. M., and Associates. *Learning to Learn Across the Life Span*. San Francisco: Jossey-Bass, 1990.

Smyth, J. "Developing Socially Critical Educators." In D. Boud and N. Miller (eds.), *Working with Experience: Animating Learning*. New York: Routledge, 1996.

Sodowsky, G. R., Kwan, K. K., and Pannu, R. "Ethnic Identity of Asians in the United States." In J. G. Ponterotto, J. M. Casas, L. A. Suzuki, and C. M. Alexander (eds.), *Handbook of Multicultural Counseling*. Thousand Oaks, Calif.: Sage, 1995.

Sork, T. J. "Exploring the Ethics of Professional Practice." In *Proceedings of the 1988 SCUTREA Conference* (pp. 393–398). Leeds, England, July 1988.

Sork, T. J. "An 'Ethical Practices Analysis' for Adult Educators." Paper presented at the American Association for Adult and Continuing Education conference, October 1990.

Sork, T. J. "Codes of Ethics and Ethical Competence." Paper presented at the American Association for Adult and Continuing Education. Anaheim, Calif., 1992.

Sork, T. J. "A Few Potholes on the Road to Salvation: Codes of Ethics in Adult Education." *Proceedings of the Adult Education Research Conference*, no. 37. Tampa: University of South Florida, 1996.

Spear, G. E. "Beyond the Organizing Circumstance: A Search for Methodology for the Study of Self-Directed Learning." In H. B. Long and others (eds.), *Self-Directed Learning: Application and Theory*. Athens: Department of Adult Education, University of Georgia, 1988.

Spear, G. E., and Mocker, D. W. "The Organizing Circumstance: Environmental Determinants in Self-Directed Learning." *Adult Education Quarterly*, 1984, *35*(1), 1–10.

Spear, G. E., and Mocker, D. W. "The Future of Adult Education." In S. B. Merriam and P. M. Cunningham (eds.), *Handbook of Adult and Continuing Education*. San Francisco: Jossey-Bass, 1989.

Spearman, C. E. "'General Intelligence' Objectively Determined and Measured." *American Journal of Psychology*, 1904, *15*, 201–293.

Spencer, B. "Old and New Social Movements as Learning Sites: Greening Labor Unions and Unionizing the Greens." *Adult Education Quarterly*, 1995, *46*(1), 31–41.

Springer, S. P. "Educating the Left and Right Sides of the Brain." *National Forum*, 1987, *67*(2), 25–28.

Squire, L. R., Knowlton, B. and Musen, G. "The Structure and Organization of Memory." *Annual Review of Psychology*, 1993, *44*, 453–495.

Stacy, N., and Duc-Le To. "Adult Education and Training Markets." In
  T. Noyelle (ed.), *Skills, Wages, and Productivity in the Service Sector.*
  Boulder, Colo.: Westview Press, 1990.

Stacy, N., and Duc-Le To. "Adult Education and Training Markets." In
  T. Husen and T. N. Postlethwaite (eds.), *The International Encyclope-*
  dia of Education (Vol. 1, pp. 106–111). (2nd ed.) New York: Pergamon Press, 1994.

Staddon, J.E.R. "Social Learning Theory and the Dynamics of Interaction."
  Psychological Review, 1984, *91*(4), 502–507.

Stalker, J. "Sexual Harassment: The Dark Side of the Adult Learner/Teacher
  Relationship." *Proceedings of the Adult Education Research Confer-*
  ence, no. 34. University Park: Penn State University, May 1993a.

Stalker, J. "Voluntary Participation: Deconstructing the Myth." *Adult Edu-*
  cation Quarterly, 1993b, *43*(2), 63–75.

Stalker, J. "Women Teachers Mentoring Women Learners: On the Inside
  Working It Out." *Proceedings of the Adult Education Research Confer-*
  ence, no. 34. University Park: Pennsylvania State University, May
  1993c.

Stalker, J. "Women and Adult Education: Rethinking Androcentric
  Research." *Adult Education Quarterly,* 1996, *46*(2), 98–113.

Stamps, D. "Learning Is Social. Training Is Irrevelant?" *Training,* 1997, *3(2)*,
  35–42.

Starkey, K. (ed.). *How Organizations Learn.* London: International
  Thomson Business Press, 1996.

Starratt, R. J. "Building an Ethical School: A Theory for Practice in Educational Leadership." *Educational Administration Quarterly,* 1991,
  27(2), 185–202.

Starratt, R. J. *Building an Ethical School: A Practical Response to the Moral*
  Crisis in Schools. Washington, D.C.: Falmer Press, 1994.

Steffe, L. P.. and Gale, J. (eds.), *Constructivism in Education.* Hillsdale, N.J.:
  Erlbaum, 1995.

Sternberg, R. J. *Beyond I.Q.: A Triarchic Theory of Human Intelligence.*
  Cambridge: Cambridge University Press, 1985.

Sternberg, R. J. *Intelligence Applied: Understanding and Increasing Your*
  Intellectual Skills. Orlando, Fla.: Harcourt Brace, 1986a.

Sternberg, R. J. "Intelligence, Wisdom, and Creativity: Three Is Better Than
  One." *Educational Psychologist,* 1986b, *21*(3), 175–190.

Sternberg, R. J. *The Triarchic Mind: A New Theory of Human Intelligence.*
  New York: Viking Penguin, 1988.

Sternberg, R. J. "Wisdom and Its Relations to Intelligence and Creativity."

In R. J. Sternberg (ed.), *Wisdom: Its Nature, Origins, and Development.* Cambridge: Cambridge University Press, 1990a.

Sternberg, R. J. (ed.), *Wisdom: Its Nature, Origins, and Development.* Cambridge: Cambridge University Press, 1990b.

Sternberg, R. J. "Allowing for Thinking Styles." *Educational Leadership,* 1994a, 52(3), 36–40.

Sternberg, R. J. "PRSVL: An Integrative Framework for Understanding Mind in Context." In R. J. Sternberg and R. K. Wagner (eds.), *Mind in Context: Interactionist Perspectives on Human Intelligence.* Cambridge: Cambridge University Press, 1994b.

Sternberg, R. J. "A Prototype View of Expert Training." *Educational Researcher,* 1995, 24(6), 9–17.

Sternberg, R. J. "Myths, Countermyths, and Truths About Intelligence." *Educational Researcher,* 1996a, 25(2), 11–16.

Sternberg, R. J. *Successful Intelligence: How Practical and Creative Intelligence Determine Success in Life.* New York: Simon & Schuster, 1996b.

Sternberg, R. J. "Styles of Thinking." In P. B. Baltes and U. M. Staudinger (eds.), *Interactive Minds: Life-Span Perspectives on the Social Foundation of Cognition.* Cambridge, Mass.: Cambridge University Press, 1996c.

Sternberg, R. J., and Berg, C. A. "What Are Theories of Adult Intellectual Development Theories Of?" In C. Schooler and K. Schaie (eds.), *Cognitive Functioning and Social Culture Over the Life Course.* Norwood, N.J.: Ablex, 1987.

Sternberg, R. J., and Wagner, R. K. (eds.). *Practical Intelligence: Nature and Origins of Competence in the Everyday World.* Cambridge: Cambridge University Press, 1986.

Sternberg, R. J., and Wagner, R. K. (eds.). *Mind in Context: Interactionist Perspectives on Human Intelligence.* Cambridge: Cambridge University Press, 1994.

Stevenson, J. J. "Load, Power and Margin in Older Adults." *Geriatric Nursing,* 1980, 1(2), 50–55.

Straka, G. A. "Cross-Cultural Validity of the Guglielmino 'Self-Directed Learning Readiness Scale.'" In W. Bos and C. Tarnai (eds.), *Ergebnisse qualitativer und quantitativer empirischer padagogischer Forschung.* Munster, Germany: Waxmann, 1996.

Straka, G. A. *European Views of Self-Directed Learning: Historical, Conceptional, Empirical, Practical, Vocational.* Munster, Germany: Waxmann, 1997.

Straka, G. A., and Hinz, I. M. "The Original SDRLS (Self-Directed Learning Readiness Scale) Reconsidered." In W. Bos and C. Tarnai (eds.),

Ergebnisse qualitativer und quantitativer empirischer padagogischer Forschung. Munster, Germany: Waxmann, 1996.

Strike, K. A., and Soltis, J. F. *The Ethics of Teaching.* New York: Teachers College Press, 1985.

Stroobants, V., and Wildemeersch, D. "Learning for Labour: Women Exploring Boundaries." In P. Armstrong, N. Miller, and M. Zukas (eds.), *Crossing Borders, Breaking Boundaries: Proceedings of the 27th Annual SCUTREA Conference.* London: Birbeck College, University of London, July 1997.

Sugarman, L. *Life-Span Development: Concepts, Theories and Interventions.* New York: Methuen, 1986.

Surrey, J. L. "The Self-in-Relation: A Theory of Women's Development." In J. V. Jordan, A. G. Kaplan, J. B. Miller, I. P. Striver, and J. L. Surrey (eds.), *Women's Growth in Connection: Writing from the Stone Center.* New York: Guilford Press, 1991.

Swanson, R. A., and Arnold, D. E. "The Purpose of Human Resource Development Is to Improve Organizational Performance." In R. W. Rowden (ed.), *Workplace Learning: Debating Five Critical Questions of Theory and Practice.* New Directions for Adult and Continuing Education, no. 72. San Francisco: Jossey-Bass, 1996.

Sylwester, R. *A Celebration of Neurons: An Educator's Guide to the Human Brain.* Alexandria, Va.: Association for Supervision and Curriculum Development, 1995.

Tatum, B. D. "Racial Identity Development and Relational Theory: The Case of Black Women in White Communities." In J. V. Jordan (ed.), *Women's Growth in Diversity.* New York: Guilford Press, 1997.

Taylor, E. W. "Intercultural Competency: A Transformative Learning Process." *Adult Education Quarterly,* 1994, *44*(3), 154–174.

Taylor, E. W. "Rationality and Emotions in Transformative Learning Theory: A Neurobiological Perspective." *Proceedings of the Adult Education Research Conference,* no. 37. Tampa: University of South Florida, 1996.

Taylor, E. W. "Building upon the Theoretical Debate: A Critical Review of the Empirical Studies of Mezirow's Transformative Learning Theory." *Adult Education Quarterly,* 1997a, *48*(1), 34–59.

Taylor, E. W. "Implicit Memory and Transformative Learning Theory: Unconscious Cognition." *Proceedings of the Adult Education Research Conference,* no. 38. Stillwater: University of Oklahoma, 1997b.

Taylor, K., and Marienau, C. (eds.). *Learning Environments for Women's Adult Development: Bridges Toward Change.* New Directions for Adult and Continuing Education, no. 65. San Francisco: Jossey-Bass, 1995.

Tennant, M. C. *Psychology and Adult Learning.* New York: Routledge, 1988.

Tennant, M. C. "The Psychology of Adult Teaching and Learning." In J. M. Peters, P. Jarvis, and Associates, *Adult Education: Evolution and Achievements in a Developing Field of Study.* San Francisco: Jossey-Bass, 1991.

Tennant, M. C. "The Staged Self-Directed Learning Model." *Adult Education Quarterly,* 1992, 42(3), 164–166.

Tennant, M. C. "Perspective Transformation and Adult Development." *Adult Education Quarterly,* 1993, 44(1), 34–42.

Tennant, M. C., and Pogson, P. *Learning and Change in the Adult Years: A Developmental Perspective.* San Franciso: Jossey-Bass, 1995.

Theil, J. P. "Successful Self-Directed Learning Styles." *Proceedings of the Adult Education Research Conference,* no. 25. Raleigh: North Carolina State University, 1984.

Thomas, J. L. *Adulthood and Aging.* Needham Heights, Mass.: Allyn and Bacon, 1992.

Thomas, L. E. " Cognitive Development and Transcendence: An Emerging Transpersonal Paradigm of Consciousness." In M. E. Miller and S. R. Cook-Greuter (eds.). *Transcendence and Mature Adult Thought in Adulthood: The Further Reaches of Adult Development.* London: Rowman & Littlefield, 1994.

Thorndike, E. L., Bregman, E. O., Tilton, J. W., and Woodyard, E. *Adult Learning.* New York: Macmillan, 1928.

Thurstone, L. L., and Thurstone, T. G. *Factorial Studies of Intelligence.* Psychometric Monographs, no. 2. Chicago: University of Chicago Press, 1941.

Tinto, V. *Leaving College: Rethinking the Causes and Cures of Student Attrition.* (2nd ed.) Chicago: University of Chicago Press, 1993.

Tisdell, E. J. "Feminism and Adult Learning: Power, Pedagogy, and Praxis." In S. B. Merriam (ed.), *An Update on Adult Learning Theory.* New Directions for Adult and Continuing Education, no. 57. San Francisco: Jossey-Bass, 1993.

Tisdell, E. J. *Creating Inclusive Adult Learning Environments: Insights from Multicultural Education and Feminist Pedagogy.* Information Series No. 361. Columbus, Ohio: ERIC Clearinghouse on Adult, Career, and Vocational Education, 1995.

Tisdell, E. J. "Feminist Pedagogy and Adult Learning: Underlying Theory and Emancipatory Practice." *Proceedings of the Adult Education Research Conference,* No. 37. Tampa: University of South Florida, May 1996a.

Tisdell, E. J. "Using Life Experience to Teach Feminist Theory." In D. Boud and N. Miller (eds.), *Working with Experience: Animating Learning.* New York: Routledge, 1996b.

Tisdell, E. J. "Poststructural Feminist Pedagogies: The Possibilities and Limitations of a Feminist Emancipatory Adult Learning Theory and Practice." *Adult Education Quarterly,* 1998, *48*(3), 139–156.

Tisdell, E. J., and Perry, C. "A Collaborative Inter-racial 'Border' Pedagogy in Adult Multicultural Education Classes." In P. Armstrong, N. Miller, and M. Zukas (eds.), *Crossing Borders, Breaking Boundaries: Proceedings of the 27th Annual SCUTREA Conference.* London: Birkbeck College, University of London, July 1997.

Tolman, E. C. Principles of Purposive Behavior." In S. Koch (ed.), *Psychology: A Study of Science.* Vol. 2. New York: McGraw-Hill, 1959.

Tomlin, M. E. "Changing What and How We Teach for a Changing World." *Adult Learning,* 1997, *8*(5 & 6), 19–21.

Torrance, E. P., and Mourad, S. "Some Creativity and Style of Learning and Thinking Correlates of Guglielmino's Self-Directed Learning Readiness Scale." *Psychological Reports,* 1978, *43*, 1167–1171.

Tough, A. "The Assistance Obtained by Adult Self-Teachers." *Adult Education U.S.,* 1966, *17*(1), 31–37.

Tough, A. *Learning Without a Teacher.* Educational Research Series, no. 3. Toronto: Ontario Institute for Studies in Education, 1967.

Tough, A. *The Adult's Learning Projects: A Fresh Approach to Theory and Practice in Adult Learning.* Toronto: Ontario Institute for Studies in Education, 1971.

Tough, A. "Major Learning Efforts: Recent Research and Future Directions." *Adult Education,* 1978, *28*(4), 250–263.

Tough, A. *The Adult's Learning Projects: A Fresh Approach to Theory and Practice in Adult Learning.* (2nd ed.) Toronto: Ontario Institute for Studies in Education, 1979.

Toye, M. "Learning Styles." In C. J. Titmus (ed.), *Lifelong Education for Adults: An International Handbook.* Oxford: Pergamon Press, 1989.

Tremblay, N. A., and Theil, J. P. "A Conceptual Model of Autodidactism." In H. B. Long and others (eds.), *Self-Directed Learning: Consensus and Conflict.* Norman: Oklahoma Research Center for Continuing Professional and Higher Education, University of Oklahoma, 1991.

Tremmel, R. "Zen and the Art of Reflective Practice in Teacher Education." *Harvard Educational Review,* 1993, *63*(4), 434–458.

Troll, L. E. *Continuations: Adult Development and Aging.* Pacific Grove, Calif.: Brooks/Cole, 1982.

Turner, C. W. "Psychosocial Barriers to Black Women's Career Development." In J. V. Jordan (ed.), *Women's Growth in Diversity.* New York: Guilford Press, 1997.

U.S. Bureau of the Census. *Sixty-Five Plus in America.* Current Population Reports, Special Studies, P23–178. Washington, D.C.: U.S. Government Printing Office, 1992.

U.S. Bureau of the Census. *Population Profile of the United States: 1995.* Current Population Reports, Series P23–189. Washington, D.C.: U.S. Government Printing Office, 1995.

U.S. Department of Education. Office of Educational Research and Improvement, Center for Statistics. *Bulletin.* Washington, D.C.: Department of Education, 1986.

Ullrich, H. E. "A Co-Constructivist Perspective on Life-Course Changes Among Havik Brahmins in a South India Village." In J. Valsiner (ed.), *Child Development Within Culturally Structured Environments: Comparative-Cultural and Constructivist Perspectives.* Norwood, N.J.: Ablex, 1995.

Ulrich, D. "A New Mandate for Human Resources." *Harvard Business Review,* 1998, *76*(1), 124–134.

Usher, R. "Experience in Adult Education: A Post-Modern Critique." *Journal of Philosophy of Education,* 1992, *26*(2), 201–214.

Usher, R., Bryant, I., and Johnston, R. *Adult Education and the Postmodern Challenge: Learning Beyond the Limits.* New York: Routledge, 1997.

Usher, R., and Edwards, R. *Postmodernism and Education.* New York: Routledge, 1994.

Vaillant, G. *Adaptation to Life.* Boston: Little, Brown, 1977.

Valentine, T. "United States of America: The Current Predominance of Learning for the Job." In P. Belanger and S. Valdivielso (eds.), *The Emergence of Learning Societies: Who Participates in Adult Learning?* New York: Elsevier, 1997.

Valentine, T., and Darkenwald, G. G. "Deterrents to Participation in Adult Education: Profiles of Potential Learners." *Adult Education Quarterly,* 1990, *41*(1), 29–42.

Valsiner, J. (ed.). *Child Development Within Culturally Structured Environments: Comparative-Cultural and Constructivist Perspectives.* Norwood, N.J.: Ablex, 1995.

Velazquez, L. C. "Voices from the Fields: Community-Based Migrant Education." In P. Sissel (ed.), *A Community-Based Approach to Literacy Programs: Taking Learners' Lives into Account.* New Directions in Adult and Continuing Education, no. 70. San Francisco: Jossey-Bass, 1996.

Vella, J. *Learning to Listen, Learning to Teach: The Power of Dialogue in Educating Adults.* San Francisco: Jossey-Bass, 1994.

Verma, J. "Transformation of Women's Social Roles in India." In J. Valsiner (ed.), *Child Development Within Culturally Structured Environments: Comparative-Cultural and Constructivist Perspectives.* Norwood, N.J.: Ablex, 1995.

Verner, C. "Definitions of Terms." In G. Jensen, A. A. Liveright, and W. Hallenbeck (eds.), *Adult Education: Outlines of an Emerging Field of University Study.* Washington, D.C.: Adult Education Association, 1964.

von Glaserfeld, E. "Sensory Experience, Abstraction, and Teaching." In L. P. Steffe and J. Gale (eds.), *Constructivism in Education.* Hillsdale, N.J.: Erlbaum, 1995.

Vygotsky, L. S. *Mind in Society: The Development of Higher Psychological Processes.* Cambridge, Mass.: Harvard University Press, 1978.

Wagschal, K. "I Became Clueless Teaching the GenXers." *Adult Learning,* 1997, *8*(4), 21–25.

Walker, B. H. "Margin-in-Life Scale: A Predictor of Persistence for Nontraditional Students in Higher Education." Unpublished doctoral dissertation, University of Georgia, 1996.

Watkins, K. "Of Course Organizations Learn!" In R. W. Rowden (ed.), *Workplace Learning: Debating Five Critical Questions of Theory and Practice.* New Directions for Adult and Continuing Education, no. 72. San Francisco: Jossey-Bass, 1996.

Watkins, K. E., and Marsick, V. J. *Sculpting the Learning Organization: Lessons in the Art and Science of Systemic Change.* San Francisco: Jossey-Bass, 1993.

Weiler, K. "Freire and a Feminist Pedagogy of Difference." In R. Edwards, A. Hanson, and P. Raggatt (eds.), *Boundaries of Adult Learning* (pp. 128–151). New York: Routledge, 1996.

Weiman, E. R. "McClusky's Power-Load-Margin Theory and Adult Students." Abstract from: *Dissertation Abstracts International:* 50–11A: 3450, 1987.

Weisinger, H. *Emotional Intelligence at Work.* San Francisco: Jossey-Bass, 1998.

Wellington, B., and Austin, P. "Orientations to Reflective Practice." *Educational Researcher,* 1996, *38*(3), 307–316.

Welton, M. R. "The Contribution of Critical Theory to Our Understanding of Adult Learning." In S. B. Merriam (ed.), *An Update on Adult Learning Theory.* New Directions for Adult and Continuing Education, no. 57. San Francisco: Jossey-Bass, 1993.

Welton, M. R. "The Critical Turn in Adult Education Theory." In M. R. Welton (ed.), *In Defense of the Lifeworld* (pp. 11–38). Albany: State University of New York Press, 1995a.

Welton, M. R. "In Defense of the Lifeworld: A Habermasian Approach to Adult Learning." In M. R. Welton (ed.), *In Defense of the Lifeworld* (pp. 127–156). Albany: State University of New York Press, 1995b.

Welton, M. R. "We Need to Have a Radical Learning Theory." In M. R. Welton (ed.), *In Defense of the Lifeworld* (pp. 218–223). Albany: State University of New York Press, 1995c.

West, C. K., Farmer, J. A., and Wolff, P. M. *Instructional Design: Implications from Cognitive Science.* Englewood Cliffs, N.J.: Prentice Hall, 1991.

West, R., and Bentley, E. L. "Relationship Between Scores on the Self-Directed Learning Readiness Scale, Oddi Continuing Learning Inventory and Participation in Continuing Professional Education." In H. B. Long and others (eds.), *Self-Directed Learning: Consensus and Conflict.* Norman: Oklahoma Research Center for Continuing Professional and Higher Education, University of Oklahoma, 1991.

Whitson, D. L., and Amstutz, D. D. *Accessing Information in a Technological Age.* Malabar, Fla.: Krieger, 1997.

Wilber, K. *A Sociable God.* New York: McGraw-Hill, 1982.

Wilber, K. *Eye to Eye.* New York: Doubleday, 1983.

Wilber, K. "Two Patterns of Transcendence: A Reply to Washburn." *Journal of Humanistic Psychology,* 1990, *30*(3), 113–136.

Wilcox, S. "Fostering Self-Directed Learning in the University Setting." *Studies in Higher Education,* 1996, *21*(2), 165–176.

Williamson, A. "You're Never Too Old to Learn! Third-Age Perspectives on Lifelong Learning." *International Journal of Lifelong Education,* 1997, *16*(3), 173–184.

Willis, S. L., and Schaie, K. W. "Practical Intelligence in Later Adulthood." In R. J. Sternberg and R. K. Wagner (eds.), *Practical Intelligence: Nature and Origins of Competence in the Everyday World.* Cambridge: Cambridge University Press, 1986.

Willis, S. L., and Schaie, K. W. "Cognitive Training in the Normal Elderly." In F. Forette, Y. Christensen, and F. Boller (eds.), *Plasticité Cerebrale et Stimulation Cognitive [Cerebral Plasticity and Cognitive Stimulation].* Paris: Fondation Nationale de Gerontologie, 1994.

Wilson, A. "How We Find Ourselves: Identity Development and Two-Spirit People." *Harvard Educational Review,* 1996, *66*(2), 303–317.

Wilson, A. L. "Adult Learning, Situated Cognition, and Authentic Activity:

Relocating Adult Education in the Context of Experience." *Proceedings of the Adult Education Research Conference,* no. 34. University Park: Pennsylvania State University, 1993a.

Wilson, A. L. "The Common Concern: Controlling the Professionalization of Adult Education." *Adult Education Quarterly,* 1993b, *44*(1), 1–16.

Wilson, A. L. "The Promise of Situated Cognition." In S. B. Merriam (ed.), *An Update on Adult Learning.* New Directions for Adult and Continuing Education, no. 57. San Francisco: Jossey-Bass, 1993c.

Wilson, A. L., and Cervero, R. M. "Who Sits at the Planning Table: Ethics and Planning Practice." *Adult Learning,* 1996, *8*(2), 20–22.

Wilson, A. L., and Cervero, R. M. "Beyond Disciplinary Consumption in Program Planning Courses: Dilemmas in Teaching with and About Power." In *Conference Proceedings,* 38th Annual Adult Education Research Conference. Stillwater: Oklahoma State University, 1997.

Wilson, B. A. "A Descriptive and Interpretive Study: The Intellectual Development of Adults." Paper presented at the Annual Meeting of the American Educational Research Association, New York, 1996. (ED 393 976)

Winner, L. "Mythinformation." In J. Zerzan and A. Carnes (eds.), *Questioning Technology.* Philadelphia: New Society, 1991.

Winters, N. W., and Long, H. B. "Uses of Guglielmino Self-Directed Learning Readiness Scale." In H. B. Long and others (eds.), *Expanding Horizons in Self-Directed Learning.* Norman: Public Managers Center, University of Oklahoma, 1997.

Wlodkowski, R. J., and Ginsberg, M. G. *Diversity and Motivation.Culturally Responsive Teaching.* San Francisco: Jossey-Bass, 1995.

Wolf, M. A., and Leahy, M. A. (eds.). *Adults in Transition.* Washington, D.C.: American Association for Adult and Continuing Education, 1998.

Wood, G. S. "A Code of Ethics for All Adult Educators?" *Adult Learning,* 1996, *8*(2), 13–14.

Yang, B. "Explaining and Predicting Participation in Adult Education: A Longitudinal Study." *Proceedings of the Adult Education Research Conference,* no. 36. Edmonton, Alberta: University of Alberta, May 1995.

Yang, B., Blunt, A., and Butler, R. S. "Prediction of Participation in Continuing Professional Education: A Test of Two Behavioral Intention Models." *Adult Education Quarterly,* 1994, *44* (2), 83–96.

Yesavage, J. A. "Imagery Pretraining and Memory Training in the Elderly." *Gerontology,* 1983, *29,* 271–275.

Young, M. F. "Instructional Design for Situated Learning." *Educational Technology Research and Development,* 1993, *41*(1), 43–58.

Youngman, F. *Adult Education and Socialist Pedagogy.* London: Croom Helm, 1986.

Youngman, F. "A Transformative Political Economy of Adult Education: An Introduction." In P. Wangoola and F. Youngman (eds.), *Towards a Transformative Political Economy of Adult Education.*" DeKalb, Ill.: LEPS Press, 1996.

Zemke, R., and Zemke, S. "30 Things We Know for Sure About Adult Learning." *Training,* 1981, *18,* 45–49.

Zemke, R., and Zemke, S. "Adult Learning: What Do We Know for Sure?" *Training,* 1995, *32*(6), 31–34, 36, 38, 40.

Ziegahn, L. "Transforming Intercultural Perspectives: Reflecting On-Line." *Proceedings of the Adult Education Research Conference,* no. 39. San Antonio, Tex: University of the Incarnate Word and Texas A&M University, 1998.

‑‑‑ Name Index

――― Subject Index